CATHOLIC SCHOOLS IN ACTION

Catholic

A REPORT

Executive Committee
REVEREND THEODORE M. HESBURGH, C.S.C.
RIGHT REVEREND MONSIGNOR FREDERICK G. HOCHWALT
DOCTOR GEORGE N. SHUSTER

Edited by
REGINALD A. NEUWIEN

Schools
in Action

**THE NOTRE DAME STUDY OF
CATHOLIC ELEMENTARY AND SECONDARY SCHOOLS
IN THE UNITED STATES**

**UNIVERSITY OF NOTRE DAME PRESS · 1966
NOTRE DAME AND LONDON**

This report was made possible by a substantial grant made by the Carnegie Corporation of New York. The report was also given financial assistance from the University of Notre Dame. The statements made and views expressed are solely the responsibility of the authors.

CONTRIBUTORS

Donald N. Barrett

John Darby, S.M.

Terry Denny

Xavier J. Harris, O.F.M.

Robert F. Harvanek, S.J.

Leonard J. Kazmier

Reginald A. Neuwien

Mary Emil Penet, I.H.M.

Mary James Rau, O.P.

George N. Shuster

John E. Walsh, C.S.C.

The National Advisory Committee to the Study of Catholic Education gave carefully considered advice to the staff of the Study, and a number of important changes were made in the operation of the Study as a result of this advice. The Advisory Committee, which was active through July 1964, had the following membership:

His Eminence
Lawrence J. Cardinal Shehan
Archbishop of Baltimore
Chairman

Most Rev. John F. Dearden
Archbishop of Detroit

Most Rev. John J. Wright
Bishop of Pittsburgh

Sister Mary Emil, I.H.M.
Marygrove College

Dr. John H. Fischer
Teachers College
Columbia University

Rev. Theodore M. Hesburgh, C.S.C.
University of Notre Dame

Mr. Carroll Hochwalt
Monsanto Chemical Company

Rt. Rev. Msgr. Frederick G. Hochwalt
National Catholic Educational
Association

Mr. Frederick H. Jackson
Carnegie Corporation (formerly)

Brother Adelbert James, F.S.C.
Manhattan College

Sister M. Josetta, R.S.M.
Conference of Major Religious
Superiors of Women's Institutes
  (formerly)

Mr. Roy Larsen
TIME Magazine

Dr. Roger T. Lennon
Harcourt, Brace & World, Inc.

Rev. Neil G. McCluskey, S.J.
Gonzaga University

Rt. Rev. Msgr. William E. McManus
Archdiocese of Chicago

Rev. Edward B. Rooney, S.J.
Jesuit Educational Association

Dr. George N. Shuster
University of Notre Dame

Mr. Alfred C. Stepan, Jr.
Stepan Chemical Company

Dr. Ralph W. Tyler
Center for Advanced Study
in the Behavioral Sciences

Rt. Rev. Msgr. John J. Voigt
Archdiocese of New York

Acknowledgments

THE STUDY EXTENDS ITS APPRECIATION TO THE FOL-
lowing who rendered extensive service in the conduct of the depth
studies and in the review of the findings:

Sister Mary Adeline, F.S.S.J., Sister Mary Adria, C.P.P.S., Sister
Louise Aimee, C.S.J., Sister Mary Aloysius, C.S.J., Sister Mary Anthony,
S.S.O., Sister Terese Augustine, S.N.D., Rt. Rev. Msgr. A. W. Behrens,
Sister Bernadine, S.N.D., Nellie Browning, Valerie Price Casey, Sister
Mary Celine, O.S.F., Sister Jean Clare, O.P., Sister M. Teresa Clare,
R.S.M., Sister Mary Clarita, S.C., Sister Mary Colleen, S.S.N.D., Robert
L. Cook, Sister Mary Cordelle, B.V.M., Sister Corinne, I.H.M., Sister
Mary Cyril, C.B.V.M., Brother John Darby, S.M., J. Alan Davitt, Sister
Mary Dolorata, C.S.C., Rev. James Donahue, Sister Mary Dorothea,
B.V.M., Brother John Driscoll, C.S.C., Sister Mary Eudes, S.C., Dolo-
rita J. Falvey, John F. Farinacci, Sister Mary Felicitas, C.P.P.S., Sister
Violetta Florio, M.P.F., Brother Cosmas Francis, F.S.C., Sister Mary
Teresa Francis, B.V.M., Sister Mary Gemma, H.H.M., Sister Mary Ger-
trude, S.L., John H. Gillick, Sister Mary Gratia, R.S.M., Rev. Andrew
Greeley, Edward J. Griffin, John A. Gutherie, Rev. Robert F. Harvanek,
S.J., Sister Mary Henrietta, C.P.P.S., Rev. Harold E. Hicks, Rev. John
M. Hynes, S.J., Sister M. Irenaea, C.T.P.S., Brother John Jansen, S.M.,
Sister Mary Jerome, R.S.M., Sister Mary John, I.H.M., William F.
Kean, Eleanor Kennard, Sister Mary Kevin, S.S.M.N., Marian Kilbane,
Helen M. Kleyle, Sister Mary Leonella, C.S.C., Very Rev. Msgr. J.
William Lester, Brother Alphonsus Maher, O.S.F., Brother C. Mark,
F.S.C., Sister Dorothy Marie, O.P., Brother Stanley Mathews, S.M.,
Sister Mary Matthew, C.S.C., Raymond McCoy, Earl A. McGovern,
Helen McKinney, F.C.M., Michael J. McLaughlin, Eleanor McMahon,
Eloise Mihills, Mary Molyneaux, Thomas J. Moran, Rev. Thomas
Mullowney, John O'Donnell, Kathryn E. O'Reilly, Brother Joseph J.
Panzer, S.M., Gordon E. Parsons, Sister Mary Paschal, C.S.C., Rev.
Henry A. Paul, O.S.F.S., Brother Bernard Peter, F.S.C., Sister Mary

Peter, I.H.M., Philip Pitruzello, Brother Thomas J. Powers, Sister Mary Reginald, O.S.F., Lawrence A. Roche, Sister Mary St. Jude, R.S.M., Sister Mary St. Rose, B.V.M., Sister Mary Sebastian, D.C., Ralph Scott, Rev. Jeremiah B. Sullivan, Florence Tarbox, Sister Mary Teresina, S.C., Sister Theodore, O.P., Sister Marie Theresa, S.C., Sister Mary Thomas, C.S.C., Jean A. Thompson, Mary T. Thorp, Douglas Van Bramer, John A. Vanderford, Sister Mary Walter, S.S.J., Joseph A. Whelan, Charles B. Willard, Elizabeth Wingerter.

Preface

The University of Notre Dame's Study of Catholic Elementary and Secondary Education in the United States was made possible by a very generous grant of assistance from the Carnegie Corporation, the fruit of the passionate interest of John Gardner, then President of the Corporation, in the improvement of education in our country. It was his hope, as it has been ours, that a truly objective view of the Catholic school would challenge those who serve it to meet as fully as possible the needs that result from the profound changes which have been taking place in our society. Another belief we shared and which has been substantiated is that the Study would spur the desire to come closer to what Mr. Gardner so aptly called the "quest for educational excellence."

The Study was officially launched on March 16, 1962. The Senior Consultants had already been at work outlining a plan of procedure likely to produce the desired results. These were the Reverend Theodore M. Hesburgh, C.S.C., President of the University, Right Reverend Monsignor Frederick G. Hochwalt, Executive Secretary of the National Catholic Educational Association, and Dr. George N. Shuster, Assistant to Father Hesburgh and President Emeritus of Hunter College of the City of New York. Monsignor Hochwalt's office not only pledged the statistical and other services of the Association, but also enlisted the support of Archbishop, now Cardinal Archbishop Lawrence J. Shehan of Baltimore, at the time Chairman of the Department of Education of the National Catholic Welfare Conference. At a memorable meeting, which Monsignor William McManus, Superintendent of Schools, Archdiocese of Chicago, generously helped to arrange, the unhesitating endorsement of the late Albert Cardinal Meyer, Archbishop of Chicago, was secured. At the same time careful attention was given to the question of finding a competent director.

These were great steps toward success, but an important question remained. Catholic schools generally had not opened their doors to investigators. What would happen if large numbers of them refused to give more than lip service to the idea of the Study? Fortunately all but a few dioceses promised full cooperation and, as time went on, gave it in a measure which no other comparable study has received: 92% of all Catholic elementary schools and 84% of the secondary schools responded.

The first director of the Study, Dr. William H. Conley, granted a leave of absence from Marquette University, began his work on May 1, 1962. Shortly thereafter a representative committee of school superintendents laid down the first guide rules. Dr. Conley resigned in 1963 to become president of Sacred Heart University, Bridgeport, Connecticut. Mr. Reginald A. Neuwien, Dr. Conley's associate, then became director of the Study and carried it to conclusion. He had previously served as Superintendent of Schools in Stamford, Connecticut, and as Director of Administrative Research for the Educational Research Council of Greater Cleveland.

A distinguished Advisory Committee was formed, with Archbishop Shehan as chairman. The Committee included members of the hierarchy, diocesan superintendents, prominent Catholic and Protestant educators, and some representatives of the public. (The membership is listed elsewhere in this Report.)

The most important of the guide rules established are the following:

Reliable statistical information concerning all the cooperating agencies and institutions (a few dioceses in one part of the country refused to cooperate) was to be collected on a nationwide basis.

Thirteen dioceses were proposed by the Senior Consultants for study in depth.

The Study was to be objective and informative, not evaluative. It was understood, of course, that information might suggest evaluation.

The Catholic school system was not to be compared with the public school system, although "national norms" would be taken into account.

Although the Study would inquire into the academic achievement of the schools, it would pay special attention to results in the area of religious and ethical education, a prime concern of the Catholic school.

Study in depth was defined as involving both educational and sociological analysis.

Such an undertaking proved to be of far greater scope than had been visualized. In addition to preparing, administering, and analyzing the statistical data, which required the joint efforts of the National Catholic Educational Association and the Education Departments of the National Catholic Welfare Conference and Notre Dame, it was necessary to test ways in which the University's new UNIVAC computer could be used to best advantage. Because no pattern for a study in depth had been established previously, the school system of the diocese of Fort Wayne-South Bend was used as a sort of experimental laboratory. We owe a great deal to Monsignor J. William Lester, Diocesan Superintendent, acting on the initiative taken by his Bishop, the Most Reverend Leo A. Pursley, for the patience and courtesy which he displayed and which was reflected in the attitudes of the schools under his direction. A staff had to be assembled and trained. We were most fortunate in securing the services of Dr. Terry Denny, who was granted a leave of absence from Purdue University for the purpose. Other members of the staff were: Dr. Bernard J. Kohlbrenner, Professor of Education, University of Notre Dame; Dr. Leonard J. Kazmier, Professor of Business Organization and Management, University of Notre Dame; Sister Maria Concepta, C.S.C., Ph.D., St. Mary's College; Rev. Xavier J. Harris, O.F.M., Ph.D., then at the University of Notre Dame; Sister Mary James, O.P., Ph.D.; and Professor Donald Barrett, of the Department of Sociology, University of Notre Dame. In addition, key personnel of the NCEA and the Education Department of the National Catholic Welfare Conference and more than one hundred professional educators—school superintendents, professors of education, supervisors, and teachers, from both public and private schools—assisted in the diocesan depth studies. (They, too, are listed elsewhere in this Report.) Finally, we had the generous, intelligent help of the Reverend John E. Walsh, C.S.C., Ph.D., Vice-President for Academic Affairs, University of Notre Dame, in preparing the manuscript. A trustee of the University, Mr. Oliver C. Carmichael, Jr., very generously made his rural estate available for staff meetings. To all we are most grateful.

The major guidelines for the Study have been indicated earlier. It remains to say that this Report could not be an exhaustive treatment of the Catholic schools of the United States. Certain interests of these schools have been dealt with, but we know that more research is required. For example, no satisfactory test of religious knowledge was available. Accordingly one was devised and proved much more valuable than we had dared to hope. It now needs to be refined, in the light of experimentation done both while the Study was in progress and subsequently. The Report sheds light on admission policies, guidance, and curriculum, but does not profess to provide exhaustive comment on any of these. We feel, however, that we have unearthed enough information to justify further inquiry.

The Study did not, in particular, have the resources of personnel and time to take more than a rather cursory look at the all-important question of Catholic school financing. We managed, however, to take some soundings, which indicate how difficult and complex a problem this is. Notable is Sister Maria Concepta's published study, *The Making of a Sister-Teacher* (University of Notre Dame Press, 1965)—prepared with the cooperation of Mr. Neuwien and others—which outlines for the first time financial problems confronted by a religious community called upon to staff elementary and secondary schools. The University hopes to inaugurate during the year that lies ahead studies in depth of the financial problem faced by Catholic education. Nor could we deal adequately with the lay teacher. The Study does, it is true, provide a great deal of information, never available before, based on extensive interviews. One may hope that more research can be devoted to this topic in the near future. There are other sections of this vast field which need tilling. We believe that research workers interested in doing so will find the data collected by the Study invaluable.

We are confident that the Report provides a picture of the Catholic educational endeavor which has hitherto been missing. It should be stressed that no one has tried to inhibit us from saying honestly what we had to say on the basis of the evidence. Instead, as has been indicated, we have profited by a brimming measure of cooperation which none of us could have anticipated. It is our hope that our findings will enable those entrusted with the welfare of Catholic education to continue effectively the many good things which have been accomplished and to initiate improvement where it seems called for.

Theodore M. Hesburgh, C.S.C.
Frederick G. Hochwalt
George N. Shuster

Contents

CHAPTER ONE

The Current Goals of Catholic Education

AS THIS STUDY OF CATHOLIC ELEMENTARY AND SECONDARY schools in the United States will clearly indicate, the Church is conducting a vast and very complex educational enterprise. This it is doing in a country which has decided that education is the most important business in which it is collectively engaged. The endeavor grows larger with each new day, in terms of the commitment of all the things which count—time, personnel, imaginativeness, planning, and, of course, money. In addition to the impressive formal establishment, ranging from the nursery school to the research institute, there are such programs as those of the Armed Forces and of industry which alone would cause the citizen of the late nineteenth century to rub his eyes in amazement, were he privileged to consider them.

This development has many causes. Doubtless the most important is social evolution, which has brought us from the days of a culture in which most of the people lived on farms and earned their bread by physical labor to a culture largely that of the mechanized city. We have leisure in abundance, so much so indeed that young people not in school become a major social problem. We need new skills, new professions, which can be provided only by careful training, extending in many instances over a long period of years. The citizenry must also be literate and reasonably well informed, if is is to know whether or not it is being governed intelligently and honestly. And finally, we all recognize more and more deeply that there is an abiding necessity for moral conduct, which some social scientists may prefer to call "civility." Unless a democracy can take it relatively for granted that those who live in it combine a measure of honesty with a leaven of unselfishness, the seeds of dissolution can quickly take root.

To all this the religious among us, and by no means Catholics only, add another dimension of concern. This is, of course, to a certain extent identifiable with ethical training, but its essence is something quite different. If indeed God exists, He must be more important than all else. What does He say to man, what does He want of man? The spokesman for religion, be he Christian or Jew, must of necessity feel that these questions are very important. Therefore, he will conclude that they cannot be asked too early in life. He may not be convinced that formal education must always and everywhere make them centers of inquiry round which all else turns, but they will certainly be of vital significance in his concept of the education of his children. Many Catholics, Protestants, and Jews also feel that the religious school alone will satisfy the need, but as we all know it is Catholics who have given fullest corporate expression to that need.

The central consideration, therefore, is this: how does the Catholic school carry out the mandate to provide religious training, while at the same time serving the purposes which are those of education for life in the United States at this period in its history? Note that the question is "how" and not "how well." Here we are attempting to explain, not to evaluate. If we can learn from the spokesmen for Catholic education just what it is they have set out to do, we should be able to determine in broad outline the basic reasons why the Catholic educational enterprise exists. It will not help greatly to formulate still another philosophy of education more or less our own. Insofar as seems possible, therefore, we shall proceed empirically.

History will be of some assistance, though unfortunately this history has not yet been written.[1] Some of the pertinent literature is listed at the close of this introduction, and much of it is valuable. But it does not present the full story. Even so, one can distinguish periods having quite different overall objectives although a thread of continuity runs through them. These periods are: first, that of education as it was thought of prior to the establishment of the common schools, later to be designated the public schools; second, the period of mass Catholic immigration; and third the period in which Catholics attempted to establish a school system that would provide a general education of the kind offered in the public schools while emphasizing religious training.

History seen in this context is interesting. The Spanish colonizers fostered in what later became the South and Southwest of the United States mission schools that retain a romantic charm even for us today. As early as 1594 Franciscans built a school in Florida and, despite numerous adversities, kept up some kind of educational effort in that area until the territory was annexed by the United States in 1817. In the Southwest the friars dotted the landscape with similar schools in which "praying, singing, playing musical instruments and other interesting things," among them various crafts, were taught.[2] But the effort was short lived because of a change in the orientation of the Spanish authorities. In the British colonies the "Papist" was greatly disadvantaged. In Maryland the Catholic gentry, for whom the colony had been chartered originally, strove in an environment which became hostile to bring up their children with the help of tutors, since anyone of their faith who sought to establish a school ran afoul of the law. The Jesuits made three unsuccessful attempts to establish educational institutions in Maryland. German and Irish Catholics in Pennsylvania fared better, and some historians say that the "mother-school of all parochial schools in the English colonies was founded by St. Mary's Church, Philadelphia."[3]

The Constitution of the newly formed United States guaranteed freedom of religion, and the pioneer bishops sought to take advantage of the new situation. John Carroll, Bishop of Baltimore, supported "George-town College" as a center from which the blessings of Catholic education could radiate.[4] To the south, John England, Bishop of Charleston, founded schools for both whites and Negroes and even established a religious community to serve the second group.[5] Elsewhere, notably in New York and New Orleans, comparable efforts were made. By 1840 there were 200 Catholic schools in the country as a whole. These continued as best they could the traditions of the Old World, where education had always been considered one of the principal missionary and caritative activities of the Catholic Church. Of course one could not hope that the tradition would be duplicated immediately in a pioneer country, any more than the founders of Harvard and Yale could fancy that these colleges would soon have the luster of Cambridge and Oxford. The Catholic tradition kept alive by the religious orders was a noble one. There were the Benedictine schools of Austria and Germany, the more popular pan-European schools of the Franciscans and Capuchins, and the academies in which the Jesuits brilliantly fostered humanistic studies. We sometimes forget how much patient thought had been expended on formulating a theory of pedagogy by the great masters of these schools and how they had sought long before Cardinal Newman's time to find formulas for effectively combining sacred and profane learning. Therefore, it was eminently natural that when the French Revolution and the Napoleonic Wars were ended new religious communities, especially those founded in France, could proceed so vigorously to restyle the principles of education to meet new and notably different social situations. Very especially the orders of women took up the educational mission. Some of this effort to achieve rejuvenation naturally spilled over into the new United States as Europe experienced a period of fervent missionary activity.

The United States also established its own communities of religious teachers, the two Negro sisterhoods created in the South prior to the abolition of slavery doubtless being the most dramatic. By far the most influential, however, were the Sisters of Charity founded by Elizabeth Bayley Seton in 1809. Mother Seton believed that education was the most important of the works of charity, and so contagious was this conviction that the community she founded eventually grew to include 8000 sisters.[6] Many of these "native" sisterhoods were diocesan. While these communities adapted Old World rules and customs to their use, it was also true that eventually almost all the teaching religious came to employ methods in keeping with the cultural outlook of the United States, even as has happened in Australia and more recently in some of the countries of Latin America.

But it was a far cry from the effort thus described to the era of the parochial school. The decision of several states, with Massachusetts in the lead at an earlier time, to establish "common schools" conducted at public expense virtually coincided with the coming of great waves of Catholic immigrants to these shores. Originally the common school, since it was a community enterprise (the Massachusetts Act of 1647 had simply ordered every township in which there dwelt 50 householders to appoint a teacher and set up a school) was tied in fact if not in principle to the dominant form of Protestant belief. But the Anglo-

Saxon settlers were not cast in a uniform religious mold, and in addition to the divergences between the Calvinist and the Anglican creeds there was a considerable body who professed no faith, as well as a number who subscribed to the deist beliefs that were the legacy of the eighteenth century. Religious instruction consequently varied a great deal from community to community, but there was a general trend toward liberalization. Therefore it was perhaps very natural that Horace Mann (1796–1859), the foremost protagonist of the public school, believed that it would be possible to give "so much religious instruction as is compatible with the rights of others and with the genius of our government." What this really meant was that the Bible was to be read in the schools, since it was "the acknowledged expositor of Christianity." But what version of the Bible should be used? Controversies about the acceptability of the King James version resounded throughout the land.[7]

Nevertheless there was a latent, generous recognition of the difficulties confronted by Catholics; and one must also bear in mind that the Romantic Movement in the ninteenth century brought an interest in the Church which later ranged all the way from the logic of Orestes Brownson to the literary interests of Henry Wadsworth Longfellow.[8] But even if good will had been abundant (as it was not always, by any means), it would have been very difficult to work out a compromise satisfactory to Catholics. The effort continued, however, and is still being made.

Although no adequate study has been undertaken, looking back we can discern a developing endeavor to foster concern with religion in the public schools. In part this was due to the presence of large numbers of teachers who were devoted to their creeds and who gradually realized that some measure of solidarity across denominational lines was desirable. In New England, where graduates from the major private universities seldom adopted teaching as a career, the sons and daughters of Catholic families, less well supplied with this world's goods, often prepared for this profession. Elsewhere, too, those who served the public schools did not divorce their private lives completely from their professional concerns. Religious education associations brought members of the several faiths into a corporate effort to be of service.

And so there almost seemed to have come into being a kind of unreported conspiracy among Catholics, Jews, and Protestants to emphasize religious values. This became especially evident after the world's ordeal with totalitarianism had stirred so many Americans to the core of their souls. Released time (as well as the more traditional Sunday School) became a national institution, legally sanctioned, and youngsters who took advantage of it were likely to find their public-school teachers also teaching the classes in religion. A network of observances, from Christmas assemblies to Seders, was introduced. And although no formal instruction was permitted in the public schools, classes in art, music, history, and literature strongly stressed religious motifs.

The situation existing in 1840 was greatly altered by the mighty tide of immigration, especially from Ireland and Germany. The number of Catholics in the United States increased from 663,000 in 1838 to 3,103,000 in 1860. Because of the famine and the collapse of the textile industry, the Irish usually arrived destitute, with children, and sought employment in the cities and the textile towns.[9] They had survived as best they could years of discrimination and persecution in their home country, and had looked upon the "mixed schools" organized there from 1831 with considerable hostility. How could they be expected to view the public schools established in this country with favor, especially since the social discrimination to which they were subjected so frequently lay heavy on them? For example, until a couple of decades after the dawn of the twentieth century no Irish Catholic could be admitted to a country club in many New England communities. Sometime during the nineteenth century, to be sure, the public education authority recognized their needs. Thus in Lowell, Massachusetts, provision was made for a time for "Irish" schools, which Catholic children only attended, to be taught by Catholic teachers. Pupils were even accorded the right to attend religious devotions in the school building.[10] But the number of anti-Catholic bigots was by no means infinitesmal. At one school in Boston, for example, an Irish pupil was badly beaten for having protested against being compelled to use the King James version of the Bible.

Priests who came from Ireland with the immigrants were often not slow to take offense. They usually ignored the well-meant, if somewhat tame, Emersonian admonition that tolerance must be shown to "the Negro, the Irishman and the Catholic," and preferred to transfer to their Protestant neighbors in the new world much of their aversion to post-Elizabethan England. Often pastors, anxious to insure the orthodoxy of their flock, lacked the means to establish a school. But when one of them had the means, the school belonged to the parish and he administered it. Even so the trend might well have been toward greater elasticity in meeting through public funds the legitimate needs of Catholic parents had it not been for the wave of anti-Catholic bigotry that swept across many sections of the nation before the Civil War. This may be attributed in some part to Catholic criticism of the public school, but its roots go far deeper. For instance, for reasons not yet clarified, the Spanish Inquisition was a major subject of conversation. Ex-priests and "escaped nuns" were widely exploited.[11] Mob action was sometimes the unfortunate result.

It was this upsurge of Protestant hostility to Rome that confronted German migrants when they began to arrive in large numbers. German Catholic immigration, like the smaller Belgian immigration, was largely a planned resettlement. That these men and women would keep the faith in a presumably hostile environment was a pledge made in the firm determination to honor it. The school was the instrumentality chiefly relied upon. That the language used in it would be German meant, of course, that preservation of ethnical group identity was considered desirable, but the major aim was keeping the Catholic faith alive by maintaining the traditional liturgy. In some areas, even rural ones, church and school stood side by side and formed the core of the parish.[12] Against what was considered a "divisive education," extremists like those who formed the American Protective Association joined hands with the more moderate advocates of Americanization.[13] But the Germans not only waged epic battles on this front, sometimes in union with their Lutheran fellow-immigrants, but also locked horns with many of their Irish brethren over the issue of education.

The historic climax was the address that Archbishop John Ireland delivered in 1890 to a convention of the National Educational Association in St. Paul.[14] His remarks may seem rather conventional today, when the Catholic public has grown accustomed to pleas for federal aid. But at that time the Archbishop's approval of the public school, his recognition of the right of the state to establish and support it, and his declaration that the parochial school was a creature of necessity seemed to undermine every educational principle to which some eastern dioceses and the German Catholics of the Middle West were committed. For these, by and large, did not even concede what to Archbishop

Ireland seemed obvious, namely, that only the state could force parents to send their children to school. On the other hand, the Archbishop was a resolute spokesman for religious instruction. He insisted that the school was obligated to provide for it and therefore that Catholic parents could expect the public authority to enforce that obligation. For did not these parents as taxpayers contribute their share to the maintenance of the public school? Nor in his view—for he was, as we would now say, ecumenically minded—were Catholics the only citizens who were committed to religious instruction.

He suggested that the problem could be approached in two ways. First, there might be general recognition of the fact that when a private school educated a child the taxpayers' burden was reduced; so a compensatory fee might be paid the school, as was (and to an increasing extent still is) the custom in some countries. Second, and for this there was a precedent in the State of New York, the parochial school might simply be reimbursed for most of the expense it incurred. It was the second proposal that was adopted in Faribault and Stillwater, Minnesota, with the cooperation of local school boards. The state supported a Catholic school in each of these cities and exercised supervision over them in a way that in the Archbishop's later view resulted in a notable improvement of educational facilities.

But he failed to carry the day. On the one hand, Catholics who had made sacrifices to help build parochial schools were, to judge from their outcries, persuaded that these schools were in jeopardy. In particular, the Germans of the Middle West were bitterly opposed, and the swelling tides of other immigrants—Poles, Italians, Hungarians, and French Canadians among them—brought with them an additional interest in schools conducted in other languages than English. It was also true that the American hierarchy generally had so often and so vigorously supported an all-out effort to creat a Catholic school system that the Archbishop of St. Paul was bound to seem a lone dissenter, although as a matter of fact he was not wholly isolated. Nor did Rome find fault with his ideas or with the methods he proposed for realizing them. But doubtless it was the barrage of disagreement and criticism that came from non-Catholics that really doomed the "Faribault Plan." Ardent and often fanatical friends of the public school were determined that the "common citizenship" principle to which they had grown accustomed was not to be undermined by a new and more subtle form of separatism.[15]

Meanwhile the views of the American hierarchy had been formulated in the resolutions adopted by the Third Plenary Council of Baltimore (1884). Two of these resolutions read:

> 1. That near every Church a parish school, where one does not yet exist, is to be built and maintained in *perpetuum* within two years of the promulgation of this council, unless the bishop should decide that because of serious difficulties a delay may be granted.
>
> 2. That all Catholic parents are bound to send their children to the parish school, unless it is evident that a sufficient training in religion is given either in their own homes, or in other Catholic schools; or when, because of a sufficient reason, approved by the bishop, with all due precautions and safeguards, it is licit to send them to other schools. What constitutes a Catholic school is left to the decision of the bishop.[16]

These resolutions prepared the way for the vigorous conclusion of the debate about what inferences were to be drawn from the inability of the public school to provide adequately for the religious instruction of youth. They were reinforced some decades later in the encyclical letter on the "Christian Education of Youth" (*Divini Illius Magistri*) of Pope Pius XI (1929). Catholics would proceed with vigor and dedication to establish a system of education that has no parallel anywhere in the world.

The question, then, became one of performance. What were the objectives of Catholic schools and how were they to be achieved? Throughout the period of pioneering and growth it was clearly recognized that answers to these questions could be given only by those who were engaged in the manifold tasks of instruction. Therefore, the emphasis was placed, at first often theoretically but then in fact, on the training of teachers. Like the public school in this respect, the parochial school was built and maintained in a climate of "liberty and diversity." For the most part it was the pastor, acting in accordance with the directives of his bishop, who took the initiative, and as rapidly as it was possible he turned to a religious community to obtain the teachers he needed. These communities, too, enjoyed a large measure of the same "liberty and diversity," so that there were many and serious differences of outlook and quality of preparation. A similar lack of uniformity was also characteristic of the public school system. It was only gradually that some of the states, to which authority in the realm of education has been reserved in the United States constitution, established standards for the licensing of teachers. It was necessary for Catholic aspirants to the profession to conform with these standards also.

Teacher training therewith became a major and often hotly debated issue. It seldom concerned the Catholic high school because this, usually conducted by a religious community, was competitive not only with other Catholic institutions but also with those organized under public or private auspices. The communities of priests and brothers were rather rapidly identified with secondary education. But the elementary school was another matter entirely. What training should the teacher receive? In general more exacting standards were insisted upon, but it took a long time to decide what they were to be. What emphasis should be placed on "content courses" and how much on "method courses"? The Normal School was slowly but surely transformed into the College of Liberal Arts, and programs designed to provide advanced and/or graduate instruction were developed. Insofar as Catholic education was concerned, there very fortunately appeared a group of able and farsighted men who greatly increased the confidence of Catholics that their schools, while maintaining separateness both of outlook and initiative, could meet the challenge of the time. John Lancaster Spalding (1840–1916), Bishop of Peoria and one of the founders of the Catholic University of America,[17] Thomas Shields (1862–1921), professor of education and author,[18] Edward Pace (1861–1938), professor and philosopher, and George Johnson (1862–1944), professor and moving spirit in the preparation of *Guiding Growth in Christian Social Living* (1954), the first significant plan for the development of a curriculum for Catholic schools,[19] provided guidance that has not lost its significance until this very day. Though not all the religious communities or all the schools could respond to the demands made by such leaders, a marked change took place.

The work of these leaders may be described briefly as designed to give Catholic teachers a sense of common purpose and objective. The traditional concept that the schools were to train "the whole man"— the body, the intelligence, and the religious sense—was brought into intimate relationship with educational needs and opportunities in many ways different from those that had previously been recognized. First, the benefits of schooling were now to be made available to far greater numbers, indeed to every child. This was a great step forward, but it required the application of psychological insights into the processes of learning and motivation. That application could not be a consequence of formulas until these had been diligently tested. Experimentation was the order of the day. Obviously this could not move forward until teacher training had been improved.

A great step toward the realization of the ideals that had been projected was taken when the National Catholic Educational Association was formed in 1904 by uniting previously existing Catholic educational societies. Since that time the Association has increased almost spectacularly in membership and influence. It owes its success in very large part to George Johnson, who served as executive secretary until his death in 1944, and his successor, Frederick G. Hochwalt, whose leadership is still vigorous as this study is being completed.

Because, as has been noted, the male teaching communities had devoted their efforts mainly to secondary education, it was the teaching sister who became the pioneer in elementary school reform. Doubtless the most impressive step forward in teacher preparation was taken when Sister Formation came into being during 1954. This dramatic and effective remedial action was primarily a consequence of initiatives taken within and without the Catholic school system. First, the National Education Association established a National Commission on Teacher Education and Professional Standards which began to wrestle with the tasks assigned to it in 1946. These tasks were quite pragmatic. How could elementary-school teachers acquire professional recognition similar to that which long since had been obtained for the faculties of secondary schools? These last received most of their training in the subjects they were to teach. The number of so-called "methods courses" they were obliged to take was minimal, unless perchance a state department of education demanded more. But in 1946 only 15 states required a Bachelor's degree for the first standard teaching certificate. By 1953, just before Sister Formation came into being, the number of states insisting on the same requirement had increased to 27. A 1952–53 inquiry into the situation in Catholic schools indicated that only 16 religious communities were equipping their candidates for elementary-school teaching with the Bachelor's degree. Obviously an effort to improve the situation would have to be made quickly.

Second, the initiative taken within the Catholic school system, following upon a good deal of more or less random discussion of the quality of teaching, resulted in the convening in 1949 by the National Catholic Educational Association of a "Symposium on Teacher Education and Teacher Training" for the purpose of considering in depth the import of the religious vocation. The results of this Symposium were published under the title *The Education of Sister Lucy*.[20] This contained a major address by Sister Mary Madeleva, C.S.C., which presented Lucy Young, "a hypothetical high school graduate." Because Sister Mary Madeleva formulated so well ideas about teacher outlook and training that were then being proposed by reformers, we shall quote rather extensively.

> She wants to be a teacher. To realize her desire on any level she knows that she will have to have a Bachelor's degree and a teacher's license. She plans on all of this under whatever difficulties and demands of time and money. She expects to fulfill the minimum professional requirements for teaching. Any other precedure would be a sort of treason disqualifying her for the thing she wishes to be and to do. Before she begins her preparation she finds that she would rather be a teacher for God's sake than for two hundred dollars a month. She enters the novitiate of a religious community dedicated to education. She is simultaneously on two thresholds of one life. She is to be educated to be a teacher. She is to be formed to be a religious teacher. The two trainings are completely compatible, complementary, and can be perfectly synchronized.
>
> For six months Lucy is a postulant and has no status save that of hope and anticipation in the community to which she has come. Her superiors, with wisdom and foresight, logically let her have her first semester of college preparation for teaching. Some superiors may give her the entire freshman year. At the end of her academic period she receives the holy habit of the community and begins her canonical year of preparation to be a religious teacher. No secular studies can intrude upon this important work. However, young Sister Lucy does study religion, Scripture, apologetics, dogma, Church history, perhaps.
>
> At the end of her canonical year of formation she still has one year before her first vows and three additional years before her final profession. These are, I believe, the regular canonical periods and are fairly uniform in all our active orders. She still has three years and a little more of college preparation for her degree and her license. These are as important to her honest professional training as her canonical years are to her religious formation. We need not evade this by arguing the superiority of religious over secular subjects. We do need to face the fact that the religious habit does not confer infused knowledge in any field nor justify the violation of the commonest requirements for teacher preparation. So let us give Sister Lucy these least qualifications.

In the second year of her religious life proper she should be allowed
to take her regular sixteen hours of college work each semester. Good
planning and budgeting of time can make this possible with an enrich-
ment of rather than an intrusion upon her religious life. During summer session she can take an additional six hours. By the time that Sister
Lucy makes her first vows she will or she can be a junior in college. Both
her religious and her academic preparation are synchronously more
than half completed. There still remain three years before her final
profession. With less than two of these plus summer schools she will
have finished her work for her Bachelor's degree and will have over a
year to go on mission as an unprofessed sister.

On the day of her final profession her religious superiors and her
community can receive her as a sister completely prepared by her religious training, her vows, her academic education, to begin at once
to carry on the work to which she is dedicated.

Sister Madeleva added:

I need not tell you that Sister Lucy does not exist. But I know that
we all should insist that she must exist.

It is probable that the Symposium would have made only a fleeting
impression had it not been for the Roman Congress of the States of Perfection, convened in 1950. This was one of the first manifestations in
the field of education of what would later be widely referred to as
aggiornamento in the Catholic Church—the bringing up to date, in
a world of social and intellectual change, of institutional and individual religious effort. Insofar as the teaching religious communities were
concerned, adaptation to the new social order fortunately did not
consist of mere external manifestations of a desire to modernize. True
enough, some habits were redesigned in conformity with common sense
so that the sister in one community or another was no longer compelled
to look at the world through a slit in starched linen. Many more sisters
were visible outside convent walls, especially on university campuses,
but the major emphasis was placed squarely on helping them to become
more adequately prepared teachers. The sister who was being trained
for elementary school instruction was to have the Bachelor's degree,
and indeed if this objective had been reached the religious generally
would have been better educated than their counterparts in the public
schools. Second, her religious formation was to be planned to provide
increased attention to the nature of her life's work in the service of
God. These modifications of traditional practice were eloquently advo-

cated by Pope Pius XII in a memorable allocution to the Roman Congress for Communities of Religious Women, convened in 1952. The Pope's counsel was seed that fell on good ground when the National Catholic Educational Association met later in that year. The Sister Formation Conference was organized, given a large measure of autonomy, and helped to work seriously in 1954. It was very fortunate in having the leadership of Sister Mary Emil, I.H.M., a remarkable woman whose comment on the achievement to date will be given later in this Report.[21]

The achievement has indeed been great. Nevertheless, as Sister Mary Emil's reflections will indicate, Sister Formation and other movements that resemble it have not succeeded in bringing about fully the improvement Pope Pius XII had advocated. There are good reasons why this is so, and even a cursory enumeration of them will indicate the need for inquiries that go beyond the scope of the present *Study of Catholic Education*. The first reason is implicit in the stated purpose of the Catholic school effort. If all children are to benefit, why are not all actually doing so? This is an obviously crucial question. Sometimes the endeavor to provide for as many as possible led to a demand for teachers greater than the ability of the communities to meet if they were to provide the kind of training to which Sister Formation was dedicated. Nor has it been possible to recruit an adequate number of well-prepared lay teachers, for whom, incidentally, no program such as Sister Formation exists. Although the data in this Report throw a great deal of light on the situation, they outline rather than assess the difficulties. Nor have we tried to compare what is happening in the Catholic school with public education. Here too, the problem has been one of providing schools for a rapidly expanding pupil population, and those in charge would candidly admit that finding wholly adequate teachers has been a matter of constant concern.

The cost factor has been especially troubling in Catholic education, but a thorough analysis of it has yet to be undertaken.[22] It has many aspects, and although attention has been focused on nearly all of them in recent comments and studies, we have nothing that resembles a comprehensive view of any one aspect, not to speak of the situation as a whole. We may refer to a few. From what sources are the revenues that support Catholic schools derived? On the one hand, these are contributions made by the laity in the form of either donations or tuition fees.

On the other hand, they are services provided by religious communities. Two recent studies by Sister Cecilia Maureen Kehoe, F.C.S.P., and Sister Maria Concepta, C.S.C.,[23] throw light on the difference between the expenditures made by the communities for the training, maintenance, and retirement of their teaching members and the stipends received. This difference is often very great. Although in some instances lay teachers are paid at the prevailing local rate for teachers' salaries in the public schools, this is by no means usually the case, so that it is frequently relevant to speak of "contributed services" in this respect also. As for contributions made by the laity, either to the parish or to the diocese, "liberty and diversity" are so dominant that no clear pattern emerges.

Inquiries into the business management of the Catholic schools have been in progress for some time, and the literature is extensive. Although this clearly reveals an increasingly greater concern for improved methodology, it is far too early to speak of a time when a general solution of management problems will be possible. The present is a period of experimentation, and a careful scrutiny of the results is eminently desirable. So far school administration has not been emphasized in Catholic centers for the training of teachers.

There are other reasons why training for work in Catholic schools, in the light of the objectives established in the early 1950s, has proved a knotty problem. Among them is one that lies outside the limits assigned to our *Study of Catholic Education.* The number of colleges and other institutions of higher learning maintained by religious communities has greatly increased, with the result that a considerable emphasis has been placed on the preparation of a relatively few to give instruction at the postsecondary-school level. Diverse factors are at work here, but it would seem on the whole that these colleges and other institutions have been of benefit to the school system in training of teachers, however problematic they may be from some other points of view, notably their financial stability.[24]

The question "why do Catholic schools exist" may now be asked at a deeper, more philosophical level. Are there valid reasons why the Church should not have been content to follow the Protestant example and establish Sunday Schools to provide the religious instruction that the public school could not usually offer? It may seem strange at first glance that the question is very difficult to answer. A simple, uncomplicated reply is readily found. But an elaboration must take into account differences of orientation that have three main identifiable sources.

The first is the "diversity" already referred to. A school "system" that is not systematic cannot easily achieve unity in terms of either philosophy or practice. Public education in the United States also does not conform with any one pattern. We can, however, identify special Catholic problems. Some of these are often referred to in the pertinent literature. Diocesan superintendents have limited authority. They have no status in the canon law, whereas the pastor of a parish does. In many instances the decision about what to do in a given local situation depends on generally silent but protracted discussions or even altercations between a bishop and his parish priests or between the bishop and religious communities. Frequently there is neither the time nor the training to deal effectively with educational problems. A considerable number of the clergy and religious of the United States read widely, take an interest in current discussion of ideas, and follow the debates that make some leading periodicals lively organs of opinion. If they do so they are likely to differ about virtually all matters that are not definitely doctrines of the Church. But in many rectories intellectual life may proceed pretty much in terms of seminary manuals and diocesan newspapers (some of which, incidentally, are better than their reputations). Therefore, although the exploration of educational objectives is being conducted vigorously at the level of university discussion, with the support of diocesan superintendents, the actual conduct of the schools may be quite routine in character.

The second of the three sources is the fact that at present the study of administrative, curricular, and guidance problems by persons serving the public school so far outstrips that under Catholic auspices that the influence of the first is dominant. There is a growing quantity of reputable Catholic research, but most of it is being conducted in collaboration with scholars who serve public and secular education. The inevitable result is that in several areas there is no recognizable difference between the two systems. For instance, new methods of teaching mathematics and physics have been adopted by Catholic and public schools alike, and there is even some reason to conclude from statistics compiled by the National Science Foundation that these methods are being used more widely in Catholic than in other schools. But they are the same methods, and on the whole approximation to common standards tends to blunt the edges of separatism. This is most noticeable in curriculum building.[25] One has only to compare the course of study used in a typical Catholic elementary or secondary school of forty years ago with that in effect today to note the influence of public education on the Catholic school.

The third source is the unevenness of teacher preparation. As has been indicated, the great efforts made to improve the training given to religious have been notably successful. But the demands made on the communities have been so heavy that young men and women have been assigned to schools far earlier than is desirable, in the hope that summer session work would fill in the educational gaps. That being the situation, it is not remarkable that differences in outlook and orientation should exist. Meanwhile the religious community itself may be undergoing a transformation of its rule and structure. The major cause of unevenness is, however, the fact that the increasing number of lay teachers are being recruited haphazardly. Even the question of whether they are truly committed to Catholic education sometimes remains open.

Of course there are manifest similarities. Every Catholic school teaches religion, although it may by no means do so in the way others do. In all, symbols associated with the liturgy and prayer are intimately associated with the school day. The very presence of the religious is in itself a dominant, unforgettable symbol. Here are persons set apart from the world reminding that world not merely of sin, of justice, and of judgment, but also of the unavoidable choice between the holy and the unholy, between the things that are of time and the things that transcend time. One may rebel against all this, as many have, but even those who do not surrender to the school cannot erase its imprint from the texture of their minds. This one remembers about Catholic education when virtually all else may have been forgotten.

But whether this unity is properly one of intensified parish life rather than of the school is a question asked more and more often.[26] It cannot be answered because research has provided no basis for a valid comparison between parish life in which the school occupies a central position and, hypothetically, parish life that exists so rich in terms of liturgy and action that a school might be of peripheral concern. Even so there is ample evidence that if what has just been said about the purpose of the Catholic school were all that could be said, the philosophical basis on which that school rests would be relatively insubstantial.

Attempts have not been lacking to formulate a Catholic educational philosophy adequate for the times in which we live. Pope Pius XI's encyclical, "The Christian Education of Youth,"[27] presented the school as an agency which, in cooperation with parents, civil society, and cultural institutions, seeks to form Christian character, so that men will think, judge, and act in accordance with right reason and the teachings of Jesus Christ. Pope John XXIII's encyclical, *Pacem in Terris* says:

> It is our opinion, too, that the above-mentioned inconsistency between the religious faith, in those who believe, and their activities in the temporal sphere, results—in great part if not entirely—from the lack of a solid Christian education. Indeed, it happens in many quarters and too often that there is no proportion between scientific training and religious instruction: the former continues and is extended until it reaches higher degrees, while the latter remains at an elementary level. It is indispensable, therefore, that in the training of youth, education should be complete and without interruption: namely, that in the minds of the young, religious values should be cultivated and the moral conscience refined, in a manner to keep pace with the continuous and ever more abundant assimilation of scientific and technical knowledge. And it is indispensable, too, that they be instructed in the proper way to carry out their actual tasks.[28]

The great "Pastoral Letter of the Archbishops and Bishops of the United States," published in 1919, restated five principles that were said to "serve as the basis of Catholic Education."[29] First, the child has a right to education, and so his elders have the duty to provide it, because the soul created by God is "endowed with capacities which need to be developed for the good of the individual and the good of society." Education, therefore, is "essentially and inevitably a moral activity," in the sense that it undertakes to satisfy certain claims to rights through the fulfillment of certain obligations. Second, the capacities of the child should be developed harmoniously: "An education which quickens the intelligence and enriches the mind with knowledge, but fails to develop the will and direct it to the practice of virtue, may produce scholars, but it cannot produce good men." Third, "Since the duties we owe our Creator take precedence of all other duties, moral training must accord the first place to religion, that is to the knowledge of God and His law." Fourth, "Religious training should be joined with instruction in other kinds of knowledge. It should so permeate these that its influence will be felt in every circumstance of life." Fifth, "An education that unites intellectual, moral and religious elements, is the best training for citizenship."

Thus one can discern a marked continuity of thought in the declarations made by the teaching authority of the Church on the subject of education. Because man is endowed by his Creator with rights that in turn impose duties, moral training in the rational use of those rights and in the performance of the duties that accompany them is inseparable from education; and religion provides the only light in which the significance of moral action can be adequately understood. But none of these statements indicates how these educational goals are to be reached. One can perhaps distinguish four main trends in thinking about this problem. There have been those for whom the pedagogical method is properly that of the traditional seminary. "The Catholic way of seeing the world" is expounded, no matter what the subject matter may be, and it is supposed that young people will docilely absorb the instruction given them. The second way is that which holds that transmitting the riches of Christian culture is the major objective of Christian education. Its proponents are persuaded that the Christian faith has flowered in a philosophy, literature, and art so rich and inspiring that being educated to share in the tradition is the worthiest of educational goals. But obviously Christian culture in the sense thus presented is primarily humanistic and does not include the scientific and technological studies that loom so large in *Pacem in Terris*. The third way is that presented in John Henry Cardinal Newman's *Idea of a University*. This recognizes the autonomy of the various disciplines but places theology at the center. Science and literature are accepted as they are. One must know them but at the same time see what happens in these realms when religion ceases to provide the light in which their relationship to man and his God becomes manifest. The fourth way is one that seems to be evolving in the United States, although it clearly reveals its indebtedness to contemporary thought in Europe and Great Britain.

The pioneer formulation of this "way" was supplied by *Guiding Growth in Christian Social Living* (1944). If all the schools to which this treatise was directed had followed the advice given, we should doubtless now be witnessing in the Catholic schools a unity of philosophical commitment that is not discernible. We have asked Sister Mary Nona, O.P., co-author with Sister Mary Joan, O.P., of this book for a summary of the position to which it might desirably have led. Sister replied that the purposes of Christian education "can be reduced to two," both of which refer to the human person. First, the school must seek to develop the "given powers of the learner," both those manifest and those it is hoped can be achieved. Second, the learner must strengthen "his kinships with all being outside himself." Commenting on the first purpose, she said in part:

> Since the senses are the pupil's gateways to learning throughout life, it is the work of the school to teach him to see, to listen, to use hands and body for learning and communication; to use his memory for various kinds of remembering; to develop his imagination as a bridge of reasoning; and to find valuable help to learning in his emotions. Greater than these powers, yet paradoxically dependent on them, are the endowments of the intellect and the will. These above all others, but always in conjunction with the others, need to be stimulated, challenged, persuaded to human purpose through school guidance and experience. For every pupil is a unity of body and soul, in whom the spiritual powers unify, direct and vitalize the activities of his whole person. According to a Christian phiosophy of education, each individual is a person to be perfected in nature and grace, called to share in the life of God and there to realize fully his latent possibilities. The work of the teacher is not so much with the structure of mathematics or the right use of a textbook or the class norms on an examination as it is with the human potential of each person in the class.

Concerning the second purpose, she wrote:

> The tie which the pupil discovers first is that with the physical world—the total environment of nature and man-made things. These range from the inanimate stones and stars, the multiple products of human workmanship, to higher forms of the natural life, including his own body. Among these creatures it is the prerogative and the responsibility of man before the Creator of the world to know them, use them reasonably, control them for human needs, appreciate and share their resources for the sake of all men. One of the fundamental objectives of the Christian school therefore is to teach the pupil to live humanely in relation to things.
> Quite different is the pupil's kinship with people, with men, women and children known and unknown. This kinship begins with his own family and grows outward and with varying degrees of affinity with and responsibility to the human race, to persons living in the present and the past, or to those yet unborn. It requires knowledge, communication

and joint action for the common good, whether it be that of a family or the entire world of men. The Christian school proposes to teach its pupils the profound meaning of their human associations, whether through social studies or through the practice, in and out of school, of the social virtues.

This statement may be (and has been) questioned by reason of its assumption that there is a tenable psychology that separates the "faculties" from each other. We need not debate the matter here. One of the merits of Sister Mary Nona's formulation, however, is that it helps to emancipate the discussion of Catholic educational theory from a long, at onetime fruitful but eventually more and more sterile, debate about whether the schools should be concerned primarily with the teaching of ethics and the "Christian formation" of character or whether their main purpose should be to train the mind. Implicit in Sister Mary Nona's methodology for attaining the two purposes of education is "problem solving," which can have persistent moral and religious implications for the Catholic educator and the children he or she serves. Whether Catholic schools have always and everywhere reckoned fully with all the help that psychological inquiry now provides is another matter, but at least there would seem to be little this does offer which cannot, or could not, be used to serve the educational purposes Sister Mary Nona has in mind.

Her comment on religious instruction as such is therefore of special interest:

> The pupil's relationship to God is not only the most eminent and mysterious but also the most unique, in that it gives other kinships a meaning. St. Paul says, "All things are yours and you are Christ and Christ is God's." It accounts for the orientation of material things to the spiritual, of all that is natural to human life, of time to eternity, and of the child in his whole life and education to God. Who can understand the bond between the creature and his Creator, the man saved and his Redeemer, the child and his Father, man and the Son of Man? The human person is bound by love to the God of love. It is the awesome privilege of the Christian school to enable pupils, through knowledge and practice, to strengthen the mysterious bond of love with God.

These reflections on the inner meaning of Christian formation capture much of the richness of the Pauline and Thomist traditions. They indicate that in this realm the objective must be *realization* and not *infor-*

mation as such. There has been much recent discussion of the meaning of realization. We cannot hope to deal here with the numerous implications of the newer literature. Perhaps one may say that on the one hand these challenge a too school-centered concept of the educational process. Certainly in a society like ours, the home, the pattern of urban living, and the mass media must somehow be correlated with the school if both the conscience of the pupil and his awareness of life in its full potential are to be served. If, indeed, the ethical habits of a child are, as many psychologists assert, formed in the home during early childhood, the school must seek whenever it is possible to continue and strengthen rather than to initiate character formation.

But the new literature indicates also that the ancient debate over whether the school is to serve intellectual ends primarily or whether in doing so it neglects the task of religious-ethical teaching has been reformulated. In the wake of Vatican II some commentators have assumed that since the study of Scripture is once more the central concern of the Church, therefore older Augustinian views of the relationship between philosophy and theology once again loom large in the discussion, the doctrine that "God is Love" and the supreme manifestation of His Affection is in Christ is paramount, and one must draw a sharp line of demarcation between *realization* thus understood and the intellectualist purposes of education. So, it is argued, since public and secular education probably serve those last-named purposes more effectively than do the Catholic schools, one may well handicap Catholic children by refusing to give them access to that education. In addition, does not the parochial school divert those who could most effectively exemplify the service of Christ and the "Theology of Love" —namely the religious—from the real reason why they have chosen their vocation? Why should they teach mathematics or linguistics when they could preach the Gospel? Besides, there will never be enough religious to make parochial education available to all Catholic children.

Therewith the ancient debate between those who refused to admit that secular culture could be thought of as an integral part of Christian wisdom and those who believed that "Jerusalem and Athens" must be conjoined has taken on a new form. However difficult it may be to conceive of a time when the teaching sister will be akin to a Salvation Army lassie, the new literature does introduce a fresh kinetic influence into the discussion of Catholic educational philosophy. Doubtless, however, the pessimism latent in it—a pessimism induced by the obvious fact that parochial schools and other forms of institutionalized education cannot serve all Catholic children, and by the less obvious but often-assumed probability that in some ways public schools may be better schools—may give way in part to a new optimism when the total situation is reviewed calmly. This report, for instance, will indicate clearly that, in their totality, Catholic schools are much better than some recent appraisals have assumed. Far more important is the probability that these schools can dedicate themselves to an objective of spiritually motivated service to the community that would be uniquely their own.

That love of God and affection for one's neighbor go hand in hand is the oldest of truths in the Christian tradition. Lip service in plenty has been paid to it. But if one can make service to the neighbor, exemplified in daily practice, the hub round which the school life turns, one will weave into it almost automatically reverence for the God of Love. Education would then be Christ-like. The dignity of man in the Catholic view rests on the belief that he is in God's image—that his intellect exists to make possible his moving away from what is beastlike in him toward participation in the Divinity from which his spirit comes. The vast numbers of men, women, and children living in towns and cities who do not have any awareness of their dignity, often through no fault of their own, is the most evident and ominous of social realities. Now some masters of the philosophy of Catholic education dream of schools in which a central purpose of the Catholic educators would be reaching out to these, in a spirit of comradeship in which disdain has no part. Here may well be a restatement of vital purposes that can give these schools new and abundant life.

It would seem far more in consonance with the steady development of a philosophy of Catholic education than any other to which Vatican II has given impetus. Sister Mary Nona's comment, on that development though more general in scope, seems pertinent:

> Like American democracy, the Christian philosophy of education is always assumed and defended though its translation into action may leave something to be desired. But its tenets have been clarified over many years and applied to new circumstances, new forms of teaching and learning. The philosophical development of Catholic teaching is in fact as interesting as that of the foundation of Catholic schools, and this history has been equally neglected.

With this outline of a developing view of the objectives of Catholic education in the United States we close. We have come a long way from a time when the major objective appeared to be giving immigrant Catholics who desired education for their children some of the advantages that monastic schools had provided in Europe. Inevitably Catholic education has become American. It is now a vital part of the great effort to bring to the citizens of this country a deepened awareness of their opportunities and responsibilities.

References

1. Burns, James, C.S.C., and Bernard Kohlbrenner, *A History of Catholic Education in the United States* (New York: 1937), a pioneer survey unfortunately never revised; McCluskey, Neil G., S.J., *Catholic Education in America: A Documentary History* (New York: 1964); McAvoy, Thomas T., C.S.C., *The Great Crisis in American Catholic History* (Washington: 1957). A number of dissertations, for the most part unpublished, also deal with segments of educational history: "The School Controversy in New York, 1840–1842, and Its Effect on the Formulation of Catholic Elementary School Policy" (Notre Dame: 1962) and Martine, Harriette A., "A History of Parochial Elementary School Education" (New York: 1955). Histories of various dioceses will also provide information.

2. Ellis, John Tracy, ed., *Documents of American Catholic History* (Milwaukee), p. 17.

3. Burns and Kohlbrenner, *op. cit.*, p. 55.

4. Guilday, Peter, *The Life and Times of the Most Rev. John Carroll, Bishop and First Archbishop of Baltimore* (New York: 1922).

5. England, John, *Life and Times of John England* (New York: 1927).

6. Melville, Annabelle, *Elizabeth Bayley Seton* (New York: 1951); Dirbin, Joseph, *Mrs. Seton, Foundress of the American Sisters of Charity* (New York: 1962).

7. McCluskey, *op. cit.*, p. 6 ff.

8. Shuster, George N., *Catholic Spirit in America* (New York: 1925).

9. Maguire, J. F., *The Irish in America*, 4th ed. (New York: 1873).

10. Lord, R. H., J. E. Sexton, and E. T. Harrington, *History of the Archdiocese of Boston* (Boston: 1944), XXI, 320.

11. Billington, Ray A., *The Protestant Crusade 1800–1860* (New York: 1938).

12. Barry, C. J., *The Catholic Church and German Americans* (Washington: 1953).

13. Kinser, Donald L., *An Episode in Anti-Catholicism* (New York: 1964).

14. In McCluskey, *op. cit.*, p. 127 ff.

15. Moynihan, James A., *The Life of Archbishop John Ireland* (New York: 1953).

16. In McCluskey, *op. cit.*, p. 178 ff.

17. See McCluskey for bibliography.

18. Ward, Justine, *Thomas Edward Shields* (New York: 1947).

19. Sister Mary Joan, O.P., and Sister Mary Nona, O.P., *Guiding Growth in Christian Social Living* (Washington: 1944).

20. St. Mary's, Indiana, 1954.

21. Sister Ritamary, C.H.M., ed., *Planning for the Formation of Sisters* (New York: 1958).

22. *Commonweal* (special issue, "Federal Aid and Catholic Schools"), LXXIX, 18.

23. McCluskey, *op. cit.,* p. 33.

24. Lee, James Michael, *Principles and Methods of Secondary Education* (New York: 1963).

25. Ryan, Mary Perkins, *Are Parochial Schools the Answer?* (New York: 1964).

26. *Five Great Encyclicals* (New York: 1939).

27. *Peace on Earth* (New York: 1964), p. 153.

28. In McCluskey, *op. cit.*

29. Mouroux, Jean, *The Meaning of Life* (New York: 1948), p. 143.

30. Vann, Gerald, O.P., *The Divine Pity* (New York: 1946), p. 66.

CHAPTER TWO

The Enrollment of Catholic Schools

ANY LOOK AT SCHOOLS IN ACTION MUST BE CONCERNED with that segment of youth being served. This Study examined the enrollment of the Catholic elementary and secondary schools in the United States for the 1962–63 school year. The enrollment statistics collected annually by the National Catholic Welfare Conference were analyzed for the 9-year period from the school year 1953–54 to the school year 1962–63. This period was used because the statistical method of collecting data was changed in 1953 and remained constant through 1962.

The enrollment data were first analyzed by individual dioceses and then by dioceses grouped into 9 standard statistical regions (Fig. 1). The analyses showed a clear pattern of continued growth in both the elementary and secondary enrollment during this 9-year period. A few individual dioceses showed a drop in enrollment, but in each of these subdivision to form new dioceses accounted for the decrease in enrollment.

The second clear outcome of the analysis was that the rate of growth of secondary enrollment greatly exceeded that of elementary enrollment. During the 9-year period secondary enrollment increased 62.8% whereas elementary enrollment increased 38.7% (Tables 1 and 2).

In further analysis the 9-year period broke down into 2 parts. The first 6 years, 1953–54 to 1959–60, showed a rather even rate of growth for both elementary and secondary enrollments. During this period the elementary enrollment increased by 27.2% and the secondary by 29.9%. However, the 3 years 1960–61 to 1962–63, show a complete change in

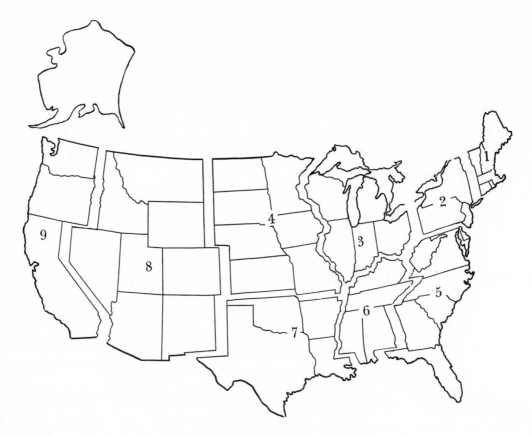

Fig. 1.   Standard statistical regions.

Region 1:   Maine, New Hampshire, Vermont, Massachusetts, Rhode Island, Connecticut.

Region 2:   New York, New Jersey, Pennsylvania.

Region 3:   Ohio, Indiana, Illinois, Michigan, Wisconsin.

Region 4:   Minnesota, Iowa, Missouri, North Dakota, South Dakota, Nebraska, Kansas.

Region 5:   Delaware, Maryland, District of Columbia, Virginia, West Virginia, North Carolina, South Carolina, Georgia, Florida.

Region 6:   Kentucky, Tennessee, Alabama, Mississippi.

Region 7:   Arkansas, Louisiana, Oklahoma, Texas.

Region 8:   Montana, Idaho, Wyoming, Colorado, New Mexico, Arizona, Utah, Nevada.

Region 9:   Washington, Oregon, California, Alaska.

the rate of enrollment growth. During this period secondary enrollment increased by 20.2% while elementary enrollment increased by only 9.0%. The average growth per year in elementary school enrollment over the full 9-year period was 138,671, and in secondary schools 43,294; for the first 6-year period the average growth per year was 146,329 in elementary schools, and 30,867 in secondary schools; during the subsequent 3-year period the elementary growth per year was 123,356, compared with 68,149 in secondary schools (Table 3); a further look at these enrollment growth rates is presented in Table 4.

From these statistics it seems clear that greater provision for secondary schools was made from about 1959, near the end of the first

Table 1

GROWTH IN ELEMENTARY ENROLLMENT BY REGIONS, 1953–62

Region	1953	1962	Change	Change %	1953	1959	Change	Change %	1959	1962	Change	Change %
1	303,693	354,779	51,086	16.8	303,693	350,020	46,327	15.2	350,020	354,779	4,759	1.3
2	1,016,167	1,365,530	349,363	34.3	1,016,167	1,236,269	220,102	21.6	1,236,269	1,365,530	129,261	11.2
3	902,696	1,264,469	361,773	40.0	902,696	1,182,486	279,790	30.9	1,182,486	1,264,469	81,983	6.9
4	293,900	425,958	132,058	44.9	293,900	378,365	84,465	28.7	378,365	425,958	47,593	12.5
5	162,999	259,556	96,557	59.2	162,999	215,289	52,290	32.0	215,289	259,556	44,267	20.5
6	78,720	116,784	38,064	48.3	78,720	110,814	32,094	40.7	110,814	116,784	5,970	5.3
7	187,280	242,278	54,998	29.3	187,280	236,873	49,593	26.4	236,873	242,278	5,405	2.3
8	66,774	98,008	31,234	46.7	66,774	95,389	28,615	42.8	95,389	98,008	2,619	2.7
9	212,099	345,013	132,914	62.6	212,099	296,800	84,701	39.9	296,800	345,013	48,213	16.2
Total	3,224,328	4,472,375	1,248,047	38.7	3,224,328	4,102,305	877,977	27.2	4,102,305	4,472,375	370,070	9.0

Table 2

GROWTH IN SECONDARY ENROLLMENT BY REGIONS, 1953–62

Region	1953	1962	Change	Change %	1953	1959	Change	Change %	1959	1962	Change	Change %
1	55,762	88,968	33,206	59.5	55,762	72,885	17,123	30.7	72,885	88,968	16,083	22.1
2	186,949	296,358	109,409	58.5	186,949	243,442	56,493	30.2	243,442	296,358	52,916	21.7
3	177,509	274,027	96,518	54.3	177,509	227,423	49,914	28.1	227,423	274,027	46,604	20.4
4	61,262	90,477	29,215	47.7	61,262	75,109	13,847	22.6	75,109	90,477	15,368	20.5
5	26,909	54,974	28,065	104.3	26,909	36,420	9,511	35.3	36,420	54,974	18,554	50.9
6	19,631	31,106	11,475	58.5	19,631	24,752	5,121	26.1	24,752	31,106	6,354	25.7
7	32,198	49,347	17,149	53.3	32,198	41,947	9,749	30.3	41,947	49,347	7,400	17.6
8	12,567	20,365	7,798	62.1	12,567	18,164	5,597	44.5	18,164	20,365	2,201	12.1
9	46,642	84,891	38,249	82.0	46,642	64,492	17,850	38.3	64,492	84,891	20,399	31.6
Total	619,429	990,513	371,084	59.9	169,429	804,634	185,205	30.0	804,634	990,513	185,879	23.0

6-year period. This change in emphasis could not have been the result of a change in total population, because the percentage of increase in upcoming secondary school population was far outstripped by the increase in the provision for secondary schools; and further, the decreased provision for elementary schools cannot be accounted for by a corresponding decrease in elementary-age population.

It is interesting that in Region 5, which consists of the South Atlantic states, from Delaware south and including West Virginia, the increase in secondary school enrollment during the 9-year period was 104.3%, an increase well beyond the total secondary school population increase in that same region. A typical example of this increase in secondary school enrollment is the Bridgeport, Connecticut, diocese, where during the 9-year period enrollment increased by 305.8%. The question that follows is whether this identified movement toward greater provision for secondary schools was an attempt to catch up to secondary school needs or the result of a decision to make greater effort to provide for secondary school pupils rather than for elementary pupils.

Table 3

AVERAGE GROWTH PER YEAR IN ELEMENTARY
AND SECONDARY ENROLLMENT

	1953–54 — 1962–63	1953–54 — 1959–60	1960–61 — 1962–63
Elementary	138,671	146,329	123,356
Secondary	43,294	30,867	68,149

Table 4

PERCENTAGE OF ENROLLMENT GROWTH BY REGIONS

Region	1953–1962		1953–1959		1959–1962	
	Elementary	Secondary	Elementary	Secondary	Elementary	Secondary
1	16.8	59.5	15.2	30.7	1.3	22.1
2	34.4	58.5	21.6	30.2	10.4	21.7
3	40.0	54.3	30.9	28.1	6.9	20.4
4	44.9	47.7	28.7	22.6	12.6	20.5
5	59.2	104.3	32.0	35.3	20.5	50.9
6	48.3	58.5	40.7	26.1	5.3	25.7
7	29.3	53.3	26.4	30.3	2.3	17.6
8	46.7	62.1	42.8	44.5	2.7	12.1
9	62.6	82.0	39.9	38.3	16.5	31.6
National	38.7	62.8	27.2	29.9	9.0	20.2

ELIGIBLE CATHOLIC YOUTH

When the current enrollment figures in Catholic schools had been evaluated, the next step was to establish the total number of Catholic youth who would be eligible for Catholic schools if they should apply. A review of logical sources of information produced only broad estimates without any statistical base.

A procedure was developed to determine the number of Catholic youth who would have been eligible to apply for entrance to Catholic elementary and secondary schools throughout the nation in the school year 1962–63. A legitimate assumption is that the number of children eligible to apply for entrance to Catholic schools would be the total of those who were baptized as Catholics and who survived to school age (indeed it is general practice for Catholic schools to demand a baptismal certificate for all children seeking admission). Therefore, the infant baptism figures as reported in *The Official Catholic Directory*[1] were accumulated from the yearly volumes of 1943 to 1962. The volumes of the *Directory* are identified by the year of publication, each reporting on diocesan affairs for the preceding year; thus the 1964 volume contains diocesan reports for the year 1963. The editor's instructions to the individual dioceses state that the infant baptisms being reported should cover the first 10 months of the current year and the last 2 months of the preceding year, so that the report covers a 12 month period, November through October. This reporting period coincides with the general admission age in Catholic schools, which for first grade is age 6 by October of the admitting year.

The yearly reported infant baptisms, as described above, were correlated with survivorship ratios, year by year, to determine the number of baptized children alive and eligible to apply for admission to Catholic schools during the school year 1962–63. The survivorship ratios were developed by the application of a series of life-table reports from the National Vital Statistics Division of the Public Health Service, United States Department of Health, Education and Welfare.[2]

The following statistical assumptions were made in processing these baptismal reports:

1. Catholic children die at the same age-specific rate as do other children in the United States;

2. the use of 1949–51 life tables is an acceptable approximation of age-specific death rates (the 1959–61 life tables were not published at the time these data were being processed);

3. the use of 1949–51 life tables for the years preceding 1949;

4. the application of "white, both sexes" death rates to all baptisms because the baptisms are not reported by sex or color.

The survivorship figures produced by the procedures outlined represent a close approximation of the number of Catholic youth eligible to apply for admission to Catholic schools. The numbers of these young people, presented by age-grade groups, are compared with the reported enrollments in Catholic schools for the school year of 1962–63 in Table 5.

By using the procedure outlined and summarizing the findings in the preceding tables, the percentage of eligible Catholic youth enrolled in Catholic schools in the school year 1962–63 was identified. Those unaccounted for were presumed to be:

1. enrolled in public schools or other independent schools;

2. under special care in institutions or classes for the handicapped, both physically and mentally;

3. or, in the upper age groups, a part of school dropouts, either employed or unemployed.

An important observation here is that of the total eligible Catholic youth as determined by the Study procedure, 52% of the elementary and 32% of the secondary eligibles were enrolled in Catholic schools. It must be emphasized that these findings represent a composite national picture, which conceals the wide differences that may exist among individual dioceses.

An original part of the design of this Study was to be a carefully planned and demographically sound diocesan census through which individual dioceses could assess the total problem involved in educating all of the Catholic children in Catholic schools, if this were the diocesan objective. The plan for such a diocesan census was developed, but because of the costs that would have been involved and because of the inability of some dioceses to cooperate, the plan was not fully implemented. However, 3 census approaches were made in which the Study design was in some part operative.

In the Fort Wayne-South Bend, Indiana, diocese the census approach used only a demographic sample of parishes and produced results at considerable variance with the regular parish reports. The variance in these results should make clear the necessity for validation of each set of parish reports. The variances suggest that parish Catholic population reports greatly underestimate (and rarely overestimate) the reality, whereas baptismal reporting tends to be highly accurate.

In 1962 the Wilmington, Delaware, diocese organized a Bishop's Lay Advisory Committee, the function of which was to advise the bishop in all areas of the diocesan operation that were not canonical. Among the many activities of this committee were the development and execution of a complete diocesan census on which to base a long-term plan for Catholic school provision directly related to the total need. The resulting picture of the total need led to many further considerations including: the possibility and method of financing the total need; the type of school organization by which the provision could best be made; the effectiveness of interparish schools in serving remote areas; and the methods of staffing possible broadly expanded school facilities.

Table 5

ELIGIBLE CATHOLIC CHILDREN AND ENROLLMENT, OCTOBER 1962–63

Grade	Eligible Catholic Children	Enrollment	%
Elementary Grades 1–8 *			
1	1,168,913	616,695	52.75
2	1,140,117	598,086	52.45
3	1,097,017	584,998	53.32
4	1,054,777	558,181	52.91
5	1,036,754	543,535	52.42
6	978,207	514,790	52.63
7	934,410	475,086	50.84
8	905,360	450,902	49.80
Total	8,315,555	4,342,273	52.21

* Does not include Kindergarten.

Grade	Eligible Catholic Children	Enrollment	%
Secondary Grades 9–12			
9	896,513	304,874	34.00
10	865,856	279,214	32.24
11	702,752	237,130	33.74
12	666,453	187,863	28.18
Total	3,131,574	1,009,081	32.22
Elementary and Secondary Grades 1–12			
	11,447,129	5,351,354	46.74

The major result was a realistic look at the total problem of providing Catholic schools for the Catholic children in that diocese. This activity required ecclesiastical and clerical confidence in the laymen and full cooperation among all groups. The considerable physical, technical, and personnel resources of the lay group and their unqualified contribution were revealed in this activity. According to the census survey plans, the information is to be kept current and will be available for use in other diocesan activities including the Catholic Charities operation.

Professor Donald Barrett, a member of the Sociology Department of the University of Notre Dame and a member of the Study staff, was invited to act as an advisor to the census development in the Lafayette, Indiana, diocese, a function which he also fulfilled in the Wilmington diocese. As this report is being written, the Lafayette census is being completed, and responsible authorities are expected to utilize the census results fully. Full-scale and well-developed censuses have been and are being conducted in other dioceses, including the Archdioceses of Baltimore and Washington, D. C. From the point of view of this Study, individual parish enumeration or mere counting of known Catholic families should not be confused with a real and legitimate census. The present general lack of diocesan information about the Catholic population is a result of such unorganized parish enumerations. This lack of diocesan information about the total Catholic population surely has some relationship to the fact that there is provision for less than 50% of all Catholic youth to attend Catholic schools, which are nevertheless very highly regarded.

ENROLLMENT PROJECTION FOR SCHOOL YEAR 1968–69

In looking toward the possible future Catholic school enrollment, the percentages of those eligible and of those who were enrolled in the school year 1962–63, as shown in Table 5, were used in making projections for the school year 1968–69. This future year was used because it was the latest for which previous infant baptism figures were available to project first-grade eligibles. The control factors in the 1962–63 enrollment were held constant. The projection assumes: that no change in the percentage of eligibles enrolled will be made; that the ratio of staff to pupils will be unchanged; and that the use of school space will continue at the 1962–63 level. The procedure was to move the "Eligible infant baptisms" for 1962–63 ahead 6 years, applying the survivorship ratios; by this method the 1962–63 elgibles for grade one became the eligibles for grade seven, the sixth-grade became the twelfth-grade eligibles and so with each grade level advanced 6 years. To complete the total eligible group, 6 yearly groups were moved into the grade 1–6 positions; the results are shown in Table 6.

Table 6

PROJECTED SCHOOL ENROLLMENT FOR 1968–69

Elementary Schools, Grades 1–8

Eligible infant baptisms	Enrollment at 1962–63 percentage (52.21)
9,770,108	5,100,973*

Secondary Schools, Grades 9–12

Eligible infant baptisms	Enrollment at 1962–63 percentage (32.22)
4,154,080	1,338,444*

* Percentage applied against total grades, not grade by grade.

These projections produce some interesting indications. For example, compared with the actual enrollments of 1962–63, they show increases of 758,700 in the elementary grades and 329,363 in the secondary grades. In the elementary grades, if the same ratio of lay teachers to religious teachers were to prevail, the additional staff needed would be 12,644 religious and 6322 lay teachers. In the secondary schools an additional 12,668 teachers would be needed, of which 8445 would be religious and 4223 would be lay teachers. These figures reflect only the need for additional teachers and do not include the numbers needed for normal replacement.

In further consideration of these projected increases in school enrollment, another item of concern would be the additional school plant facilities needed. The projected costs of providing these physical facilities are also based on the situation existing in 1962–63. To provide for the 758,700 additional elementary pupils as projected would require 16,860 additional elementary classrooms at the 1962–63 average classroom usage. At a conservative estimate, using the 1962–63 cost of $13,500 per room, the total cost of providing space for elementary children would be $227,610,000.

To determine the cost of facilities for the projected increases in secondary school enrollments, it is necessary to use a cost per pupil because of the varying nature of secondary school facilities. If an arbitrary and conservative cost per pupil of $1500 were used, it would make necessary a capital expenditure of $494,000,000 to provide for the projected increase of 329,363 secondary pupils by the 1968–69 school year.

In summary, this projection into the 1968–69 school year, based on all the conditions controlling the enrollment of the 1962–63 school year, produces the following:

1968–69 Projection Summary

Elementary schools, grades 1–8

Increased enrollment		758,700	
Increased staff need	18,966		
Religious		12,644	
Lay		6,322	
Capital expenditure			
16,860 rooms			$227,610,000

Secondary schools, grades 9–12

Increased enrollment		329,363	
Increased staff need	12,315		
Religious		8,445	
Lay		4,223	
Capital expenditure			
329,363 pupils			$494,000,000

In considering this statistical projection, the following factors should be emphasized:

1. The total projection concept was based on a national picture of Catholic school enrollment.

2. There are wide differences in the way in which the projection applies to individual dioceses.

3. No diocese can say the projection does not apply until that diocese

has made a diagnostic study of its needs.

4. Because this was a national projection, it was not necessary to identify locality growth rates, industrial development, zoning controls, area population migration and immigration, public and private housing plans, large property sales, highway development, and the myriad controls on population location and growth.

5. The items mentioned in 4 above, and many others, become of high importance in determining potential population growth when individual geographic areas are being considered.

6. The cost figures used in estimating the capital expenditure figures of the projection were based on 1962 construction cost estimates and did not include financing charges. In some areas of the country these costs might be either lower or higher.

7. As dioceses are concerned with the provision of schools for Catholic youth, they cannot take the position that the implications of this projection do not apply to their problems.

In further observation, the following seem to be continuing pertinent questions:

1. For whom shall Catholic education be provided?

2. Perhaps more important, what is the purpose of Catholic schools?

3. What part should the Catholic laity have in considering items 1 and 2?

4. What part should the religious communities have in considering the purposes of the Catholic schools? And also, what part should they play in determining the ways in which future school staffing needs should be met?

5. What part will lay staffing play in the future development of Catholic schools?

ADMISSION POLICIES

At this point a review of the schools' admission policies as of 1962 is in order. The review of these policies is based on responses from 9451 elementary school principals and 2075 secondary principals which were recorded on Study Questionnaire Schedules II and III, referred to earlier in this report.

The general admission policies can be summarized as follows, with the percentage of schools using each policy:

1. Attendance limited to parish membership
   Elementary schools   70%
   Secondary schools   14%
2. Limitation of space
   Elementary schools   42%
   Secondary schools   52%
3. Limited to Catholics
   Elementary schools   20%
   Secondary schools   17%
4. Academic standards
   Elementary schools   13%
   Secondary schools   53%
5. Lack of maturity of students
   Elementary schools   25%
   Secondary schools   26%
6. Admission tests
   Elementary schools   16%
   Secondary schools   68%
7. Direct tuition charges
   Elementary schools   50%
   Secondary schools   77%

The use of parish membership as a requisite for school enrollment is more common among elementary schools because the parish-administered school is the usual type of elementary school; 86% of the reporting elementary schools were parish schools, whereas only 37% of the reporting secondary schools were parish administered.

When space is a factor in limiting enrollment, the policies are usually established by the individual schools. However, a growing number of dioceses have diocesan policies governing class size in the elementary schools, and in most of these the policy is followed strictly. This definite trend seems to go through 2 stages: the control is first a strong suggestion and then a strict policy. This trend is not so evident at the secondary level, because in most dioceses such administrative control of secondary schools is slight.

Only a small percentage of the reporting schools indicated a policy of limiting attendance to Catholic children. This Study did not collect information on the number of non-Catholic students in the schools, but it was not rare to find schools which had non-Catholic boys and girls in enrollment. In some systems that had separate schools for Negroes, which were in the process of integration, there were secondary schools that had non-Catholic enrollments as high as 50%. The policy of not enrolling a non-Catholic child was most often effected when there was a lack of space for Catholic applicants.

Admission tests in the elementary schools are used primarily to assist in better placement of the child, although in some of the private elementary schools the admission test is used as a screening for enrollment. Only 4% of the 9541 elementary schools reporting were classed as private schools, and only some of these screened applicants by testing. Tests administered prior to admission to the secondary schools are also used for student placement, but in 53% they are used chiefly for acceptance or rejection of the applicants (Tables 7 and 8).

Additional admission policies are developed in parish schools when in spite of the policies outlined there are too many eligible applicants for the available space. In many of these schools the parish membership requirement is extended to include some or all of the following qualifications:

1. Parents of applicants must be regular envelope contributors to the support of the parish.

2. Longer parish membership receives priority for enrollment.

3. Parish activity and service of parents also establish priority.

4. In some parishes having a child already in the school establishes priority for the younger children; in others only one child in a family is admitted.

In some parish elementary schools 4 times as many children are enrolled in the Confraternity of Christian Doctrine classes as are enrolled in the full-time elementary school because of lack of space. In a lighter vein, some pastors have observed that the school enrollment period would be the ideal time for pastors to take their annual vacations.

As applicants for admission to Catholic schools were processed for the 1961–62 school year the responding schools reported the following:

1. 3999 of the 9451 elementary schools, 42% of the total, found it necessary to reject 91,400 applicants. These were mostly applicants for

grade 1; the total rejected was equal to 20% of the number enrolled in grade 1.

2. 942, or 45%, of the 2075 secondary schools reported it necessary to reject 76,000 applicants.

In the admission procedures for the 1962–63 school year the responding schools reported the following:

1. 5015 elementary schools, 53% of the total, reported it necessary to reject 110,000 applicants, mostly first-grade applicants, equal to 20% of first-grade enrollment.

2. 1371 secondary schools, 66% of the total, found it necessary to

Table 7

ELEMENTARY SCHOOL ADMISSION POLICIES, 1962–63*

	Total schools	%	Not identified	%	Parish	%	Private	%	Inter-parish	%	Diocesan	%
Admit all applicants	9451	100.0	288	3.0	8211	86.9	394	4.2	80	0.8	359	3.8
No response	174	1.8	8	2.8	141	1.7	7	1.8	2	2.5	5	1.4
Yes	3039	32.2	93	32.3	2728	33.2	40	10.2	32	40.0	102	28.4
No	6238	66.0	187	64.9	5342	65.1	347	88.1	46	57.5	252	70.2
Parish only	9451	100.0	288	3.0	8211	86.9	394	4.2	80	0.8	359	3.8
Yes	2861	30.3	67	23.3	2672	32.5	7	1.8	12	15.0	102	28.4
No	6590	69.7	221	76.7	5539	67.5	387	98.2	68	85.0	257	71.6
Lack space	9451	100.0	288	3.0	8211	86.9	394	4.2	80	0.8	359	3.8
Yes	3969	42.0	110	38.2	3383	41.2	278	70.6	19	23.8	144	40.1
No	5482	58.0	178	61.8	4828	58.8	116	29.4	61	76.3	215	59.9
Catholic only	9451	100.0	288	3.0	8211	86.9	394	4.2	80	0.8	359	3.8
Yes	1965	20.8	62	21.5	1775	21.6	23	5.8	11	13.8	81	22.6
No	7486	79.2	226	78.5	6436	78.4	371	94.2	69	86.3	278	77.4
Academic standards	9451	100.0	288	3.0	8211	86.9	394	4.2	80	0.8	359	3.8
Yes	1258	13.3	40	13.9	930	11.3	235	59.6	11	13.8	25	7.0
No	8193	86.7	248	86.1	7281	88.7	159	40.4	69	86.3	334	93.0
Lack maturity	9451	100.0	288	3.0	8211	86.9	394	4.2	80	0.8	359	3.8
Yes	2381	25.2	73	25.3	2001	24.4	161	40.9	26	32.5	97	27.0
No	7070	74.8	215	74.7	6210	75.6	233	59.1	54	67.5	262	73.0
Admission test	9451	100.0	288	3.0	8211	86.9	394	4.2	80	0.8	359	3.8
No response	152	1.6	9	3.1	124	1.5	3	0.8	2	2.5	8	2.2
Yes	1477	15.6	56	19.4	1178	14.3	155	39.3	11	13.8	61	17.0
No	7822	82.8	223	77.4	6909	84.1	236	59.9	67	83.8	290	80.8

* Not included, 119 institutional schools, 1.3% of total.

reject 86,787 applicants, almost equal to 30% of the ninth-grade enrollment.

In summary of this 2-year admission picture, we see that the elementary schools had to reject 20% more applicants in 1963–64 than they did in 1962–63, and that 11% more of the schools had to reject applicants. In the secondary schools 14% more applicants were rejected, and an additional 21% of the schools had to reject some applicants. Most of the youngsters rejected at the elementary school level probably entered public schools. At the secondary school level, it is possible that some of these rejected by a private Catholic school were able to enter

Table 8

SECONDARY SCHOOL ADMISSION POLICIES, 1962–63*

	Total schools	%	Not identified	%	Parish	%	Private	%	Inter-parish	%	Diocesan	%
Admit all applicants	2075	100.0	64	3.1	770	37.1	763	36.8	105	5.1	344	16.6
No response	28	1.3	3	4.7	9	1.2	10	1.3	1	1.0	5	1.5
Yes	448	21.6	15	23.4	192	24.9	91	11.9	46	43.8	102	29.7
No	1599	77.1	46	71.9	569	73.9	662	86.8	58	55.2	237	68.9
Parish only	2075	100.0	64	3.1	770	37.1	763	36.8	105	5.1	344	16.6
Yes	289	13.9	7	10.9	127	16.5	25	3.3	19	18.1	109	31.7
No	1786	86.1	57	89.1	643	83.5	738	96.7	86	81.9	235	68.3
Lack space	2075	100.0	64	3.1	770	37.1	763	36.8	105	5.1	344	16.6
Yes	1089	52.5	26	40.6	381	49.5	495	64.9	30	28.6	148	43.0
No	986	47.5	38	59.4	389	50.5	268	35.1	75	71.4	196	57.0
Catholic only	2075	100.0	64	3.1	770	37.1	763	36.8	105	5.1	344	16.6
Yes	357	17.2	11	17.2	147	19.1	81	10.6	18	17.1	98	28.5
No	1718	82.8	53	82.8	623	80.9	682	89.4	87	82.9	246	71.5
Academic standards	2075	100.0	64	3.1	770	37.1	763	36.8	105	5.1	344	16.6
Yes	1095	52.8	28	43.8	343	44.5	534	70.0	32	30.5	150	43.6
No	980	47.2	36	56.3	427	55.5	229	30.0	73	69.5	194	56.4
Lack maturity	2075	100.0	64	3.1	770	37.1	763	36.8	105	5.1	344	16.6
Yes	546	26.3	23	35.9	158	20.5	265	34.7	21	20.0	64	18.6
No	1529	73.7	41	64.1	612	79.5	498	65.3	84	80.0	280	81.4
Admission test	2075	100.0	64	3.1	770	37.1	763	36.8	105	5.1	344	16.6
No response	27	1.3	1	1.6	11	1.4	7	0.9	3	2.9	5	1.5
Yes	1408	67.9	32	50.0	448	58.2	612	80.2	55	52.4	255	74.1
No	640	30.8	31	48.4	311	40.4	144	18.9	47	44.8	84	24.4

* Not included, 29 institutional schools, 1.4% of total.

a diocesan Catholic school other than the school of their first choice.

Applicants for admission to Catholic secondary schools in 1962–63 found it most difficult to gain admission to the private secondary schools, of which only 21% admitted all applicants.

It seems important to make an observation here that cannot be entirely supported by statistics but which has been the experience of the Study staff. There are 2 distinct groups of parents of Catholic children as defined by their children's school attendance:

1. those parents who presented their children for enrollment in Catholic schools and whose children were either accepted or rejected;

2. those parents of Catholic children who did not present their children for enrollment in Catholic schools because they preferred other schools, or because they felt the children did not have a chance for acceptance, or because they were indifferent toward the religious development program of the Catholic schools.

This observation is developed in a later section of this report dealing with parents' expectations.

It seems clear that if the purposes of the Catholic schools are well founded and are completely accepted by those responsible for school operation, neither of the 2 groups of Catholic youth mentioned above, nor any one of their subgroups, is more important or less important than any other.

TUITION COSTS

The additional factor in the enrollment of children in Catholic schools is the direct payment of tuition and fees by the parents to assist in financing the school operation. Fifty percent of the elementary schools reported direct tuition charges, with the median payment at $25 or less. Among private elementary schools, accounting for only 4% of the total, the median tuition payment was between $76 and $100. Also in the elementary schools, fees in addition to tuition were reported by 69% of the schools, the median fee being $25 or less. Direct tuition payment is more common at the secondary school level, where this is levied in 77% of the reporting schools, with the median tuition between $76 and $100. In the private secondary schools the median tuition charge is between $150 and $200. The median additional fee charge in 79% of all secondary schools is $25 or less.

In many elementary schools and in some secondary schools tuition charges are scaled down when more than one child in a family attends the school. Principals of 61% of the elementary schools estimated that income from tuition covered less than 25% of the cost of school operation. Principals of 38% of the secondary schools estimated that tuition income covered between 76% and 100% of the cost of school operation.

SCHOOL ORGANIZATION PATTERNS

The Study considered the organization of Catholic schools under 3 classifications. The first identification was by ownership, the second by administrative grade organization, and the third by student organization. Elementary and secondary schools were considered separately, and the information reported here has been processed from the responses of 9451 elementary and 2075 secondary schools to Schedule II —Elementary Principal's Report, and to Schedule III—Secondary Principal's Report (these schedules are reproduced in the Appendix). The aim of the Schedules was to produce a reflection of the schools' operation during the 1962–63 school year.

Ownership Patterns

Broken down by ownership there are 4 groups of schools: those owned by individual parishes; those owned by a group of parishes; those owned by individual religious communities; and those owned by the dioceses. One rather clear way of identifying ownership is to determine which agency would receive insurance benefits in case of fire or other damage.

The principals' reports on ownership of elementary schools in 1962–63 are given in Table 9.

It is obvious from the summary of ownership of elementary schools that the most common is the parish-owned school. This is understandable because these schools are located closest to the homes of the young elementary school children. The establishment of the parish elementary

Table 9

OWNERSHIP OF CATHOLIC ELEMENTARY SCHOOLS IN 1962–63

Elementary	Totals	%
Total reporting	9451	100.0
No response	288	3.0
Parish	8211	86.9
Private	394	4.2
Diocesan	359	3.8
Interparish	80	0.8
Institutional	119	1.3

school also tends to provide some social and recreational facilities that could be used by both the school and the parish.

Most of the private elementary schools are downward extensions of existing private secondary schools; only a few operate as separate elementary schools.

Diocesan elementary schools represent efforts to provide elementary school facilities for sparsely populated areas and areas where diocesan financial assistance is necessary. When the statistics on diocesan elementary schools are considered by Standard Statistical Regions (Table 10), no definite trend appears. However, there might be some diocesan trends concealed within Regions 1, 2, 4, and 9.

Table 10

DIOCESAN-OWNED ELEMENTARY SCHOOLS
BY STANDARD STATISTICAL REGIONS

	Total schools	Diocesan schools	
		Total	%
National	9451	359	3.8
Region			
1	773	36	4.7
2	2138	98	4.6
3	2504	91	3.6
4	1343	55	4.1
5	545	18	3.3
6	415	12	2.9
7	687	6	0.9
8	247	8	3.2
9	718	35	4.9

The breakdown of interparish elementary schools by Standard Statistical Regions, as presented in Table 11, shows no significant trend toward this type of school ownership. We find the same lack of evidence when analyzing the age of school buildings; the median age of these schools buildings is the same as the median of all elementary buildings. However, these buildings might previously have had another type of ownership.

Table 11

INTERPARISH-OWNED ELEMENTARY SCHOOLS
BY STANDARD STATISTICAL REGIONS

	Total schools	Interparish schools	
		Total	%
National	9451	80	0.8
Region			
1	773	5	0.6
2	2138	17	0.8
3	2504	25	1.0
4	1343	7	0.5
5	545	13	2.5
6	415	3	0.7
7	687	5	0.7
8	247	1	0.4
9	718	4	0.6

It is clear and understandable that the prevailing type of elementary school is connected with the parish organizations.

No statistical treatment will be given to institutional schools. This lack of consideration is not related to the high importance of these schools. Those many readers who have an interest in them are referred to the reports of the Special Education Department of the National Catholic Educational Association.[3]

The same classifications of ownership are followed for the secondary schools. As might be reasonably expected, however, pattern of ownership of secondary schools differs considerably from that of elementary schools.

The numerical and proportional relationships show that whereas in the elementary schools, parish ownership far outdistanced the other types, at the secondary level private school ownership came within 0.3% of parish ownership. Other increases in types of ownership were shared by the interparish and the diocesan-owned schools. The following is a breakdown of secondary school ownership for the 1962–63 school year:

	Total	%
Total responding	2075	100.0
No identification	64	3.0
Parish	770	37.1
Private	763	36.8
Interparish	105	5.1
Diocesan	344	16.6
Institutional	29	1.4

Table 12 shows that the median age of the original buildings that house interparish schools is 6–10 years and the diocesan schools 11–15 years, whereas the median age for both parish and private school buildings is 21–40 years. Even making the slight allowance that some parish schools have been transferred to diocesan or interparish ownership and that some diocesan schools have been transferred to private ownership, the picture of secondary school ownership would not be changed substantially.

The patterns established in the foregoing analysis show ownership of secondary schools more evenly distributed than that of elementary

Table 12

AGE OF THE ORIGINAL SECONDARY SCHOOL BUILDINGS

Age interval	Total schools	%	Not identified	%	Parish	%	Private	%	Inter-parish	%	Diocesan	%
No response	87	4.2	6	9.4	29	3.8	33	4.3	3	2.9	16	4.7
1– 5 years	282	13.6	7	10.9	61	7.9	91	11.9	29	27.6	91	26.5
6–10 years	286	13.8	8	12.5	97	12.6	98	12.8	26*	24.8	55	16.0
11–15 years	161	7.8	8	12.5	64	8.3	48	6.3	8	7.6	31*	9.0
16–20 years	39	1.9	0	0.0	14	1.8	13	1.7	1	1.0	9	2.6
21–40 years	565*	27.2	11*	17.2	238*	30.9	211*	27.7	20	19.0	76	22.1
41–60 years	412	19.9	16	25.0	185	24.0	146	19.1	12	11.4	45	13.1
61–80 years	162	7.8	6	9.4	58	7.5	77	10.1	5	4.8	15	4.4
Over 80 years	81	3.9	2	3.1	24	3.1	46	6.0	1	1.0	6	1.7
Total	2075	100.0	64	3.1	770	37.1	763	36.8	105	5.1	344	16.6

* Median.

schools, with 37% classified as parish schools, 36% as private, 16% as diocesan, and 5% as interparish.

A closer look at the ownership pattern of secondary schools shows that the total number of students enrolled in the different types of schools produces a different alignment. We find that 38.6% of the total enrollment is in private, 30.8% in diocesan, 23.5% in parish, 4.4% in interparish, and 2.5% in schools not identified by ownership. The average enrollments by types are diocesan 753, private 426, interparish 351, and parish schools 256.

In summary of the ownership patterns of secondary schools, parish and private schools represent the largest number, the highest total enrollment is in private schools, and the largest average enrollment is in diocesan schools.

Grade Organization Patterns

In the elementary schools the prevailing administrative organization is by grades 1 through 8. However, 22% of the reporting schools indicated that they had kindergartens in their programs. The organization by sexes is primarily coeducational, although approximately 6% of the schools limited enrollment to either boys or girls.

Grade organization at the secondary school level is slightly more complicated than at the elementary school level (Table 13).

Table 13

GRADE ORGANIZATION OF SECONDARY SCHOOLS*

	Total schools	%	Not identified	%	Parish	%	Private	%	Inter-parish	%	Diocesan	%
Grade organization												
No response	47	2.3	6	9.4	23	3.0	10	1.3	2	1.9	2	0.6
7– 8	0	0.0	0	0.0	0	0.0	0	0.0	0	0.0	0	0.0
7– 9	26	1.3	0	0.0	25	3.2	0	0.0	1	1.0	0	0.0
7–12	84	4.0	0	0.0	21	2.7	45	5.9	4	3.8	3	0.9
8–12	192	9.3	4	6.3	67	8.7	79	10.4	6	5.7	34	9.9
9–12	1666	80.3	52	81.3	607	78.8	610	79.9	91	86.7	297	86.3
10–12	14	0.7	1	1.6	5	0.6	5	0.7	1	1.0	2	0.6
Others	46	2.2	1	1.6	22	2.9	14	1.8	0	0.0	6	1.7
Total	2075	100.0	64	3.1	770	37.1	763	36.8	105	5.1	344	16.6

* Not included, 29 institutional schools, 1.4% of total.

Table 13 shows that although there is a wide variety of grade organization in secondary schools, the predominant organization is by grades 9 through 12, which matches with the elementary structure of kindergarten or grade 1 through grade 8. We can assume that other grade spans are provided to meet local situations, such as 7–12 and 8–12 organizations, which probably serve parish and private schools that have corresponding elementary divisions.

It is interesting that the junior high school organization, which is part of that popularly known as the 6–3–3 breakdown, is not present in appreciable numbers; only 26 schools, or 1.3%, report this organization. In numbers enrolled, only 1.5% of the total secondary enrollment is designated as grades 7 and 8.

Student Organization Patterns

The more complicated structure within the secondary school pattern is the organization by sexes. This includes 4 types of school organization, which we will define, although they might appear obvious.

1. *All-boy schools* enroll boys only.

2. *All-girl schools* enroll girls only.

3. *Coeducational schools* enroll boys and girls and provide a common education program for boys and girls in the same classrooms under the same instructors. The obvious exception to this type of instruction would be physical education, intramural and extramural.

4. *Coinstitutional schools* are almost unique to Catholic secondary school organization. In this type of organization, 2 schools share a single administrative structure. The total educational program is offered separately to boys and girls, with women instructors for girls and men instructors for boys. In the general academic program separate physical facilities are used for boys and girls, although they make use of the same specialized facilities, such as science laboratories, but under separate instruction. Somewhat less clear are the conditions under which boys and girls use such facilities as diningrooms, libraries, and auditoriums. The aim is to provide a separate education for boys and girls more economically in a single school plant than could be provided in 2 separate schools.

A slight variance of the coinstitutional school is the coinstructional school, in which the organization remains the same for the faculty, men or women serving boys or girls or both in separate classes. The purpose of this type of organization is to provide separate education and to take advantage of the special abilities of the teaching staff, most frequently in science, mathematics, foreign languages, art, and music. This plan is limited by the fact that the constitutions of many religious communities for men do not allow their members to teach girls, and some religious communities for women have a similar prohibition.

Later in this section we will present the position of the Catholic Church on coeducation and its effect on the structure of the Catholic schools. At this point it seems desirable to summarize the organization of the secondary schools reporting to the Study (Table 14).

Table 14 shows that the prevailing type of secondary school is the coeducational school, with 44.8% of all secondary schools organized on this basis. Only the private school had a high commitment to separate education for boys and girls. Among the privately owned schools, 659, or 86.4%, were organized for boys only, for girls only, or as co-institutional schools. Only 74, or 9.7%, of the private schools were organized as coeducational.

Although the coinstitutional school represents a very small percentage of the total secondary schools, this type of organization seems to indicate an important effort of the Catholic school leadership to provide a separate education for boys and for girls in tune with the desires of the Catholic Church (Table 15).

Table 15 shows no identifiable pattern for the coinstitutional school other than the fact that this type of school does appear in each region

Table 14

STUDENT ORGANIZATION OF SECONDARY SCHOOLS

	Total schools	%	Not identified	%	Parish	%	Private	%	Inter-parish	%	Diocesan	%
Student organization	2075	100.0	64	3.1	770	37.1	763	36.8	105	5.1	344	16.6
No response	82	4.0	7	10.9	37	4.8	30	3.9	0	0.0	8	2.3
Boys only	301	14.5	2	3.1	21	2.7	189	24.8	6	5.7	78	22.7
Coeducational	930	44.8	35	54.7	567	73.6	74	9.7	88	83.8	165	48.0
Girls only	691	33.3	17	26.6	131	17.0	465	60.9	8	7.6	47	13.7
Coinstitutional	71	3.4	3	4.7	14	1.8	5	0.7	3	2.9	46	13.4

Table 15

DISTRIBUTION OF COINSTITUTIONAL SCHOOLS BY
STANDARD STATISTICAL REGIONS AS REPORTED BY 2075 SCHOOLS

Region	Total schools	Coinstitutional	% of total
1	221	9	4.0
2	442	18	4.0
3	469	15	3.0
4	280	6	2.1
5	141	8	5.6
6	110	4	3.6
7	164	9	5.4
8	55	1	1.8
9	151	9	5.9

of the country although not in each of the dioceses. This fact seems in tune with the lag that occurs in all areas of American educational innovation and helps prove that Catholic schools are as resistant to new departures as public and other schools. According to our research the first coinstitutional Catholic school was organized in 1952, and it is interesting that this first coinstitutional school is being reorganized currently into 2 separate schools, 1 for boys only and 1 for girls only.

Two additional interesting factors related to the secondary schools are the average size of the units and the assignment of full-time principals to schools (Table 16).

Reference was made earlier to the position of the Catholic Church concerning the coeducation of Catholic youth. Pope Pius XI's encyclical, "Christian Education of Youth,"[4] in dealing with the whole matter

Table 16

AVERAGE ENROLLMENTS OF SECONDARY SCHOOLS BY STUDENT
ORGANIZATION AND THE FULL-TIME PRINCIPAL ASSIGNMENT TO EACH TYPE

School type	Total number	Average enrollment	Full-time principal	%
All-boy	301	686	201	66.8
All-girl	691	366	347	50.2
Coeducational	931	330	337	36.2
Coinstitutional	71	777	42	59.2
No response	82	—	—	—

of coeducation warns of the moral dangers involved in it. The "Instruction on Mixed Education"[5] issued by the *Sacred Congregation of Religious* also advises that the hierarchy should seek alternatives to coeducation in providing educational opportunities for Catholic youth. Basil Frison[6] interprets the position of the Church on coeducation and supports the organization of the coinstitutional high school as an economical approach to the problem. Because of the relative newness of the coinstitutional concept extensive research material is not available on the operation of this type of school.[7]

SIZE OF CATHOLIC SCHOOLS

The size of a school is not in itself the most important factor in controlling quality or effectiveness of the school. In fact, an ideal school was described in earlier times as "Mark Hopkins on one end of a log and a student on the other," a description that implies that the complete education exists in a one-to-one relationship of teacher to student. Because our society makes ever-broadening demands for more and better education for an ever-increasing number of students, the one-to-one relationship becomes more and more impossible. The picture of Mark Hopkins and his student emphasizes the continuing importance of the quality of the teacher. The importance of the teacher and his effectiveness are controlled by the circumstances under which he meets his students. The good teacher's effectiveness will be conditioned by good or bad physical surroundings. A good first-grade teacher can produce good results in good physical surroundings, with good instructional tools, working with a reasonable number of children; the same first-grade teacher working under less favorable circumstances will not achieve optimum results. The completely good or the very poor first-grade situation, each with the same good teacher, can occur in either a very small school or a very large school. The parallel exists at the secondary school level. Because some of the factors controlling effectiveness can arise from school size, an analysis of the size of the elementary and secondary schools that reported to the Study is presented in Tables 17 and 18.

The median size for elementary schools reporting falls in the inter-

val of 301–400 in enrollment. It is interesting that the combined enrollment of 802 schools reporting enrollments at 100 or less, 8.6% of all
schools, is only 1.1% of the enrollment of all schools. Also notable is
the fact that the 12 schools reporting enrollments of over 2000 enroll
more than half as many as the 802 small schools.

The greater number of the large schools, those with enrollments in
excess of 800 students, are in Regions 2 and 3. This is a natural result
of the large, heavily populated metropolitan areas in these regions.

Among the chief drawbacks of the small elementary schools, those
with 400 or less enrollment, are the lack of a nonteaching principal
and of adequate clerical assistance. An elementary school of this size
usually has 8 classrooms and a total staff of 8, 1 of whom has the
responsibility of the principalship as well as a full-time teaching load.
The function of the elementary school principal will be treated more
fully in the chapter devoted to school staff.

The Study has found little evidence of any movement toward inter-

Table 17

ENROLLMENT OF ELEMENTARY SCHOOLS, OCTOBER 1962

Enrollment intervals	Number of schools by Regions									Total
	1	2	3	4	5	6	7	8	9	
1–25	6	8	7	3	5	4	2	1	1	37
26–50	7	14	23	35	11	24	21	7	4	146
51–75	9	37	40	65	10	33	38	14	10	256
76–100	16	40	78	121	24	27	38	8	11	363
101–125	14	59	84	121	35	20	45	8	13	399
126–150	17	75	106	115	27	32	33	9	22	436
151–175	31	90	130	73	20	22	34	16	19	435
176–200	25	92	117	74	26	25	46	17	17	439
201–300	120	337	375	213*	102	75*	132*	43	93	1490
301–400	196*	357*	410*	160	84*	57	117	58*	238*	1677*
401–500	94	243	274	99	48	26	61	20	95	960
501–600	69	147	202	74	39	27	37	14	45	654
601–800	123	238	317	109	45	28	48	23	94	1025
801–1200	37	265	237	60	48	13	20	7	51	738
1201–1600	5	94	77	7	13	0	7	0	0	203
1601–2000	0	24	12	0	4	0	1	0	0	41
2001–over	0	7	5	0	0	0	0	0	0	12
Total schools responding	769	2127	2494	1329	541	413	680	245	713	9311

* Median.

parish school planning or toward diocesan central schools for the elementary school population. The advantages of such planning might outweigh any disadvantages and might even make it possible to provide Catholic schools for a larger number of the youth.

In common with other types of American secondary schools, the Catholic secondary schools reviewed here have an appreciable number of small schools and a significant number of very small schools. The *very small* schools are those with an enrollment of 100 or less. There are 258 of these schools among those reporting, or 12.9% of the total 1997 schools being considered. The small schools are those with an enrollment between 101 and 200; these added to the very small schools make a total of 704 schools, or 35.3% of all secondary schools reporting. The group with an enrollment between 101 and 200 considered separately were 446, or 22.4% of the total schools reporting. However, the small and very small schools enroll only 10% of the total students. The median enrollment figure for all schools is in the interval of 201–300 (Table 18).

Table 18

ENROLLMENT OF SECONDARY SCHOOLS, OCTOBER 1962

Enrollment intervals	Number of schools by Regions									Total
	1	2	3	4	5	6	7	8	9	
1–25	2	2	0	1	3	1	2	0	2	13
26–50	5	2	5	11	4	8	3	1	2	41
51–75	2	16	8	29	5	11	19	1	5	96
76–100	6	16	20	28	5	9	14	5	6	109
101–125	16	17	14	26	9	7	12	2	7	110
126–150	16	17	25	19	17	8	13	8	4	127
151–175	23	24	16	24	8	10*	10	5	5	125
176–200	9	21	16	13*	5	2	7	4	7	84
201–300	49*	61	71	28	30*	20	30*	9*	27	325*
301–400	26	53*	58*	29	19	8	16	4	22*	235
401–500	17	35	51	21	9	5	16	1	21	176
501–600	15	32	28	11	7	6	5	7	9	120
601–800	14	49	50	12	10	8	9	7	16	175
801–1200	13	38	66	14	8	4	6	1	15	165
1201–1600	2	25	20	7	2	1	0	0	1	58
1601–2000	0	6	13	2	0	0	0	0	0	21
2001–over	2	13	1	1	0	0	0	0	0	17
Total schools responding	217	427	462	276	141	108	162	55	149	1997

* Median.

The problems in the operation of the small and very small secondary schools can be overcome, but too often they are not. Both groups are seriously handicapped in attempting to provide a broad curriculum. It is almost impossible to maintain a thoroughly competent staff within a reasonable ratio of total staff to students to provide: a full program of English in language structure, literature, and development of writing ability; the social sciences; mathematics; the sciences in biology, chemistry, and physics; more than one modern foreign language; art, and music.

A further necessity for a good secondary school is an adequate library with a competent person to operate it. The library needs of a small secondary school are not greatly different from those of a secondary school with 500 students. The major difference might be less need for multiple copies of volumes.

Other special competent staff are necessary in physical education, guidance, and school administration. Intermural sports, if considered important, also need staff and pupil personnel.

Specialized space, facilities, and equipment necessary to implement the total school program are also among the problems of the small schools.

Each of these problems and others not identified can be overcome. If adequate finances were available most of the problems could be eliminated, but in view of the short supply of well-trained teachers staffing problems would remain. In other situations, interschool cooperative programs for sharing staff and facilities have been developed. One of these is the Western States Small Schools Project,[8] by which the departments of education of several Rocky Mountain states have attempted to improve the educational offering in the small high schools.

In a number of dioceses, long-term plans have been implemented to develop central schools and to replace small parish high schools with new interparish schools. One of these plans is described in a monograph prepared by Monsignor Justin A. Driscoll of the Archdiocesan Schools of Dubuque, Iowa.[9]

Medium-sized secondary schools, with enrollments between 201 and 600, number 856, 42.8% of the responding schools with 38% of the total enrollment in all schools.

The greater part of the total enrollment is served by the large school group, those with enrollments of 601 or more, which enroll 52% of all secondary students. There are only 436 of these schools, which is 21.8% of the total. The enrollment of these large schools extends from just over 600 to over 4000 students.

Just as size is not an absolute factor limiting quality in the small schools, it does not guarantee quality in the largest school. The control of positive factors can be illustrated by a closer look at the largest schools in the secondary group, the 38 with enrollments in excess of 1600. Of the 38 schools, 16 are located in 1 archdiocese and the remaining 22 in 13 individual dioceses. Using the ratio of staff to students as an indicator of quality, there is a wide range in the 38 schools, from 1 staff to 20 students in the most favorable school, to 1 to 42 in the 2 least favorable schools. The ratio in the 16 schools in the single archdiocese ranges from 1 staff member to 38 students to 1 staff member to 42 students, and in the remaining 13 dioceses the range is from 1 to 20 up to 1 to 34. It would seem that in the single large archdiocese there is a policy of establishing very large schools with a limited faculty. This combination policy could be a deterrent to operating a quality school. One of the potential advantages of the large school is the possibility of having highly trained and specialized teachers in such fields as physical science, biological sciences, modern language, religion, and other subject areas. However, some of this advantage could be dissipated by seriously handicapping the teachers with heavy student loads. This overload would be likely in secondary schools with a staff to student ratio of 1 to 42, where academic class size would be regularly in excess of 60 students.

One other gauge of secondary school size is the twelfth-grade enrollment. Of the total number of schools reporting, 907 schools, or 47%, identified their twelfth-grade enrollment at less than 39 students. This group represented 17% of the total twelfth-grade enrollment.

Classrooms Not in Use

School principals reporting in October 1962 showed very little extra available classroom space in either elementary or secondary schools.

In the elementary school reports, 6806 schools, 72% of the total, showed no unused classrooms, and the remaining 2645 schools, 28% of the total, showed 5551 classrooms not in use. Analysis of the reports did not show greater unused space in any regions or in any particular type of elementary school. This is not surprising since the average number of unused rooms for all schools reporting such space was only slightly more than 2 per school. Only 49 schools reported more than 6 vacant classrooms.

In observation, not based on statistical accumulation, another type of unused elementary school space showed primarily in inner-city parishes. These parishes are located in downtown city areas where housing has been eliminated with a consequent diminishing or even elimination of parish rolls. Some schools in these areas have been adapted to other parish uses, some have been abandoned, and some have been leased or sold for use by other schools.

A similar analysis of secondary school reports shows 1805, or 87%, with no unused classrooms, and 270 schools with a total of 746 unused classrooms. As in the elementary schools, the unused classrooms were not associated with regions or with type of school. Presumably a large number of these classrooms are in high schools that are just beginning their operation and admit 1 class a year until all 4 grades are housed. These reports point up the reasons why admission to Catholic high schools is a severe problem.

Double Sessions

For the school year 1962–63, the elementary principals reported 210, or 2.2%, of the 9451 schools with double sessions; secondary principals reported only 13, or 0.6%, of the 2075 schools with double sessions. It is clear that double sessions are not prevalent in Catholic schools. This can be accounted for by admission policies whereby first applicants are admitted until a maximum class size has been reached and then admission is closed.

SCHOOL PLANT FACILITIES

The principals of both elementary and secondary schools were asked to describe the educational facilities beyond regular classrooms available in their schools.

Elementary principals were presented with 5 groupings of special facilities that might be found in elementary schools and asked to identify the grouping that most closely represented the special facilities available in their schools. The groupings proceeded from the most extensive to the least extensive provision as shown below, and the responses of the principals are given in Table 19.

ELEMENTARY SCHOOL SPECIAL FACILITIES GROUPINGS

Group 1
Gymnasium
Auditorium
Cafeteria
Library
Audiovisual
Music
Art
Home economics
Industrial arts

Group 2
Gymnasium
Auditorium
Cafeteria
Library
Music
Art

Group 3
Multipurpose
Cafeteria
Library
Music
Art

Group 4
Multipurpose
Cafeteria
Library

Group 5
Multipurpose

Table 19

ELEMENTARY SCHOOL FACILITIES, OCTOBER 1962

	Total reporting		Not identified		Parish		Private		Diocesan		Interparish	
	Number	%	Number	%	Number	%	Number	%	Number	%	Number	%
Group 1	347	4.0	22	8.4	273	3.6	40	10.6	12	3.6	0	0.0
Group 2	1841	21.4	52	19.8	1570	20.8	147	39.1	57	17.1	15	20.5
Group 3	943	11.0	17	6.4	806	10.7	73	19.4	41	12.3	6	8.2
Group 4	2827	32.9	89	33.9	2514	33.4	73	19.4	120	36.1	31	42.4
Group 5	2611	30.4	82	31.3	2363	31.3	43	11.4	102	30.7	21	28.7
Total	8569	100.0	262	3.0	7526	87.8	376	4.3	332	3.8	73	0.8

Sixty-three per cent of the elementary principals classified their facilities in groups 4 and 5, the least extensive provision. As could be expected, the available facilities seem to relate to school size: the 63% reporting the least extensive facilities relates closely to 60% reporting enrollments of 400 or less. The private schools follow a different pattern from that of the other 3 types of schools; almost 50% of private schools identify their facilities in the 2 most extensive groupings. This difference probably reflects the fact that many of the private elementary schools are downward extensions of secondary schools to which the more extensive secondary facilities are available.

A library facility is constant through the first 4 groupings. Almost 70% of the schools fall into these groups, which leaves 30% of the schools without a separate library. A general observation by the Study staff was that library collections in many schools were very modest, and there was little evidence of the use of loan collections or library service from local public libraries.

Secondary school principals were asked to describe their special facilities beyond regular classrooms through the use of 2 groupings, the first related to the curricular offerings of the schools and the second to those facilities that support the general school program.

SECONDARY SCHOOL ACADEMIC SERVICE FACILITIES

Group 1

Library
Language laboratory
Reading laboratory
Typing
Office practice
Drafting (mechanical drawing)
Home economics
Industrial arts
Choral room
Band and orchestra
Audiovisual

Group 2

Library
Language laboratory
Reading laboratory
Typing
Office practice
Drafting (mechanical drawing)
Home economics
Industrial arts

Group 3

Library
Language laboratory
Reading laboratory
Drafting (mechanical drawing)
Typing
Office practice

Group 4

Library
Language laboratory
Reading laboratory
Typing

Group 5

Library
Typing

SECONDARY SCHOOL PROGRAM SUPPORT FACILITIES

Group 1
Gymnasium
Auditorium
Cafeteria
Chapel
Pool

Group 2
Gymnasium
Auditorium
Cafeteria
Chapel

Group 3
Gymnasium-auditorium
Cafeteria
Chapel

Group 4
Multipurpose
Cafeteria or auditorium
Chapel

Group 5
Multipurpose

An analysis of the reports on academic service facilities (Table 20) indicates that among the total schools there is limited availability of academic services. 49.4 percent of the schools classify their academic services in groups 4 and 5, which represent the most limited services. However, this identification is strongly influenced by the large number of parish high schools in groups 4 and 5; the larger interparish, private, and diocesan schools present a more favorable picture. The relationship between school size and school operation seems clear: the total parish high schools, with average enrollment of 250 students, report the most

Table 20

SECONDARY SCHOOL ACADEMIC SERVICE FACILITIES, OCTOBER 1962

	Respondents		Not identified		Parish		Private		Interparish		Diocesan	
	Total	%	Total	%	Total	%	Total	%	Total	%	Total	%
Group 1	562	27.9	19	30.1	124	16.4	257	34.2	30	29.1	132	38.7
Group 2	285	14.1	11	17.4	112	14.8	93	12.4	19	18.4	50	14.6
Group 3	168	8.3	5	7.9	61	8.1	45	6.0	16	15.5	41	12.0
Group 4	257	12.7	6	9.5	80	10.6	132	17.6	8	7.7	31	9.0
Group 5	738	36.7	22	34.9	376	49.9	223	29.7	30	29.1	87	25.5
Total	2010	100.0	63	3.1	753	37.4	750	37.3	103	5.1	341	16.9

limited facilities; the total diocesan schools, with an average enrollment of 780 students, report the most extensive facilities. This is also true for interparish and private schools, which have average enrollments of 350 and 425 students, respectively.

The same general relationship of size and type of school applies to provision of program support facilities (Table 21). The parish schools are again most limited and the private schools most extensive in their provisions. The private schools hold this position on the basis of a 43.1 percentage in groups 1 and 2. The private schools in this percentage have a swimming pool as well as separate gymnasium and auditorium facilities. In addition to the size of enrollment, the potential of financial support for capital investment by the private school is undoubtedly effective in providing more extensive physical facilities.

GRADUATES OF CATHOLIC SCHOOLS

At the end of grade 8 Catholic school students and their parents must make a decision about the continuation of their education. That some students make this decision at the end of either grade 6 or 7 is evidenced by a consistent drop in enrollment from grade 6 to 7 and from

Table 21

SECONDARY SCHOOL PROGRAM SUPPORT FACILITIES, OCTOBER 1962

	Respondents		Not identified		Parish		Private		Interparish		Diocesan	
	Total	%	Total	%	Total	%	Total	%	Total	%	Total	%
Group 1	104	5.2	2	3.1	14	1.8	78	10.4	1	1.0	9	2.7
Group 2	510	25.5	14	21.8	142	19.0	245	32.7	15	15.0	94	28.2
Group 3	868	43.5	34	53.1	292	39.0	312	41.6	63	63.0	167	50.1
Group 4	235	11.7	6	9.3	96	12.8	87	11.6	11	11.0	35	10.5
Group 5	276	13.8	8	12.4	203	27.1	27	3.6	10	10.0	28	8.4
Total	1993	100.0	64	3.2	747	37.4	749	37.5	100	5.0	333	16.7

grade 7 to 8. It is highly improbable that these students are giving up further education; they are entering either a Catholic secondary school with a different grade organization or a public school with a junior high school organization. Validating this assumption, 11.4% of parish secondary schools begin with grade 7 or 8 and 16.3% of the private secondary schools begin with grade 7 or 8.

Elementary schools responding to an inquiry about their graduates of June 1962 reported that 61.5% of those graduates went on to Catholic secondary schools, boys and girls in about equal percentages (Table 22).

Table 22

SECONDARY SCHOOL DIRECTION OF CATHOLIC
ELEMENTARY SCHOOL GRADUATES, JUNE 1962

	Graduates	%	To Catholic high schools	%
Total	388,683	100.0	239,351	61.5
Boys	189,843	48.8	114,005	60.0
Girls	198,840	51.2	125,346	63.0

The graduates of parish, interparish, and diocesan elementary schools went to Catholic high schools in about equal percentages, but of the private school graduates 73.9% entered Catholic high schools, in comparison with the total percentage of 61.5 This difference might indicate the greater ability and willingness of the parents of private students to provide for tuition costs.

Secondary school principals were asked to identify the type of degree-granting institution their graduates planned to attend. The request, made in October 1962, did not require a follow-up to determine whether the graduates' intentions were fulfilled. An analysis of the principals' responses is given in Table 23.

The figures indicating the postsecondary directions of Catholic high school graduates of 1962 include an appreciable number of young people whose next step was to a junior college. This is increasingly true in areas where state-supported and community junior colleges make higher education financially possible for increasing numbers of our youth. Under these circumstances the junior college is becoming less a terminal institution and more an intermediate institution between secondary education and the possible achieving of a degree.

There is the possibility that the plans of the graduate will change, that he may never continue a program of further formal education, or that he will follow his plans on a deferred-time basis. There is also the possibility, although true of smaller numbers, that some graduates who do not have this as their plan in June of their graduating year, will go on to higher education.

Table 23

POSTSECONDARY DIRECTION OF CATHOLIC HIGH SCHOOL GRADUATES
JUNE 1962 (2075 schools)

Total graduates	155,698	
To college:		
Catholic college	40,922	48.42%
Private college	7,773	9.20%
Public college	30,401	35.97%
Religious life	4,441	5.60%
Diocesan seminary	968	.20%
Total postsecondary	84,505	
54.29% of the total graduates planned to go on to postsecondary education.		
Total girl graduates	87,177	
To college:		
Catholic college	19,529	48.14%
Private college	3,151	7.80%
Public college	14,681	36.21%
Religious life	3,205	8.00%
Total	40,566	
46.53% of the total of girl graduates planned to go on to postsecondary education.		
Total boy graduates	68,521	
To college:		
Catholic college	21,393	48.76%
Private college	4,622	10.51%
Public college	15,720	35.77%
Religious life	1,236	2.30%
Diocesan seminary	968	2.01%
Total	43,939	
64.15% of the total of boy graduates planned to go on to postsecondary education.		

On the premise that it is important to know what the graduates of secondary schools do after their graduation and, more important, how well they succeed, the Study developed a means by which success of the college-bound graduates could be judged. Although educators are interested in the in-school progress and success of their students, the purpose of this follow-up was to determine how well the graduates had been prepared for success in their later study. The Study did not assume that only the college-bound were important in a follow-up. The inquiry checked the graduates of June 1956 and June 1958 in their college graduating years, June of 1960 and 1962. The areas of inquiry considered most significant included: did the student graduate; did he transfer; was he dropped; grade point average at leaving or graduation; grade point average of his graduating class; persistency rate of entering class; did the student go on to graduate work; honors achieved. These items were selected not only because of their importance but also because of their general availability in college student records.

The 104 secondary schools involved in this follow-up procedure were willing to cooperate but the accumulated returns were so few that they could not produce significant results. The major problem was that the high-school pupil records generally did not show the college into which the graduate was accepted and subsequently entered but only showed the colleges to which transcripts had been sent. Because most students requested more than one transcript and some as many as 8, the follow-up went no further.

As the Study staff visited high schools in the 13 selected dioceses, conferences with principals and guidance personnel showed that a strong effort was made to guide the college-bound students toward Catholic colleges; the success of these efforts can be seen in Table 23. Some principals and guidance counselors indicated that very strong guidance was given the academically superior graduates toward Catholic colleges. It is difficult to evaluate the success of this guidance activity; if it were completely effective large numbers of the academically apt would continue their future education in Catholic colleges and the lesser academically apt graduates' success in non-Catholic colleges, on a comparative basis, would be somewhat obscured. Thus a new dimension would have to be added to any comparative studies of the college success of Catholic high-school graduates.

SOURCES OF FINANCIAL SUPPORT

The original design of the Study considered the problem of financing Catholic schools of utmost importance. However, it became evident that this aspect could not be given adequate treatment within the time of the Study. The fiscal information presented here is limited to identification of major sources of income for current operation of the schools.

The principals of the elementary and secondary schools were asked to estimate the sources of finance for their operation. The request included a suggestion that they reinforce their estimates with the judgment of others who might be more knowledgeable. The request did not require any validation by the principal, and it represented his conditioned thinking. Whether these estimates would be proved by a complete financial analysis or not, the importance of the summary is that it shows what the principals think.

The principals were asked to estimate the percentage of financial support derived from the following sources: tuition and fees, parish subsidy, diocesan subsidy, and miscellaneous—endowments, gifts, et cetera. A fifth category presented to the secondary principals only was the percentage of their operating expenditure subsidized by their religious communities; this percentage was not to include any allowance for contributed services.

The analysis of the elementary principals' responses in Table 24 shows 2 general patterns: first, the parish, interparish, and diocesan schools get their major support from parish subsidy; second, the private schools get their major support from direct tuition. It can also be seen that very little financial support for the elementary schools comes from the diocesan level. Surprising was the small number of parish, interparish and diocesan schools that ascribed any considerable income to miscellaneous receipts including gifts and money-raising events. The surprise is occasioned by the stereotype of the Catholic school and its bingo games.

At the secondary level a similar pattern of income source prevails, although direct tuition becomes more important for the parish, interparish, and diocesan high schools. Parish subsidy remains the greatest source of income for the parish and interparish schools, and it is the second most important source for the diocesan high school. The private schools report direct tuition as the major source of income; the other important sources are the operating religious communities and miscellaneous receipts, although, in the elementary schools, these were reported as a relatively unimportant source of support. Secondary principals' responses are shown in Table 25.

This analysis of the sources of income reported by the principals should be considered very carefully. The principals were in fact estimating, by request, what might be considered a cash statement. In both elementary and secondary schools there probably are actual costs that were not included in these estimates. These costs would include interest and amortization on capital investments and costs of operation and

Table 24

SOURCE OF FINANCIAL SUPPORT
ELEMENTARY PRINCIPALS' ESTIMATES FOR 9451 SCHOOLS

	Total	%	Not identified	%	Parish	%	Private	%	Diocesan	%	Interparish	%
1. % tuition												
None	2493	26.4	113	39.2	2128	25.9	22	5.6	129	35.9	22	27.5
Less than 25	3274	34.6	82	28.5	2991	36.4	31	7.9	119	33.1	35	43.8
25–50	1696	17.9	33	11.5	1551	18.9	41	10.4	51	14.2	11	13.8
51–75	997	10.5	27	9.4	870	10.6	52	13.2	35	9.7	8	10.0
76–100	991	10.5	33	11.5	671	8.2	248	62.9	25	7.0	4	5.0
2. % parish subsidy												
None	2000	21.1	104	36.1	1329	16.1	358	90.9	84	23.4	11	13.8
Less than 25	723	7.6	24	8.3	639	7.8	23	5.8	26	7.2	7	8.8
25–50	1461	15.5	32	11.1	1359	16.6	7	1.8	50	13.9	12	15.0
51–75	1270	13.4	30	10.4	1195	14.6	4	1.0	33	9.2	8	10.0
76–100	3997	42.3	98	34.0	3689	44.9	2	0.5	166	46.2	42	52.5
3. % diocesan subsidy												
None	9243	97.8	276	95.8	8079	98.4	388	98.5	326	90.8	79	98.8
Less than 25	110	1.2	6	2.1	77	0.9	6	1.5	8	2.2	1	1.3
25–50	39	0.4	1	0.3	27	0.3	0	0.0	9	2.5	0	0.0
51–75	17	0.2	0	0.0	9	0.1	0	0.0	6	1.7	0	0.0
76–100	42	0.4	5	1.7	19	0.2	0	0.0	10	2.8	0	0.0
4. % miscellaneous receipts												
None	8005	84.7	237	82.2	7139	87.0	203	51.5	294	81.9	70	87.6
Less than 25	1208	12.8	39	13.5	925	11.3	152	38.6	53	14.8	9	11.3
25–50	144	1.5	6	2.1	101	1.2	20	5.1	7	1.9	0	0.0
51–75	37	0.4	1	0.3	22	0.3	7	1.8	2	0.6	0	0.0
76–100	57	0.6	5	1.7	24	0.3	12	3.0	3	0.8	1	1.3

Table 25

SOURCE OF FINANCIAL SUPPORT

SECONDARY PRINCIPALS' ESTIMATE FOR 2075 SCHOOLS

	Total	%	Not identified	%	Parish	%	Private	%	Diocesan	%	Interparish	%
1. % tuition												
None	157	7.6	8	12.5	95	12.3	16	2.1	15	4.4	6	5.7
Less than 25	373	18.0	16	25.0	232	30.1	43	5.6	48	14.0	29	27.6
25–50	358	17.3	13	20.3	186	24.2	60	7.9	65	18.9	31	29.5
51–75	408	19.7	10	15.6	120	15.6	131	17.2	121	35.2	25	23.8
76–100	779	37.5	17	26.6	137	17.8	513	67.2	95	27.6	14	13.3
2. % parish subsidy												
None	1057	50.9	25	39.1	137	17.8	713	93.4	142	41.3	11	10.5
Less than 25	203	9.8	7	10.9	99	12.9	36	4.7	48	14.0	13	12.4
25–50	297	14.3	11	17.2	160	20.8	9	1.2	86	25.0	31	29.5
51–75	212	10.2	11	17.2	143	18.6	4	0.5	31	9.0	23	21.9
76–100	306	14.7	10	15.6	231	30.0	1	0.1	37	10.8	27	25.7
3. % diocesan subsidy												
None	1879	90.6	61	95.3	747	97.0	748	98.0	195	56.7	99	94.3
Less than 25	108	5.2	0	0.0	17	2.2	13	1.7	74	21.5	4	3.8
25–50	54	2.6	1	1.6	3	0.4	1	0.1	48	14.0	1	1.0
51–75	15	0.7	1	1.6	2	0.3	1	0.1	11	3.2	0	0.0
76–100	19	0.9	1	1.6	1	0.1	0	0.0	16	4.7	1	1.0
4. % miscellaneous receipts												
None	1233	59.4	43	67.2	625	81.2	293	38.4	191	55.5	70	66.7
Less than 25	727	35.0	18	28.1	129	16.8	402	52.7	137	39.8	31	29.5
25–50	83	4.0	2	3.1	12	1.6	50	6.6	12	3.5	3	2.9
51–75	13	0.6	0	0.0	2	0.3	6	0.8	3	0.9	1	1.0
76–100	19	0.9	1	1.6	2	0.3	12	1.6	1	0.3	0	0.0
5. % religious communities												
None	1748	84.2	58	90.6	748	97.1	483	63.3	334	97.1	103	98.1
Less than 25	161	7.8	2	3.1	16	2.1	134	17.6	6	1.7	1	1.0
25–50	89	4.3	3	4.7	4	0.5	78	10.2	2	0.6	0	0.0
51–75	33	1.6	0	0.0	2	0.3	29	3.8	1	0.3	0	0.0
76–100	44	2.1	1	1.6	0	0.0	39	5.1	1	0.3	1	1.0

maintenance which in many parish schools are included in the regular parish budget for heat, power, cleaning, and care of grounds. Other costs not normally included would be the real costs to religious communities not covered by the nominal stipend paid for each sister, brother, or priest who works in the school. These hidden costs absorbed by the community include the cost of educating each teacher, health care costs, and retirement costs for community members.

Perhaps the basic information in this analysis will stimulate further interest in the total fiscal operation of the schools.

ACADEMIC ACHIEVEMENT

The Study considered it of prime importance to examine the way the schools are meeting their goals. Broadly the goals are twofold: those that derive from the special reasons for the existence of Catholic schools and those goals that are common to all schools. The ways in which the special goals are met are presented later in this report, under the heading "Inventory of Catholic School Outcomes." The goals common to all schools considered here can be most easily classified under the heading "academic achievements."

The academic achievement in Catholic schools was evaluated by analysis of the results of nationally standardized achievement tests at both elementary and secondary levels. The results of standardized mental ability measures were also analyzed so that the learning potential of the students in the schools could be considered at the same time their achievements were reviewed. This review of academic achievement covers the same sample schools in the 13 selected dioceses that participated in other aspects of the depth study inquiries.

The test results were accumulated from existing testing programs in 192 of the possible 218 elementary schools. Because the existing testing programs in the secondary schools did not produce sufficient common factors to be used in an analysis, it was necessary to administer a common test battery in these schools. This was administered to approximately 7300 twelfth-grade pupils in 44 sample secondary schools in 5 of the 13 selected dioceses.

Table 26

STANFORD ACHIEVEMENT TEST NORMS AND MEDIANS
FOR GRADES 1–4, BY SCHOOLS

Grade 1			Grade 2			Grade 3			Grade 4		
Ach.	Norm	Freq.	Ach.	Norm	Freq.	Ach.	Norm	Freq.	Ach.	Norm	Freq.
2.7		1	3.4		1	4.7		1	6.0		1
2.6		1	3.0		2	4.6		2	5.9		1
2.4		2	2.7	2	1	4.5		2	5.8		2
2.3		4*	2.6	7*		4.4		2	5.7		2
2.2		2	2.3		1*	4.3		5	5.6		2
2.1		1	2.2		1	4.2		7*	5.4		1
2.0		2	1.9		2	4.1		2	5.3		2
1.8	1	1	1.7		1	4.0		5	5.2		3*
1.7	11*					3.9		2	5.1		1
1.6	2					3.8		2	5.0		2
						3.7	9	1	4.9		1
						3.6	1		4.8		1
						3.5	23*	1	4.7	3	
						3.4		1	4.6	3	1
									4.5	20*	1
									4.4		3
									3.7		1
									3.4		1
Number of school grades											
14	14			9	9		33	33		26	26
Number of school grades above median norm											
	14				4			31			20
Number of school grades at median norm and below											
	0				5			2			6

* Median column values.

Table 27

STANFORD ACHIEVEMENT TEST NORMS AND MEDIANS
FOR GRADES 5–8, BY SCHOOLS

Grade 5			Grade 6			Grade 7			Grade 8		
Ach.	Norm	Freq.	Ach.	Norm	Freq.	Ach.	Norm	Freq.	Ach.	Norm	Freq.
7.1		1	8.6		1	9.5		2	11.0		1
6.7		1	8.3		2	9.3		1	10.7		1
6.5		2	8.2		2	9.1		3	10.5		3
6.3		2*	8.1		1	8.9		2*	10.2		1
6.2		1	8.0		4	8.8		1	10.1		3
6.1		2	7.9		2	8.6		2	10.0		2
6.0		1	7.8		2	8.4		1	9.8		1
5.9		1	7.7		2	8.2		1	9.7		4*
5.7	9*		7.6		5	8.1		1	9.6		1
5.6	2		7.4		4	7.7	12*		9.3		1
			7.3		4*	7.6	2		9.0		1
			7.2		3				8.9		1
			7.1		3				8.7	4	1
			6.9		2				8.6	2	
			6.8		2				8.5	21*	1
			6.7	4					8.3		1
			6.6	5	2				8.2	1	
			6.5	43*					7.9		1
			6.4		2				7.4		1
			6.3		1				7.1		1
			6.2		1				6.9		2
			6.1		1						
			5.9		1						
			5.7		2						
			5.5		1						
			5.2		1						
			4.9		1						
Number of school grades											
	11	11		52	52		14	14		28	28
Number of school grades above median norm											
	11			41			14			21	
Number of school grades at median norm and below											
	0			11			0			7	

* Median column values.

Table 28

OTIS MENTAL ABILITY TEST MEDIANS,
BY SCHOOLS AND ELEMENTARY GRADE LEVEL

Median I.Q.	Percentile norms, † graaes 1–4	Percentile norms, † grades 1–5	Grade level 2	4	6	8
126	98	98	1			
119	93	94		3	1	1
118	92	93	1			2
117	90	92	2	2	1	
116	89	91		2		2
115	88	89		1	4	4
114	86	88	1	5	2	2
113	84	86		1	3	1
112	82	84	1	5	5*	4
111	80	82	1	4*	2	2*
110	78	80				1
109	76	77	2*	1	3	1
108	73	75		4	3	2
107	70	72	2	1	1	4
106	68	69				1
105	65	66		2		1
104	62	63	2			1
103	59	60		1	2	2
102	56	57		1	1	2
100	50	50		2	1	
99	47	47	1			1
98	44	43		1	1	
95	35	34		1	1	
93	30	28		1		
92	27	25	1			
89	20	18	1			
88	18	16				1
86	14	12	1			
Number reporting			17	38	31	35
Number above 50th percentile point			13	33	28	33
Number at 50th percentile point and below			4	5	3	2

* Median column values.

† Source: *Test Data Report No. 14.* New York: Harcourt, Brace & World, Inc., May, 1961.

Table 29

KUHLMANN-ANDERSON INTELLIGENCE TEST MEDIANS,
BY SCHOOLS AND ELEMENTARY GRADE LEVEL

Median I.Q.	Percentile † norms	Grade level					
		1	3	5	6	7	8
123	92						1
121	91					1	
119	88					1	
118	87					1	
117	86					1	
116	84				1		3
115	83				1		1
114	81	1	1		3	1	1
113	79	1			1	1	
112	77		3		2	1	3
111	75	1	5	4	5*	2	
110	73	4	4	1	3	1*	6*
109	71	2*	5	1*		4	2
108	69	1	6	1	4	3	2
107	67	3	8*	1			1
106	65		3	1	2		1
105	62	1	6		1		1
104	60		2				2
103	57		1	2	1		
102	55		3				1
101	52		2				
100	50		1				
99	48		1			1	
98	45		1			1	
97	43		1				
Number reporting		14	53	11	24	19	25
Number above 50th percentile point		14	49	11	24	17	25
Number at 50th percentile or below		0	4	0	0	2	0

* Median column values.

† Source: *Norms Manual for the Kuhlmann-Anderson Test, Seventh Edition, Booklets D and E F.* Princeton, N. J., Personnel Press, Inc., 1961.

Elementary School Testing Analysis

In the analysis of the elementary school results only those tests that were in most general use are reported: one achievement battery, the *Stanford Achievement Test*[10] and 2 mental ability measures, the *Kuhlman-Anderson Test*[11] and the *Otis Mental Ability Test.*[12]

The accumulated results of the Stanford Achievement Test are presented in Tables 26 and 27. These tables include pupils who were in grades 1–8 during the school year 1962–63. In the first column the achievement results are reported in terms of the grade level by years and months, for example, in the first-grade report, 2.7 in the first column means achievement at the seventh month of grade 2. The second column shows the norm, which is the month of the school year during which the test was administered; for the first grade 1.7 shows that the test was administered during March, or the seventh month of the first-grade year. Column 3 shows the number of grades achieving at the achievement intervals. In the first grade summary 4 grades are shown at the 2.3 interval; this is the median achievement for the 14 grades in the first-grade analysis.

Tables 26 and 27 show that the median achievement at each grade level, except grade 2, is significantly above the norm, ranging from 6 months at the first-grade level to 1 year and 2 months at the seventh- and eighth-grade levels. A further indication of the superior achievement of these students is that 84% of the grades reported have a median achievement above the test norm. Each grade reported includes all pupils at that grade level whether in a single classroom or in as many as 6 classrooms. The total number of students is approximately 17,000.

The most commonly used mental ability measures were the Kuhlman-Anderson and the Otis tests. The results of the Kuhlman-Anderson test covers 6 grade levels and 146 grades; the Otis test covers 4 grade levels and 121 grades. The results of these tests, covering a total of approximately 26,000 students, are presented in Tables 28 and 29.

These tables present the median I. Q. scores, the publishers' percentile norms, and the number of grades at each incident level. On the Otis test we find the median I. Q. value at the second grade as 109, at the fourth and eighth grade 111, and the sixth grade 112, and the median for all 4 grades as 111. The Kuhlman-Anderson test shows median I. Q.'s of 109 for grades 1 and 5, 107 for grade 3, 111 for grade

6, and 110 for grades 7 and 8. The median for all 6 grades is 109. These mental ability measures indicate that pupils in the Catholic elementary schools under consideration are superior in academic learning potential. Further analysis of these measures shows that in the Otis test only 14 grades are below the fiftieth percentile and that only 6 are below the Kuhlman-Anderson fiftieth percentile. This means that of the total 267 grades tested only 20 have a median I. Q. below the fiftieth percentile, and in terms of the mental ability measures this group of students has a significantly superior learning potential.

It is important to point out that in the combined analyses of the 2 mental ability measures reported, 90% of the grades had median I. Q.'s at or above the fiftieth percentile and 84% had achievement scores at or above the national norms. Any review of the academic results of a group of schools must consider both academic achievement and learning potential; this group of elementary schools shows superior student results and challenging efforts by the schools.

Secondary School Testing Analysis

The test battery administered under the auspices of the Study in the sample secondary schools consisted of the Metropolitan Achievement Test: High School Battery, and the Otis Mental Ability Test (both published by Harcourt, Brace and World). Approximately 7300 twelfth-grade pupils in 44 high schools in 5 of the selected dioceses participated in this testing program. In 3 of the schools the results were incomplete; consequently the results for only 41 schools are presented in the analysis. As was true of the elementary schools, the schools in the secondary testing program were the same schools that participated in other depth-study activities conducted by the Study staff. Of the 41 schools, 11 were all-boy schools, 14 were all-girl schools, 14 were coeducational, and 2 were coinstitutional. The largest twelfth-grade enrollment was 413 pupils and the smallest 17. Eight of the schools had twelfth-grade enrollments of more than 300, and 14 fewer than 100.

The high-school battery of the Metropolitan Achievement Tests consists of 11 subtests covering the areas of language, social studies, mathematics, and science:

The *language* subtests are reading, spelling, language structure, and language study skills.

The *social studies* subtests are social studies study skills, social studies vocabulary, and social studies information.

The *mathematics* subtests are mathematics computation and concepts, mathematics analysis, and problem-solving.

The *science* subtests are science concepts and understandings and science information.

The results of the testing are presented in Table 30.

The first column shows the twelfth-grade norms in percentile ranks. The following 11 columns record the mean score for the twelfth-grade class in each of the 41 high schools. The numbers in parenthesis identify the highest, median, and lowest mean score for each of the 11 subtests.

In each of the subtests the median value of the scores for the 41 schools is above the fiftieth percentile on the twelfth-grade norms. In addition, the school medians are significantly above the fiftieth percentile in each of the subtests except spelling, indicating that as a group these schools displayed superior achievement. In accumulating all of the subtests, 79% of the schools were above the fiftieth percentile and 55% were above the sixtieth percentile. Further analysis shows that the same 6 schools were among the lowest achievers in each of the 11 subtests; at the other end of the scale 14 schools were always among the highest achievers in each of the subtests.

The results of the Otis Mental Ability Test administered to the twelfth-grade pupils are reported in Table 31; these are the same respondents whose achievement test results are reported in Table 30.

The mean Otis I. Q. is reported in the first column, the corresponding twelfth-grade norm by percentile rank is given in the second column, and the number of schools at each interval is shown in the third column. The table gives a clear picture of the superior potential of the pupils in the Catholic high schools considered in this analysis. The median Otis I. Q. for the 41 schools is 116 at the 74th percentile of the twelfth-grade norm. This indicates that only 26% of the pupils who participated in this developed national norm exceed the median I. Q. of the pupils in the 41 schools. It should be noted that although the lowest median I. Q. reported in Table 31 is 101, many students' I. Q. falls considerably below this point.

This table does not prove that Catholic students per se are superior in ability, merely that the students in these Catholic schools are superior when compared with national norms. Some of the reasons for this indicated superiority can be traced to the relative selectivity of the admission policies of the Catholic elementary schools. At the secondary level the admissions become more selective in a number of ways. Admission to private Catholic high schools is nearly always based on academic potential; these schools represent 37% of all Catholic high schools and serve 38% of the total enrollment. Admission to other types of Catholic high schools such as the parish or diocesan school is frequently based on a competitive entrance examination, although parish high schools more frequently have a universal admission policy for parish members and graduates of the parish elementary school. How-

Table 30
METROPOLITAN ACHIEVEMENT TEST, 12th-GRADE MEANS BY SUBTEST

	1	2	3	4	5	6	7	8	9	10	11
Percentile † rank (12th-grade norms)	Reading	Spelling	Language	Lang. study skills	Social studies study skills	Social studies vocab.	Social studies inform.	Math. compt. & concpt.	Math. analysis & prob.-solv.	Science concpt. unders.	Science inform.
93–95						2(93)					
90–92						1					
87–89						3					
84–86						6		2(85)		1(86)	
81–83			1(81)		1(82)	4	3	3(83)	3(83)		
78–80	3(79)		1	3(80)		7*(79)	2	1	1	1	
75–77	3	3(76)	2	2	2	7	1	1	3	1	2(77)
72–74	5	2	1	2	1	1	1	2	1	5	1
69–71	4	1	3	3	3	1	4	1		6	2
66–68	7*(66)	6	4	3	2	3	5	6	2	3	2
63–65	5	3	4	2	1		10*(65)	3	2	5*(64)	4
60–62	5	3	2	9*(61)	1	3	3	2	7	2	2
57–59	3	2	3*(57)	4	10*(57)	1	2	8*(59)	3*(58)	3	8*(58)
54–56	1	4*(55)	6	3	3			1	5	2	3
51–53	1	1	3	4	3		5	4	3	5	3
48–50	1	3	2	1	3			1	1	1	1
45–47		8	3		4	1	1	1	1	4	4
42–44	1	2	2	1				4	1		
39–41		1	1	2	2			1	2	1	1
36–38	1		1			1(36)	1	1	1		2
33–35			1		1				2	1(34)	2
30–32	1(31)	1	1(32)		2				1		2
27–29								1(28)			2(27)
24–26		1(26)		2(24)			1(26)				
21–23					1						
18–20					1(18)				1(18)		
No. of Schs.	41	41	41	41	41	41	41	41	41	41	41
Above 50th Percentile	37	25	30	35	27	39	38	32	31	34	27
Below 50th Percentile	4	16	11	6	14	2	3	9	10	7	14

* Median class; numbers in parentheses indicate the minimum, median, and maximum values for each column.
† Source: *Booklet of Norms, Metropolitan Achievement Tests: High School Battery.* New York: Harcourt, Brace & World, Inc., 1962.

ever, parish high schools enroll only 23% of the total national Catholic high school enrollment. A few dioceses have a universal admission policy, but frequently this is used in conjunction with a diocesan admission test for all Catholic high schools including private schools; the diocesan high school is often a second choice for the applicant. Another factor in the selectivity of Catholic high school enrollment is the strong academic emphasis of the curriculum—with very little emphasis on vocational and prevocational offering—which tends to attract the college-bound student. Many Catholic high schools have a high rate of academic failure, resulting in withdrawals and transfers to other schools. Tuition payments are another factor; 76% of these high schools have tuition charges and other fees. There is no indication of an attempt to admit only an academic elite; rather, lack of space and other factors make it impossible to admit all applicants.

Table 31

TWELFTH-GRADE OTIS MENTAL ABILITY TEST MEANS BY SCHOOLS

Mean Otis I.Q.	Percentile rank † (12th-grade norm)	Frequency
124	89	1
122	86	3
120	83	3
119	81	2
118	79	4
117	76	3
116	74	5*
115	71	2
114	69	3
113	66	4
112	62	3
111	59	2
110	56	3
107	47	1
103	33	1
101	27	1
Number of schools		41
Number above 50th percentile point		38
Number at 50th percentile point or below		3

* Median column value.

† Source: *Booklet of Norms, Metropolitan Achievement Tests: High School Battery.* New York: Harcourt, Brace & World, 1962.

In further analysis the results of the achievement battery and the results of the mental ability measure were considered comparatively. The median I. Q. of each twelfth-grade group in the 41 high schools was used in a regression equation to project the expected achievement for each of the groups. Although this procedure was used in full realization of current questioning of mental ability measures and the tendency to classify them as another form of achievement measures, the study assumed that there is sufficient differentiation in the mental ability measure to make it useful in establishing expected achievement levels for groups of students. The development procedure was influenced by current studies of over-achievers and under-achievers.[13]

The developed achievement expectancy for each twelfth-grade group was compared with the actual median achievement of the same group. If the actual median exceeded significantly the achievement expect-

Table 32

ACHIEVEMENT OF TWELFTH GRADERS, BY TYPE OF SCHOOL AND AREA OF ACHIEVEMENT

Achievement area	Type of school				Total
	All-boy	All-girl	Coeduca-tional	Coinstitu-tional	
Language Arts					
High-achieving schools	0	8	3	0	11
Schools with expected achievement	3	5	10	1	19
Low-achieving schools	8	1	1	1	11
Social Studies					
High-achieving schools	4	1	0	0	5
Schools with expected achievement	7	9	12	2	30
Low-achieving schools	0	4	2	0	6
Mathematics					
High-achieving schools	5	2	1	0	8
Schools with expected achievement	6	6	13	2	27
Low-achieving schools	0	6	0	0	6
Science					
High-achieving schools	1	0	4	0	5
Schools with expected achievement	9	8	10	0	27
Low-achieving schools	1	6	0	2	9
Schools in the analysis	11	14	14	2	41

ancy, the group was identified as "high-achieving"; if the median fell within the normal range of the achievement expectancy, the group was identified as "expected-achieving"; and if the actual achievement median fell significantly below the expectancy, the group was identified as "low-achieving." For this analysis the 11 subtests of the Metropolitan Achievement Test were combined into the 4 areas of language, social studies, mathematics, and science. The results of this procedure are presented by secondary school type in Table 32.

In the terms of the analysis these groups of twelfth-grade pupils are meeting their indicated potential in a more than satisfactory degree.

A summary of this comparative achievement follows:

Language arts

Above potential	26.8%	
At potential	46.3%	
Total at or above		73.1%
Below potential		26.8%

Social Studies

Above potential	12.2%	
At potential	73.1%	
Total at or above		85.3%
Below potential		14.6%

Mathematics

Above potential	19.5%	
At potential	65.8%	
Total at or above		85.3%
Below potential		14.6%

Science

Above potential	12.2%	
At potential	65.8%	
Total at or above		78.0%
Below potential		21.9%

Total of all areas

Above potential	17.7%	
At potential	62.7%	
Total at or above		80.4%
Below potential		19.5%

In looking at the comparative achievement as presented in Table 32 only a few positive indications stand out: the all-boy schools are well behind the all-girl and coeducational schools in language arts; the all-boy schools are superior to the other schools in social studies; and the coeducational schools are superior in mathematics and science. It is important when comparing student achievement with student academic potential to remember the relation to the stimulation which the school brings to student effort.

In this analysis of academic achievement in the Catholic elementary and secondary schools studied, the mental ability measures show the students as superior on the scale of national norms, and more important the measures of achievement showed a comparable superior achievement.

References

[1] P. J. Kenedy & Sons, New York, Vols. 1943–1963.

[2] *Life Tables For 1949–51,* U. S. Department of Health, Education and Welfare, Public Health Service, National Office of Vital Statistics.

[3] *Directory of Catholic Special Facilities and Programs in the United States for Handicapped Children and Adults,* Monsignor Elmer H. Behrmann, Sister Ann Dolores, S.L., National Catholic Educational Association, Washington, D. C., February 1965.

[4] Pope Pius XI, "Christian Education of Youth," Encyclical, December 1929.

[5] Sacred Congregation of Religious, "Instructio de Uneum Utrisque Promiscua Institutione," *Acta Apostolicae Sedis,* (1958).

[6] Frison, Basil, C.M.F., *Coeducation in Catholic Schools* (Boston: Daughters of St. Paul, 1959).

[7] Dorn, Anthony, O.F.M., "The Organization and Administration of the Co-institutional High School" (doctoral dissertation, Catholic University, 1962).

[8] Western States Small Schools Project: *Progress Report 1963,* Arizona State Department of Public Instruction, Phoenix, Arizona; *Project Roster 1963–64,* Colorado State Department of Education, Denver, Colorado; *New Dimensions for the Small Schools of Nevada,* Department of Education, Carson City, Nevada; *Annual Progress Report 1962–63,* Utah State Department of Public Instruction, Salt Lake City, Utah.

[9] Right Reverend Monsignor Justin A. Driscoll, Superintendent, Archdiocesan Schools, Dubuque, Iowa.

[10] New York, Harcourt, Brace and World Publishing Co.

[11] Princeton, N. J., Personnel Press Inc.

[12] New York, N. Y., Harcourt, Brace and World Publishing Co.

[13] Thorndike, Robert L., *The Concepts of Over- and Underachievement* (New York: Teachers College, Columbia University, 1963); Blythe C. Mitchell, "A Comparison of Achievement-Intelligence Relationship for Pupils with that for School Systems," *The Journal of Educational Research,* 57 (1963), 172–180.

CHAPTER THREE

The Staff of
Catholic Schools

THIS SECTION OF THE STUDY, CONCERNED WITH THE staffing of Catholic elementary and secondary schools, is based on 2 separate activities. The first was an attempt to gather statistical data about each of the staff members in the schools. Since this was a first attempt, only information that is most fundamental and informative and could be most reliably determined in a national survey was requested. The Study staff hopes that these basic findings might stimulate further inquiry.

The second activity was a more intimate view of teachers and administrators as the Study staff met them face to face in a representative group of Catholic schools in action. This firsthand experience also gave the staff an opportunity to observe the interesting relationship of students and schools.

This depth study of Catholic schools in action observed 218 elementary and 104 secondary representative schools in 13 dioceses. The results will not be presented statistically but will be offered as observations to support and broaden the statistical reports.

In each of the 2 activities the Study staff met with wholehearted cooperation from all the people concerned with the schools—the hierarchy, the diocesan superintendents, the religious communities, the principals and teachers, and the pastors of parish schools. Only 3 dioceses and 1 archdiocese—in New Jersey—decided not to cooperate with the Study. This decision affected returns from approximately 100 secondary and 475 elementary schools, served by about 8500 staff members.

In the nationwide collection of data 92% of the total elementary staff, 84% of the secondary staff, 88% of the elementary schools, and 85% of the secondary schools made returns that could be handled in the processing of national data. There were other returns in each category that could not be handled in the Study's data-processing procedure.

In processing the accumulated data, elementary and secondary staff are treated separately, and each staff group is presented under 5 categories: priest, brother, sister, layman, and laywoman. The same instrument was used in gathering data for each of the 2 groups: Schedule I, Faculty Data, included in the Appendix.

Tables 33 and 34 present the basic findings: total number reporting, the category of each, and the position of each respondent.

Table 33 shows the responses of 103,779 elementary school staff members that could be processed. The largest number of staff members consists of sisters, who represent 66.2% of the total; the second largest

Table 33

TOTAL ELEMENTARY STAFF RESPONDENTS BY CATEGORY AND POSITION, OCTOBER 1962

Position	Total	No response No.	%	Priest No.	%	Brother No.	%	Sister No.	%	Layman No.	%	Laywoman No.	%
No response	5,152	123	14.4	953	46.8	23	4.8	2,470	3.6	163	5.8	1,420	4.9
Teacher	89,576	660	77.4	968	47.5	389	81.9	57,449	83.7	2,645	93.9	27,465	94.9
Administrator	2,055	22	2.6	40	2.0	38	8.0	1,947	2.8	2	0.1	6	0.0
Teacher and administrator	6,996	48	5.6	75	3.7	25	5.3	6,807	9.9	6	0.2	35	0.1
Total	103,779	853	0.8	2,036	2.0	475	0.5	68,673	66.2	2,816	2.7	28,926	27.9

Table 34

TOTAL SECONDARY STAFF RESPONDENTS BY CATEGORY AND POSITION, OCTOBER 1962

Position	Total	No response No.	%	Priest No.	%	Brother No.	%	Sister No.	%	Layman No.	%	Laywoman No.	%
No response	2,984	75	16.9	906	16.5	264	7.9	1,162	5.9	273	4.6	304	6.3
Teacher	34,310	350	78.8	4,001	72.8	2,839	84.5	16,931	85.9	5,654	95.0	4,535	93.5
Administrator	1,290	3	0.7	352	6.4	188	5.6	719	3.6	19	0.3	9	0.2
Teacher and administrator	1,225	16	3.6	238	4.3	68	2.0	896	4.5	5	0.1	2	0.0
Total	39,809	444	1.1	5,497	13.8	3,359	8.4	19,708	49.5	5,951	14.9	4,850	12.2

group is laywomen, 27.9% of the total. The small number of priests is somewhat surprising; these reports came from 9451 schools, and one might assume that the number of priests who render some teaching or supervisory service would be closer to 9500 than the 2036 shown here. It is clear that communities of teaching brothers are not extensively engaged in elementary education; they represent only 0.5% of the total elementary group.

A gross ratio of lay to religious teachers developed from Table 33, shows 1 lay teacher to 2.24 religious in the elementary schools. This ratio is based on the total number of persons reporting and does not take into account the fact that some of them participate only on a part-time basis.

Statistical Regions 2, 3, 4, 5, 8 and 9 are very close to the national ratio of 1 lay teacher to 2.24 religious in the elementary schools. However, Region 1, the New England States, shows the lowest ratio of lay to religious, 1 to 6.43; Region 6, with 1 to 1.72, and Region 7, with 1 to 1.33, show the highest lay to religious ratio. These regions include the states of Kentucky, Tennessee, Alabama, Mississippi, Arkansas, Louisiana, Oklahoma, and Texas. The median training level for the teachers in each of these 3 regions is the same as the national median. In Region 1, the median salary for laywomen is the same as the national median and the median salary for laymen is above the national median, whereas in Regions 6 and 7 the median salary for both laymen and laywomen is below the national median by almost $1000.

In a later analysis in this section, (Tables 50 and 51), lay to religious ratios are based on full-time equivalency rather than total numbers in each group. As an example, of the 2036 priests reported in Table 33, only 90, or 4.4%, are engaged full time in the schools. The rest devote from one-tenth to nine-tenths of their time to school work.

Table 33 also shows that only 2055 of the respondents from the 9451 schools reported as full-time principals. This would indicate that only 21% of the elementary schools reporting had nonteaching principals; this will be considered more fully later in this chapter.

Table 34 shows 39,809 secondary staff members responding, 84% of the total that could have responded. Here too, the sisters make up the largest category, 49.5% of the total, and the women out-number the men 62% to 38%. The gross ratio of lay to religious teachers is 1 lay to 2.64 religious, a slightly lower lay ratio than that of 1 to 2.24 for the elementary schools. In comparing the regional with the national figures, Region 1 shows, as it did for the elementary schools, a lower ratio of lay to religious teachers of 1 to 4.6, and Region 7 shows the highest ratio of 1 lay to 2.02 religious teachers.

Although the sisters make up the largest staff category in the secondary schools, the other categories show an alignment different from that in the elementary schools. There is an increase in each of the male categories and a decrease in the laywomen category. Although the brothers still have the smallest total number, they represent 8.4% of the total staff.

Table 35

AGES OF ELEMENTARY SCHOOL STAFF, OCTOBER 1962

Age	Total	No response		Priest		Brother		Sister		Layman		Laywoman	
		No.	%	No.	%	No.	%	No.	%	No.	%	No.	%
No response	923	39	4.6	240	11.8	6	1.3	64	0.1	54	1.9	520	1.8
Under 20	1,553	8	0.9	1	0.0	2	0.4	311	0.5	42	1.5	1,189	4.1
20–24	17,369	105	12.3	5	0.2	149	31.4	9,690	14.1	784	27.8	6,636	22.9
25–34	26,653	173	20.3	797	39.1	170*	35.8	19,670	28.6	1,030*	36.6	4,813	16.6
35–44	18,081*	154	18.1	467*	22.9	61	12.8	11,278*	16.4	376	13.4	5,745*	19.9
45–54	19,150	174	20.4	314	15.4	43	9.1	12,474	18.2	292	10.4	5,853	20.2
55–64	12,868	130	15.2	157	7.7	33	6.9	9,273	13.5	169	6.0	3,106	10.7
65–69	4,264	43	5.0	34	1.7	3	0.6	3,455	5.0	46	1.6	683	2.4
Over 69	2,918	27	3.2	21	1.0	8	1.7	2,458	3.6	23	0.8	381	1.3
Total	103,779	853	0.8	2,036	2.0	475	0.5	68,673	66.2	2,816	2.7	28,926	27.9

* Medians, not including "No response."

Table 36

AGES OF SECONDARY SCHOOL STAFF, OCTOBER 1962

Age	Total	No response		Priest		Brother		Sister		Layman		Laywoman	
		No.	%	No.	%	No.	%	No.	%	No.	%	No.	%
No response	573	34	7.7	186	3.4	56	1.7	44	0.2	100	1.7	153	3.2
Under 20	34	1	0.2	1	0.0	2	0.1	7	0.0	4	0.1	19	0.4
20–24	3,967	43	9.7	21	0.4	563	16.8	721	3.7	1,307	22.0	1,312	27.1
25–34	12,308	158	35.6	2,452	44.6	1,405*	41.8	4,115	20.9	2,986*	50.2	1,192*	24.6
35–44	8,690*	78	17.6	1,755*	31.9	614	18.3	4,459	22.6	902	15.3	882	18.2
45–54	7,567	64	14.4	814	14.8	481	14.3	5,056*	25.7	382	6.4	770	15.9
55–64	4,517	44	9.9	218	4.0	172	5.1	3,518	17.9	203	3.4	362	7.5
65–69	1,362	17	3.8	29	0.5	43	1.3	1,120	5.7	36	0.6	117	2.4
Over 69	791	5	1.1	21	0.4	23	0.7	668	3.4	31	0.5	43	0.9
Total	39,809	444	1.1	5,497	13.8	3,359	8.4	19,708	49.5	5,951	14.9	4,850	12.2

* Median, not including "No response."

AGE OF TEACHERS

The median age of the total elementary staff falls in the interval of 35–44 years, as does the median age of the priests, sisters, and laywomen, whereas the median age of brothers and laymen falls in the younger interval of 25–34 years. The staff is not heavily weighted with elderly people; only 19.3% are 55 years or older. The laywoman group does not seem heavily weighted with teachers who have retired from other teaching positions because of age; only 14.4% are in the over-55 category (Table 35).

Table 36 shows the median age of the secondary school staff in the same interval, 35–44, as the elementary staff. However, the sisters, who make up 49.5% of the total, are older; their median age is in the 45–54 interval. Apparently they enter teaching later, as only 24.6% are under age 34. It is surprising that the laywomen are younger than their counterparts in the elementary schools; their median age falls in the 25–34 interval, whereas the elementary laywomen's median falls in the 35–44 interval.

PREPARATION OF TEACHERS

Tables 37 and 38 show the degree of preparation of staff members in elementary and secondary schools.

The median training level of the total elementary staff is the B. S. degree, with 49.8% having less than a degree and 50.2% having a bachelor's degree or more. As noted in Table 37, the medians are developed without including the "no response" category. Laywomen teaching in the elementary school have less formal training than any of the other 4 categories, 23.2% having only 1 year of college or less and only 31.8% having a bachelor's degree or better. 56.7% of the sisters have a bachelor's degree or better.

Table 38 shows that the secondary staff has more training than does the elementary staff. The median training level for the total group is the B. S. degree plus and is the same for each of the 5 categories. The sisters have the highest percentage of 47.7% at the advanced training

Table 37

PREPARATION OF ELEMENTARY SCHOOL STAFF, OCTOBER 1962

Education	Total	No response		Priest		Brother		Sister		Layman		Laywoman	
		No.	%	No.	%	No.	%	No.	%	No.	%	No.	%
No response	1,439	42	4.9	254	12.5	6	1.3	767	1.1	29	1.0	341	1.2
High school only	2,669	32	3.8	4	0.2	12	2.5	1,065	1.6	40	1.4	1,516	5.2
Less than 1 yr. college	3,977	39	4.6	1	0.0	6	1.3	1,383	2.0	51	1.8	2,497	8.6
1 yr. college	5,131	40	4.7	3	0.1	16	3.4	2,341	3.4	95	3.4	2,636	9.1
2 yr. college	39,209	318	37.3	219	10.8	142	29.9	24,603	35.8	1,108	39.3	12,819*	44.3
B.S. degree	17,408*	153	17.9	314	15.4	72*	15.2	12,123*	17.7	475*	16.9	4,271	14.8
B.S. +	27,005	179	21.0	680*	33.4	146	30.7	21,078	30.7	827	29.4	4,095	14.2
M.S.	4,994	33	3.9	292	14.3	48	10.1	3,936	5.7	123	4.4	562	1.9
M.S. +	1,947	17	2.0	269	13.2	27	5.7	1,377	2.0	68	2.4	189	0.7
Total	103,779	853	0.8	2,036	2.0	475	0.5	68,673	66.2	2,816	2.7	28,926	27.9

* Median, not including "No response."

Table 38

PREPARATION OF SECONDARY SCHOOL STAFF, OCTOBER 1962

Education	Total	No response		Priest		Brother		Sister		Layman		Laywoman	
		No.	%	No.	%	No.	%	No.	%	No.	%	No.	%
No response	305	23	5.2	101	1.8	9	0.3	76	0.4	28	0.5	68	1.4
High school only	153	5	1.1	5	0.1	13	0.4	18	0.1	38	0.6	74	1.5
Less than 1 yr. college	115	1	0.2	0	0.0	6	0.2	33	0.2	21	0.4	54	1.1
1 yr. college	132	3	0.7	1	0.0	6	0.2	35	0.2	17	0.3	70	1.4
2 yr. college	2,246	35	7.9	237	4.3	172	5.1	1,050	5.3	291	4.9	461	9.5
B.S. degree	5,851	57	12.8	660	12.0	424	12.6	1,591	8.1	1,599	26.9	1,520	31.3
B.S. +	15,901*	153	34.5	2,227*	40.5	1,333*	39.7	7,523*	38.2	2,794*	47.0	1,871*	38.6
M.S.	9,447	113	25.5	1,378	25.1	827	24.6	5,866	29.8	762	12.8	501	10.3
M.S. +	5,659	54	12.2	888	16.2	569	16.9	3,516	17.8	401	6.7	231	4.8
Total	39,809	444	1.1	5,497	13.8	3,359	8.4	19,708	49.5	5,951	14.9	4,850	12.2

* Median, not including "No response."

level of a master's degree or more. Also, each of the religious categories outranks the lay teachers in advanced training. Of the brothers and priests, 41.5% and 41.3%, respectively, have master's degrees or more, whereas only 19.5% of the laymen and 15.1% of the laywomen have this advanced training.

In a separate analysis not presented in tabular form, the Study identified those elementary and secondary staff members who earned their undergraduate diplomas from Catholic institutions. Of the total elementary group, 85% were awarded their undergraduate degrees by a Catholic institution, whereas only 50.8% of the lay teachers were awarded undergraduate degrees in a Catholic institution. Similarly, in the total secondary group, 84% were graduates of Catholic institutions, whereas only 55% of the lay teachers got their undergraduate degrees from a Catholic college or university. A similar inquiry aimed at identifying the number of non-Catholic teachers in the schools showed that in the elementary schools 3.8% of laymen teachers and 4.4% of laywomen teachers were non-Catholic. In the secondary schools there was a much larger percentage of non-Catholic teachers, 6.8% of the laymen and 15.1% of the laywomen.

Tables 39, 40, 41, and 42 present a more complete understanding of the formal preparation of teachers in Catholic schools. These tables, developed through cross-tabulation of staff ages and formal preparation, include sisters and laywomen at both elementary and secondary levels.

Tables 39 and 40 show that preparation for sisters and laywomen in the elementary schools is about equal in the 20–24 age interval, but the in-service advancement of the sisters brings them to the bachelor's degree plus in the 35–44 age interval. The median preparation level for laywomen in the 20–24 year interval is 2 years of college, and it remains at that level throughout the scale. On the other hand, although the median preparation level of the sisters has the same beginning, it increases continuously throughout the age scale, up to the 69-or-over age group. The required educational programs of religious communities and the lack of comparable programs for lay teachers, either required or highly motivated, probably account for this difference in continuing in-service training. Also, the cost of this additional formal education might be a deterrent to lay teachers, in view of the level of their salaries. A summary of lay teachers' salaries is presented later in this chapter.

It seems important to establish the important characteristics of the 2 parts of this dichotomous staff of the Catholic schools, the religious members and lay members. In this identification of characteristics of staff at both the elementary and secondary levels, the sisters will be used as representative of all religious and the laywomen as representative of all lay teachers. In most important characteristics, the sisters are truly representative of the religious and the laywomen of the lay faculty. The characteristics considered are age, preparation, and experience.

Tables 39 and 40 show a small but significant number of sisters

Table 39

CROSS-TABULATION OF AGE AND PREPARATION OF ELEMENTARY SISTERS
OCTOBER 1962

Education	No response		<20		20–24		25–34		35–44	
	No.	%	No.	%	No.	%	No.	%	No.	%
No response	10	15.6	3	1.0	55	0.6	78	0.4	75	0.7
H. S. only	2	3.1	33	10.6	130	1.3	121	0.6	98	0.9
<1 yr. col.	1	1.6	88	28.3	407	4.2	238	1.2	122	1.1
1 yr. col.	4	6.3	92*	29.6	880	9.1	504	2.6	192	1.7
2 yr. col.	18	28.1	95	29.9	6550*	67.6	10,505*	53.4	2,346	20.8
B.S.	7	10.9	0	0.0	1057	10.9	3,322	16.9	2,335	20.7
B.S. +	19	29.7	0	0.0	598	6.2	4,562	23.2	4,705*	41.7
M.S.	1	1.6	0	0.0	9	0.1	277	1.4	1,118	9.9
M.S. +	2	3.1	0	0.0	4	0.0	63	0.3	287	2.5
Total (68,673)	64	0.1	311	0.5	9690	14.1	19,670	28.6	11,278	16.4

Education	45–54		55–64		65–69		Over 69	
	No.	%	No.	%	No.	%	No.	%
No response	120	1.0	214	2.3	113	3.3	99	4.0
H. S. only	172	1.4	235	2.5	132	3.8	142	5.8
<1 yr. col.	162	1.3	162	1.7	127	3.7	76	3.1
1 yr. col.	209	1.7	228	2.5	123	3.6	109	4.4
2 yr. col.	1,711	13.7	1759	19.0	903	26.1	718	29.2
B.S.	2,480	19.9	1817	19.6	638	18.5	467*	19.0
B.S. +	5,611*	45.0	3722*	40.1	1145*	33.1	714	29.0
M.S.	1,464	11.7	790	8.5	193	5.6	84	3.4
M.S. +	545	4.4	346	3.7	81	2.3	49	2.0
Total (68,673)	12,474	18.2	9273	13.5	3455	5.0	2458	3.6

* Median, not including "No response."

and laywomen in the elementary schools less than 20 years of age, and for the teachers in each of these categories the median preparation level is 1 year of college. The presence of these very young and lesser trained people seems to prove the difficulty of Catholic schools to secure an adequate supply of teachers.

As a group the sisters in the elementary schools are older than the laywomen; only 14.6% of the sisters are less than 25 years of age, whereas 27% of the lay teachers fall in that age group. The largest number of sisters, 28.6%, are in the 25–34 year category.

The median training level of the elementary sisters does not rise

Table 40

CROSS-TABULATION OF AGE AND PREPARATION OF ELEMENTARY LAYWOMEN
OCTOBER 1962

Education	No response No.	%	<20 No.	%	20–24 No.	%	25–34 No.	%	35–44 No.	%
No response	27	5.2	5	0.4	25	0.4	34	0.7	74	1.3
H. S. only	28	5.4	76	6.4	103	1.6	187	3.9	529	9.2
<1 yr. col.	30	5.8	511	43.0	480	7.2	292	6.1	599	10.4
1 yr. col.	43	8.3	265*	22.3	658	9.9	313	6.5	489	8.5
2 yr. col.	223	42.9	329	27.7	3487*	52.5	2007*	41.7	2005*	34.9
B.S.	62	11.9	0	0.0	1311	19.8	917	19.1	911	15.9
B.S. +	81	15.6	0	0.0	553	8.3	931	19.3	955	16.6
M.S.	18	3.5	3	0.3	15	0.2	100	2.1	141	2.5
M.S. +	8	1.5	0	0.0	4	0.1	32	0.7	42	0.7
Total (28,926)	520	0.5	1189	4.1	6636	22.9	4813	16.6	5745	19.9

Education	45–54 No.	%	55–64 No.	%	65–69 No.	%	Over 69 No.	%
No response	79	1.3	67	2.2	19	2.8	11	2.9
H. S. only	386	6.6	166	5.3	32	4.7	9	2.4
<1 yr. col.	366	6.3	178	5.7	28	4.1	13	3.4
1 yr. col.	536	9.2	275	8.9	43	6.3	14	3.7
2 yr. col.	2584*	44.1	1721*	55.4	293*	42.9	170*	44.6
B.S.	726	12.4	235	7.6	71	10.4	38	10.0
B.S. +	1010	17.3	348	11.2	138	20.2	79	20.7
M.S.	128	2.2	86	2.8	36	5.3	35	9.2
M.S. +	38	0.6	30	1.0	23	3.4	12	3.1
Total (28,926)	5853	20.2	3106	10.7	683	2.4	381	1.3

* Median, not including "No response."

above 2 years of college until age 35–44 years. The training level of sisters moves from the 2-year college level in the 25–34 year interval to a bachelor's degree plus in the 35–44 interval. This slow but steady movement up by the sisters can be ascribed in great part to the positive influence of the Sister Formation movement. This movement, which has its beginnings only 10 years ago, is explained fully later.

In Tables 41 and 42 we find that the sisters are considerably older than the laywomen in the secondary schools. Only 24.6% of the sisters are younger than 35 years, compared with 52.1% of the laywomen, and at the upper age levels only 10.8% of the laywomen are older than 54

Table 41

CROSS-TABULATION OF AGE AND PREPARATION OF SECONDARY SISTERS
OCTOBER 1962

Education	No response No.	No response %	20 No.	20 %	20–24 No.	20–24 %	25–34 No.	25–34 %	35–44 No.	35–44 %
No response	18	40.9	0	0.0	0	0.0	12	0.3	4	0.1
H. S. only	0	0.0	0	0.0	0	0.0	1	0.0	2	0.0
<1 yr. col.	0	0.0	2	28.5	4	0.6	6	0.1	5	0.1
1 yr. col.	0	0.0	4*	47.1	11	1.5	10	0.2	4	0.1
2 yr. col.	1	2.3	1	14.3	194	26.9	590	14.3	114	2.6
B.S.	1	2.3	0	0.0	242*	33.6	505	12.3	283	6.3
B.S. +	5	11.4	0	0.0	244	33.8	2372*	57.6	1787*	40.1
M.S.	14	31.8	0	0.0	10	1.4	460	11.2	1610	36.1
M.S. +	5	11.4	0	0.0	16	2.2	159	3.9	650	14.6
Total (19,708)	44	0.1	7	0.0	721	3.7	4115	20.9	4459	22.6

Education	45–54 No.	45–54 %	55–64 No.	55–64 %	65–69 No.	65–69 %	Over 69 No.	Over 69 %
No response	10	0.2	16	0.5	11	1.0	5	0.7
H. S. only	3	0.1	8	0.2	1	0.1	3	0.4
<1 yr. col.	8	0.2	6	0.2	2	0.2	1	0.1
1 yr. col.	2	0.0	2	0.1	3	0.3	1	0.1
2 yr. col.	60	1.2	50	1.4	19	1.7	22	3.3
B.S.	219	4.3	199	5.7	85	7.6	57	8.5
B.S. +	1444	28.6	1031	29.3	395	35.3	244	36.5
M.S.	1982*	39.2	1250*	35.5	350*	31.2	188*	28.1
M.S. +	1328	26.3	956	27.2	254	22.7	147	22.0
Total (19,708)	5056	25.7	3518	17.9	11.20	5.7	668	3.4

* Median, not including "No response."

years, compared with 27.0% of the sisters. The median training level for both sisters and laywomen is the same through the interval of 35–44 years. Beyond this point the median training level of the sisters advances to the master's degree plus. In addition the sisters' training beyond the master's degree far exceeds that of the laywomen.

Table 42

CROSS-TABULATION OF AGE AND PREPARATION OF SECONDARY LAYWOMEN
OCTOBER 1962

Education	No response No.	%	20 No.	%	20–24 No.	%	25–34 No.	%	35–44 No.	%
No response	14	9.2	0	0.0	13	1.0	13	1.1	10	1.1
H. S. only	6	3.9	3	15.8	3	0.2	8	0.7	24	2.7
<1 yr. col.	3	2.0	1	5.3	7	0.5	10	0.8	17	1.9
1 yr. col.	4	2.6	5	26.3	12	0.9	8	0.7	19	2.2
2 yr. col.	16	10.5	10*	52.6	113	8.6	91	7.6	93	10.5
B.S.	37	24.2	0	0.0	707*	53.9	352	29.5	226	25.6
B.S. +	45	29.4	0	0.0	413	31.5	528*	44.3	332*	37.6
M.S.	20	13.1	0	0.0	39	3.0	133	11.2	105	11.9
M.S. +	8	5.2	0	0.0	5	0.4	49	4.1	56	6.3
Total (4850)	153	0.4	19	0.4	1312	27.1	1192	24.6	882	18.2

Education	45–54 No.	%	55–64 No.	%	65–69 No.	%	Over 69 No.	%
No response	8	1.0	7	1.9	2	1.7	1	2.3
H. S. only	18	2.3	10	2.8	2	1.7	0	0.0
<1 yr. col.	10	1.3	4	1.1	1	0.9	1	2.3
1 yr. col.	13	1.7	8	2.2	0	0.0	1	2.3
2 yr. col.	79	10.3	40	11.0	16	13.7	3	7.0
B.S.	149	19.4	40	11.0	5	4.3	4	9.3
B.S. +	334*	43.4	158*	43.6	48*	41.0	13*	30.2
M.S.	104	13.5	58	16.0	30	25.6	12	27.9
M.S. +	55	7.1	37	10.2	13	11.1	8	18.6
Total (4850)	770	15.9	362	7.5	117	2.4	43	0.9

* Median, not including "No response."

EXPERIENCE OF TEACHERS

Experience is an important characteristic of any school staff; Tables 43 and 44 present this characteristic of the staff in the Catholic elementary and secondary schools. The types of experience presented are years in Catholic schools, in public schools, in other independent schools, total experience, and years in present position. Some respondents (the number is not known) did not count the school year 1962–63, the year within which they were teaching, as a year of experience. This might affect the figures in these tables in the first 3 experience ranges: years in Catholic schools, total experience, and years in present position.

Most easily identified is the high median of sisters' total years of experience in both elementary and secondary schools. The sisters' median for total experience in elementary schools is 15–19 years. In secondary schools, sisters' medians for total experience and experience in Catholic schools is 20–29 years.

It is important that in the elementary schools only 19.6% of the laywomen and 21.7% of the sisters have been in their present positions for more than 4 years. In the secondary schools, only 36.2% of the

Table 43

EXPERIENCE OF ELEMENTARY SCHOOL SISTERS AND LAYWOMEN, OCTOBER 1962

	Catholic schools		Public schools		Independent schools		Total experience		Years in present position	
	No.	%	No.	%	No.	%	No.	%	No.	%
Sisters (68,673)										
No response & 0	1,774	2.6	65,179*	94.9	68,141*	99.2	1,560	2.3	11,859	17.3
1– 2 years	5,603	8.2	1,131	1.6	201	0.3	5,406	7.9	28,046*	40.8
3– 4 years	5,089	7.4	687	1.0	90	0.1	4,992	7.3	13,842	20.2
5– 9 years	11,557	16.8	927	1.3	123	0.2	11,417	16.6	10,819	15.8
10–14 years	9,441*	13.7	410	0.6	51	0.1	9,323	13.6	2,346	3.4
15–19 years	5,942	8.7	147	0.2	29	0.0	5,857*	8.5	785	1.1
20–29 years	11,200	16.3	126	0.2	23	0.0	11,141	16.2	629	0.9
30–39 years	10,960	16.0	55	0.1	10	0.0	11,236	16.4	254	0.4
More than 39 years	7,107	10.3	11	0.0	5	0.0	7,741	11.3	93	0.1
Laywomen (28,926)										
No response and 0	4,645	16.1	18,881*	65.0	27,427*	94.8	3,677	12.7	7,734	26.7
1– 2 years	8,947	30.9	2,378	8.2	716	2.5	6,523	22.6	10,194*	35.2
3– 4 years	5,673*	19.6	1,724	6.0	296	1.0	4,547*	15.7	5,063	17.5
5– 9 years	6,517	22.5	2,761	9.5	291	1.0	6,099	21.1	4,609	15.9
10–14 years	1,790	6.2	1,329	4.6	108	0.4	3,196	11.0	869	3.0
15–19 years	602	2.1	616	2.1	42	0.1	1,861	6.4	235	0.8
20–29 years	472	1.6	572	2.0	35	0.1	1,702	5.9	120	0.4
30–39 years	225	0.8	413	1.4	7	0.0	768	2.7	85	0.3
More than 39 years	55	0.2	322	1.1	4	0.0	553	1.9	17	0.1

* Median, including "No response and 0."

sisters and 18.5% of the laywomen have been in their present positions for more than 4 years. Even considering the number of newly established schools, this is a relatively high rate of turnover that must cause serious problems at both levels. The median total experience of laywomen in secondary schools is the 3–4 year interval.

The short tenure of the sisters can be ascribed partly to the policy of religious communities to review annually the assignments of each of their members. Many changes in assignments are made to meet the overall needs and commitments of the individual communities. This change in assignment particularly affects school principals who often are also the spiritual superiors of local communities. The canonical rules that govern religious communities require that a spiritual superior may not continue in this capacity for a period longer than 6 years. Some communities have adopted a policy under which a religious

Table 44

EXPERIENCE OF SECONDARY SCHOOL SISTERS AND LAYWOMEN, OCTOBER 1962

	Catholic schools		Public schools		Independent schools		Total experience		Years in present position	
	No.	%	No.	%	No.	%	No.	%	No.	%
Sisters (19,708)										
No response & 0	254	1.3	17,980*	91.2	19,440*	98.6	166	0.8	2,564	13.0
1– 2 years	658	3.3	621	3.2	82	0.4	632	3.2	5,993	30.4
3– 4 years	724	3.7	370	1.9	41	0.2	674	3.4	4,020*	20.4
5– 9 years	1,974	10.0	478	2.4	62	0.3	1,891	9.6	4,117	20.9
10–14 years	2,618	13.3	148	0.8	37	0.2	2,563	13.0	1,435	7.3
15–19 years	2,244	11.4	62	0.3	14	0.1	2,192	11.1	664	3.4
20–29 years	4,955*	25.1	40	0.2	14	0.1	4,932*	25.0	648	3.3
30–39 years	4,126	20.9	8	0.0	13	0.1	4,231	21.5	201	1.0
More than 39 years	2,155	10.9	1	0.0	5	0.0	2,427	12.3	66	0.3
Laywomen (4,850)										
No response & 0	1,008	20.8	3,041*	62.7	4,338*	89.4	773	15.9	1,516	31.3
1– 2 years	1,613*	33.3	638	13.2	196	4.0	1,135	23.4	1,721*	35.5
3– 4 years	815	16.8	342	7.1	125	2.6	734*	15.1	711	14.7
5– 9 years	889	18.3	379	7.8	89	1.8	965	19.9	622	12.8
10–14 years	264	5.4	162	3.3	40	0.8	466	9.6	143	2.9
15–19 years	116	2.4	84	1.7	28	0.6	269	5.5	69	1.4
20–29 years	99	2.0	77	1.6	26	0.5	261	5.4	55	1.1
30–39 years	44	0.9	71	1.5	6	0.1	153	3.2	13	0.3
More than 39 years	2	0.0	56	1.2	2	0.0	94	1.9	0	0.0

* Median, including "No response and 0."

other than the superior is assigned the responsibility of principal. This usually happens at the secondary school level and in larger schools.

In the elementary schools 35% of the laywomen and 23.3% of the laymen have had some teaching experience in public schools, and 5.1% of the sisters also have had public school teaching experience. At the secondary school level, 37.3% of the laywomen, and 24.2% of the laymen, and 8.8% of the sisters have taught in public schools.

SCHOOL PRINCIPALS

Tables 33 and 34 show 2055 elementary and 1290 secondary full-time principals. In a later item in Schedule I, the personnel questionnaire, the respondents were requested to establish full-time equivalency. A respondent who spent full time in a position reported as 1.0, and a person who spent 1 day a week in a position reported as .2 or one-fifth of a week. In this analysis, 1752 elementary principals served full time; the remaining 303 spent from one-tenth to nine-tenths of their time as principals. Here secondary principal respondents dropped from 1290 to 1077; the remaining 213 were classified as part-time principals.

We find, then, that 1752 of the 9451 elementary schools are staffed by full-time nonteaching principals. Of the 2075 secondary schools reporting, 1077 are staffed by full-time nonteaching principals. The assignment of full-time principals in both elementary and secondary schools is conditioned by the size of the schools; Tables 17 and 18 in the earlier chapter on enrollment showed 5870 elementary schools with enrollments of 400 or less and 705 secondary schools with 200 or less. Considering the financial pressures on these small schools, one can understand the lack of full-time administrators and supervisors.

In the elementary schools some additional administrative assistance available to the school principal was reported under the heading "Assistant Principals." 444 schools, or 4.7% of the total, showed from one-tenth to 1 full-time assistant. Similarly, 606, or 29.2% of the secondary schools showed from one-tenth to 4 full-time assistants. Although this item was not cross-tabulated with school size, we assume that these assistant principals are in the larger schools.

Part of the administrative duties within any school is purely clerical, so we attempted to determine the availability of clerical assistance in elementary and secondary schools. Of the 9451 elementary schools, 86.1% reported they had no full-time clerical help, and 80.9% reported they had no full- or part-time clerical help. Among 2075 secondary schools 53.7% had no full-time clerical help, and 69.1% had no full- or part-time clerical help. It was a firsthand observation of the Study staff that the small schools with full-time teaching principals had no clerical assistance, and the schools that were fairly staffed and had at least a part-time nonteaching principal also had clerical help.

The Study staff had planned to survey the persistency rate of students in Catholic elementary schools, but the plan was abandoned because of the method by which student records were filed. All former students, both graduates and transfers, were placed in a single alphabetical file. A complete reorganization of files by year in schools that were in many cases 25 years old or older was obviously impossible. As mentioned earlier, a planned follow-up of college-bound high school graduates was not completed because most school records showed the colleges to which students requested transcripts be sent, but not the schools they eventually entered. The Study staff ascribed these inadequacies not only to lack of adequate clerical help but also to lack of guidance personnel.

Table 45

GUIDANCE PERSONNEL IN SECONDARY SCHOOLS, OCTOBER 1962

Full-time equivalency	Total No.	%	Not identified No.	%	Parish No.	%	Private No.	%	Interparish No.	%	Diocesan No.	%
0.0	911	44.5	36	56.3	453*	58.8	272	35.6	46	43.8	104	30.2
0.1–0.5	334*	16.3	10	15.6	140	18.2	117*	15.3	19*	18.1	48	14.0
0.6–1.0	289	14.2	9	14.1	84	10.9	110	14.4	15	14.3	71*	20.6
1.1–1.5	163	7.4	3	4.7	35	4.5	72	9.4	10	9.5	43	12.5
1.6–2.0	131	6.4	2	3.1	25	3.2	68	8.9	4	3.8	32	9.3
2.1–2.5	57	2.7	1	1.6	9	1.2	24	3.1	9	8.6	14	4.1
2.6–3.0	56	2.7	0	0.0	9	1.2	34	4.5	1	1.0	12	3.5
3.1–3.5	28	1.3	0	0.0	3	0.4	16	2.1	0	0.0	9	2.6
3.6–4.0	30	1.4	2	3.1	4	0.5	21	2.8	0	0.0	3	0.9
4.1–4.5	11	0.5	0	0.0	0	0.0	8	1.0	1	1.0	2	0.6
4.6–5.0	14	0.6	1	1.6	2	0.3	7	0.9	0	0.0	4	1.2
> 5.0	22	1.0	0	0.0	6	0.8	14	1.8	0	0.0	2	0.6
Total	2046	100.0	64	3.1	770	37.6	763	37.2	105	5.1	344	16.8

* Median.

Secondary Guidance Personnel

Secondary school responses showed that of the 2075, 44.3% had no staff member assigned for any time to the guidance function (Table 45). In 30.4% of the schools assignments for guidance ranged from one-tenth to 1 full-time person. In the remaining 25.3% of the schools, guidance assignments ranged from more than 1 to more than 5 full-time assignments.

RATIO OF STAFF TO STUDENTS

A review of the schoolday organization and the teaching load assignment in the secondary schools is presented in Table 46.

Table 46

SECONDARY TEACHERS' CLASS LOAD, SCHOOL DAY ORGANIZATION,
OCTOBER 1962

Teaching load (2075 schools)								
Teaching periods			Other assigned periods			Total periods		
	Total	%		Total	%		Total	%
No response	124	6.0	No response	465	22.4	No response	237	11.4
4	189	9.1	1	1226	59.1	4	32	1.5
5	1035	49.9	2	305	14.7	5	275	13.3
6	510	24.6	3	46	2.2	6	799	38.5
>6	217	10.5	>3	33	1.6	7	535	25.8
						8	165	8.0
						9	32	1.5

School day					
Daily hours			Daily periods		
	Total	%		Total	%
No response	41	2.0	No response	32	1.5
4	2	0.1	4	0	0.0
5	162	7.8	5	35	1.7
6	1246	60.0	6	331	16.0
7	569	27.4	7	910	43.9
>7	55	2.7	8	676	32.6
			9	91	4.4

The teaching load medians appear normal—5 teaching periods and 1 additional assigned period in a 6- or 7-period day. However, 35% of the schools report 6 or more teaching periods, and an additional 35% report 7 or more total assignment periods. These loads would be excessive for teachers who must make varied preparation and evaluate written work of students.

In considering the numerical relationship of teachers to pupils, the Study first developed the ratio of total staff to total enrollment within each school. This was followed by a digest of the practices followed by each school to control the number of students assigned to a single class. Tables 47, 48, 49, and 50 show the results of applying these approaches to both elementary and secondary schools.

Table 47, which presents the ratio of total staff to pupils in elementary schools, shows the national median in the interval of 36–40 pupils.

Table 47

ELEMENTARY SCHOOL PRINCIPALS' REPORTS,
STUDENT PER STAFF MEMBER, OCTOBER 1962
(9280 Schools)

Number of students per staff member	Number of schools	% of schools
25 or less	853	9.2
26–30	832	8.9
31–35	1490	16.0
36–40*	2068	22.2
41–45	1990	21.4
46–50	1207	13.0
51–55	415	4.4
56–60	187	2.0
61–65	86	.9
66–70	34	.3
71 or more	118	1.2

* Median.

Similar analyses prepared by the nine national regions show regional medians and the number of schools reporting as:

Region 1	36–40	768 schools
Region 2	41–45	2124 schools
Region 3	41–45	2484 schools
Region 4	36–40	1331 schools
Region 5	36–40	532 schools
Region 6	31–35	412 schools

Region 7	31–35	672 schools
Region 8	36–40	244 schools
Region 9	41–45	649 schools

The national median of 36–40 is influenced by the large number of schools in regions other than 2, 3, and 9 with ratios in the lower intervals.

The staff to pupil ratios reported in Table 47 are not synonymous with class size. These ratios reflect the relation of total number of staff members to total number of students in each school. This procedure includes all staff members, both full- and part-time. Part-time teachers are included on the basis of their full-time equivalency; if they work 1 day a week they are included as 0.2. The class-size figures would be the number of pupils in each of the classrooms in each of the elementary schools. The questionnaire included an item intended to gather this information (see item 14, Schedule II, Elementary Principal Report in Appendix), but the returns on this item were not processed because the request was variously misinterpreted.

Table 48 gives a strong indication of class size in its report of the maximum size control in each school. Although the table does not tabulate enrollment room by room in each school, one can assume that individual room enrollments will not be greatly above or below the indicated maximum control figure. In this light the median class size for grades 1–3 falls in the interval of 46–50 pupils; 21.4% of the schools report maximum controls above 50 pupils.

Table 48

ELEMENTARY SCHOOL PRINCIPALS' REPORTS,
CONTROL OF MAXIMUM CLASS SIZE, OCTOBER 1962

Maximum size	Total schools	%	Maximum size	Total schools	%
Grades 1–3	8179	100.0	Grades 4–8	8159	100.0
Less than 26	748	9.1	Less than 26	823	10.0
26–30	399	4.8	26–30	403	4.9
31–35	477	5.8	31–35	521	6.3
36–40	1135	13.8	36–40	1265	15.5
41–45	1039	12.7	41–45*	1126	13.8
46–50*	2604	31.8	46–50	2621	32.1
51–55	878	10.7	51–55	775	9.4
56–60	563	6.8	56–60	386	4.7
61–65	112	1.3	61–65	93	1.1
66–70	86	1.0	66–70	61	0.7
More than 70	138	1.6	More than 70	85	1.0

* Median.

A second approach to the numerical relationship of teachers to students was an inquiry aimed at determining practices in controlling class size in grades 1 through 8. In reviewing these reports by the 9 regions some variation is found:

Region	Grades 1–3 median	Grades 4–8 median
1	41–45	36–40
2	51–55	46–50
3	46–50	46–50
4	41–45	41–45
5	46–50	41–45
6	36–40	36–40
7	36–40	36–40
8	46–50	46–50
9	46–50	46–50

In observation beyond the gathered statistics, the Study found very large classes, 60 and above, in elementary schools in each of the statistical regions and in almost all of the dioceses. The greatest number of very large classes is found in Region 2, where the very large classes occur with the highest frequency in a single diocesan organization. In this large diocesan organization, the relationship of total staff to total elementary enrollment is 1 staff member to 62 students, which means that there are many classrooms where the ratio exceeds 1 teacher to 70 pupils.

Many dioceses have policies on class size in the elementary school which vary from strong directives to suggested practices. Frequently these are newly developed policies being implemented by control of the registration of the incoming first grades. From observation and discussions with many educators, the Study staff is certain of a growing concern in Catholic schools about the size of classes in the elementary schools. The major block to the control and reduction of class size is at the parish level, where more children are applying for admission than can be accommodated at existing class sizes. The problem of expanding facilities at the parish level is a serious one because of the financial difficulties and the difficulty of obtaining adequate staff. The supply of religious teachers is limited, and it is frequently difficult to find a religious community able to accept the staffing of a new school or the expansion of an existing one. If a religious community does accept the responsibility of a school, it is usually with the understanding that the staff will include a certain number of lay teachers. This increases the operating costs because the direct salary payment to a lay teacher greatly exceeds the stipend to a religious.

Large classes are not new to the religious communities that prepare teachers for the Catholic elementary schools. Although the sister who faces a first-grade class of 60 or more would probably rather have fewer, in her training she has been exposed to techniques for minimizing the problems in handling such large groups. Members of the Study staff visited first grades in 218 elementary schools at various times in the school year from October through May, and it was a rare classroom with fewer than 40 students. The majority had more than 50 youngsters and many had more than 60. The most evident characteristic was the prevailing order and the ready response of the children to a change in classroom activity. The order, necessary for any effective instruction, did not seem oppressive and seemed easily accepted by the children.

In some first grades of 60 or more, the teacher had as many as 5 reading groups. While she worked with each of these groups separately, the rest of the class was busy with reading workbooks and other assigned work. As the teacher spent about 15 minutes with each group, by the time the fifth group came for its reading activity the youngsters had been at work independently for more than an hour. Although there was no evidence of unrest among the children, there surely can be some question of the effectiveness of this hour of independent work. However, the reading achievement of pupils in these schools, as measured by standard tests at the second-, fourth-, and sixth-grade levels, was significantly above their grade norms.

In the middle and upper grades of the elementary schools a great part of the educational program is carried on within a catechetical framework, a procedure adopted as an answer to the very large class. As in the primary grades, the results of standard achievement batteries show that the students are achieving at better than an acceptable level. The observer cannot help wondering how much more these same teachers could do with smaller classes and the opportunity to give more attention to the individual.

In order to get an understanding of the staff to pupil ratio and the class size in Catholic secondary schools, secondary school principals were requested to report on staff and enrollment statistics and on class size policies. Analyses of these data are presented in Tables 49 and 50.

Table 49

SECONDARY SCHOOL PRINCIPALS' REPORTS,
STUDENTS PER STAFF MEMBER, OCTOBER 1962
(1976 Schools)

Number of students per staff member	Number of schools	% of schools
< 26*	1119	56.7
26–30	480	24.3
31–35	231	11.7
36–40	79	4.0
41–45	23	1.1
46–50	21	1.0
51–55	11	0.5
56–60	5	0.2
61–65	1	0.0
66–70	1	0.0
> 70	5	0.2

* Median.

The inquiry reported in Table 49 was based on an interval that did not discriminate below 1 staff member to 25 pupils. But according to the inquiry the median ratio of total staff to total students fell in the interval of 1 to 25 or fewer. By inspection of the raw reports the ratio can be placed more exactly at 1 staff member to 21.9 pupils in the schools reporting. As explained earlier for the elementary schools, the total number of staff, including administrators and educational specialists both full-time and part-time, is included in this ratio. There is no attempt to establish a class-size figure.

Because of the way in which secondary schools are organized, a general overall class-size figure has little meaning. While classes in such subjects as English, social sciences, and mathematics might be limited to 35 or 40 by the size of a classroom, physical education classes might be as large as 90. In other situations different kinds of controls might operate: size of industrial arts classes might be limited by safety and number of pupil stations; classes such as the fourth year of a foreign language would be limited by the number of pupils who elect to participate. For these reasons the Study decided to direct its inquiry to the maximum class size in the academic subject areas including English, mathematics, social sciences. The analysis of this inquiry is presented in Table 50.

Table 50

MAXIMUM CLASS SIZE, SECONDARY PRINCIPALS' REPORTS, OCTOBER 1962
(2075 Schools)

Class size	Total	%	Not identified		Parish		Private		Interparish		Diocesan	
			No.	%	No.	%	No.	%	No.	%	No.	%
Less than 26	248	12.0	9	14.1	88	11.4	111	14.5	7	6.7	13	3.8
26–30	343	16.5	12	18.8	107	13.9	156	20.4	21	20.0	41	11.9
31–35	672*	32.4	18*	28.1	257*	33.4	264*	34.6	40*	38.1	91	26.5
36–40	511	24.6	20	31.3	161	20.9	173	22.7	23	21.9	133*	38.7
41–45	167	8.0	2	3.1	77	10.0	48	6.3	6	5.7	34	9.9
46–50	104	5.0	3	4.7	64	8.3	8	1.0	6	5.7	23	6.7
51–55	23	1.1	0	0.0	13	1.7	2	0.3	1	1.0	7	2.0
56–60	5	0.2	0	0.0	2	0.3	0	0.0	1	1.0	2	0.6
61–65	1	0.0	0	0.0	0	0.0	1	0.1	0	0.0	0	0.0
66–70	1	0.0	0	0.0	1	0.1	0	0.0	0	0.0	0	0.0
More than 70	0	0.0	0	0.0	0	0.0	0	0.0	0	0.0	0	0.0

* Median.

The principals' responses to this item made it possible for 100% of the responses to be processed. The median academic class-size control falls in the 31–35 pupil interval at 33.6 pupils. This might be the place to point out that no single index related to class size can be used as a determinant of what is desirable or undesirable. However, if a single indicator could be used, the ratio of total staff to total students would be most reliable as a beginning at the secondary level.

THE LAY TEACHER

The rapid growth of Catholic schools during the past 10 years has made necessary an expanded use of the lay teacher at both the elementary and the secondary school levels. During this period the number of religious who became available as teachers did not keep pace with the expanding needs of the schools. In 1950 there was a total of 27,770 teachers in the secondary schools, 23,147 religious and 4623 lay teachers. By 1961 the total number of teachers had risen to 46,623, an increase of 67.9%. In this period the number of religious increased from 23,147 to 34,153, a growth of 47.5%, while the number of lay teachers advanced from 4623 to 12,470, an increase of 169%.

A similar expansion took place in the elementary schools, with an increase of total staff from 66,525 in 1950 to 110,911 in 1961, a growth of 66.7%. The number of religious increased 26.5% from 61,778 to 78,188, but the great increase was in the number of lay teachers from 4747 to 32,723, a 589% increase. This meant that whereas there were 13 religious for every lay teacher in 1950, in 1961 there were 2.38 religious for each lay teacher.

As reported earlier, this increase in the number of lay teachers continued into the 1962–63 school year, which showed national ratios of lay to religious at 1 to 2.24 for elementary schools and 1 to 2.64 for secondary schools.

An analysis of the ratio of lay to religious teachers in the schools that reported to the Study is presented in Tables 51 and 52. This analysis of staff members is on the basis of full-time equivalency; a part-time teacher who spends one-half time in the school is represented as 0.5 in the computation. Also, the analysis is presented in terms of number of schools and is not related to the size of individual school faculties. For example, in Table 52 the 228 secondary schools at the median had staffs ranging from less than 10 members to over 100.

It is apparent from the wide range of the ratios of lay to religious in Tables 51 and 52 that one can make no generalization about the numer-

Table 51

ELEMENTARY SCHOOLS' RATIO OF LAY TO RELIGIOUS, OCTOBER 1962

Lay	Religious	No. of schools	% of schools
All	0	51	0.5
1	Less than 0.5	125	1.2
1	0.5–0.9	652	6.6
1	1.0–1.9	2268	23.2
1	2.0–2.9	1524	15.5
1	3.0–3.9	1400*	14.3
1	4.0–4.9	552	5.6
1	5.0–5.9	288	2.9
1	6.0–6.9	200	2.0
1	7.0–7.9	312	3.2
1	8.0–8.9	162	1.6
1	9.0–9.9	41	0.4
1	More than 9.9	260	2.6
0	All	1938	19.8

ical relationship between lay and religious staff members. However, there did seem to be a significant regional variation in Region 1, where the ratio of lay to religious is 1 to more than 9 in both elementary and secondary schools, but even with a median differing so sharply from the national medians, there is the same wide range of ratios in this region.

It seems worth noting that lay teachers outnumber the religious in 7.8% of the elementary schools and in 5.4% of the secondary schools. In addition, 51 elementary schools, 0.5% of the total, and only 3 secondary schools, 0.1% of the total, are totally staffed by lay teachers. At the other end of the scale, 19.8% of the elementary schools and 16.0% of the secondary schools are staffed entirely by religious, and in an additional 18.3% of the elementary schools and 29.7% of the secondary schools the staffing is 4 or more to 1 in favor of the religious.

A review of Tables 33 and 34 shows that of the total 31,742 lay teachers reporting from 9451 elementary schools, only 49 are classified as administrators, either full- or part-time. The same situation exists in secondary schools, where of 10,801 lay teachers reporting from 2075 schools, only 35 are classified as administrators. The administrator classification includes principals, assistant principals, and department heads, either full- or part-time.

Table 52

SECONDARY SCHOOLS' RATIO OF LAY TO RELIGIOUS TEACHERS, OCTOBER 1962

Lay	Religious	No. of schools	% of schools
All	0	3	0.1
1	Less than 0.5	18	0.8
1	0.5–0.9	97	4.6
1	1.0–1.9	419	20.2
1	2.0–2.9	354	17.0
1	3.0–3.9	228*	10.9
1	4.0–4.9	163	7.9
1	5.0–5.9	91	4.3
1	6.0–6.9	81	3.9
1	7.0–7.9	48	2.3
1	8.0–8.9	38	1.7
1	9.0–9.9	16	0.7
1	More than 9.9	185	8.9
0	All	333	16.0

Because of the increasing numbers of lay teachers in Catholic schools, an inquiry was made to determine the salary levels of lay teachers during the 1962–63 school year. The results are given in Tables 53, 54, 55, and 56, where elementary and secondary schools are presented separately, as are men and women, and salary intervals are cross-tabulated against total teaching experience. It is easily determined that teachers in the secondary schools receive salaries higher than those paid to elementary teachers.

Table 53

LAYMEN TEACHERS' SALARIES AND TOTAL TEACHING EXPERIENCE,
ELEMENTARY SCHOOLS, OCTOBER 1962

Salary	< $2500		2500–2999		3000–3499*		3500–3999		4000–4499	
	No.	%	No.	%	No.	%	No.	%	No.	%
No resp. & 0	66	2.38	48	19.0	145	25.3	141	25.1	76	18.5
1– 2 years	84†	30.3	85†	33.6	168†	29.4	190†	33.8	150†	36.5
3– 4 years	35	12.6	35	13.8	91	15.9	84	14.9	93	22.6
5– 9 years	40	14.4	36	14.2	78	13.6	63	11.2	51	12.4
10–14 years	18	6.5	21	8.3	33	5.8	37	6.6	22	5.4
15–19 years	9	3.2	9	3.6	20	3.5	20	3.6	5	1.2
20–29 years	11	4.0	7	2.8	21	3.7	15	2.7	10	2.4
30–39 years	5	1.8	5	2.0	8	1.4	6	1.1	2	0.5
>39 years	9	3.2	7	2.8	8	1.4	6	1.1	2	0.5
Total (2338)	277	11.8	253	10.8	572	24.4	562	24.0	411	17.6

Salary	4500–4999		5000–5499		5500–5999		6000 +	
	No.	%	No.	%	No.	%	No.	%
No resp. & 0	24	16.9	1	1.3	0	0.0	0	0.0
1– 2 years	52†	36.6	23	29.9	2	14.3	2	6.7
3– 4 years	29	20.4	23†	29.9	3	21.4	2	6.7
5– 9 years	26	18.3	23	29.9	7†	50.0	12†	40.0
10–14 years	8	5.6	2	2.6	0	0.0	11	36.7
15–19 years	0	0.0	0	0.0	1	7.1	1	3.3
20–29 years	2	1.4	5	6.5	1	7.1	0	0.0
30–39 years	0	0.0	0	0.0	0	0.0	2	6.7
>39 years	1	0.7	0	0.0	0	0.0	0	0.0
Total (2338)	142	6.1	77	3.3	14	0.6	30	1.3

* Median salary interval.
† Median experience interval.

Table 54

LAYWOMEN TEACHERS' SALARIES AND TOTAL TEACHING EXPERIENCE,
ELEMENTARY SCHOOLS, OCTOBER 1962

Salary	< $2500		2500–2999		3000–3499*		3500–3999		4000–4499	
	No.	%	No.	%	No.	%	No.	%	No.	%
No resp. & 0	876	13.9	539	12.3	1021	12.9	565	11.1	143	7.5
1– 2 years	1675	26.5	997	22.8	1906	24.0	1008	19.8	305	16.1
3– 4 years	1030†	16.3	736†	16.9	1255	15.8	820	16.1	262	13.8
5– 9 years	1240	19.6	921	21.1	1629	20.5	1158†	22.8	474†	25.0
10–14 years	606	9.6	489	11.2	861	10.9	597	11.7	270	14.2
15–19 years	321	5.1	289	6.6	519	6.5	354	7.0	154	8.1
20–29 years	281	4.4	236	5.4	431	5.4	339	6.7	172	9.1
30–39 years	156	2.5	89	2.0	185	2.3	142	2.8	83	4.4
>39 years	131	2.1	70	1.6	126	1.6	105	2.1	36	1.9
Total (26,028)	6316	24.2	4366	16.8	7933	30.5	5088	19.5	1899	7.3

Salary	4500–4999		5000–5499		5500–5999		6000 +	
	No.	%	No.	%	No.	%	No.	%
No resp. & 0	28	9.7	5	6.2	2	9.5	0	0.0
1– 2 years	35	12.2	15	18.5	1	4.8	3	8.3
3– 4 years	41	14.2	7	8.6	7	33.3	4	11.1
5– 9 years	59†	20.5	16†	19.8	4†	19.0	9	25.0
10–14 years	41	14.2	15	18.5	4	19.0	8†	22.2
15–19 years	24	8.3	6	7.4	0	0.0	2	5.6
20–29 years	38	13.2	12	14.8	2	9.5	4	11.1
30–39 years	17	5.9	5	6.2	0	0.0	3	8.3
>39 years	5	1.7	0	0.0	1	4.8	3	8.3
Total (26,028)	288	1.1	81	0.3	21	1.0	36	0.1

* Median salary interval.

† Median experience interval.

Table 55

LAYMEN TEACHERS' SALARIES AND TOTAL TEACHING EXPERIENCE,
SECONDARY SCHOOLS, OCTOBER 1962

Salary	< $2500		2500–2999		3000–3499*		3500–3999		4000–4499	
	No.	%	No.	%	No.	%	No.	%	No.	%
No resp. & 0	20	19.4	9	22.5	33	28.4	115	33.0	330	24.6
1– 2 years	19	18.4	16†	40.0	27†	23.3	143†	41.1	566†	42.1
3– 4 years	14†	13.6	1	2.5	19	16.4	41	11.8	239	17.8
5– 9 years	15	14.6	9	22.5	12	10.3	27	7.8	148	11.0
10–14 years	11	10.7	1	2.5	9	7.8	10	2.9	31	2.3
15–19 years	6	5.8	2	5.0	5	4.3	2	0.6	14	1.0
20–29 years	2	1.9	1	2.5	9	7.8	4	1.1	3	0.2
30–39 years	7	6.8	0	0.0	1	0.9	2	0.6	10	0.7
>39 years	9	8.7	1	2.5	1	0.9	4	1.1	2	0.1
Total (5260)	103	1.9	40	0.7	116	2.2	348	6.6	1343	25.5

Salary	4500–4999		5000–5499		5500–5999		6000 +	
	No.	%	No.	%	No.	%	No.	%
No resp. & 0	133	11.7	40	4.4	7	1.4	7	0.9
1– 2 years	393	34.6	195	21.4	49	10.0	22	2.9
3– 4 years	312†	27.4	279	30.6	104	21.2	54	7.0
5– 9 years	209	18.4	276†	30.3	199†	40.5	251	32.6
10–14 years	50	4.4	74	8.1	73	14.9	229†	29.7
15–19 years	10	0.9	20	2.2	30	6.1	68	8.8
20–29 years	11	1.0	18	2.0	17	3.5	79	10.2
30–39 years	9	0.8	6	0.7	9	1.8	53	6.9
>39 years	10	0.9	3	0.3	3	0.6	8	1.0
Total (5260)	1137	21.6	911	17.3	491	9.3	771	14.6

* Median salary interval.
† Median experience interval.

The median salaries fall in the following intervals: for elementary women, $3000–3499, by inspection $3145; elementary men, $3500–3999, by inspection $3555; secondary women, $4000–4499, by inspection $4010; secondary men, $4500–4999, by inspection $4803. Combining men and women, 2.4% of the teachers at the elementary level are paid more than $4500, whereas 46.4% of the teachers at the secondary level receive more. In addition, 0.2% of all elementary teachers and 9.4% of all secondary teachers receive salaries greater than $6000.

Table 56

LAYWOMEN TEACHERS' SALARIES AND TOTAL TEACHING EXPERIENCE, SECONDARY SCHOOLS, OCTOBER 1962

Salary	< $2500		2500–2999		3000–3499*		3500–3999		4000–4499	
	No.	%	No.	%	No.	%	No.	%	No.	%
No resp. & 0	48	12.3	24	14.0	79	19.1	175	20.3	196	19.3
1– 2 years	81	20.8	31	18.0	104	25.2	257†	29.8	291	28.7
3– 4 years	64	16.5	23	13.4	58†	14.0	122	14.2	185†	18.2
5– 9 years	81†	20.8	36†	20.9	74	17.9	145	16.8	167	16.5
10–14 years	42	10.8	17	9.9	40	9.7	63	7.3	67	6.6
15–19 years	22	5.7	16	9.3	17	4.1	40	4.6	37	3.6
20–29 years	24	6.2	14	8.1	18	4.4	33	3.8	39	3.8
30–39 years	12	3.1	7	4.1	9	2.2	18	2.1	22	2.2
>39 years	15	3.9	4	2.3	14	3.4	8	0.9	11	1.1
Total (3696)	389	10.5	172	4.6	413	11.2	861	23.3	1015	26.1

Salary	4500–4999		5000–5499		5500–5999		6000 +	
	No.	%	No.	%	No.	%	No.	%
No resp. & 0	55	11.7	14	6.4	3	3.7	0	0.0
1– 2 years	102	21.7	30	13.7	5	6.2	2	2.7
3– 4 years	88†	18.7	38	17.4	9	11.1	3	4.0
5– 9 years	119	25.3	60†	27.4	26†	32.1	19	25.3
10–14 years	42	8.9	37	16.9	20	24.7	12	16.0
15–19 years	21	4.5	19	8.7	5	6.2	16†	21.3
20–29 years	27	5.7	10	4.6	9	11.1	13	17.3
30–39 years	12	2.5	9	4.1	4	4.9	8	10.7
>39 years	5	1.1	2	0.9	0	0.0	2	2.7
Total (3696)	471	12.7	219	5.9	81	2.2	75	2.0

* Median salary interval.

† Median experience interval.

48% of the elementary principals and 65% of the secondary principals indicated that lay teachers were paid on a salary schedule determined by training and teaching experience. However, analysis of the relation between salary payments and teaching experience presented in Tables 53, 54, 55, and 56 and a further analysis related to teacher training, showed little connection between the training and experience of the teachers and salaries paid. This lack of correlation may be due to the slight spread between the minimum and maximum salaries reported.

In an attempt to determine the role and status of lay teachers, the Study staff held small group conferences with them in 218 elementary and 104 secondary schools.

These conferences were with groups varying from 3 to 8 teachers, totalling approximately 1200 elementary and 650 secondary teachers. The conferences were structured around 3 areas of inquiry; the teachers' opinion of their status in the schools, their career possibilities, and their special functions. As checks, similar conferences were held with groups of religious teachers in the same schools and the concept of the lay teacher was discussed with the school principals. Because of the subjective nature of the interviews, no attempt was made to evaluate the conference outcomes statistically. The findings are presented as the consensus of the Study staff's observations.

In general, the lay teachers felt that they were accepted kindly and with gratitude by the religious teachers, but they also felt that they were not accepted as professional coequals by these same teachers. Many of the lay teachers pointed out that the faculty meetings they attended were administrative routine; at other faculty meetings which they did not attend development and school policy were discussed, and they were informed of the outcomes. However, there was some evidence that a small segment of the secondary teachers felt they were fully accepted by the staffs with which they worked. Teachers in the elementary schools pointed out that parents were grudging in their acceptance of lay teachers to the extent that school principals made special efforts to see that pupils were not assigned to lay teachers for 2 years in a row.

A number of lay teachers in the elementary schools felt that their status was affected negatively when completely unqualified lay teachers were employed merely to fill vacancies. In their view, lay teachers were hired only because of the unavailability of sufficient religious teachers to staff the schools. These lay teachers pointed out further that there was little if any effort to provide special in-service programs for lay teachers that might enable them to compete as coequals with the religious.

The greater number of lay teachers did not consider teaching in a Catholic school as a career. Those who considered teaching as a career indicated that they were in their positions temporarily while waiting for other teaching assignments or completing requirements to qualify for other teaching positions. Among the reasons they offered for not considering Catholic school teaching as a career were low salaries, lack of job security, absence of fringe benefits including retirement programs, and small opportunity for promotion. Those who considered Catholic school teaching as a career were mostly in secondary schools; these pointed out that efforts are being made by Catholic school authorities to make salaries and other financial benefits competitive with other teaching positions. These same teachers felt that their status in the schools was approaching the level of equality with the religious.

Lay teachers pointed out that as lay persons they had the opportunity to provide examples of Christian life in a way different from and beyond that of the religious. They also felt that because of their greater social freedom they could represent Catholic schools more effectively in general community life and in specific community activities. At the secondary level, particularly, the lay teachers believed that they could supplement the guidance programs more effectively in the areas of social and personal guidance. Many of the lay teachers felt that their presence in the schools should provide a positive opportunity for constructive dialogue among lay and religious teachers. There was, however, a general feeling that little effort was being made to explore and capitalize on the special functions lay teachers could fulfill.

Conferences with religious teachers and principals in these same schools involved approximately as many persons as those with the lay teachers. They were firm in their belief that lay teachers were fully accepted in the schools. They pointed out that the lay teacher was at some disadvantage in participating fully in the school operation because religious community life provided an opportunity of continuing school interests long after the school day had ended and when the lay teacher was not available. Many of the religious in the elementary schools felt that low salaries affected the supply of lay teachers, making it necessary to employ inadequately prepared people; this in turn affected the acceptance of lay teachers by parents.

There was almost general agreement that no special orientation or in-service programs were provided for lay teachers, and the religious did not feel that such programs were necessary. The religious further stated that adjustment to the purposes of the Catholic schools developed in the day-to-day contacts within the school.

There was not a great or ready response to the question of what functions lay teachers could fulfill better than the religious. However, in a number of instances members of the Study staff were approached by individual religious teachers who indicated that they had been thinking about the special functions of lay teachers and identified what they thought were strengths peculiar to the lay teachers. The strengths most frequently mentioned were the special guidance functions that could be served better by the lay teacher, the lay person as an example of good Christian living, and the greater freedom of social living possible for the lay teacher.

Based on the interviews just discussed, observations of the lay teachers at work in the schools, and evaluation of the statistical data related to the lay teacher, the Study staff identified factors that seem to control the most effective utilization of these teachers in Catholic schools and that need consideration by Catholic school leaders.

1. As the number of lay teachers continues to grow, greater efforts must be made to provide more adequate salaries to attract and retain better-trained teachers. This effort should be aimed at both elementary and secondary schools but more intensely at the elementary level.

2. There is a general lack of organized orientation and in-service programs for lay teachers to assist them in reaching a level equal to that of the religious. The training of religious teachers prepares them to work toward the special goals of Catholic schools that are the only reason for their existence. To work effectively toward these goals the lay teacher must first be made aware of them and then be assisted in developing the methods by which they can be achieved.

3. Almost always the number of lay teachers in a given school is the result of a problem of numbers. The first factor is the total number of teachers needed for the school staff; the second factor is the number of religious teachers available. The number of lay teachers that must be employed is determined by subtracting. To improve the position of

lay teachers in Catholic schools and to capitalize best on their potential, an evaluation should be made of those contributions that are peculiar to them and those they can accomplish more effectively than could the religious.

4. The negligible participation by lay teachers in the administration of Catholic schools strongly affects the status of the lay teacher. Careful consideration should be given to determining whether a lay principal is anomalous to the concept of a Catholic school staffed by lay and religious teachers.

5. In the elementary schools particularly, parents do not understand or accept fully the concept of the lay teacher. If the lay teacher is accepted by Catholic school leadership as something more than a necessity, a program informing parents of the true place of these teachers should be developed.

CHAPTER FOUR

The Preparation of Religious for Teaching

THIS CHAPTER CONTAINS 3 PRESENTATIONS THAT DEAL with the preparation of religious for teaching. In the first Sister Mary Emil, I.H.M., president of Marygrove College, draws on her knowledge of sister education. In the other two presentations Father Robert F. Harvanek, S.J., and Brother John Darby, S.M., deal respectively with the education of Jesuits and Marianists as they are prepared for teaching.

SISTER FORMATION

As the recent Conant study on teacher education, the agitation over the existence and standards of the National Council for the Accreditation of Teacher Education, and many hundreds, if not thousands, of journal articles will readily attest, perhaps the most controversial area in higher education today is teacher education. Analysis of the polemic shows a relatively small part concerned with the preparation of secondary teachers. The training of the nations's high school teachers has traditionally been accepted as the responsibility of the liberal arts colleges and universities. And although minimum background in professional education courses and methodology has usually been insisted on—by state departments of education if by no other agencies—curricula for these teachers were largely in the hands of subject departments, which made sure that their "majors" went out into the schools with some competence in the subjects they were destined to teach.

Most of the controversy over whether teacher should "teach Johnny" or "teach arithmetic," whether her college preparation should consist of "content" courses or "how-to" courses, has concerned the training of elementary teachers. And what is often overlooked is that the reasons for the conflict are considerably more historical than ideological.

The preparation of elementary teachers in the United States grew up, for the most part, as a function of "normal schools" or teachers' colleges. Until well into this century the standard program was not a 4-year but a 2-year course, and since this was terminal education designed immediately to equip young teachers for the classroom, emphasis was naturally put on how to do the job at hand. When the 2-year programs for elementary teachers grew into 4-year programs, there was time for the psychological and sociological foundations of education and time to provide instruction on a college level in the general areas to be covered in the elementary school, but the conviction that an elementary teacher should study explicitly not only the structure of mathematics but also arithmetic-as-taught-in-the-elementary-school tended to remain. And the end of this problem is not yet. Nor is it the purpose of this chapter to solve it. It is raised here to point up the historical fact that acceptance of the principle that an elementary teacher should be a professional man or woman who should not enter the classroom without at least a Bachelor's degree is very recent.

The struggle to upgrade the elementary teacher was begun by the National Education Association through its National Commission on Teacher Education and Professional Standards. When this commission, commonly referred to as NCTEPS, began its activities in 1946, only 15 states[1] required a Bachelor's degree for the first standard teaching certificate. By 1953 27 states had such a requirement, and by 1961 44 states required it.[2] In spite of all the efforts of NCTEPS, which has behind it the total resources of NEA and the full cooperation of the National Association of State Directors of Teacher Education and Certification, to say nothing of departments of education in all the colleges and universities and numerous professional agencies of all kinds, there were still 93,917, or 1 out of 15, teachers operating on substandard or emergency certificates in 1961, the year before the present Study.[3]

Sister teachers are recruited, are trained, and operate within the general context of American education, and there is nothing surprising about the fact that until very recently leaders in Catholic schools and otherwise enlightened representatives of higher education judged that 2 years of college constituted entirely respectable preparation for a sister *beginning* to teach in a "grammar" school—particularly in view of the known fact that almost all sisters regularly attend summer school for the whole of their lives. When it is recalled that the turnover among sister teachers is much less than among public school personnel because of the comparatively large number of lay teachers who remain in the profession only until marriage, it might be expected that a larger number of holders of life certificates earned in the 2-year normal schools would remain in the ranks of the sisters. This is not to say, of course, that Catholic schools are filled with superannuated sisters. In this respect the findings of the Study are very encouraging.

This judgment is no longer respectable. The rather sudden shift of opinion, among bishops, pastors, school superintendents, and the heads of the sisters' communities, had many causes. Catholic education was influenced by public education, both in its practice and in the demands of certifying agencies. The urge to excellence that struck American education in the fifties called for a beginning with the education of teachers. The prime cause, however, was probably the Sister Formation movement.

The Sister Formation movement can be traced to a number of causes. One was the great movement of *aggiornamento* in the Catholic Church —a term actually first used in connection with religious and popularized by the great Roman Congress of the States of Perfection in 1950. Then, as now, there were some who saw "adaptation" in a shortsighted and superficial way as consisting primarily in such changes as modification of sisters' dress or extension of visiting privileges. From 1950 there were many to say, as does Elio Gambari, S.M.M., consultant to the Sister Formation Conference and member of the Sacred Congregation of Religious, that adaptation is "90% formation" and 10%, perhaps, lesser changes needed to modernize religious life. In 1952 the emphasis upon improved education for sister teachers and improvement in the intellectual tools available to them was insisted upon expressly by Pope Pius XII in the Roman Congress for Communities of Religious Women. It was this emphasis of the Holy Father, discussed by the sisters in the Teacher Education Section of the National Catholic Educational Association at its Kansas City Convention of 1952, that led eventually to the establishment of the Sister Formation Conference.

From the Pope's insistence that sister teachers should be at least as well trained as their secular colleagues, the delegates concluded quickly that degree-level initial preparation was surely minimal in the United States. And when a survey authorized at the 1952 NCEA Convention revealed that only 16 religious communities in the United States actually required a Bachelor's degree of elementary teachers before entrance to the classroom, it became obvious that something like NEA's NCTEPS was necessary in the Catholic educational system. Because a sister's training was seen to be something more than academic preparation—an integrated process, in fact, of fusing intellectual and spiritual preparation, the new NCEA section was called, not a Conference on Sister Education and Professional Standards but the Sister Formation Conference. The main operations of the new organization were decentralized and began with a series of 3-day conferences for the major superiors of women's institutes in 1954.

It is important to note that the formal movement toward professional standards in the preparation of sister teachers began in the NCEA only 8 years after a similar movement began in NEA. The current Study of Catholic Education collected statistics for the school year 1962–63, 8 years after the first year in which the major superiors of women's institutes met to discuss the problem of providing degree training for their members. Therefore, this current Study cannot reflect, statistically, much change brought about by the Sister Formation movement.

The standard acceptable program for the training of sisters is now a 5-year program consisting of various combinations of postulancy, novitiate, and juniorate (or "scholasticate"). The most common patterns are a 1-year postulancy, 2-year novitiate, and 2-year juniorate, or a 1-year postulancy, 1-year novitiate, and 3-year juniorate. This 5-calendar-year period includes 4 academic years, leading to a Bachelor's degree. The extra calendar year, that of the canonical novitiate, is devoted largely to spiritual training. The 5-year period usually includes a number of summer sessions, so that most of these programs total more than the number of credit hours usually considered minimal for a bachelor's degree. Since most of the communities or independent provinces of sisters began their Sister Formation programs with a class of entering postulants (or freshmen), the 1962 figures would normally show an influx of degree-holding teachers only from those communities that began their programs in 1957 or before. Since this was only 3 years after the first set of SF Conferences and since the programs for most communities were only in the planning stage at this time, it is understandable that the crucial age group from 20 to 24 years does not show a dramatic or even appreciable drop in the number of teachers with only 2 years of college preparation. This is not to say that there was not actually a sizable drop in the number and percentage of sisters in this age group with substandard preparation. No reliable comparisons can be made because there are no statistics available on a national basis for earlier years. All that can be deduced from the current Study is that the age group 20–24 having only 2 years of college includes about as many sisters, per year, as does the age group 25–34. Although the younger group, which might have been expected to show the effects of a 3-year-old Sister Formation program in the United States, does not seem to be better situated than the older group, it is still possible that without the agitation for Sister Formation, median preparation for these sisters would have been less than 2 years! Still another possibility is that some communities may have replaced a certain number of sisters, travelling to their degrees by the summer-school route, by new recruits. If these older religious thus given the opportunity for full-time study during the school year were among those nearest their degrees, enough might have fallen in the age bracket 25–34 to cancel out the improvement in the 20–24 group.

In my opinion there is but one respect in which the statistics collected by the Study of Catholic Education show progress in the preparation of sister teachers, and this comparison offers only relative comfort to anyone interested in the system as a whole. Sister Rose Matthew's study, the sole major research effort covering some of the areas touched upon in the current study with which the data at hand could be compared, indicated that in 1956, 47% of all sister teachers at whatever level held bachelor's degrees and an additional 14% held master's degrees.[4]

Sister Rose Matthew worked with an official Catholic Directory population of 93,518 sister teachers, which included college teachers, community and diocesan supervisors, community administrators, full-time CCD personnel, and other persons listed as "teachers" by their communities but not working in elementary or secondary schools. The Study of Catholic Education worked with a population of 88,381 sister teachers actually in elementary and secondary schools in a year in which the Official Catholic Directory listed 100,871 sister teachers. In other words, there are about 12,000 sister "teachers" not covered by the Study of Catholic Education; these may reasonably be supposed to be the most highly trained of all, including almost the entire number of those with doctorates. Sister Rose Matthew's figures are suprisingly duplicated in this Study—47% holding Bachelor's degrees and an additional 16% holding Master's degrees or more—but the Study of Catholic Education statistics do not include what are presumably the best-educated members of all the groups. There would seem, then, to have been a decided improvement in the period 1956–62.

However, this improvement is only relative. If, as the Study shows, only 57,010 out of 88,381 elementary and secondary teachers are degree-holders, there are still 35% of the total teaching force of elementary and secondary sister teachers whose preparation is substandard, and the Sister Formation Conference still has a great deal of work to do. In 1960, 2 years prior to the Study of Catholic Education, only 75% of all employed elementary teachers in the United States held a degree (NEA Research Division, *Teacher Supply and Demand in Public Schools*, quoted in Stinnett and Huggett). Moreover, the ratio of sisters training at the elementary level to all sister teachers is larger than the ratio of elementary teachers to all teachers nationally. This is due to the fact that the parochial school system has emphasized elementary and secondary schools. The Study's figure of 44% of sister elementary teachers having no degree is not so startling, then, when compared with the percentage of elementary teachers without degrees in some low-ranking states such as Minnesota, with 43% in this group, Maine, with 57%, and Iowa, with 62% (Stinnett and Huggett, p. 62).

This can be illustrated by considering what is perhaps the single most disturbing figure revealed by this Study, namely, that in the 20–24 age group there are 7967 elementary sister teachers without degrees but only 1168 with and that the median for those without is 2 years of college. The problem occurs only at the elementary level. In 1962 there were only 721 sister teachers between the ages of 20-24 teaching at the secondary level—out of an entire population of high school sister teachers of 19,708. Of this 721, only 209 did not have degrees. Most communities prefer to give beginning sister teachers some experience at the elementary level before assigning them to high schools.

This undoubtedly accounts for the relatively small number beginning teaching in high school. These figures do not mean that in the period 1957-1962 only one-fifth of all young sisters were in Sister Formation programs. The figures developed in the Study do not tell us anything at all about the number in pre-service study. We can learn from the Study only how many sisters were actually teaching in elementary and secondary schools.

Really to determine the extent to which the Sister Formation movement had affected community practice by 1962, it would be necessary to know how many prospective sister teachers in the various communities, between the ages of 20 and 24, were not in elementary and secondary schools and who were in full-time study programs. These figures, to the writer's best knowledge, are not available anywhere. Available listings, community by community, list postulants, novices, and juniors. The communities have not yet been induced to distinguish juniors (temporarily professed sisters in full-time study in a house of formation) from temporarily professed in full-time teaching situations. Adding to this source of confusion the fact that the postulancy varies in length from 6 months to 2 years, the novitiate from 1 to 2 years, and the juniorate from 2 to 5 years, makes it clear that comparable statistics are difficult to gather.

In an effort to throw some light on the problem of the 7967 elementary teachers between the ages of 20–24 without degrees and in the belief that the number of young sisters making first profession in the years 1960 and 1961 might yield the most reliable information on how many sisters could have been either in formation or in the schools in the critical period 1958–62, in the summer of 1964 this writer, with the assistance of the National Secretariat of the Conference of Major Superiors of Women, inquired of 478 major superiors how many sisters made first profession in those years. Responses came from 243, reporting a total of 4230 sisters in 1960 and 4377 in 1961. On the assumption that the mean of these figures can give us the average increase of all new sisters in the period 1958–62, and on the further assumption that about 60% of all sisters go into teaching, the communities responding account at the very least for 20% of all sisters in this age bracket being in Sister Formation programs. Here, "the very least" represents the impossible supposition that the communities not responding had *no* sisters making first profession in either of the years mentioned.

On the supposition that the communities not responding had an average of as many sisters in the 1960 and 1961 profession groups as those who did answer, as many as 60% of the total number of sisters in the 20–24 age bracket could have been in full-time teacher-preparation programs. Both percentages were arrived at by subtracting the total number of sisters we know to have been in the schools in 1962 (10,411) from the total number reckoned to be in this age bracket and to be destined for the teaching profession (12,907–25,814). This rather rough calculation is not given to match the kind of data produced by the Notre Dame computer but to suggest a way in which the statistics of this Study should be supplemented if they are to yield meaningful information about the present extent of the Sister Formation program.

There is another and perhaps enlightening way in which the statistics could be analyzed. According to the Official Catholic Directory, the number of teaching sisters increased from 95,919 in 1958 to 100,871 in 1962. This represents a total addition of 4952 teaching sisters in the 5-year period. This does not mean that only 4952 new teachers entered the orders. As we have seen, a number somewhere between 13,- and 25,000 new prospective teachers actually entered the communities. From this number the 10,411 sisters in the age group 20–24 and present in the elementary and secondary schools in 1962 must have been drawn. What we do not know is whether these 10,411 represent new positions—additions to the school system—or substitutions of these young sisters for sisters withdrawn from the schools by death, illness, retirement, or other causes. Since the total increase in the sister teaching force was only 4952 in a period when 10,411 young sisters entered the schools, it would seem that 5459 represented replacements. It is assumed that the number entering the schools and older than age 25 is not statistically significant for this argument.

Some of the 4952 additional sisters reported by the Catholic Directory may have been previously pledged to replace lay teachers and represent no additions to the system. But even if every one of the additional sisters represented a concession by major superiors to expansion in a period in which formation needs urged consolidation, and even if it be granted that the major superiors would have been free to keep these sisters in formation programs had they been sufficiently determined to do so, the total number of such averaged over the communities would hardly have been more than 10 sisters per community for the 5-year period, or 2 per year. This is hardly a mass defection from the Sister Formation ideal.

These explanations of what may be the significance of the Study's data on the number of young sisters with 2 years' college preparation still in the schools is not an attempt to defend the fact. The fact in itself is not to be defended but, rather, changed as quickly as possible. We may attempt, however, to reconcile this fact with the equally true fact of widespread acceptance of the Sister Formation program by the religious superiors of the country, by detailing some of the reasons that have operated until now to delay complete installation of degree training in certain communities. If these reasons are valid now, they were most certainly operative in the period prior to 1957, which would have affected this Study.

In most communities it has been the major superior herself who has made the decision to try to institute a pre-service degree program. The 3-day regional SF conferences, of which 6 sets have now been held in the 6 NCEA regions, were limited to major superiors and 2 or 3 key members of the community. Sometimes the major superiors sent representatives, usually members of the general or provincial councils, who initiated discussions in their communities. The Sister Formation *Bulletin,* quarterly organ of the Sister Formation Conference which began publication in October 1954 and has since attained a paid subscription list of over 11,000 readers, together with 5 sets of published *Proceedings* of regional conferences, built up a corpus of Sister Formation literature that has been read and reread, quoted and requoted in the sisterhoods. The annual NCEA Convention provided another forum in which the necessity and desirability of the Sister Formation program could be set forth. Fortunately, the Sister Formation Conference was begun and knew its early flowering in a decade still marked by faith in Catholic education and respect for teaching sisters, so that the cooperation of the colleges and universities of NCEA and NCWA and of priests who were asked to write for the Conference publications and to serve as consultants was given generously and readily. Each new papal pronouncement or edict of the Sacred Congregation was echoed from many lecture platforms, and although few could remember who first called Sister Formation the most important movement in Catholic education during the last 25 years, this was repeated many times over and the lesson was not lost on the sisterhoods. There may still be among the almost 500 independent or semi-independent congregations or provinces that make SF policy some that do not believe in the Sister Formation program, but it would be difficult to name 5 anywhere in the country.

But the road from conviction to fulfillment is strewn with obstacles, some of them considerable. A major superior and her council who may decide definitely on a community policy of equipping all sisters with degree training before permitting them to begin teaching are not always in a position to implement the decision the following September. Some communities have made the decision overnight, as it were, and implemented it in a few months with no exceptions, but this rare phenomenon requires a very strong organization.

If the community has a college of its own with living facilities for the young sisters, the problem is reduced to sparing the sisters and assuming the cost of their upkeep. If the community has no college of its own, it is often possible to send the sisters to a nearby Catholic college or university. Sometimes, however, a motherhouse will be located out of the convenient reach of any Cahtolic college or university. The 1953 Survey, as a matter of fact, found 118 such communities. The problem for these groups is to find financial resources to support the sisters as resident students in another community's college or to provide a residence of their own near a college or university. In both cases the continued religious formation that is one of the essential requirements of the Sister Formation program and has to be given by the community's own formation personnel must be provided for. This is not easy. Some communities have decided to establish new colleges of their own for sister students solely. The Sister Formation Conference has taken the position that such institutions are capable of providing integrated education of a quality that could be truly exciting and that mere size or lack of it is not a fatal flaw in an institution. Several all-sister colleges established within the decade are already achieving remarkable results. However, the investment in preparing college teachers and in equipping libraries for first-rate small colleges is beyond either the imagination or the reach of many communities, which would do well to seek some cooperative arrangements.

The sisters received much encouragement to set up their formation programs, which meant somehow extending the 2-year programs most of them already had to degree programs of some kind or other, and the

Sister Formation Conference, as a voluntary self-help organization, provided a good deal of consultation and exhortation. However, the communities were very much on their own in what they set up. There are less than half a dozen cases known to the writer in which there was diocesan financial help. It is true that subsistence stipends for teaching sisters were raised rather spectacularly during the period following the initiation of the Sister Formation movement, so that the average sister teacher's annual stipend moved from $550 in 1962 to $853 in 1963. But a most meticulous, recent national survey of data from every community of sisters in the United States demonstrated that actual costs of educating the young sisters and maintaining the sick and retired when added to subsistence costs for teachers in the schools would require an annual income of $2015 for each active member of a given teaching order. This is the conclusion of Sister Cecilia Maureen Kehoe, F.C.S.P., in her unpublished Master's thesis, "Economic Contribution of Religious Communities of Women in the United States to Parochial Education through the Parochial Teaching Sister."

The community planning to extend its Sister Formation program faces some real problems of arrangements and some grim problems of finance. Actually, the grimmest problems of all have occurred in simply "hanging on" to the sisters to be educated. This is hard to explain on paper but very easy to see in a convent parlor when discussing a program to be established, with a general superior who may have only a few years of experience in general administration and who has spent a lifetime in generous and unquestioning service to the schools of a parish or diocese. If the Sister Formation movement had enjoyed an intellectual climate in the sisterhoods which understood that the young sister "belonged" to the apostolic works of the Church only when she was professionally prepared, the task of promoting the SF "idea" would have been infinitely easier than it was. As a matter of fact, the unwritten understanding—neither canonical nor logical, but almost unbelievably strong—was that the young sister belonged to the works of the diocese or parish, if not from the day of her entrance into the convent, at least from the end of her novitiate on; time devoted after that to education was seen as somehow "taken" from the children waiting to be taught.

Some semantic verification of the persistence of this attitude may be seen in the expressions still used even by those Catholic educators outside the sisterhoods who praise the Sister Formation movement but praise it precisely for "holding the sisters back" from the schools until their training is completed. This notion of "holding back" would never be applied to seminarians in training, to soldiers in boot camp or military academy, or to any professionals being readied for their profession, but it is dying a hard death with sister teachers. It *is* dying now. There has been a 721% increase in lay teachers in the period 1943–1963, during which sister teachers increased their numbers by only 33%, and a 129% student population increase in Catholic parochial schools in a period (1945–62) in which public schools increased their population by only 69%.[5] It is understood now—in most if not in all regions of the country—that sisters alone cannot assume the responsibility for every vacancy in a Catholic school, whether a new school waiting to be staffed or an old one expanding to meet the population bulge. But it is an understanding of quite recent crystallization, and what we are trying to explain is why many communities were moving with such apparent ponderousness in establishing their Sister Formation programs in the fifties, when the trends and the comprehensions were not yet clear.

A final set of difficulties. Some communities of diocesan rather than pontifical status actually did not have the canonical power to implement their Sister Formation programs, even though they were convinced of the necessity and could have financed them somehow. They were required by their dioceses to take new schools year after year, and this to an extent "used up" all the sisters who became available after first profession. Other major superiors found themselves bound by promises made by their predecessors in office, who had contracted to take new schools to be opened after their own terms had expired. Still other communities—and this was a most common difficulty—took no new schools during the period in which they were trying to establish their programs, refused even to staff additional classrooms in old schools, but still felt obligated to supply replacements for sisters who died, became ill, or had to be retired. Often this meant that although a degree program was established, not all of the young sisters could be put into it. Or a program was begun and interrupted. Sometimes there was regression. The stories are as numerous and as varied almost as the more than 400 congregations or provinces, which might react, each in its own way, to the Sister Formation message. What is important is that they did react. This current Study of 1962 shows mainly the results of the period of planting and watering; the Study of 1972 should show the harvest.

To summarize the present state of sister preparation as the Study of Catholic Education depicts it, results for the elementary teachers under 35 years of age are understandable but disappointing. A similar study made for 1965 should show a remarkable change, and the present decade should bring median preparation at the Bachelor's level down into the 20–24 group. Median preparation for this group is more than the Bachelor's degree but less than the Master's and remains so through the 45–54 and the 55–64 group. In the groups over 65 years of age, median preparation is again at the Bachelor's level. "Average" preparation for sisters in elementary schools continues to improve at both Bachelor's and Master's level until these teachers attain age 55, after which there is a tapering off. Only a small group of the elementary teachers, 2% of the total number of sisters, have continued their studies beyond the Master's degree.

The picture of the 19,708 sister teachers in secondary schools is much more encouraging. Median preparation is at least at the Bachelor's level for all age groups and is beyond the Bachelor's level for the sisters aged 25–34. It reaches the Master's level by age 35–44 and remains there for all succeeding groups, even for those over 65. Here, as with the elementary teachers, "average" preparation at the Master's level continues to improve until the 55 age group is reached, but the percentage in the classification of Master's degree plus increases up to age 65.

There is a clearly discernible pattern of study through a lifetime, hampered by a late start. The Sister Formation movement proposes to eliminate the late start, but to cherish and retain the habit of continuing education. The late start will have been eliminated when every community of sisters in the country has installed the pre-service degree program. This would be expedited if we had more exact statistics by which to estimate progress, if the financial condition of the sisterhoods and of their colleges was improved, and above all if some ecclesiastical legislation should do for the formation of sisters what the Constitution on the Sacred Liturgy is effecting with dramatic speed in its area.

Continuing education is surely the prime field for Sister Formation activity in the future. Two sets of regional SF conferences have already been held on the theme of "The In-service Sister." More will undoubtedly be held. Of prime importance in each order, after the establishment of the juniorate, is the appointment of a director of continuing education and individualized help and consultative service for the sisters in planning the lifetime programs that will be necessary in an age of exploding knowledge and accelerating change. Many communities already have established individualized in-service programs, and more will surely do so. In many communities, too, normal preparation for a teacher is already set at 5 years (Bachelor's plus 1 year), followed by a Master's degree in an area of specialization. Public school teachers now spend 2 summers out of 3 in some kind of in-service study. If the sisters of the country add to a sound pre-service training their present practices of continuing education through a lifetime, there is every solid expectation that within 10 to 15 years they may yet be the best-prepared single group of teachers on the American scene.)

THE TRAINING OF JESUITS FOR TEACHING

There are several ways in which one could give an account of the training of Jesuits for the apostolate of teaching. One would be simply to describe the course of studies in the Society of Jesus and point out those elements directly or indirectly related to the teaching profession. Another would be to give an historical account of the Society's beginnings in the field of education and the modifications and developments that have been introduced over the years. A third would be to compare the education of Jesuits with the general education of priests as regulated by the (Latin) Church and show how the special features of Jesuit education contribute to the training of teachers. We will follow the third procedure.

The General Education of a Priest

The education of a priest in the Latin Church irrespective of his status as a diocesan or religious priest has 3 aspects: the moral and religious training proper to the priestly life; the academic or intellectual formation; and training in the exercise of the priestly ministry, which includes the arts of communication. Part of the priestly office is the function of teaching. It is ordered, of course, to instruction in Christian doctrine and the Christian life of prayer and virtue, but it is a teaching office. Thus, a certain amount of teacher training is part of the education of every priest (except, perhaps, in some ascetical and contemplative orders that do not engage in any public ministry).

All 3 parts of the education of a priest are pursued concomitantly, but the core of the program is the academic education. This is divided into a sequence of 3 periods, which until recently in the United States have followed the organization of studies inherited from the late Middle Ages. The first period is given over to the arts and sciences, with emphasis on language and literature, especially Latin and the vernacular. In the United States this period corresponds to the liberal arts education given in high school and college up to the end of the first or second college year. The second period, which concentrates on the study of philosophy, is the first division of the studies of the major seminary. This period lasts for at least 2 years. It aims to give the students an understanding of the general system of philosophy as it was developed by the Scholastics with special attention to those features that pertain to theology. A special character of the Scholastic system of philosophy is that it develops an overall view of the world and human existence. Consequently, many of the areas of modern science, physical and social, are discussed. A kind of general education is the result, which could not be developed within the perspectives of experimental science.

In recent years there has been a movement in the United States to realign these first 2 periods of the education of a priest in the direction of the American division of a 4-year high school and 4-year liberal arts college. This movement includes the tendency to reduce the overall requirement of a full philosophy program and to introduce the variety of an American college, with a diversity of majors for the Bachelor's degree according to the talents and dispositions of the individual students. In other words the pre-theology academic program will be something like the present pre-law program.

The third period is that of the study of theology, which continues for 4 years and generally does not allow room for anything besides the various aspects of theology. This includes, of course, training in the communication arts mentioned above.

The Education of a Jesuit

For a member of a religious order the general education of a priest is within the *special* education of the religious in the mode of spirituality and practice of the religious life proper to his institute and also in the special forms of the apostolate characteristic of his particular order or congregation. For religious orders differ from the diocesan clergy in that they generally pursue Christian perfection according to a particular pattern of spirituality and are dedicated to one or another special form of the apostolate. Thus, the Society of Jesus does not consider parish work one of its ministries, but rather looks upon itself as a missionary order ready to undertake special missions both at home and abroad. One of the special missions that history has given to the Society is education, on the secondary, collegiate, and university levels. This work has become so large a part of the Society's apostolate that the Society is popularly known as a teaching order. Even its work in the foreign missions frequently takes the form of conducting educational institutions.

The Society likewise has a characteristic spirituality inherited from its founder, St. Ignatius of Loyola, which is not unrelated to its educational apostolate, as will be discussed later.

In comparison then with the general education of a priest, there are some differences and special emphases. First of all, the period of academic training is preceded by the novitiate, the period of induction and first training in the way of Christian perfection. In the Society this lasts for 2 years. Candidates are not accepted until they have completed their secondary education. Because in the United States this education does not lay a sufficient foundation for the higher studies of philosophy and theology, in the Society a 2-year course in classical and literary education is interposed before the period of philosophy. Since some study was done in the novitiate, the student has usually accumulated about 100 credit hours toward a Bachelor's degree.

The period of philosophy lasts for 3 years; its goal is a licentiate in philosophy, an ecclesiastical degree that roughly corresponds to a Master's degree in philosophy in the American pattern. During this period the student usually completes his Bachelor's degree at the affiliated American college. He then begins part-time work toward an American Master's degree in one of the arts or sciences such as English, history, sociology, or classics, according to his talents and interests and the possibilities of his situation. He may not be able to complete the Master's degree during the 2-year philosophy period; he may need a year of "special studies," taken out of his 3 years of teaching, for concentrated graduate work to obtain the degree. Most of the scholastics, however, have obtained their master's degree by the time they return for their theology studies. Thus, Jesuit teachers at this time have the equivalent of two Master's degrees, one in philosophy and one in some liberal art or science. If his second degree is in one of the physical or social sciences, this is usually in addition to the general literary education given to all. In some cases another degree may be added.

Several things about this early education of the Jesuit are in contrast to general seminary training. First of all, the 2 years of novitiate, during which some language study is done, particularly in the second year, postpone the student's entry into philosophical studies by at least 2 years. The 2 years of liberal arts education in the classics, English, and history provide a further foundation for philosophy. The result is that the students are more mature than if they had begun the study of philosophy 1 or 2 years after high school, and their studies can be pursued at a higher level. At the time the young Jesuit begins his first teaching period he is almost as old as the average young priest ordained in the normal seminary program, and he has not yet begun his professional theology studies. Although his whole outlook is religious, the young Jesuit's orientation is much more in the direction of liberal education and the pursuit of knowledge for its own sake than toward a pragmatically ordered professional education. His outlook approximates that of the secular university student more than that of a seminarian. In fact, it probably is much less pragmatic than that of many university students. He is already adjusted to transmit the type of liberal education the Society aims at in its schools and colleges.

This ideal of liberal education remains a permanent possession of the Jesuit. It is an inheritance from the Middle Ages and the University of Paris and is considered an essential element in his formation. Part of this ideal is respect for human science and learning as it has developed outside of specifically Christian studies. Thus, the Society has always resisted the argument that the "pagan" classics should be dropped in favor of Christian literature. It is for this reason, too, that the Society, perhaps more than other religious orders, has always given a large place in its educational enterprise to the humane arts and sciences.

This is consonant with the spirituality of St. Ignatius. One of the features of this spirituality is the recognition that all human things have a relationship to man's service to God and that it is possible to "find God" in all things and not only in the specifically religious or Christian. Perhaps this view is founded in a mystical experience early in the conversion of St. Ignatius, in which he saw the whole of creation proceeding out from and ordered to the most Blessed Trinity. In any case, the Jesuit is moved by his very spiritual formation to see value in the humane arts and sciences, thus to share in the spirit of the humanists and scientists without any violation of his religious orientation, and to enter into the education of young people in these areas with the true sense of fulfilling his vocation. (That is, this was true until recently. Part of the shifting spirit of the times is the discussion going on in the Church about the relative functions of the priest and layman. The idea that teaching secular subjects is "priestly work" is being challenged. As a result these questions are being raised also in the Society.)

Though the Society of Jesus was not founded as a "teaching order," it has to a large extent developed into one. Consequently, success in classroom teaching is considered one of the criteria of suitability for the Society's apostolate. Candidates for the Society recognize from the beginning that part of their work will be teaching. They know that they will spend 3 years teaching in a high school while still scholastics and that after their ordination they very likely will be engaged in school work on the high school or college and university level. While they are studying the arts and sciences, they and their teachers know that they will themselves teach one or other of these subjects.

There are some formal courses in education, those generally prescribed by the local accrediting associations. Thus, in the North Central area, the history of education and the principles of education are studied in the liberal arts period (juniorate). At this time the Jesuit tradition in education is studied formally. Besides the theory of liberal education spoken of, this tradition includes a methodology. In fact, the *Ratio Studiorum* so often mentioned as the Jesuit code of education is not a statement of a philosophy but a set of rules of method for teaching, especially for teaching the classical languages. The *Ratio* is not very much studied today, and its techniques are seldom directly and literally followed, but it established a spirit of teaching and study that is still recognizable in a Jesuit high school. Emphasis is on student work. The classroom operation is largely a matter of preparation for private study and a verification of its accuracy and thoroughness. The student is constantly urged to surpass himself and to compete with others in his category.

A young Jesuit who attended a Jesuit school before coming to the Society (as many have) has already begun his teacher-training by going through the process. His teachers in the Society have been formed by the same methods. Since it is probably true that most young teachers teach as they have been taught and strive to imitate those teachers who most impressed them in their own education, it is likely that the most significant preparation for teaching comes from the experience of Jesuit education.

However, in the years immediately preceding the teaching period there is usually some instruction in teaching methods and some study of adolescent psychology and the psychology of learning. If philosophy studies are done in a scholasticate in which theology is also taught, the theology students newly returned from their teaching experience frequently conduct private seminars in the teaching of their particular subjects, in the general conduct of schools, in cocurricular activities, and in all the operations of the high schools in which they have worked and in which their younger brothers will teach.

In addition, throughout the 7 years from the novitiate through the philosophate, there has been a graduated program in the communication arts. This both exercises the students in the arts of presenting ideas and motivating others and gives them the theory that is frequently applicable to classroom teaching. Jesuit education has traditionally stressed both the written and spoken arts of communication in the old classical rhetorical tradition. This is true of the training of the Jesuits themselves, and it naturally develops their potential for teaching and for teaching others the arts of communication. The final period preceding the first teaching assignment is given over to practice teaching under supervision in a Jesuit school.

During the teaching years, all the teachers are visited by either one principal or some veteran teacher in their subject, who advises them in solving problems and improving their methods. Once annually there is a visit by a district (province) director of education, who visits the classrooms and confers with the teachers afterwards about their teaching.

When a scholastic returns to the study of theology after his 3 years of teaching, the decision is made as to whether he will continue in secondary education or go on to university or seminary education, or turn to one of the other ministries of the Society. Usually, however, he will spend several years in a school or college before turning to other works. If the theologian (student) is expected to continue in secondary education, he is encouraged to use his summers during his theology studies and what time he has during the year to prepare himself further for work in the school. If his Master's degree is completed, he may broaden and deepen his preparation in his special teaching field. Frequently he will do additional work in educational and psychological counseling or in educational administration, and perhaps eventually take another Master's degree in one of these areas. At this time, also, he will give special attention to the teaching of religion and to the techniques of religious and moral formation of the high school boy. Although he may continue to teach the art or science that was his first specialization, he can expect to teach some religion and do some counseling. Some will specialize in the teaching of religion and of counseling. If "special studies" (full-time graduate study) are needed to perfect the preparation, they are sometimes done after the seminary course is completed. A practice has recently begun of sending some on for the doctorate in preparation for high school teaching or administration.

A peculiarity of the common course of training for Jesuits (which has begun to be imitated by other religious communities in one form or another) is the tertianship. This is a full year of religious and spiritual formation comparable to the 2 years of novitiate at the beginning of the course. In both of these periods part of the training includes some experience in what might be called the area of social work. In the final year, of course, because the men are older and are priests, this work will take on the forms more proper to priests. Such social work is set in the context of the development of the life of prayer and asceticism in the pursuit of Christian perfection.

The year of the tertianship is not unrelated to the preparation of teachers for Jesuit schools. It is, in fact, very intimately related to the aims and purposes of Jesuit education. These aims may be expressed in 2 sets of dualities. There is first the duality of moral and religious formation on the one hand, and intellectual and academic formation on the other. It is the aim of the general training of the Jesuit himself and then of the students he helps to educate in the Jesuit school to merge these into a unity where "piety" and "doctrine" (the terms used in the Jesuit literature) combine into a harmonious personality.

The second duality is between religious doctrine or theology and philosophy on the one hand, and human learning or the arts and sciences on the other. The aim of Jesuit education is not merely to add courses in theological instruction to the curriculum of the arts and sciences, but actually to inform the teaching of the humane disciplines with Catholic theological and philosophical teaching so that a unity of total truth results rather than an unnatural dichotomy and separation. In other words, Jesuit education rests on a theory of Christian culture that says it makes a difference whether a subject is studied completely apart from Christian life and doctrine or whether it is constantly joined to these in harmonious integration.

For this reason the ideal teacher in a Jesuit school is one who embodies in himself the fullness of the Jesuit course of training itself; that is: training in the spiritual life and the practice of prayer and Christian virtue; the knowledge of Catholic doctrine that is imparted primarily in the theological disciplines; and the knowledge of the arts and sciences with a special knowledge in one or two of these that is comparable to that of teachers in secular schools of the same level and type. Clearly the training of the Jesuit teacher is to be measured not only by his preparation in the subject he teaches but also by the general theological and religious formation he receives as a Jesuit.

It is for these reasons that an important part of the process of the education and formation of the student in the Jesuit theory is the personal contact and association of the teacher with the student (*personalis cura alumnorum*). This is expected to take place in the classroom and study situation. In the older pattern in which the same teacher had the class for 2 or 3 subjects and even moved up with his class, it probably obtained more than it does now. Today, our larger schools, the development of specialization in teaching, and shifting class schedules make it more difficult for a close personal association to develop from the classroom alone. However, this is balanced by the cocurricular program of the school, in which there is much more opportunity for personal association between teacher and pupil. The informal character of much of this work also helps balance off the objective and regularized instruction of the classroom. Although it is true that the central educational activity of the school takes place in the classroom and in curricular learning, the full effect of Jesuit education would be lost if there were not a parallel program of activity and study in private and free groups in addition to the curriculum. Among these the religious activities of the Sodality and the Apostleship of Prayer have a high place as a support to and extension of the liturgical program of the school. Jesuit education also has traditionally put a special emphasis on the communication arts, as they are called today, on public speaking and debate and the theater. Ideally the center of the school's activity is the Mass, but physical and social circumstances have frequently made it necessary to forego the practice of daily attendance at Mass by the whole student body.

It should be clear that although the scholastics in their "regency" (the 3-year period of high school teaching) contribute important elements to the total educational activity of the school, the complete Jesuit teacher is the Jesuit priest. He has served his apprenticeship and gone through the period of studying and teaching the arts and sciences. But he has completed this with the study of theology, the reception of the priesthood, and the final year of spiritual formation. He has been able to fill out his professional training for secondary education. Moreover, he is more finally dedicated to the work of secondary education than the general group of regents, many of whom will not return to the high schools after tertianship.

The third group, in addition to the priests and scholastics, that takes part in the educational activity of the Jesuit school, is the laymen. This is a sizable group, usually about one-third of the staff and faculty. Obviously there is not as much control over their preparation for teaching as over that of the Jesuits. Many have had part or all of their own education in a Jesuit high school and college and are familiar with the aims and methods in this way. They participate in all the in-service training given in the school such as classroom visitation and guidance, special workshops and institutes for teachers of different subjects, etc. Some regions have a short introductory program of a week or so for new teachers in which the Jesuit aims and methods are studied. The laymen usually become an important part of the faculty. Those that persevere usually are excellent teachers in their fields. They tend to be more permanent members of the staff since they are not subject to the shifts of religious assignments. And they give an example of lay

Catholicism that fills out the pattern of Christian life for the students in a way not possible for the religious and priests.

One thing that we have learned in our time is that a teacher's preparation is never finished. There is continuous need to become acquainted with new developments, to learn new procedures. Jesuit teachers are encouraged to study at one of the universities during the summer. Occasionally special workshops are set up for teachers in Jesuit schools. In the Midwest region, for instance, a regular sequence of summer institutes has been established for the different subject areas.

Education is a human enterprise at both ends of the operation. This means that it always falls short of complete achievement and is always dissatisfied with itself. Yet something is accomplished, possibly in the long run a great deal, if the goal is kept in mind and the spirit of constant striving is kept alive.

PREPARATION OF A MARIANIST FOR TEACHING

The Society of Mary

In the wake of a devastating revolution, the traditional social and economic structures of France lay in ruins. The life of the Church was at ebb tide. Resurgence and revitalization would depend largely on new approaches, new means of attaining time-tested objectives for the Church and society.

One of the instruments that an Omniscient Providence raised up at this critical moment in history was William Joseph Chaminade, a French priest of the diocese of Bordeaux. He spent his early priestly years disguised as a tinker and a chimneysweep, a tense prelude to the quiet, prayerful period of exile at the shrine of Our Lady of the Pillar, Saragossa, Spain, where Our Lady revealed to him the "nova bella" She would have him engage in at a future appointed hour.

The hour struck in 1817, years after Chaminade's return from exile; after he had founded sodalities throughout Bordeaux for people of all ages; after he had established apostolically oriented youth centers, study groups, professional groups, and organizations of skilled and semiskilled workers. From the sodalities emerged 2 religious orders: the Daughters of Mary and the Society of Mary (Marianists). The members of the Society of Mary include both priests and brothers, consecrated by vow to the Blessed Mother, living exactly the same rule of life, engaged by and large in education but under a rule that has always been structured to be adaptable to a universal apostolate. "The Society of Mary excludes no kind of undertaking, no means which Divine Providence might ordain to attain the end it proposes. *Quodcumque dixerit vobis;* this is its maxim" (Chaminade).

The universality of the Marianist mission did not mean that Father Chaminade placed an equal value on every apostolic work. He was interested predominantly in any form of the apostolate that would most effectively contribute to the regeneration of society. His principal preoccupation was the multiplication of Christians. The best way to multiply Christians was to make Christians dynamic apostles to their fellowmen.

Only this total mission of the Society adequately explains why the Marianists entered the field of education. The Society of Mary was not founded to teach; it is not restricted to this form of the apostolate. The Society of Mary conducts schools because today, as in the past, imparting a true Christian education is the best possible means to convert, to remake the world. The Society of Mary conducts schools in order to raise up apostolic Christians who will take on essentially the responsibility of influencing those around them.

This apostolic orientation of youth, we submit, is the central motive for properly focusing and guaranteeing the achievement of all the secondary goals of education, such as academic excellence, professional training, moral values, financial self-sufficiency. We do not downgrade any of these secondary ends, for each is a means to reach the perfection of human existence. On the contrary, far from deflecting the Society from academic excellence, the *Constitutions* clearly pinpoint that "it is the duty of every member of the Society to attain the highest possible skill in the branches he has to teach and to turn his modest talent to the best advantage" (Article 276). "The Society gives all possible care to the good management of its schools and to the perfection of its methods" (Article 275). "The great principles of education and teaching do not vary; but the application of these principles and the methods must necessarily be adapted to the needs and requirements of human society" (Article 277).

To forestall any distraction, let me say there is no thought of creat-ing, say, a Marianist method of teaching algebra, Latin, or chemistry. The Marianist method is rather the total educational system itself that endeavors to produce truly free persons who will effectively influence the society around them. Every decision we make must be directed to the ultimate conversion of the world. "How will this help to Christianize, to remake the world?" must be the constant query of the Marianist teacher in the classroom.

Classroom instruction, therefore, is to serve as a means to an end. Included in the broader concept of education and in the ultimate objective of multiplying Christians—men of principle, zealous leaders, disciplined, sainted laymen—included in this broader concept, classroom instruction demands teachers who are themselves disciplined and trained in a spiritual, cultural, academic, and professional tradition. The student, a product of such a program, has to become delicately attuned to the needs of his time, sensitive to the demands of his profession and responsive to the inner pressures of dynamic growth.

The Marianist provincial superior who approves the candidacy of a young man seeking admission to the Society of Mary must satisfy himself that there is in the applicant seminal evidence of this vitally important socio-missionary vocation, supported by a corresponding intellectual capacity and a sound religious spirit.

Two major areas are emphasized in the program for training a Marianist, the spiritual and the academic-professional. Add to these the important aspects of apostolic, cultural, and social formation and discern that the 2 major areas blend into a harmonious system for developing the whole Marianist.

Spiritual Formation

Let us consider each of these areas in the training program of the Marianist. A candidate for the religious life must learn to know and understand the spirit of the institute to which he aspires. The maturation of this knowledge and understanding is a lifelong process; it is burnished and buffeted in varying degrees of severity and intensity as the years tumble into eternity; it flowers in peace of soul and serenity of spirit as the disciplined life bears fruit. A young man may evidence signs of a generous religious spirit while he is in high school. The alert teacher notices these signs, speaks to the boy, consults with others who know him. Through the grace of God the young man responds favorably to the suggestion that he seems to have the qualifications to serve God and our Blessed Mother as a Marianist. He is accepted into the Aspirancy Program designed to test his spirit of generosity and his ability to respond to a firm and regular spiritual direction befitting his status and the goals in mind. After a few months or a year at this level, he is encouraged to make the first major step toward the fulfillment of his goal, to leave home. When he does this before graduating from high school, he enters the postulate.

In the postulate he continues and completes his high school course of studies, fulfills all requirements for the academic high school diploma, and, in the Marianist Preparatory School, Beacon, New York, qualifies for the New York State Regents diploma. At this level due emphasis is placed on the basic principles of the Marianist way of life: obedience, generosity, devotedness to duty, efficient use of time, and family spirit. The mistake of teaching him as though he were a professed religious is avoided. However, through a system of regular spiritual and external direction, the chaplain and the director encourage the young man to cultivate well-defined motives in his spiritual life and an apostolic sense of values in his daily life. Social and cultural experiences enrich the program; group and individual recreation programs and work programs supplement the official physical fitness instruction. Upon completion of his high school studies the candidate is ready for the novitiate.

The canonical year of novitiate aims to test and to develop the tenacity of purpose of the candidate and his capacity for deep personal commitment to the life of a Marianist. His studies include The Constitutions of the Society of Mary, interior life for a Marianist, history and principles of religious life, Mariology, Church history, dynamics of the Marianist apostolate (Sodality, etc.), moral, dogma, liturgy, spirit of the foundation of the Society of Mary, history of the Society of Mary, life and writings of Father William Joseph Chaminade, Gregorian chant, music and art appreciation. The intensity of the program is relieved by daily periods of organized recreation and manual labor and by seasonal features, such as picnics, bus trips to nearby spots of interest, historic or religious, and hikes. The canonical year climaxes on Profession Day. Henceforth, the young man is a Marianist.

His training in religion continues at the next level, the scholasticate, where the young Marianist, who is now called a scholastic, pursues his university studies. In the scholasticate the emphasis on the spiritual and ascetical shifts from the intensity and specialization of the novitiate to allow for the pressures and responsibilities inseparable from the academic and professional rhythms of university life. There is a shift in emphasis, but there is not a fragmentation. The spiritual and ascetical life must mature and develop together with the intellectual life, for the one properly depends upon and complements the other. The collapse of a vocation usually may be traced to an imbalance among these elements; an unevenness in the blend brings distortion that suggests immaturity in the young religious being serviced or formed.

During the years of his scholasticate training program the Marianist is directed into a deeper understanding of the Society of Mary and its apostolic role in the Church. Lectures, conferences, guided and graded reading programs with followup personal interviews and consultations with experienced and trained Marianist staff members lead the scholastics further and deeper into such fields as Mariology and the meaning of Consecration to our Blessed Mother, the Sodality, theology of the Marianist apostolate, the liturgy, Gregorian chant. These subjects supplement the regular 4-year theology program of studies that is required of all scholastics with but rare exceptions.

The theology course of studies meets a twofold objective, the objective of the professor and the objective of the course itself. The professor of theology has a complex viewpoint, ascetical, apostolic, and academic. The theology course nourishes the faith of the young religious by giving him a deeper understanding and a broader experience in Christian doctrine. The syllabus allows the student a scriptural and liturgical orientation. Scripture and the liturgy are vital factors in the lives of young religious and offer an approach to theology that is a witness to the act of faith. Since faith completes understanding, the functional aim of our faith is inseparable from the practical objective of grasping the whole mystery of Christ. Such an understanding contributes much to and highlights the principle of integration for our 3 areas of formation, the spiritual, the apostolic, and the academic.

The professor of theology is mindful of the second objective, the apostolic. He is to train his students to share in the teaching apostolate of the Church and to form them as "men of their time." This objective demands a dynamic response to the developments and demands of contemporary society.

Finally, the professor of theology shapes his course so that its end result is a contribution to the intellectual discipline and formation of the young religious. This discipline presents its own fields of understanding and its own formation of mental habits. The reading program aims to quicken the desire for further personal investigation. In no way is this discipline to be regarded as "second-rate" or as a discipline in isolation. Combined with the required philosophy program, theology is a prime factor in helping the young religious to form his own personal synthesis of learning and of life. It is not unusual that scholastics claim in their fourth year that they see "how things fit in."

The objectives of the course itself are likewise twofold: (a) to provide the young religious with a knowledge and understanding of the teachings of the Church in each of the areas in the course of studies (theology of the Old Testament, theology of the New Testament, theology of the Word Incarnate, theology of the Sacraments, general moral theology of the Christian life, virtues of the Chrisitan life, social teaching of the Church, survey of Mariology); and (b) to foster an intelligent acquaintance with the authors and works listed as basic readings for each semester.

Experts in specific fields related to theology are invited as guest lecturers to supplement course offerings. Training in C.C.D. teaching techniques and in C.C.D. field work are additional experiences reserved for fourth-year men.

The Marianist pursues his study of religion on a formal and organized basis for the first 10 years of his religious life. Each year the theme and the content of the annual program are outlined by provincial authority and the results are evaluated by an examination. Individual Marianists engage in graduate studies leading to advanced degrees in religious education and theology. Almost 30 years ago religion was departmentalized in the secondary schools taught by Marianists in the Cincinnati Provinces.

Academic and Professional Training

The scholastic pursues his academic and professional training at one of the three Marianist universities in the United States: the University of Dayton for the scholastics of the Cincinnati and New York Provinces; St. Mary's University, San Antonio, Texas, for the scholastics of the St. Louis Province; and Chaminade College, Honolulu, for the scholastics of the Pacific Province. In each the program covers a period of 8 semesters and 3 summers. The personal talents and interests of the scholastic and the needs of the province guide the provincial supervisor in determining each scholastic's program of studies leading to the Bachelor's degree in arts, science, or business administration.

Supplementing the requirements for the Bachelor's degree, the scholastic includes professional education courses and the student-teaching program to qualify for teacher certification in whatever state he may be assigned to teach after his graduation.

Scholastics of the Cincinnati and New York Provinces who major in modern languages are required to spend a summer at the Marianist Language Institute, Mineola, New York, to develop fluency in speaking the language. Modern language laboratory facilities are used, and the F.S.I. method of language drill and teaching is followed in this intensive 280-clock-hour institute program. The faculty is composed of Marianists from the Cincinnati, New York, Canadian, and Madrid Provinces and laymen from the New York area. For the past 5 summers the program has been available to non-Marianists. Latin majors follow a similar program during a summer at Marianist College in Dayton. One of the important outcomes of the program is now clearly in evidence; direct method of teaching modern languages and the use of language laboratory equipment have become routine procedures in several of our secondary schools.

Once the young Marianist has completed his undergraduate studies, he is assigned to a teaching position in a secondary school in his home province. The assignment is in his major field or in both his major and minor fields. Usually no later than the second summer following his graduation from the university, the Marianist will begin his graduate studies for the Master's degree. Occasionally it is possible and feasible to release the man for full-time study for the Master's degree, particularly when there is an opportunity to accommodate a Woodrow Wilson Fellow or someone who has merited a graduate scholarship or fellowship. Graduate studies are done at home or abroad in some 50 colleges throughout the United States and selected centers abroad at Fribourg, Rome, Louvain. Marianists who pursue graduate studies leading to the Doctor's degree are assigned full time.

Marianists who are accepted for the clerical category do undergraduate studies leading to the B.A. degree. The general prescriptions outlined in *Sedes Sapientiae* are the guidelines for the program of studies for these students. Their B.A. program includes Greek and Latin and a minimum 33 hours of philosophy. Two of these courses are given in Latin, and the students are required to write their final examination for each of the 2 courses in Latin. These brothers teach for a period of 4 to 6 years before they are assigned to Regina Mundi, the Marianist International Seminary, Fribourg, Switzerland, for their theological studies. Some of these men add a fifth or sixth year to their program to complete the requirements for the Doctor's degree in theology or philosophy.

Obviously, the areas of training that we have highlighted are neither isolated nor all inclusive. The object of the training program is a *person,* a person who is privileged, through the grace of God to be a religious, in this instance a Marianist, another son of Mary, another apostle. The training program is adequate only in this light.

There is no one more conscious of this fact than the master of scholastics and his immediate staff of 4 prefects and 4 chaplains (for each of the 4 divisions). Under the direction of these Marianists the young religious learns to live the religious life and in the process to find himself, to develop a religious personality, to root the conviction of his vocation. This process of personal realization unfolds gradually as the young Marianist cultivates habits of prayer and work, as he develops the spirit of obedience and generosity, and engenders family spirit, as well as the basic attitudes toward the Marianist apostolate. It is the spirit that gives life.

There are additional elements that breathe a life of culture, refinement, of genuine Christian charity into the program.

1. Leisure. Its proper use flows from a careful analysis of self coupled with a firm willpower to utilize time as a most precious treasure. Recreations, formal and informal, "free time," vacation periods, library browsing cannot be excluded from an all-embracing training program if the young religious is to learn the meaning of this principle of renewal in his life.

2. Liturgy. Study club groups spark discussion of the liturgy. The awesome richness of the liturgical life is experienced by the scholastics

in a variety of ceremonies that sparkle throughout the calendar of the liturgical year. The inspiration of the daily high Mass, the splendor of the occasional Solemn Mass, the quiet impressive lesson of a Bible Vigil, the magnificence of the liturgy of Holy Week, the liturgical touch in the departure ceremony of each newly assigned religious as he goes forth to take up his lifework for Our Lady are all participated in and quicken the pulse of the apostolic heart. Directly related to these experiences is the training in liturgical music, chant, organ, and choir.

3. Personal responsibility. The basic administrative framework in every Marianist community is built on the "Four Offices:" Head of Zeal, Head of Instruction, Head of Apostolic Action, Head of Temporalities. The Scholastic Council is so structured, and it serves as an instrument for developing personal responsibility, initiative, and family spirit among the scholastics. Projects and programs under the general supervision of the Council include music appreciation "hours," art appreciation displays and lectures, fine arts festivals, radio, television, and movie evaluation training, feature lectures by university professors and visiting guests, annual dramatic productions (e.g., "A Man for All Seasons"), book review programs, Science Day Program of lectures and demonstrations, modern language clubs, *The Scholastic* (literary publication), and study clubs.

4. Manual work. Training in the correct attitude toward manual labor is regarded as extremely important to foster successful community living. The weekly schedule in the scholasticate offers many opportunities for this type of experience. Shop practice in carpentry and automotive skills are offered on a casual but systematic basis.

The Marianist in-service training program includes the intern-teacher program, weekly school conferences, monthly faculty meetings, regional administrator and academic workshops. The entire program as it relates to instruction is under the general supervision of the provincial supervisor, who is also responsible for the study program of each religious in his province and the academic tone of each school under his jurisdiction. He maintains contact with each school and each teacher through his annual visitation. This visitation program includes classroom visitation and an immediate followup personal interview with each teacher and administrator of the faculty, both religious and lay.

The Marianist training program for young religious is not the same as it was 5 years ago, nor is it a carbon copy of last year's program. It can't be. Life moves too swiftly. The principle of growth and development must be honored. The process of refinement and adjustment is held in high regard. Ultimate goals are kept in sharp focus while current practices undergo regular severe and critical scrutiny.

References

[1] *Milestones in the Professional Standards Movement* (Washington: NCTEPS, NEA, 1961).

[2] *TEPS Newsletter*, V1, 3 (April 1963), 5.

[3] Stinnett, T. M., and Albert J. Huggett, *Professional Problems of Teachers* (New York: Macmillan, 1963).

[4] Sister Rose Matthew, I.H.M., "Sister Teachers in the United States," in Sister Ritamary, C.H.M., ed., *Planning for the Formation of Sisters* (New York: Fordham University Press, 1958), p. 162.

[5] *U. S. News and World Report,* February 3, 1964.

CHAPTER FIVE

ICSO-1:
Religious Understanding

IN ITS ATTEMPT TO EXPLORE AS MANY AS POSSIBLE OF the various aspects of Catholic elementary and secondary education in the United States, the Study was particularly interested in some evaluation of the schools' effectiveness in religious education. If there is any one chief reason for the existence of a separate Catholic school system, it is religious education in its broadest dimensions. It would be impossible to determine what portion of a student's total religious education or instruction has taken place in the classroom or even in the total school environment. Religious education, like education in general, is carried on in the home, at church, and in a variety of other social situations, as well as in the classroom and school.

By means of a special instrument, the Inventory of Catholic School Outcomes, the study therefore sought to find out what the students in Catholic schools know about their religion (ICSO-1); what their attitudes are to certain questions either directly or indirectly religious in nature (ICSO-2); and what their opinions are about their religious and general education in the Catholic schools (ICSO-3).

We are concerned here only with religious understanding; ICSO-2 and ICSO-3 will be discussed in turn. The development of an instrument to measure religious knowledge and understanding may be the most significant single achievement of the entire Study. Because the staff of the Study of Catholic Education could find no current nationally standardized test of religious knowledge, it was necessary to construct one. Earlier experiments in designing and producing a standardized test of religious understanding had, for a variety of reasons, long since been abandoned. The fascinating story of the development of the test of religious understanding finally used by the Study, together with some of the principal findings revealed by that test follows.

The Inventory of Catholic School Outcomes grew out of several sets of circumstances, each of which calls for a brief review and analysis. First, the *Study of Catholic Education* took place at a time when religious education in Catholic schools was being seriously reexamined from many points of view.

Second, at the time certain groups of educators believed that a test of religious understanding might be designed to reveal not only *what* the students knew about their religion, but also their comprehension of this knowledge. It was generally agreed that no test could measure precisely the role of the school in the religious education of the student, although some conclusions concerning the quality, emphasis, and direction of religious education in Catholic schools might be drawn by inference.

Third, such a test would have to be usable by the Study of Catholic Education before it had been as fully pretested and standardized as the Study staff would have liked. The following section discusses each of these 3 points and outlines the procedure by which ICSO-1 was finally constructed.

THE STATUS OF RELIGIOUS INSTRUCTION AT THE TIME OF THE STUDY

Religious instruction both within the Catholic schools and also as it was carried on outside the schools, for example, in the Confraternity of Christian Doctrine, has had several different changes of emphasis in the history of the Church in this country. These correspond roughly to certain historical periods, and they will be treated in this light. However, it must be understood that these are, in fact, changes of emphasis rather than changes in the basic content of the instruction. As will be seen later, ICSO-1 assumes that the fundamental content of religious instruction, since it involves the beliefs, the laws, and the liturgy of the Church, varies little from school to school.

All types of instruction, including religious instruction, change to meet the particular circumstances of the times in which the instruction takes place. There have been at least 3 distinct changes of emphasis in instruction in the Catholic religion in this country since the middle of the last century. For ease of identification these will be referred to as the intellectual emphasis, the practical or applied emphasis, and the catechesis emphasis. The period of intellectual emphasis extends roughly from the Third Council of Baltimore (1884) to the end of World War I; the period of practical or applied emphasis from World War I to the end of World War II; the period of catechesis emphasis from the end of World War II through the present. These divisions are, of course, overlapping, but they are made to help identify some of the sociopolitical and economic circumstances that influenced the changes of emphasis in Catholic religious instruction.

What exactly is meant by "change of emphasis in religious instruction"? First of all, the phrase does not necessarily imply that one emphasis is better or worse than another. Nor does it mean simply a change of teaching methods; although there is a clear relationship between teaching methods and desired outcomes, it is not the techniques that determine which outcomes are possible or desirable. It does imply that the instruction is aimed at different goals. In this sense, if one emphasis is found to achieve all that is achieved by another approach and also to achieve some additional goals, this particular emphasis would be considered better or at least preferable.

Religion can be taught in any number of ways and directed toward any number of desired goals. Teachers of religion will ordinarily emphasize those goals they deem most important. One would expect little difference in the extent of the knowledge or content of religion to be imparted. All teachers try to make sure that students grasp the meaning and importance of any religious concept with which they are working. "A change of emphasis," then, means a change in goals as well as a change in the approach to the subject matter.

The Intellectual Emphasis

From the Third Council of Baltimore to the end of World War I, the emphasis was on an intellectual comprehension of the content of the Catholic religion, in making sure the students knew the answers—

namely, the teachings of the Church. The hope was that a firm intellectual grasp would lead to thoughtful and inspired practice of religion. The Baltimore Catechism, so familiar to American Catholics, is the classic prototype of this emphasis. It consisted of a series of questions and set answers graded according to the presumed intellectual ability of the students. The questions start with, "Who made the world?" and range through the entire body of Church doctrine and practice. The students learned the answers to the questions, often by rote; they were evaluated on the basis of how accurately they could give back, in written or oral form, the precise answers in the Catechism.

The Baltimore Catechism served a very important function, and its intellectual emphasis is understandable in that period. We realize that many deny that the teaching of religion according to the formula of the Catechism is "intellectual" in any acceptable sense of the word.

The Church was greatly concerned that young American Catholic boys and girls should grow up aware of the intellectual heritage of the Church—at a time when many persons outside the Church were coming to regard religion as a completely subjective or emotional matter. The Church was also anxious that students have a proper answer if their beliefs were questioned, as they were almost certain to be, since Catholics tended more and more to move freely throughout American society. Catholics would be called on often to define their faith; it was crucial that they know their faith. Since at this period few Catholics were going to college or even to high school, it was thought important that they complete their formal religious instruction in a coherent and unified way. Finally, the catechism was regarded as a means, through its clear, simple, systematic answers, of safeguarding Church teaching against the various "heresies" finding such fertile soil in America, as one sect after another split away from its parent creed.

During this period Catholic religious instruction was not alone in its intellectual emphasis. Most subjects in most schools in America were taught with a strictly content-centered approach. Few, if any other subjects were taught in strict catechetical form, to be sure, but the traditional textbook was not far removed from the catechism. Many teachers of all subjects at this time used, and still do, some form of the question-and-answer method.

Although this approach can easily be defended against the charge, many people who studied religion at the time came to identify its teaching with a listing of "do's" and "don'ts." Although there is no theoretical connection between an intellectual emphasis in the teaching of religion and a restrictive, regimented, negative, or fear-dominated interpretation of religion, this interpretation emerged in some, if not many, instances. Unless the intellectual approach is properly handled by an inspiring and enthusiastic teacher, there seems to be danger the student will develop a cold, aloof, and indifferent attitude toward religion.

The Practical or Applied Emphasis

The period between World War I and World War II saw a great change in American pedagogy. This change was bound to and did affect the teaching of religion in the Catholic schools. John Dewey's *Democracy in Education,* with the newer psychology-based theories of learning, set the stage for this change and determined its pace. Without oversimplifying too greatly we can say that the change was from knowing to doing. The question was how one really comes to know—the new emphasis being based on the theory that the only way to know is to do. In this theory a person who cannot apply the knowledge he claims to possess does not have a valid claim to knowledge. The textbook was replaced by "problem-solving," and the curriculum became "child-centered" rather than "subject-centered."

The catechism came to be regarded as the almost perfect example of how not to teach. The catechism and the intellectual approach were thought of as the most extreme forms of naive intellectualism. Catholic educators were not unimpressed by the claim that there is something more to knowledge than the ability to memorize and recite answers. Nonetheless, accepted forms die slowly, and many Catholic educators saw no sufficient reason for abandoning the method that had served so well and for so long.

What, then, happened to religious instruction in Catholic schools during this period? Although it is impossible to measure how extensive the new emphasis became, it is clear that religious instruction in Catholic schools took on a new look. An essential distinction was made by Catholic educators between the teaching of religion and the teaching of other subjects. Religion, it was held, has a "given" subject matter. The psychological principles that can be applied to the teaching of other subjects do not apply entirely, or if they do, they apply in another way to the teaching of religion.

On the other hand, it was argued, some insights based on the new psychology and even on "life adjustment" theory might be helpful in the teaching of religion. The subject matter that should be drawn most completely from and penetrate most deeply the "experience" of the student should be religion. Perhaps, without adopting the philosophy of pragmatism or experimentalism, some changes in the teaching of religion could relate the whole subject matter more closely to the life experiences, the problems, and the needs of the student. As a result of such thinking the practical or applied emphasis in teaching of religion emerged.

This new emphasis never became problem-solving in the sense that the curriculum began with the problems of the student rather than, for example, with the questions of the existence of God or the mystery of the Eucharist. But throughout the period there were many efforts, some highly successful, to teach religion in the practical mode and as a way of life. How do the mysteries and facts of the Church enter into the concrete family and other social experiences of the student? How does religion relate to citizenship? How does one make the teaching of religion meaningful and the reality of religion joyful, rich, and positive? What are the Church's teachings regarding the social and economic order? What does the Mystical Body mean as a doctrine of world order and human community? How does the doctrine of the Presence of God enter into study, work, play, and leisure life? These questions and many more like them the Catholic educators asked not of their pupils but of themselves. Religion was to be applied and practiced, not merely known.

The attempt to make the teaching of religion a vital, significant, and deeply personal experience for the student in a practical way brought 2 obvious results. The first, and more important, was to help the student develop his ability to reason and judge for himself in matters of his religion. He wasn't simply "told"; he was assisted to discover. The pupil cannot judge for himself in matters of "defined doctrine," but he can search out the deeper meanings behind such doctrines and plunge more deeply into his reasons for assenting to them. The second result was a great openness to audiovisual devices and equipment as these became available. The teaching of religion does not readily lend itself to the use of pictures, maps, charts, slides, movies, the radio, and sound recordings, but perhaps because of the inherent difficulty, there was truly creative and imaginative use of audiovisual teaching aids, particularly at the elementary school level. The Audiovisual Department of the National Catholic Educational Association has long been one of its most active departments, and many of the teaching sisters show exceptional ability in adapting audiovisual techniques to the teaching of religion.

Those educators who favored the practical emphasis in the teaching of religion (and most did in one form or another) never for a moment admitted that this was any less intellectual than the previous emphasis. Rather, they saw it as a culmination of the intellectual emphasis. They thought that only through making religion significant, real, and immediate could there be a genuine learning experience for the student. The teaching of religion in the classroom or under the aegis of the school aimed to make sure that the pupil applied and practiced his religion.

Evidence of this redirected emphasis is found in *"Guiding Growth for Christian Social Living."* The foundations and purposes of their curriculum program are stated in the prefaces of each of the 3 volumes:

> In an Apostolic Letter to the Catholic University dated September 21, 1938, our late Holy Father, Pope Pius XI, instructed the university to draw up for the people of our country a constructive social program of education based on Christian principles. It was the intention of the Holy Father that this program should clarify and re-emphasize the teachings of Christ in their application to the problems of contemporary American life. In immediate compliance with this request the bishops of the United States meeting at Washington in October, 1938, launched an education program designed to "build an enlightened, conscientious American citizenship," by instructing people on all levels "in the true nature of Christian democracy . . . ." The major objective in building the curriculum for the elementary school has been the direction of the school program toward the growth of each child in Christian social living. The term curriclum admits of diverse interpretations. It is here taken to mean all the guided experiences of the child under the direction of the school. The curriculum therefore, is broader than a syllabus or a course of study in subject-matter. It is a guide for directing the child's living in the light of Christian principles, with a detailed plan of the learning activities that are basic to that living.[1]

The Catechesis Emphasis

The catechesis emphasis in the teaching of the Catholic religion is perhaps still too recent to have a universally accepted name or label. "Catechesis" is most commonly used but other names are also used; for example, "charismatic" and "kerygma" are also sometimes used to epitomize this new emphasis. The emphasis has been more noticeable since World War II, although its roots are much more ancient. It is unfortunate, perhaps, for the present analysis that the words catechesis and catechism are so similar. Of course they both derive from the same Greek word meaning to teach or instruct.

In its simplest and most generic sense, catechesis emphasis is a combination of the intellectual and practical emphases and at the same time is quite distinct from both. It is intellectual in that it leads the student to probe deeply into the origins and meanings of his religion; it is practical in that it aims explicitly at helping the student to live fully the Christian message. However, it differs from them and transcends them in that it emphasizes the beauty and the joy of Christian faith at the very moment it seeks its truth. It emphasizes that the Christian religion is not something simply to be known or even merely to be practiced; it is rather a total spirit, or better, an inspiration or a life process. It is a view of the Christian person, as it were, from within. Only by recognizing and responding to the "good tidings" of the gospel can the Christian enter into a living awareness of the mysteries of his faith.

Catechesis seeks to combine information, formation, and initiation. Religion, it maintains, cannot properly be studied like other academic subjects. Religious instruction must strive to enlighten the mind, to form the soul and character, and to lead the student ever more deeply into the inner life of the Divine Mysteries in and through the Church.

The catechesis emphasis does not imply rampant emotionalism, but it does recognize that emotions are a valid part of human religious experience. On the other hand, it is anxious that the fundamental intellectual content of the Catholic religion is not minimized or neglected; it is fully aware that a "revealed religion" has to adhere closely to the content of that which is revealed. Finally, as the word charisma, sometimes used to identify this emphasis, connotes, the catechesis emphasis takes fully into account the fact that the student either already shares or will share in the life of divine grace because of the "character" or charisma that results from the fact of his baptism.

The approach is an outgrowth of several different factors that have profoundly influenced the life and thought of the Church, and indeed of the world, since the end of World War II. This is not the place to enlarge on these factors, but the teaching of religion could not fail to be affected by the recent developments in scripture studies, by the liturgical renewal, by the postwar spirit of ecumenism, by Christian existentialism, by the new investigations into the sociology of religion and the psychology of religion and comparative religion, and by a general religious "openness." The 20 years since World War II have seen, within the Church and outside it, a turning toward religion with a genuine quest for convincing and relevant solutions to the problems of the person and of society. The leadership was taken by European theologians and educators, but theologians and teachers of religion in this country, although somewhat more cautious than their European counterparts, have followed their lead enthusiastically.

THE THEORY BEHIND ICSO-1

The foregoing makes clear the Study staff's problem of how to measure or evaluate the religious understanding of the students in Catholic schools. Although all the Catholic schools were presenting the same content in their religious instruction, they were not, by any means, emphasizing the same things. A study that did not concentrate a great deal of attention on the principal distinctive difference between Catholic and other schools would certainly be most superficial. A quick examination showed that no testing instrument suitable to the purposes of the Study was available. In fact, no depth research into the religious understanding of Catholic school students had ever been undertaken in this country. It was clear that the Study would have to design the testing instrument to be used.

Obviously, it would have to be what is known in testing circles as a "pen-and-paper" test. Even if it were theoretically possible, within the limits of time and money, to use some other testing technique, an oral test or a depth interview, the problems of standardization and comparison appeared insurmountable. Even the pen-and-paper test would have to be designed to make it possible for the students to indicate the different ways or degrees in which they understood their religion.

To take the clearest possible example, such questions as "Who made the world?" or "What is the Mass?" or "What is the Beatific Vision?" would have been of little value. Since an early decision had been made to test both eighth-and twelfth-grade students, the Study assumed that all students would either know or at least be able to recognize the answers to such direct questions. The Study was interested in finding out whether the students understood their religion: whether they could reason about religious questions, discriminate sharply among proposed or possible answers, make sound judgments about questions that might appear novel or out of context, and see the relationships between their theoretical knowledge about their religion and certain practical conclusions or directions.

A multiple-choice, pen-and-paper test seemed the most practicable. The Study staff thought that questions could be worded so that in selecting their answers, students would reveal the level or depth of their religious understanding. The choice would not be among answers that were right or wrong but rather that showed the degree of understanding. Although the Study did not intend an evaluation of religious instruction in the schools, it was evident that the student's choices among possible answers would indicate the particular emphasis in religious instruction to which he had been exposed.

The unusual quality of the Inventory of Catholic School Outcomes, Part I, consists principally in the fact that for each of the 50 proposed items in ICSO-1, the student had the opportunity of selecting his response from 5 proposals representing 5 different levels of understanding: "advanced," "moderate," "conventional," "moralistic," and "nominalistic." Further, the items were distributed over the areas of Church law, Church doctrine, and the liturgy, and were equally divided between theory and practice.

A word of explanation about the terms selected to distinguish the different types of possible responses. Although the test was composed with these distinctions in mind, at the time the students took the test they were not aware that the responses had been coded in any way. These terms, which will be used in analyzing the data produced by the test, are not necessarily the best or most appropriate terms, but they have proved eminently satisfactory for the purposes of the Study.

"Advanced" is used to designate the possible answer most in keeping with the catechesis emphasis and should be understood only in this sense. It does not, for example, necessarily reflect an advanced number of years in school. These answers were deliberately phrased so that, taken individually and collectively, they would reveal whether the instruction had been in accord with the newer theories of religious pedagogy and with the most significant trends in modern Catholic theology.

"Moderate" responses stand somewhere between the "advanced" responses and "conventional" responses. The theory was that some schools had not had time to acquaint themselves and their students with the full meaning and importance of the catechesis emphasis. These students would show some awareness and understanding of the new emphasis, but their preferences would be for those responses that fall somewhat short of the "advanced" responses and somewhat beyond the "conventional" responses.

"Conventional" implies that the response was traditional and rather formalized. Again, in no way disparaging the conventional responses, they would be very similar to those found in the Baltimore Catechism or in other catechisms. They would not be expected to reflect (or only to a small degree) the changes taking place in Catholic theology and Catholic religious instruction. They would be good enough but nevertheless stock responses. To put it another way, they would be responses that might well have been considered reasonably advanced at the time of the Council of Baltimore or even well into the twentieth century.

"Moralistic" as a category has something of an emotional connotation. The moralistic responses are not of themselves incorrect, but they are not acceptable within the context of the individual items.

"Nominalistic" responses are rationalistic and sound logical, but like the moralistic responses they are not acceptable within the item context.

To recapitulate, the theory was that the test would give a reasonably accurate picture not only of *what* the students knew or understood about their religion but also the *way in which* they knew and understood it. The test was also interested in discovering whether and how well the students knew both theoretical and practical aspects of their religion. And as further refinements, appropriate distinctions were made between doctrine, law, and worship, in the test construction referred to as Creed, Code, and Cult. (See Fig. 2 for a model of the test construction.)

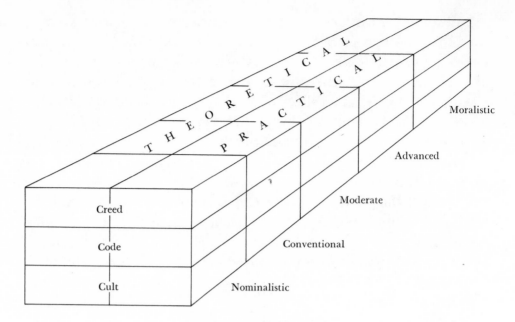

Fig. 2. Model of ICSO-1.

THE CONSTRUCTION AND USE OF ICSO-1

The staff used *A Catholic Catechism*[2] as the major source in preparing items. This English translation of the most recent revision of the German Catechism[3] was used in preference to the revised Baltimore Catechism[4] because the less familiar wording would be less likely to evoke a response based on rote memory and because it had not been widely used in classrooms in the United States. The language, approach, and content of *A Catholic Catechism* have won the respect of catechists throughout the world.

The 50 items ultimately selected were drawn from an original body of 170 and included only items passed by a jury of 3 theologians for accuracy and discrimination. The number passed was reduced by screening for difficulty of concept and language. Curricular coverage and representativeness were the final criteria. The items were tested with groups of elementary and secondary students and then subjected to intensive criticism by a panel of 23 experts in education and child development.

Once ICSO-1 had been put into a final, although tentative, form, it was pretested in various ways. It was important to know, for example, what time limits should be placed and whether the attention span of respondents would hold throughout the entire length of the test. It was essential that the possibility of indifference, carelessness, or casualness, be reduced to a minimum. Since this was the first test of its type, there were no means for comparison or standardization. Future tests will have ICSO-1 as a basis for standardization and for constant improvement.

The test in its final form (see Appendix) was administered to a carefully selected but relatively large and representative sampling of both boys and girls in both elementary and secondary schools throughout the United States—14,519 students in the eighth and twelfth grades of 104 secondary schools and 218 elementary schools within 13 representative dioceses. The dioceses were selected as representative on the basis of geographic location, size, Catholic population, urban-suburban-rural characteristics, extent of school provision, and potential financial resources. The schools within each diocese were a purposive sampling representing the various important characteristics that distinguish Catholic schools. These included size, ownership and operation, student organization, socioeconomic backgrounds of the students, geographic location, ratios of lay to religious teachers, and religious communities staffing the schools.

THE RESULTS OF ICSO-1

With the help of the University of Notre Dame's Univac 1107 Computer, the results of ICSO-1 have been analyzed and cross-correlated in a vast number of ways. The results of these extensive internal analyses are not presented within this volume because of space and possible limited interest to the general reader. The cross-tabulation and paradigm treatment of the student's responses to ICSO-1 produced results concerning his personal and family characteristics which are in usable research form in the Study's office at the University of Notre Dame. These materials should be of interest and value to scholars, students of Catholic education, and those who have the responsibility of the leadership of Catholic schools.

Although the general reader may not be seeking such precise or detailed information, it is appropriate that he have some overall view of the results of ICSO-1. What follows is an attempt to present in broad terms the findings of the inventory and their most significant interpretations. We will follow the outline presented earlier, analyzing inventory results according to the differences between the advanced, moderate, conventional, moralistic, and nominalistic choices of the students. This approach should give a good picture of the students' present thinking and also make possible, by inference, some conclusions regarding the success of religious instruction in the Catholic schools.

It would be impractical, even in this general way, to analyze each of the 50 items in ICSO-1. But the general trend can be seen by the percentages of students opting for the advanced, moderate, conventional moralistic, or nominalistic responses to selected representative items. One item dealing with doctrine, one with law, and one with worship have been selected. Item 23, doctrine, item 18, law, and item 23, worship, are chosen both because they illustrate clearly how the Inventory worked and because each deals with a central fact of Catholic life and faith. Item 47 is also reviewed because of its special difficulty.

ITEM 23   (doctrine)

The chief value of the life, sufferings, and death of Our Lord is that He thereby:

a. earned for us God's grace and everlasting life
b. showed His unlimited love for us
c. taught us how to live, suffer, and die
d. set us free from sin and sin's penalty
e. proved to doubters that He was a real man

Nothing could be more central to the Catholic religion than the knowledge of who and what Christ is. However, the item *does not ask* who Christ is or what He is; rather, it asks the value and meaning of His life and death. The item is phrased to make it impossible to give a pat response. Thought and understanding, as well as knowledge, are needed in choosing among the responses.

In this item (a) was regarded as the advanced response, (b) the moderate, (c) the moralistic, (d) the conventional, (e) the nominalistic.

Of the 14,519 respondents, i.e., all eighth- and twelfth-grade students, 36.74% selected the advanced response, 40.57% the moderate, 8.26%

the conventional, 13.40% the moralistic, and 1.44% the nominalistic; 2.59% did not respond.

The students were clearly instructed to choose 1 and only 1 response which in their understanding, was the best, the most complete, the most appropriate, or the most to be preferred. All 5 types of responses were randomly mixed.

In analyzing the responses to Item 23, it was somewhat surprising to find that 32.65% of the 7479 elementary school pupils selected the advanced response. This percentage seems remarkably high, especially in light of the fact that only 39.58% of the high school students selected the advanced response. Although an evident growing in depth of understanding is indicated in these percentages, the spread is not as great as might have been anticipated. Since there was no basis for any prior assumptions regarding the differences in depth of religious knowledge between eighth- and twelfth-grade students, it is impossible to say whether the eighth-graders were unexpectedly good or the twelfth-graders were somewhat below expectations.

Evidence for the generalization that girls tended "to do better" on the inventory than boys is gained from a close look at the results for Item 23. 36.34% of all those who took the test chose the advanced response. When the "all-girls" category, i.e., all girls in both elementary and secondary schools, is compared with this percentage, there is only a very slight advantage in favor of the girls. The actual figure is 36.50%. But when only the responses from girls in all-girl high schools are considered, the advantage is clear and appreciable; 42.1% of the girls in all-girl high schools selected the advanced response. The figure for boys in all-boy high schools is 38.60%, and it is 38.00% for boys and girls in coeducational high schools.

On this particular item over 40% of those responding selected the moderate response, "showed His unlimited love for us." Moderate, when compared with the advanced response, "earned for us God's grace and everlasting life," is probably only a shade less appropriate or complete. No doubt many had great difficulty in choosing between the moderate and advanced responses.

Only 8.26% of all respondents selected the conventional response. The conventional response, like all others, is a perfectly valid response to the item. It is conventional in the sense that it corresponds most closely to what would have been found in a standard catechism. The fact that fewer than 10% selected this response would seem to reveal that on this item at least, the students' understanding and the teaching reflected are in the direction of the moderate or advanced.

ITEM 18 (law)

We prove our love for God especially by:

a. repaying His love for us with gratitude
b. never missing our daily prayers
c. avoiding sin and keeping His commandments
d. seeking to love Him on account of His goodness
e. forgetting ourselves and going against our natural desires

In this item (d) was the advanced response, (a) the moderate, (c) the conventional, (b) the moralistic, and (e) the nominalistic.

11.91% of the 14,519 respondents selected the advanced response, 5.02% the moderate, 78.47% the conventional, 1.64% the moralistic, and 2.9% the nominalistic.

Here again, the item is particularly apt. Its great importance is immediately clear if one thinks only of Christ's statement to the effect that the most basic law of Christianity is the commandment to love God and to love one's neighbor. The item does not ask *whether we should* love God. That all Catholics know they should love God would be assumed and a response to such an item would not reveal any depth of understanding or any special emphasis in religious instruction. Rather, the item asks *how we prove* our love for God.

Further, the item involves law or moral code, and the answer involves doing something, not simply knowing something. In Catholic thinking, the moral code derives from and is contained, either explicitly or implicitly, in the Creed, the doctrine, or the system of beliefs of the Church. But it is entirely possible to separate doctrine and law, at least for analysis, and this is commonly done, even in major seminaries, where courses in dogmatic theology are often distinct from those in moral theology.

The fact that stands out, almost glaringly, in the results is that 78.4% of the respondents selected the conventional response. Considerably more than three-fourths of all who took the test felt that "we prove our love for God especially by avoiding sin and keeping His commandments." Only 11.91% selected the advanced response, "seeking to love

Him on account of His goodness." That such an overwhelming majority had selected the conventional response led the designers of the Inventory to suspect that something might be wrong with the wording of the item or of the responses, even though great care had been taken for precise wording of this, as well as all items. But even allowing for some possible confusion in the minds of those taking the test, there is no escaping the significance of the fact that the understanding of most of the students of how we prove our love for God was at the conventional level. The only other example in the entire ICSO-1 that parallels this is Item 7, dealing with worship, where 73.05% of the students gave the conventional response.

Interestingly, the girls in all-girl high schools deviated on this item from their usual pattern. On almost all items in ICSO-1 girls in all-girl high schools tended to select more of the advanced and moderate responses than any other single group. But on Item 18 the girls in all-girl high schools were below the percentage of the whole group in selecting advanced and moderate responses and they were above the whole group in selecting the conventional responses—83.2% contrasted to 78.47% of all respondents. For some reason, on this item, it was boys in all-boy high schools who showed greater preference for the advanced response; 19% of the boys in all-boy high schools picked the advanced response, whereas only 11.91% of the whole group did. On the other hand, only 68.5% of the boys in all-boy high schools selected the conventional response, against 78.47% of the whole group.

Again on Item 18, there did not seem to be any significant differences between the responses of all students, boys and girls, in elementary schools from those in secondary schools. In each category of response, the elementary percentage is practically identical to that of the entire group. Any expectation that this item would sharply differentiate high school from elementary school students was not fulfilled.

Is there an explanation, other than some possible deficiency in the test itself, for the fact that 78.47% of all respondents chose the conventional response on Item 18? There may be. The easiest explanation would be that within the catechesis or kerygmatic emphasis in the teaching of religion, more attention is paid to love of neighbor than to love of God per se. Whether this is actually true and whether, if so, it is desirable or undesirable, would be the subject of a separate study.

Some corroborative evidence appears by comparison of responses to Item 18 with those to Items 25 and 26, each of which deals with love of neighbor.

Item 25 states, *"We should practice the corporal and spiritual works of mercy"* and then lists the 5 possible responses. Each response presumes a knowledge of the meaning and nature of the corporal and spiritual works of mercy. Similarly, Item 26 states, *"We can best prove our love for our neighbor by"* and lists the 5 responses. Here, too, the responses aim at determining how deeply the student understands his responsibility for loving his neighbor.

The responses to Items 25 and 26 are much more in keeping with the general pattern of ICSO-1 results than are those to Item 18. On Item 25, 38.47% of all respondents selected the advanced response and 45.55% selected the moderate response. Only 3.03% selected the conventional response. On Item 26, 26.69% of all respondents selected the advanced response and 25.48% selected the moderate response, although 37.45% selected the moralistic response. The point is that most seem to understand what it is to love one's neighbor and what this commandment implies and entails.

There is some reasonable ground, then, for suspecting that if the advanced response in the item *"We prove our love for God especially by"* had been "by showing or proving our love for our neighbor," most students would have made that selection. In other words, if it is true that the catechesis or kerygmatic emphasis in the teaching of religion stresses the love of neighbor as the best way of proving our love for God, it is more understandable why the great majority of students thought that, in their *direct* relationship with God they could prove their love for Him best by "avoiding sin and keeping His commandments."

Another possible explanation would be that questions relating to the love of God are, in fact, handled in the elementary schools in a conventional or traditional manner. It is altogether possible that students are taught that the best way to prove their love for God is to avoid sin and keep His commandments. The results on Item 18 taken at face value would tend to confirm this. In any event, Item 18 proved very valuable to the Study. It showed that the students were seriously trying to give what they considered the best possible responses, not simply checking responses that appeared to be subtle or different or unusual.

ITEM 28 (worship)

The best way to join in the liturgy (Mass, sacraments, and so forth) is:
  a. to attend Church services regularly
  b. to read about the vestments, music and ceremonies
  c. to follow the rites and rituals in approved books
  d. to learn how to serve Mass or help in the sacristy
  e. to take an active part in performing the liturgical acts

In this item (e) was the advanced response, (c) the moderate, (a) the conventional, (d) the moralistic, and (b) the nominalistic.

Of the 14,514 respondents, 59.19% selected the advanced response, 15.88% the moderate, 21.77% the conventional, 1.72% the moralistic, and 1.44% the nominalistic; 2.83% either did not respond or their responses were unusable.

First, a few words about the item itself. Since it deals with worship or the liturgy, it seeks to determine not only how well the students understand the theory of the liturgy but also how well they understand their own active role in it. The item assumes, and rightly so, 2 things, that all Catholics should join in the liturgy and that there is a best way for all Catholics to do this. It asks, in effect, "what is the best way?" On analysis, this item seems more blunt and direct than most of the others in ICSO-1. It is probably easier than most because the alternative choices are more clear-cut and definite. Most likely the student was able to make his choice rather quickly and to feel confident he had made the best choice.

The fact that almost 60% of the students selected the advanced response reflects the current emphasis, both in the school and in the Church, on active participation of the laity in the liturgy. As the public worship of the Church, the liturgy is important both in itself and in its educative effect. Almost 60% of the students considered that the best way to join in the liturgical spirit is to participate actively in the acts of the liturgy. They realized that one can attend Church services regularly and still not join in the liturgy.

In answering Item 28, girls in all-girl high schools were once again well ahead of the group of all respondents in their selection of the advanced response. The difference was a marked one—59.19% for the group as a whole, 66.30% for girls in all-girl high schools. Boys in all-boy high schools were slightly below all respondents in their choice of the advanced response, 57.20%. The group "boys and girls in coeducational high schools" was a few percentage points ahead of the group as a whole, 62.10%.

A significant difference was also observable between the group "all elementary students" and the group "all secondary school students"; 56.95% of elementary students selected the advanced response, against 62.44% of secondary school students. The biggest difference, however, is that 26.91% of the elementary school students selected the conventional response, whereas only 15.71% of the secondary school students did.

The results for Item 28 were interesting in another way. It seems somewhat strange that a much higher percentage of students did not select the advanced response. The moralistic and nominalistic answers did not attract a significant response. On the other hand, the difference between the quality of the advanced response and that of either the moderate or the conventional is patently clear. It is more than a little difficult to diagnose why any twelfth-grade student in a Catholic school would prefer the moderate response, "to follow the rites and rituals in approved books," rather than "to take an active part in performing the liturgical acts." Yet 19.02% of all high school respondents did! Even more difficult to explain is why 15.71% of all high school respondents chose the conventional response, "to attend Church services regularly." In view of the current emphasis on the liturgy and on liturgical reform throughout the Church, it would not have been surprising if 80% or more of the students had selected the advanced response.

The last item to be considered revealed some of the strength of the Inventory in a way perhaps no other item did. It is taken from the general category of doctrine or belief; it is unique in several ways, but especially so because of its extreme difficulty and subtlety. If Item 28 is considered easy, Item 47 must be considered as exactly the opposite.

ITEM 47

The bible teaching that God created man "in His own image and likeness" means:
   a. man's spiritual powers of intellect and will are God-like
   b. all men are equal in God's eyes
   c. man's soul somehow looks like God

   d. man's spirit has a capacity for the divine

   e. man reflects the qualities of God

In this item, (d) was the advanced response, (a) the moderate, (e) the conventional, (b) the moralistic, and (c) the nominalistic.

In making their choice, 8.59% of the 14,519 students selected the advanced response, 19.80% the moderate, 29.12% the conventional, 33.33% the moralistic, and 9.25% the nominalistic. For one reason or another, 4.48% did not respond.

Here the student is asked to deal, first of all, with a figure of speech. The phrase "in His image and likeness," although very familiar to Catholics, attempts to put into words a spiritual reality of the first magnitude. Second, the student is sure to realize as soon as he looks at the item that he is treating a matter of prime importance in the Church of the modern world. Third, the distinctions among the choices of answers are exceptionally subtle and the responses tend to overlap. All of this notwithstanding, it is an item almost exactly right for determining in the most genuine way how deeply and how well the students understand their religion.

The first significant result was that only 8.59% of the 14,519 students selected the advanced response, "man's spirit has a capacity for the divine." On most of the other items a much higher percentage chose the advanced response. But here there seemed to be a marked tendency away from the advanced response and a rather definite attraction to the moralistic response; 33.33% of all the students thought the best response to *"The bible teaching that God created man 'in His own image and likeness' means"* was "all men are equal in God's eyes." It could be that students saw this answer as a good concretization or practical application of the expression "in His own image and likeness." It could be, too, that they are reflecting again our present emphasis on human equality.

As might be expected, there was a substantial difference between the percentages of "all elementary school students" and "all high school students" in the selection of the advanced response: 6.64% for the elementary school group, 11.03% for the secondary school group. An even greater differential might have been anticipated.

The response of girls in all-girl high schools shows a somewhat unusual pattern. Although the percentage of these girls selecting the advanced response was only slightly higher than the percentage for the group as a whole, the percentage of girls in all-girl high schools who picked the moralistic response was much lower than the percentage of the group as a whole; 33.23% of the whole group chose the moralistic response; only 19.80% of the girls in all-girl high schools did. The girls in all-girl high schools in moving away from the advanced response tended to cluster around the conventional response: 35.30% of these girls preferred the conventional response that "man reflects the qualities of God."

SUMMARY OF ICSO-1 FINDINGS

It remains to draw some general conclusions from the experience of the Study with ICSO-1. These conclusions are not necessarily fully substantiated by the foregoing illustrations; rather they have been arrived at by a complete analysis of the data compiled, much of which is included in the full analysis referred to earlier.

Neither are the conclusions held up as absolute or final in any sense. They are general conclusions, which the directors of the Study and the staff members have agreed are made inescapable by any careful consideration of the data. Five of the 6 conclusions pertain to the content of the inventory; one conclusion pertains to the test, ICSO-1, itself.

The conclusions are:

1. The group as a whole, the 14,519 students, did well on ICSO-1.

2. There was no distinguishable pattern among the responses of the group as a whole, based on the type of item—those relating to Catholic belief, those to Catholic moral teaching, and those to Catholic worship.

3. The differences between the performances of the eighth- and twelfth-grade students was, in general, statistically significant but by no means as great as might have been expected.

4. As a group, girls in all-girl high schools showed the best understanding of their religion.

5. ICSO-1 showed a somewhat equal distribution among responses classified as advanced, moderate, and conventional.

6. Based on results thus far and with continual improvement and refinement, ICSO-1 can become a most valuable testing instrument for Catholic educators.

The focus throughout these chapters dealing with the Inventory of Catholic School Outcomes is on the student in the Catholic school, not on the school itself. The Inventory could "get at" what the student understands, what his attitudes are, and what his opinions are, but there was no way of determining the extent to which the school is the determining or formative influence. We would assume that the school is a strong influence, but just *how strong* it is impossible to tell. However, it is probably valid to assume that the school is a much more important factor in the acquiring of knowledge and understanding than in the forming of attitudes. To impart knowledge and understanding, particularly of those matters that require formal, systematic preparation and presentation, demands the time and expertise found only in the schools.

1. *The group as a whole did well in ICSO-1.* Perhaps the most important thing the inventory set out to determine was whether and how well students in Catholic schools understand their religion. In this sense, ICSO-1 was an achievement test in much the same way a similar test would seek to determine whether and how well students knew and understood history, mathematics, or English grammar.

As pointed out, the theory of ICSO-1 was that in each item the advanced response showed a clearer or more complete understanding by the student and a reflection of a different instructional emphasis. According to this theory the maximum recordable result would occur if a student selected the advanced response in each of the 50 items. At the other end of the scale would have been the student who selected the moralistic or nominalistic response or combination of these to each of the 50 items.

Of the total group responding to the total 50 items, approximately 56% selected the advanced and moderate responses combined, 32% selected the conventional responses, and 12% selected the moralistic and nominalistic responses combined.

2. *There was no distinguishable pattern among the responses of the group as a whole, based on the type of item—those relating to Catholic belief, those to Catholic moral teaching, and those to Catholic worship.* The items in ICSO-1 were divided approximately equally among the 3 major categories of knowledge or understanding within the Catholic religion. These categories of religious knowledge are regarded as logically and pedagogically distinct, although in fact in the Catholic system they are inextricably interrelated. There were 15 items relating

to Catholic belief, 15 relating to moral practice, and 20 relating.to Catholic worship. The distinctions were based on the fact that the Church requires Catholics to believe certain things, to do certain things, and to worship in certain ways. For example, the Catholic believes in the mystery of the Eucharist, he receives Holy Communion, according to Church law at least once a year, and he joins in certain liturgical acts honoring or worshiping Christ in the Eucharist.

The Study had no presuppositions of how the students would respond to the different types of items. It was chiefly concerned to make sure that the inventory sampled the entire range of knowledge within the Catholic system. But it would not have been surprising if a pattern had developed showing a better or deeper understanding of matters pertaining to moral teaching and worship than of Church doctrine or belief. Church law and the practice of the liturgy enter much more directly and immediately into the life of the Catholic than does Catholic doctrine itself. However, no such pattern is ascertainable.

A careful analysis of the responses shows that a high percentage of those choosing the advanced or moderate response is just as likely to occur in an item relating to doctrine as in an item relating to practice or worship. The reverse is also true; the lowest percentage of those choosing the advanced response will sometimes appear on a question relating to moral practice or one relating to the liturgy. Thus it is impossible, to take an extreme example, to generalize that the respondents were advanced in matters of the liturgy, moderate in matters of practice, and conventional in matters of belief. The distinguishing feature in attempting to determine whether students were advanced, moderate, conventional, moralistic, or nominalistic in their religious understanding was not the type of question asked.

The important conclusion here is that religious education, at home and in the school, does not appear to be segmented into the 3 categories used in the inventory construction. So far as ICSO-1 could determine, religious instruction does not stress one form of religious knowledge to the detriment of the other forms.

3. *The difference between the performances of the eighth- and the twelfth-grade students was, in general, statistically significant but not as great as might be expected.* The clear purpose in giving the inventory to both eighth-grade students and to seniors in high school was to get some picture of the difference in religious understanding between

the groups. Over 96% of those taking the inventory had had their full eight or twelve years of schooling in Catholic schools. There was no attempt to match eighth- and twelfth-grade students in intelligence or in any other way.

The assumption was that the high school seniors would show a deeper understanding of their religion, and this assumption was verified. Also the difference in religious understanding of the groups was statistically significant. Put another way, 4 additional years of religious schooling does make a difference in ICSO-1 responses. The surprising result was that the degree of difference was by no means as great as had been anticipated.

This conclusion will only be illustrated here, not fully explored. Let us posit the percentage of those selecting the advanced response as the single criterion of deeper religious understanding. It is clear that on almost every item a higher percentage of high school seniors than of eighth-grade students selected the advanced response. Yet on several items a higher percentage of eighth-grade students selected the advanced response. And on several other items the difference is only a few percentage points. On the average the high school seniors range only 5–10% ahead of the eighth-grade students in their selection of advanced response.

Although ICSO-1 results are clear on this point, much further evidence would be needed to risk any valid explanation for the fact that the eighth-grade students did almost as well as the high school seniors.

4. *As a group, the girls in all-girl schools showed the best understanding of their religion.* In analyzing the results on ICSO-1 according to type of school, particular attention was paid to 5 subgroups: (a) all boys and girls in elementary schools; (b) girls in coeducational high schools; (c) boys in coeducational high schools; (d) boys in all-boy high schools; and (e) girls in all-girl high schools.

Whether in comparison with the group as a whole or in comparison with any of the other subgroups, girls in all-girl high schools showed the greatest consistency in selecting advanced responses. There were some variations, to be sure, but on almost all questions these girls set the pace. Here again, although the pattern was evident and steady, the difference was not spectacular. In item after item, these girls led in choice of the advanced response by percentage points ranging from a few to several. The significance is the consistency with which they exceeded all other groups in selection of advanced responses.

5. *To the degree that students' performance on ICSO-1 reflects the emphasis of teaching of religion in Catholic schools, the emphasis is clearly in the direction of catechesis or kerygmatic.* We have classified as advanced those responses that best exemplified the catechesis emphasis in Catholic religious instruction. The advanced responses were worded in such a way that those who had been so instructed would recognize and choose them. Those who had not been so instructed would probably prefer one of the other responses.

It was not known at the outset of the Study how widespread or pervasive the catechesis emphasis was in Catholic religious instruction in this country. The inventory helps greatly to clarify this question. If the figures are rounded out to the nearest percentage point, 31% of the elementary school and 35% of the high school students selected the advanced responses. An additional 23% of elementary school students and 24% of the high school students selected the moderate responses, which represented a position between the conventional and the advanced. However, the moderate response, in the minds of the test designers and in the minds of the students also, it would seem, shows a strong tendency toward the advanced response. It was, in effect, moderately advanced. Therefore, in drawing conclusions it is both possible and logical to combine the percentages of those choosing the advanced and moderate response. If this is done, 54% of all elementary school students and 59% of all secondary school students reflected the catechesis emphasis in their response to ICSO-1 items.

31% of elementary school students selected the conventional position; 8% selected the moralistic responses; and 6% selected the nominalistic responses.

Interestingly enough, 31% of secondary school students also selected the conventional responses; 6% of them selected the moralistic responses; and 4% selected the nominalistic respones.

Thus, although it is true that the results definitely reflect the catechesis emphasis in the teaching of religion in this country, it is by no means correct that this is the only emphasis. Among elementary school pupils, 45% preferred the conventional, moralistic, or nominalistic positions. Among secondary school students these positions were preferred by 40% of the students.

This raises again the question of the quality of the teaching in Catholic schools. The Study cannot say with complete confidence that much of the teaching in the Catholic schools is still conventional. The Study has no precise way of measuring the relationship between the religious instruction in the schools and the responses of the Catholic school students to ICSO-1. But if we assume that there is a positive relationship between the effects of religious instruction in the schools and the student responses to the inventory, the indication is that a significant amount of this teaching is at the conventional level.

However, it appears that the principal emphasis now, and for the future, if the percentage of moderate responses is taken as the criterion, is the catechesis or kerygmatic. No doubt much remains to be done to improve the quality of religious instruction, but we can be certain that the next generation of students in the Catholic schools will have a much better understanding of their religion than those of former generations had.

6. *Based on results thus far and with continual improvement and refinement, ICSO-1 can become a valuable testing instrument for Catholic educators.* In conjunction with the analysis of the results produced from the administration of ICSO-1, the Study staff has made a critical analysis of the instrument. Further steps are planned to standardize the instrument for use in Catholic schools. These plans are based on the obvious need for some orderly method by which Catholic schools can evaluate the degree to which they are serving the functions that are peculiar to them.

When the relatively small increment in advanced responses by twelfth-grade students over eighth-grade students became evident, the Study staff first became concerned with the ICSO-1 instrument. This concern was based on the original concept of the instrument, which aimed at developing a single test that could be administered to both eighth- and twelfth-grade students. This concern was finally centered on the fact that the test might have been adequate excepting that the ceiling was too low to measure the more mature understandings the additional religion instructional programs developed for twelfth-grade students. As a check against this possible weakness of the instrument, the staff was fortunate enough to secure permission from a number of religious communities for women to administer ICSO-1 to their novices and juniors. These communities concentrate most of their efforts in training sisters for teaching. Nine communities were willing to participate and 429 sisters in formation were tested. The analysis of the test results showed the sisters in formation selecting 25.7% more advanced responses, and 21.6% more combined advanced and moderate responses than did the twelfth-grade students. These increments compare to the twelfth-grade students exceeding eighth-grade students by 3.7% in advanced responses and 4.1% in advanced plus moderate responses. With these results the Study staff felt comfortable that the test ceiling was not too low and that it was not geared to or close to eighth-grade expectation. The most likely speculation is that some careful and fruitful review might be made of the religion education program in grades 9 through 12 as a step in determining the effectiveness of the program.

References

[1] Sister Mary Joan, O.P., and Sister Mary Nona, O.P., *Guiding Growth in Christian Social Living* (Washington: The Catholic University of America Press, 1944 and 1952).

[2] *A Catholic Catechism,* Clemens Tilman, ed. (New York: Herder and Herder, 1958).

[3] *Katholischer Katechismus der Bistumer Deutschlands,* Clemens Tilman, ed. (Freiburg: Herder, 1957).

[4] *The New Confraternity Edition Revised Baltimore Catechism No. 3,* Francis J. Connell, ed. (New York: Benziger Brothers, 1949).

CHAPTER SIX

ICSO-2:
The Student Attitude Index

THE STUDENT ATTITUDE INDEX WAS DEVISED IN THE belief that assessment of Catholic students' scholastic achievement and religious knowledge would be incomplete without some data on student attitudes and values. How they feel about religious vocations, minority groups, mixed marriages, and other parts of the total Catholic value system was considered equally important as what they know.

Research into the effects of Catholic schooling on students' attitudes is badly needed. Statements based on assumptions favorable or unfavorable to the parochial school system are more plentiful than hard facts. Current questions concern federal aid, decisions about dropping grades, and whether the Catholic school system ultimately represents the best use of available material resources and personnel for the religious formation of youth.

The objectives of the Index were to discover the attitudes most common among the students and to correlate them with student backgrounds. The attitudes selected were related to the declared aims of the Catholic schools as stated in general by Pope Pius XI's encyclical,[1] in the statement of the Commission on American Citizenship,[2] in statements of individual bishops and educators, and in a more detailed way in such texts as the *Guiding Growth in Christian Living Series*.[3] An additional source was the objectives identified during the course of our own depth studies.

The theoretical model of these objectives is the "complete Christian" of Pius XI's encyclical. In order to encompass the most important facets of such a model, attitudes were categorized according to their content into 5 major areas: religious-moral attitudes, occupational aspirations, civic-social attitudes, attitudes toward family values, educational aspirations. As with any theoretical model, wide variations in approximation to the "pure type" occur. Considerable deviation from the norms was anticipated because of the many variables, such as age, sex, family background, regional variations, individual personality, and specific school experiences.

The Student Attitude Index reflects the literature in attitudinal studies, with particular regard to the attitudes of youth. Potential index items were culled from the literature, discussed, and adapted to the categories indicated above. Reduced by an assiduous refining process from 200, 50 items were subjected to the judgment and criticism of 25 experts in the fields of religion, education, and behavioral science. Their comments and evaluations were analyzed and used in further refining and reducing the items to 45. The instrument was pretested at a Catholic elementary school and a Catholic high school and in elementary and high school CCD classes. Further pilot work was done in use of the instrument as the basis for a doctoral dissertation.

The problems of measuring and interpreting attitudinal and behavioral data need no elaboration. It is easy to exaggerate both the actual and possible contributions of formal educational institutions to consensus in society, whether in terms of formation of basic personality or of inculcation of a common set of values.[4] Many variables must be taken into consideration in interpretation of attitudinal data. Students at any level of educational development are subject to a host of influences, some mutually reinforcing, others at variance. The present research assumes that very probably family and school have the most important influence on the attitudes of students and that other influences, such as those of peer groups and community, are normally mediated by these institutions.

As indicated, a control was attempted for the influence of the family, especially the degree of religious interest and practice in the home. To some extent this control also served for selective factors that determine which families send their children to Catholic schools, since a high degree of variability is observed with regard to the frequency of attention to religion and religious practices in the home.

The second control variable, personal religiosity as measured by frequency of Mass attendance, is closely associated with Catholic school attendance, since the school often provides opportunity to attend Mass daily, especially for elementary school children, and encourages the practice. (Some schools retain the policy of compulsory Mass attendance on school days, but this practice apparently is diminishing rapidly. There is internal evidence that our respondents are not obliged to attend daily Mass.) The remarkable relationships between Mass attendance and specific attitudes discussed later in this report may be of interest to parents and educators.

SELECTION OF ITEMS FOR ANALYSIS

The total analysis of each item in the Index will not be presented here. Certain items have been selected for analysis to present a meaningful picture of students' attitudes in the areas of religious-moral values, social-civic attitudes, family values, educational aspirations.

Religious-Moral Values

This grouping investigates attitudes that are at the very core of the Catholic value system. It examines the reactions of students to the proposal that one of their best friends enters the seminary to become a priest or announces her intention of becoming a sister. It seeks to discover how much importance they assign to the virtue of charity, the essential Christian virtue, by asking if they believe salvation can be attained by merely living one's life well, without seeking to help others. Finally, it classifies students according to their devotion to the Mass, by asking whether they attend Mass regularly or more frequently than the Church requires. In addition, the responses to items concerning public welfare, aid to other nations, strong interest in money and things as related to the spiritual life, and the degree to which they feel certain about Catholic moral teaching are presented.

Social-Civic Attitudes

This section examines responses to questions dealing with attitudes toward minority groups. One item assays the degree to which the students accept the stereotype of the Negro as inferior intellectually to the white and fitted only for positions calling for little responsibility. Another asks whether the students are so racially prejudiced that it would really bother them to sit near someone of another race in school. A third uses a stereotype of the Jew as a shrewd, scheming person to test its acceptability to the students. Finally, bringing the racial question into the sanctuary of the Catholic Church itself, the students are asked whether it would make any difference to them whether they received the Eucharist from the hands of a white or Negro priest.

Family Values

The Catholic Church endorses the sanctity of home and family. Many influences in modern culture, however, militate against the preservation of family values. For this reason the students were questioned concerning their attitudes toward divorce with remarriage. They were also asked to indicate whether they thought strong personal ties more important for family success than money and possessions, and whether, given their preference, they would choose activities with their families, their school friends, or their out-of-school friends.

Marriage within Church membership, highly valued in Catholic circles, was also presented for evaluation, on a scale ranging from strong commitment to marrying a Catholic to complete indifference to the religion of the one they might marry. They were also given a set of characteristics of a potential marriage partner and asked to assign degrees of importance.

Related to marriage and family life is the dating behavior of young people, which today appears progressively more sophisticated for younger age groups. Students were asked to indicate whether they dated one person to the exclusion of all others. They were asked to agree or disagree with the proposition that "necking and petting" are not objectionable, since they are merely part of the growing-up process.

The degree that parents actively encourage and support religion through family religious practices, discussions, and observances has served as a control variable in analyzing many of the other attitudes in this Study and is an index of the value placed on religion by the parents.

Educational Aspirations

Much of the students' evaluation of education, its goals, the success of Catholic schools in general and of their own schools in particular is analyzed and discussed in ICSO-3, which follows this chapter. Some measure of their intellectual quality and aspirations came from answers to questions about how much importance was placed on the opportunity to go to college and whether they preferred memorization of answers about religious matters to class discussions.

PROCEDURES

The procedure for analysis was (1) specifying the modal responses of the entire student population for each questionnaire and (2) identifying the background variables associated with the various responses. Each analysis was related to the SC-RB paradigm (described below) to discover what association, if any, existed between the attitudes indicated and the social class and religious background of the students. Other background factors that will be presented when pertinent to specific index items are sex, grade level, type of high school attended, number of years of Catholic schooling, size of family, religion, education, nationality, occupation of parents, scholastic standing, future school plans, and type of school attended by the respondents' friends.

In the SC-RB paradigm the respondents were divided into 3 social classes, SC-1, SC-2, and SC-3, based on the occupation of the respondent's father, as follows:

Social Class 1—professional, semiprofessional, business executives
Social Class 2—managerial, clerical, white collar, skilled
Social Class 3—semiskilled and unskilled

Respondents were further classified according to 6 religious background categories, RB-1, RB-2, RB-3, RB-4, RB-5, RB-6, as follows:

Religious Background 1—both parents are Catholics, both had a Catholic education (at least 8 years), and the child has had some Catholic education (at least 5 years if in the elementary school, at least 8 years if in high school)

Religious Background 2—same as RB-1 except that the father has a
    Catholic education but not the mother
Religious Background 3—same as RB-1 except that the mother has a
    Catholic education but not the father
Religious Background 4—both parents are Catholics, neither has a Catho-
    lic education, but the child has
Religious Background 5—one parent is Catholic, the other is not, but the
    child has had Catholic education
Religious Background 6—both parents are Catholics, neither has had a
    Catholic education, nor has the child

Analyses of particular questionnaire items will be based on a specific
response, for example, "strongly agree" or "strongly disagree," according to the above classifications of the students. The analyses, therefore,
will consider responses according to the pattern of round numbers of
students shown in Table 57, when these respondent characteristics are
meaningful.

Table 57

SOCIAL CLASS-RELIGIOUS BACKGROUND PARADIGM

	Total	RB-1	RB-2	RB-3	RB-4	RB-5	RB-6
SC-1	2125	440	250	370	760	200	105
SC-2	4950	960	560	860	1980	330	260
SC-3	4970	750	470	900	2220	370	280
Total	12,045	2150	1280	2130	4940	900	645

The total respondents was 14,519; whenever total response is reported, that is the number (less "no response"). The SC-RB paradigm
was set up to include the maximum possible students; 12,045 children
are involved whenever this paradigm is analyzed. Subcategories of
social class and religious background are enumerated in Table 57.

Differential sex responses refer to about 6500 boys and 7900 girls.
When elementary school responses are compared with high school
responses, 7479 elementary and 6855 secondary school students are
responding. These are distributed according to sex and type of school
as follows:

Elementary school boys	3,476
Elementary school girls	4,003
All-boy high schools	1,504
All-girl high schools	2,275
Coeducational high school boys	1,472
Coeducational high school girls	1,604
Total	14,334

Not all 45 questions in the Student Attitude Index are thoroughly analyzed in this report. This chapter explains the disposition made of specific questions. The subject matter of the total questions appears in the instrument in the Appendix.

RELIGIOUS-MORAL VALUES

Catholic schools differ from other schools as they inculcate religious values, thus continuing and reinforcing the family's efforts to introduce children to their Christian heritage. For Catholic families the Catholic value system is central to that heritage. Our analysis turns first, therefore, to 3 questions of a religious-moral nature:

1. Do the students in Catholic schools feel that charity in the form of helping other people is really necessary?

2. What are the attitudes of the students toward vocations?

3. What are the students' practices in Mass attendance?

The Necessity of Helping Others

Several questions in the Student Attitude Index (referred to hereafter as SAI) aimed at measuring the value placed by Catholic students on helping others. The doctrine of brotherly love and mutual assistance is central to Christianity, yet Catholic education may not be assigning to this doctrine the focus it deserves. Ritual observances, memorizing answers, and stock solutions to religious problems may divert attention from the essence of Christ's Gospel, which is primarily a message of active love. Recent research has raised the question whether the Catholic subculture places obedience ahead of charity—whether, for instance, it is considered more important for children to learn to obey than to learn to help others."[5]

ITEM 15

To reach heaven, it is enough to live our own lives well without looking for ways of helping others.

The response choices, as for almost all index items, was the following continuum: "strongly agree"; "agree somewhat"; "not certain"; "disagree somewhat"; "strongly disagree." At first glance, it appears that most of the respondents realize the importance of helping others, since 55% reject the statement by disagreeing strongly and another 28% by disagreeing somewhat. This puts 83% on the "Gospel side," with 4% not certain. Strongly agreeing with this isolationist statement are 5%, with an additional 8% agreeing somewhat (see Table 58). The analysis is concerned with those who take the most Christian position, who repudiate (by disagreeing strongly) the idea that an eternal reward is to be won without regard to the welfare of others.

In Table 58 the division according to sex shows that the 55% consensus is more apparent than real, as the boys' responses drop to 46% for strong disagreement with the idea of getting to heaven without regard for others, and the girls' increase to 63%. This item is one of the few in which grade level makes no significant difference in response percentages. Both elementary and secondary show 55% in the "strongly disagree" category. When both grade level and sex are constant, the percentage of girls' over boys' response can be seen in perspective: elementary school girls reject the idea of winning heaven by "only living one's own life well" 13% more than elementary school boys (61% to 48%); 22% more high school girls than high school boys (65% to 43%).

Table 58

DISTRIBUTION OF RESPONSES TO QUESTION
ABOUT THE NECESSITY OF HELPING OTHERS

Response	Frequency	%
Strongly agree	656	4.6
Agree somewhat	1227	8.5
Uncertain	602	4.2
Disagree somewhat	3940	27.4
Strongly disagree	7948	55.3
Total	14,373	100.0

The type of high school attended makes some difference in the response pattern. At the high school level 20% more girls than boys reject the solitary path to heaven, but girls in the all-girl schools are in advance of those in coeducational schools, and boys in all-boy schools hold a slight edge over coeducational school boys. The responses of the 4 types of high schools are ranked in Table 59.

Table 59

RESPONSES REJECTING THE IDEA OF GETTING TO HEAVEN
WITHOUT HELPING OTHERS, BY TYPE OF SCHOOL

Rank	School type	% strongly disagreeing
1	All-girl schools	67.1
2	Coed school girls	61.2
3	All-boy schools	45.0
4	Coed school boys	41.6

Analysis of the Social Class-Religious Background (SC-RB) paradigm gives evidence that the higher the social class, the greater the proportion of students who reject the isolationist path to heaven. SC-1 has 59% rejecting the isolationist position, SC-2, 56% and SC-3, 54%.

The characteristic of the respondents' academic achievement was developed from a self-rating academic classification that proved to be a very effective discriminator in all areas of the instrument. Recent national studies have demonstrated the validity of assuming that self-reports of students are a good measure of their real academic accomplishments. The data for Davidsen's (1963) study of a national population indicate a correlation of .92 between self-reported grades, even when the students' reports were obtained under conditions comparable to those used for this Study.[6] As the students classify themselves academically and reject the "narrow path" to heaven, we find 68% of the A students rejecting and 40% of the D students rejecting.

The analysis has shown that whereas four-fifths of the students express the attitude that "living one's life well without helping others" is not enough to insure a heavenly reward, certain backgrounds are associated with higher percentages expressing the truly Christian attitude toward brotherly help. Children who express such attitudes are from families of high social class; their parents have more than an average amount of education, especially of Catholic education. They have 6 or more brothers and sisters. Their parents actively encourage interest in religion and religious practice in the home every day. They are more likely to be girls than boys, to be elementary rather than high school students. A considerable proportion of their education has been in Catholic schools; they rate themselves high in scholastic achievement; and they assist at Mass beyond their Sunday obligation, some of them almost everyday of the week.

Just where the line divides family from school influences is impossible to say, but these associated variables cannot fail to interest Catholic parents and educators.

Responses to several other questions in the SAI that probed attitudes tend to follow the same general pattern described. An overall 57% strongly agree with Item 24.

ITEM 24

Wherever I work, I hope that I will be able to help the people I work with to be good Christians.

Again the girls agreed more than the boys, 64% to 48%, with the high school boys reporting the lowest degree of agreement, 39%.

On the community level of helping others, close to half the respondents strongly rejected the statement.

ITEM 5

Generally, I do not believe in all these community drives, like the Community Chest or the United Fund. People on relief and in need should be taken care of by their own relatives.

Girls exceed boys in strongly disagreeing with this statement, but both remain fairly close to the general mean of 51% (girls, 54%; boys, 46%). Elementary school students disagree 5% more than high school students. High school boys rank lowest, with 42% disagreeing strongly.

Helping others on an international level is not seen by these students as of great value, especially when the use of tax money is the means suggested. Only 8% of both boys and girls agree strongly with the proposal in Item 30.

ITEM 30

America would be more of a Christian nation if it used more of its tax money to help other nations of the world.

Elementary students are twice as ready to approve this statement than are high school students (11% to 5%).

Finally, on a more generally global scale, we again observe more than half the respondents strongly agreeing with item 19.

ITEM 19

We have a responsibility in Christian charity to give money and make sacrifices to help oppressed people in other parts of the world.

The general mean here is 55%, with the elementary exceeding the high school students 59% to 50%. Girls exceed boys in general and at each grade level; elementary girls report 10% more agreeing than elementary boys (63% to 53%) and the high school girls 20% more than high school boys (59% to 39%).

It should be restated that in this brief examination of responses to items about helping others, only the "strongly agree" category has been included to make the percentages comparable with those analyzed for "getting to heaven without helping others." An additional sizeable proportion of respondents selected the "agree somewhat" response; combining "agree" responses, we find a substantial majority supporting all forms of help except that of using "tax money to help other nations."

Related to love of one's neighbor is recognition that Christians must try to be kind toward every human being, no matter how unattractive or unprepossessing, simply because all are children of God and brothers of Christ. The respondents in this Study were asked to react to the following statement embodying such a Christian attitude in Item 28.

ITEM 28

No matter how stupid or vulgar a person may be, we should still try to be kindly toward him because he is a son of God.

Three-fifths of the student respondents heartily endorsed this statement by strongly agreeing. However, only half of the boys (52%) took that attitude, whereas two-thirds of the girls, or 67%, did so. The high school students gave this sentiment far less support than the elementary students, the latter agreeing 69% compared with 52% for the older students.

When the type of high school is constant, a strong commitment to the Christian attitude of "charity toward all" characterizes only 2 out of every 5 high school boys, whereas closer to 3 out of every 5 girls express such an attitude. The all-girl schools once more give evidence of more strongly "Catholic" attitudes than the other high school students. The all-boy schools show the lowest percentage strongly agreeing.

Table 60

PERCENTAGE OF "STRONGLY AGREE" RESPONSES TO THE
IDEAL OF "CHARITY TOWARD ALL," BY TYPE OF HIGH SCHOOL

Type of school	%
All-girl	63
Coed girls	57
Coed boys	41
All-boy	38

Attitudes Toward Vocations

The Catholic schools are considered the most fruitful source of religious vocations. Most of the young people who enter the priestly or religious life have had the greater part of their education in Catholic institutions, where they have been taught by priests, brothers, sisters, and lay teachers.[7] To discover how the respondents felt about religion as a life career, they were asked in Items 9 and 10 how they would react if one of their best friends chose such a career.

ITEM 9

If one of my best friends said she wanted to become a sister, I would pray that she would succeed in that vocation.

ITEM 10

It makes me happy to hear that one of my best friends is going to the seminary to become a priest.

The reason for specifying a friend's vocation was that some youngsters are reluctant to admit a personal interest in the religious life. Moreover, the point of inquiry was not how many were contemplating a religious life, but rather the respondents' general attitudes toward such careers. In order to measure commitment to this way of life, they were asked not for mere approval but if they would rejoice over their hypothetical friend's plans and pray for their successful fulfillment. The responses appear in Table 61.

Table 61

DISTRIBUTION OF RESPONSES FAVORABLE TO A
FRIEND'S VOCATION TO THE PRIESTHOOD OR SISTERHOOD

Response	Priest vocation %	Sister vocation %
Agree strongly	61.5	65.0
Agree somewhat	23.6	18.9
Uncertain	9.4	10.6
Disagree somewhat	3.7	3.3
Strongly disagree	1.8	2.2
Total	100.0	100.0

Relatively few children react negatively to the questions; more indicate uncertainty than disapproval. Close to two-thirds would agree strongly. Adding those who agree somewhat brings to 85% those who react positively to the idea of a friend's religious vocation. There is a tendency to be more supportive of the sister vocation.

To discover which students indicate favorable reactions, we turn first to the SC-RB paradigm. No substantial social class differences are observable for attitudes toward the friend's priest vocation, although children in SC-1 were somewhat less favorable than SC-2 and SC-3. Lower social class is related to favoring the sister vocation also. It may be that the children of high social status have been oriented toward a style of life and pattern of achievement more consonant with affluence and secular values than the children in the other classes.

There is a tendency for children of one or both parents educated in Catholic schools to report higher percentages favorable to both vocations. Thus, the RB-1, 2 and 3 children average 64% supportive of the priest vocation, compared with 60% of the RB-4, 5, and 6 children. Comparable approval of the sister's vocation is at 66.0% and 64.1%. Other than the noted differences based on social class and Catholic education of parents, the use of the paradigm yields little insight into the variables in attitudes toward vocations.

Cross-tabulations show how age and sex affect these attitudes. Girls give more favorable responses than boys toward both vocations, as do elementary students over high school students. Table 62 shows the rank in which the various groups express strong support of a friend's vocation.

Table 62

RANK IN WHICH STUDENTS EXPRESS SUPPORTIVE
ATTITUDES TOWARD A FRIEND'S PRIEST OR SISTER VOCATION

Priest %		Sister %	
Elementary school girls	69	High school girls	77
High school girls	67	Elementary school girls	74
Elementary school boys	62	Elementary school boys	60
High school boys	45	High school boys	42
Total	61	Total	65

Controlling for both sex and grade level reveals substantial differences among these groups. The high school boys show the least support of either of the vocations. The data also underscore how misleading it is to speak indiscriminately about the attitudes of "Catholic school children"; unless age and sex are specified, the picture may be blurred.

There are some interesting differences among high school students, based on the type of high school they attend. Girls in all-girl schools show the highest percentage strongly agreeing about both vocations; boys in all-boy schools are lowest for both. The girls are 10% or 11% more favorable to a friend's vocation to the sisterhood than to the priesthood; the case is reversed for the boys, but they favor a friend's priestly vocation only a little more than that of the sister candidate. The rank in which these 4 groups express attitudes supporting a friend's career in religion is the same for both vocations, as may be seen in Table 63.

Table 63

RANK IN WHICH 4 TYPES OF HIGH SCHOOL STUDENTS
EXPRESS STRONG SUPPORT FOR A FRIEND'S RELIGIOUS VOCATION

Rank	Type of school	Priest %	Sister %
1	All-girl schools	69.1	79.1
2	Coeducational school girls	63.1	74.6
3	Coeducational school boys	48.2	44.9
4	All-boy schools	41.2	39.2

When one parent is not a Catholic, a significantly lower percentage of children express support of vocations than when both parents are Catholic. This difference is largest in the middle class, SC-2, where the agreement of children with both Catholic parents is 15% greater than that of the children with one non-Catholic parent, who might not be expected to have the same enthusiasm for a religious vocation as a career as does the parent who accepts the total Catholic value system. Apparently the lesser evaluation by non-Catholic parents is conveyed to children, consciously or not, so that it is evident in their responses even when they have had a Catholic education.

Examination of the cross-tabulation of "strongly agree" responses with the scholastic average the students think best fits them shows that the best students are most likely to be happy over a friend going to become a priest and to pray for a friend going to become a sister. The percentages for the poorer students fall linearly, although even among the D students more than half give strong support to both vocations. The favorable percentages range linearly from 71% for the A students to 52% for the D students.

In summary, the students who express strong positive support for a friend's religious vocation will sound familiar: in most respects they resemble the students who reject the idea of saving their souls without looking for ways of helping other people. They are more likely to be girls than boys, and elementary rather than high school students. They perceive themselves as having high scholastic averages, associate chiefly with friends in Catholic schools, and assist frequently at Mass when not obliged to.

Family characteristics differ from those of the previously analyzed questions in that lower class (SC-3) reflects a more ideally Catholic attitude toward religion as a career. Moreover, a slightly more favorable attitude toward the sisterhood is observed among respondents with non-Catholic mothers. Mother's total years of education is associated with decreasing rather than increasing percentages approving, although mothers' Catholic education beyond 12 years brings increased percentages approving the sisterhood. Children both of whose parents are Catholic are more favorable to the priesthood than are those who have one non-Catholic parent. A high level of father's general education and father's Catholic education, larger families, and a high degree of active promotion of religious interest and practice in the home are all associated with higher proportions of children expressing strong support for religious vocations.

Mass Attendance

The discussion of background explained the use of Mass attendance as an index of personal religious practice and a correlate of Catholic attitudes. The question proposed in Item 39 measures attitude behaviorally, by asking students about their actual practice. The distribution of responses is shown in Table 64.

Table 64 shows 3 groups of Catholic school students: those who meet their obligation by attending Mass regularly on Sundays and on holy days; a second group which attends Mass more frequently than their obligation; and a third group which does not regularly meet its Mass

Table 64

FREQUENCY OF MASS ATTENDANCE

Responses	Frequency	%
Occasionally on Sundays and holy days	581	4.1
Regularly on Sundays and holy days	6,171	43.4
Besides Sundays and holy days:		
1–3 times a month	4,199	29.5
2–3 times a week	1,550	10.9
4 or more times a week	1,712	12.0
Total	14,213	100.0

obligations. The regular attenders are 43.4% of the total, the frequent attenders 52.4%, and the irregular attenders 4.1%.

In considering the frequent attenders by age, grade, and sex a pattern similar to other positive attitude responses is identified: elementary girls have the highest percentage among the frequent attenders, 67%; 60% of the elementary boys report in this group; high school girls show 49%; and high school boys show 30%.

The SC-RB paradigm shows that higher percentages of SC-1 students are frequent attenders than in the other classes. Other characteristics of the frequent attenders are that they have had all of their education in Catholic schools; they plan to continue their education in Catholic schools; they also report themselves as academically successful. Their families provide and encourage discussion and practice of religion in the home; mother and father are Catholics and have at least a high school education in Catholic schools.

The obverse characteristics hold for the irregular Mass attenders. When the age, grade, and sex of the irregular attenders is considered, 9% of the high school boys fall in this group, 4% of the elementary boys, 3% of the high school girls, and 2% of the elementary girls. Stated another way, boys account for 70% of the irregular attenders; high school boys alone account for 45%. Those who attend all-boy high schools report greater laxity than do boys in coeducational high schools, and girls are divided about equally between all-girl and coeducational schools.

SOCIAL-CIVIC ATTITUDES

Attitudes Toward Racial and Other Minority Groups

Closely related to the Christian spirit of "helping others" is the ideal of brotherly love. A Christian cannot in conscience harbor ill feelings, suspicion, or prejudice against any group because of race, color, ethnic origin, or economic status. Presumably this doctrine is emphasized in Catholic schools, although the value placed upon it may vary among students of various backgrounds and from one region to another.

To discover to what degree the spirit of Christian love for all men characterized these students, 3 items were provided with which they could agree or disagree along the usual continuum.

ITEM 7

Manual labor and unskilled jobs seem to fit the Negro's mental and physical ability better than more skilled or responsible work.

ITEM 34

It would bother me to sit next to or near a person of another race in school.

ITEM 17

There is something strange and different about Jews; it is hard to know what they are thinking or planning, or what makes them tick.

The first of these is obviously ill-founded from the point of view of Christian teaching and of civil rights. Students who believe the statement have perhaps grown up in an environment where racial bias has superseded the principle of rating each person on his merits. If they maintain this attitude, they are not likely to work toward building a world of understanding in which job opportunities are equal for all qualified persons. The social encyclicals of the Popes afford Catholics no support for the idea that Negroes are natively inferior.

The item questioning how they would feel about sitting next to someone of another race was generalized to apply equally to respondents of all races, but since our sample is made up overwhelmingly of white children, the answers can be interpreted as typical of their reactions to sitting near a Negro child.

The stereotype in the third item presenting Jews as strange, crafty, and scheming was included to measure anti-Semitism among the students and to discover what background factors are associated with anti-Semitic attitudes. The new spirit of ecumenism embraces Jews as well as Protestants, and recent years have seen cooperative efforts among the 3 major faiths toward achieving better interfaith understanding and acceptance. The inquiry here is whether or not that spirit has "trickled down" to the secondary and elementary level of Catholic schools.

The questions were placed randomly in the questionnaire. They are combined here in Table 65 for easy comparison.

It appears that 7% of our students give strong assent to these prejudiced statements, and an additional 9% to 15% accept them somewhat. The majority express unbiased attitudes toward the Negro, although

Table 65

DISTRIBUTION OF BIASED AND UNBIASED RESPONSES
TO QUESTIONS ON ATTITUDES TOWARD MINORITIES

Response	Unskilled jobs fit the Negro %	Dislike sitting near another race %	Jewish stereotype %
Agree strongly	7.6	7.3	6.9
Biased			
Agree somewhat	14.9	8.7	13.0
Combined biased	22.5	16.0	19.9
Disagree somewhat	20.9	15.0	15.8
Unbiased			
Strongly disagree	45.9	61.0	31.6
Combined unbiased	66.8	76.0	47.4
Uncertain	10.7	8.0	32.7

the majorities do not exceed two-thirds and three-fourths of the students. Most surprising is the high proportion selecting the "uncertain" response for the Jewish stereotype; 33% did not know how to answer. This is the highest "uncertain" percentage reported in the entire SAI. Indications are that students in Catholic schools know very little about Jews, since over half of them (53%) either agree with the cliché or say they are not sure. Even the "give-away" wording of the statement did not help the uncertain 33%.

Only the "strongly disagree" response will be analyzed. At least the emphasis will be on that response, since it indicates the lowest degree of bias toward minorities, and we wish to see what backgrounds are associated with unbiased attitudes.

In all instances girls are less biased than boys, although the difference is not so great at the elementary as at the high school level. There is little difference between elementary and high school students in agreeing with Negro inferiority, but the high school students are 4% less biased about sitting near someone of another race or thinking of Jews as strange. On all 3 items the one-sex high school displays less bias than the coeducational high school, as may be seen in Table 66.

Girls, then, in general are 12% less likely than boys to say that sitting near a Negro disturbs them, and high school girls are least disturbed.

Table 66

DISTRIBUTION OF UNBIASED RESPONSES ON
ATTITUDES TOWARD MINORITIES, BY TYPE OF HIGH SCHOOL

Strongly disagree	Coed boys %	All-boy %	Total boys %	Coed girls %	All-girl %	Total girls %
Unskilled work fits Negro mentality	33.5	34.1	33.8	53.0	58.2	56.1
Dislike sitting near another race	50.7	56.2	53.5	65.7	73.3	70.2
Jews are strange, etc.	23.2	28.2	25.7	35.4	42.8	39.7

The same relationships hold for attitudes toward the Jewish stereotype, girls rejecting it 10% more than boys.

Table 66 shows the all-girl schools highest in rejecting Negro inferiority, with coed girls 5% below them. There is little difference in the 2 types of schools for boys, but the boys in both types are twice as likely as the girls to agree with the biased statement.

Again, feelings that cause a student to be disturbed by having to sit near one of another race characterize the coed boys and girls more than the one-sex school students. Coed boys are least likely (50.7%) to adopt the most Christian attitude; all-girl school students are the most likely. Percentage gaps by types of high school may partly reflect social class differences. We shall see in the SC-RB analysis that higher social class is characterized by less bias, and it may be that the all-boy and all-girl schools, some of which are privately operated, costly, and selective, imply higher socioeconomic status than the coeducational high schools. It is not known whether any Negroes or Jews attend these more selective schools.

A substantial proportion of the high school boys, who will enter colleges, occupy administrative positions, serve the professions, or join the labor force in the next decade, will carry with them anti-Negro prejudice or at least convictions of Negro inferiority.

Recognition of the possibility that Negroes may have abilities equal to those of other races does not increase linearly with years of Catholic schooling. It lurches upward irregularly, beginning with 47% rejection of Negro inferiority by those who have had 1–4 years of Catholic schooling, to 52% of those who have had 13 years. The fact that children who have had 12 years reject this statement 3% less than those with only 1–4 years (44% to 47%) casts some doubt on the influence of Catholic schooling in reducing the amount of prejudice.]

Increasing years of Catholic education are associated, however, with somewhat larger proportions disagreeing strongly that it would bother them to sit near a student of another race in school. The increase, though small, is progressively upward from 60% of those with 1–4 years to 68% of those with 13 years, except for the 8-year category, which drops 4% below the categories on either side of it. The Jewish stereotype also tends to be rejected more with increased years of Catholic schooling. A linear increase is observed from 45% of those with 1–4 years strongly rejecting the statement to 51% of those with 13 years (these percentages combine the "disagree strongly" and "disagree somewhat" responses).

The percentage differences between boys and girls, however, also increase with years; elementary students were noted to be only 7 percentage points apart, whereas high school students are 13 points apart.

The evidence from the SC-RB paradigm is unanimous for all 3 questions in indicating that social class is negatively associated with biased responses. Descending proportions reject the biased statements as we move from SC-1 to SC-3 (Table 67).

It is possible, of course, that the lower social classes are more likely to view the Negro as a potential threat in job competition and to favor the status quo, which treats the Negro as if he really were inferior in mental ability and capacity for assuming responsibility. Children may pick up this attitude from conversations reflecting the attitudes of their parents and peers. That this has an occupational more than a social basis seems indicated by the comparatively larger percentages of

Table 67

MEAN PERCENTAGE REJECTING BIASED ATTITUDES
TOWARD MINORITY GROUPS, BY SOCIAL CLASS

Strongly disagree	SC-1 %	SC-2 %	SC-3 %
Negro is inferior mentally	49.2	46.2	44.8
Dislike sitting near another race	63.6	60.1	61.2
Jews are strange, etc.	40.9	32.3	27.3

respondents who say it would not bother them to sit near someone of another race. About 15% more in each social class take that position than reject Negro inferiority.

At first look it seems that the students are more likely to express bias against Jews than against Negroes, but the relatively small numbers rejecting the Jewish stereotype result in part from the very high number who select the "not certain" response. In any case it is clear that upper class status is related to less prejudice toward either minority group.

Religious background as a variable in the SC-RB paradigm does not show any consistent relationship to any of the 3 attitudes toward minorities, each social class being idiosyncratic in this respect. In each of the attitudes toward Negroes, however, the children of SC-1 who have one non-Catholic parent show the least prejudice, and the children with one non-Catholic parent in SC-2 show the most prejudice. A constant and consistent relationship, already noted, is the percentage gap between girls and boys, which within certain cells of the paradigm (SC-2, RB-5 and RB-6) widens to as much as 38%. This suggests that boys may be more conditioned, even at the eighth-grade level, to job competition and economic threat (and perhaps also to cultural aura surrounding sex between the races) than are girls.

Just as the children of better-educated parents are shown to bear less prejudice against minorities, so the evidence is incontrovertible that the best-educated students, whom we arbitrarily assume to be our self-styled A and B students, show significantly less prejudice in their responses than do the C and D students. That A students are the least biased is not surprising since a large proportion of the A students are girls, who show themselves less biased on all minority group items. The combined table indicates the declining unbiased percentages associated with progressively lower scholastic averages.

Religion of parents makes little difference in attitudes toward Negro inferiority. However, examination of each parent's religion cross-tabulated separately against those who would not mind sitting near a Negro reveals that apparently the mother's religion makes some difference, but not in the expected direction. Children of non-Catholic mothers are 3% more likely to express unprejudiced attitudes than are children of Catholic mothers in willingness to sit near someone of another race. Fathers' being Catholic or not makes no significant difference.

Table 68

STUDENT RESPONSES UNBIASED TOWARD MINORITIES,
BY SCHOLASTIC AVERAGE

Strongly disagree (unbiased)	A %	B %	C %	D %
Negro inferiority	53.0	48.4	40.6	36.6
Anti-racial feelings	66.1	60.9	59.5	55.8
Jewish stereotype	40.3	34.1	25.6	22.2

The education of parents evidently has considerable effect on attitudes of prejudice in children. The more (total) education parents have, the more their children strongly disagree with the biased statements. This applies to Catholic education of parents chiefly with respect to anti-Semitism. Each attitude is analyzed separately for its relationship to parents' education.

Total education of parents seems to contribute more to increased unprejudiced attitudes toward Negro inferiority than does Catholic education of parents. Increased years of Catholic education of the fathers have no perceptible effect on percentages of unbiased responses among their children, which hover between 46% and 49% throughout whether the father has had no Catholic schooling or 16 years or more. However, the children increasingly reject this idea as the father's total years of education increase, from 43.6% of the children whose fathers had 1–7 years, to 50.2% of those whose fathers had 16 or more years.

Children whose mothers did not attend Catholic schools show a slightly higher unbiased percentage (48.3%) than those whose mothers had 1–12 years of Catholic schooling (46.0%). If the mothers have had 13–15 years of education in Catholic institutions the unprejudiced percentage rises to 46.0%. The general educational level makes more difference. If the mother had 1–12 years of schooling, 45% of the children are unprejudiced; beyond that level, from 13–17 years or more, the percentages rise to 50.9%. If Catholic schooling has had any effect on parents in reducing biased judgments about Negro ability, it is not consistently reflected in the attitudes expressed by their children. Greater total education, however, is associated with less prejudiced judgment by children.

Total education of parents also has a more consistent relationship to unbiased feelings about sitting near a Negro than does Catholic education. Fathers' total education seems to effect an increase in unprejudiced attitudes for each consecutive span of years, from 58.7% for 1–7 years to 63.7% for 16 years or more. Fathers' Catholic education, however, shows a declining or stationary rate of unprejudiced attitudes from 62.2% if the fathers had no Catholic schooling to 60.2% if they had 16 years or more. Mothers' education shows a similar but even less regular pattern. The conclusion seems that Catholic-educated parents are not conveying unprejudiced attitudes about physical proximity to other races in any degree proportionate to their years of Catholic education, unless the proportion be a negative one. Indeed, considering both fathers and mothers, children whose parents had no Catholic schooling at all are less prejudiced than children of parents with 16 years or more of Catholic schooling (fathers, 62.2%; mothers, 63.1% to 59.4%). The message of brotherly love seems not to have got through to these parents, or at least they do not convey it to their offspring. An alternative explanation is that their social education is deficient to that given in secular schools. Perhaps the social message of the Gospel has not been given the attention it deserves in Catholic schools; perhaps it is taught in an abstract way without application to daily life and concomitant social interaction. One final possibility is that since there are relatively few Negroes in Catholic schools, parents who have been educated in secular schools have had more experience mingling with other races and their children have consequently been less affected by prejudice.

The education of parents shows a definite relationship to attitudes of anti-Semitism. The more education parents have, the more children manifest unbiased attitudes toward the Jews. The patterns of relationship are similar for fathers and mothers with few exceptions. For fathers' education from 1–16 years or more, the total percentage increase in the children's unbiased responses is 19% (from 22.6% to 41.8%); for mothers' it is 18% (from 22.4% to 40.5%). In other words, more education of parents tends to reduce anti-Semitism in children. Education beyond high school is especially influential in increasing unbiased responses in the children.

We observe, too, that the more Catholic education parents have the less anti-Semitism their children express. Catholic-college-educated-mothers induce a 10% increase in unbiased responses over mothers who are Catholic high school graduates (42% to 32%). In comparison, Catholic-college-educated fathers induce a 3.6% increase in children's unbiased responses over fathers who are Catholic high school graduates (38.3% to 34.7%) but still remain below Catholic-college-educated mothers. Children show slightly more bias if their fathers attended Catholic colleges, but slightly less bias if their mothers attended Catholic colleges.

The point is that Catholic education of parents is not as important a variable in the family's influence on attitudes toward race as the degree of interest in and encouragement of the practice of religion within the family. When family religiosity is held constant, we find children of highly religious families rejecting the racially biased statements more frequently than do children of medium and low religious families. In the reduction of racial bias whether the parents are Catholic or whether they have been educated in Catholic schools is not nearly so important as the degree of family religious practice. Attitudes associated with family religious interest and practice are shown in Table 69.

Whether a family is highly religious or not makes little difference, however, in the percentage of children who reject the stereotype of the Jew. Nor does the degree of religiosity seem to relate in any way

Table 69

PERCENTAGES UNCERTAIN OR STRONGLY DISAGREEING WITH BIASED
ATTITUDES TOWARD MINORITY GROUPS, BY FAMILY RELIGIOSITY

| | Family religiosity | | |
Response	High %	Medium %	Low %
Negro is mentally inferior			
Strongly disagree	49.3	45.2	44.2
Not certain	9.9	10.2	11.3
Dislike sitting near another race			
Strongly disagree	66.7	58.8	58.5
Not certain	6.4	9.1	8.2
Something strange about Jews, etc.			
Strongly disagree	32.2	31.4	31.7
Not certain	32.8	31.2	33.2

to the proportions who are uncertain about this question. In both the high and low levels of religiosity 1 out of 3 students select the response "not certain." It seems that even the most religious families do not instill in their children an open-minded attitude toward Jews. The children are as likely to select the uncertain responses as to reject the stereotype by strongly disagreeing. Apparently Catholic school children do not so much have an unfavorable image of Jews as that they have no image at all. This may be accounted for to some extent by infrequency of social contacts between Catholics and Jews.

The final background characteristic to be measured against attitudes of prejudice toward minority groups is frequency of attendance at Mass, which is used as an index of personal religiosity. The more often students attend Mass, the less prejudice they express. Among irregular attenders 31% reject Negro inferiority; among regular attenders the percentage rises to 44%; it rises again to 49% for frequent attenders. Those who accept Negro inferiority drop from 21% of the irregular attenders to 9% of the regular attenders, to 6% for frequent attenders. The children who value the Mass show a stronger disposition to judge Negroes in a Christian way than children who fail to attend Mass regularly (see Table 70).

Even if they sincerely believed in Negro inferiority, it could be expected that those who attend Mass frequently would express the least bias about the proximity of a member of another race, since for Catholics the Mass is a symbol of Christian unity. To participate in the Mass while harboring unfriendly feelings toward any individual or group would cast serious doubts on the sincerity of the worshipper.

Table 70

BIASED AND UNBIASED ATTITUDES TOWARD SITTING NEAR
SOMEONE OF ANOTHER RACE, BY MASS ATTENDANCE

	Irregular	Regular	1–3 per month %	Sunday plus 2–3 per week %	4 or more per week %
Biased responses (strongly agree)	15	8	6	7	7
Unbiased responses (strongly disagree)	49	58	63	64	66

Two inferences can be made from these data: first a clear and consistent progression is observable toward less acceptance and greater rejection of the biased statement as Mass attendance becomes more frequent; second, this observation strengthens the reliability of using Mass attendance as an index of religiosity for Catholic children, since it discriminates the most from the least biased group by a 17% difference. It seems from this and from other analyses that frequent attenders at Mass differ from others in their attitudes as well as in their Mass attendance. The 66% of the Mass attenders represents one of the highest observed percentages of unbiased responses to sitting near someone of another race.

A more tangible relationship is found between the students' personal religiosity and their attitude toward Jews than between family religiosity and attitudes. Of the students who report not attending Mass regularly on Sundays, 24% are unbiased toward Jews; of the regular attenders, 31%, an increase of 7% over the irregular attenders. The students who show the least prejudice are those who attend Mass several times a month besides Sunday; 34% of them reject the Jewish stereotype. We might expect those who go to Mass several times weekly to exceed those who go only several times a month in kindly attitudes toward Jews, but actually the percentages drop from 34% to 29%. This brings the daily Mass attenders 2% below the regular attenders—the only time in our entire Study when the latter group displays more desirable attitudes than the frequent attenders.

More of the frequent attenders select the "not certain" response than do any other group, an unprecedented 38%. This means that nearly 2 out of 5 of these very religious young people do not know how to react when confronted with what would seem an obviously extreme generalization. Many of the most frequent attenders are elementary students, who are as a group 6% more uncertain about how to answer this item than high school students. One wonders whether those most devoted to the Mass feel vaguely that they should not be too favorable toward Jews, and therefore take refuge in the "safe" category of not certain. It is even more puzzling when we recall that the daily attenders at Mass report the least prejudiced attitudes toward Negroes.

One final item dealing with minority groups attempted to discover whether prejudice was strong enough in some instances to overcome the deepest convictions concerning Catholic faith.

ITEM 14

It makes no difference to me whether I receive Holy Communion from a white or a colored priest.

Overwhelmingly the respondents said it makes no difference, 81% agreeing strongly. Girls exceed boys by 4%; elementary students surpass high school students by 5% in agreeing. Very few (2%) disagree strongly. Some interesting differences occur, however, at the secondary level; whereas elementary boys and girls and high school girls all approach 83% agreeing strongly, high school boys are significantly lower, with 74% agreeing strongly. Examination of cross-tabulations against type of high school reveals that coed boys are lowest of all in agreeing that reception of the Holy Communion at the hands of a colored priest makes no difference to them. Their percentage agreeing strongly is 72%, that of the all-boy schools 76%; the coed girls report 81%, and the all-girl schools 84%, strongly agreeing. These differences are due, in part, to sampling from heavy city populations where more Negroes are likely to attend schools with white Catholic children. Diocesan differences are marked and noteworthy, as Table 71 illustrates. This table shows the reaction of 14,519 students in 13 dioceses to attitude questions about minority groups. In general, averages of 5% to 22% expressed prejudiced attitudes toward Negroes and Jews in the context of the 4 statements.

Those who considered manual labor befitting the Negro mental and physical ability average 22% of the entire sample, but the dioceses vary widely in prejudicial answers (from 16% to 37%) around the average. Two-thirds of the respondents reject this statement, although the dioceses vary from one-half to three-fourths disagreeing.

Relatively few students would care whether they receive Holy Communion from a white or a colored priest; 90% of them said it made no difference to them. Another 10% from the same diocese were uncertain (average uncertain response was 5%).

Most of the students (three-fourths) say it would not bother them to sit near a person of another race. Those who say it would bother them range from 11% to 31% by diocese.

The response patterns to the cliché about Jews presents a quite different picture. The children are less likely to take extreme positions on this statement and 3 times as likely to say they are uncertain about it. About 20% agree that Jews are "strange and different"; those who reject this idea range from 34% in 1 diocese to 61% in another. Uncertain responses are as high as 50% in 1 diocese, and only in 1 diocese are less than one-fourth uncertain.

Although the percentages of prejudiced answers vary among the statements and among the dioceses, a general mean shows that 16% of the responses reflect biased attitudes toward the 2 minority groups. In a number of the dioceses it is clear that the degree of bias expressed is related to the proportions of the minority group in the diocese. Schools in these areas can infer from the present data the tasks they face in applying the Christian principle of the brotherhood of all men to their specific situations.

Table 71

RESPONSES TO QUESTIONS ABOUT MINORITY GROUPS, BY DIOCESES

Dioceses	1	2	3	4	5	6	7	8	9	10	11	12	13
(1) Manual labor and unskilled jobs seem to fit the Negro mental and physical ability better than more skilled or responsible work.													
Biased %	17	29	21	20	26	16	37	21	24	17	19	16	23
Unbiased	72	61	67	67	62	68	51	70	66	73	75	75	64
Uncertain	11	10	12	13	12	16	12	9	10	11	6	9	13
(2) It makes no difference to me whether I receive Holy Communion from a white or colored priest.													
Biased %	4	5	4	2	4	1	14	4	6	2	3	3	4
Unbiased	92	87	91	93	92	97	76	93	89	95	93	94	91
Uncertain	4	8	5	5	4	2	10	3	5	3	4	3	5
(3) There is something different and strange about Jews; it is hard to tell what they are thinking and planning, and what makes them tick.													
Biased %	18	20	22	18	19	16	21	23	26	20	12	18	20
Unbiased	50	49	56	46	54	34	38	58	47	47	61	54	54
Uncertain	32	31	34	46	37	50	41	19	27	33	27	28	26
(4) It would bother me to sit next or near a person of another race (e.g., a Negro, a white person) in school.													
Biased %	15	17	15	13	17	16	31	14	18	11	11	11	16
Unbiased	77	72	77	77	76	79	58	80	73	83	86	85	75
Uncertain	8	11	8	10	7	5	11	6	9	6	3	4	9

	All Dioceses combined			
	Total (1)	Total (2)	Total (3)	Total (4)
Biased %	22	5	20	16
Unbiased	67	90	47	76
Uncertain	11	5	33	8

FAMILY VALUES

One of the institutions on which Catholic teaching places the highest value is the family. The Church has consistently abhorred divorce and resisted any social change that seemed to threaten or undermine the stability of the home. Catholic parents are expected to teach their children to value family life, and they expect the Catholic schools to reinforce that teaching. A number of questions were included to get some index of the family values held by Catholic school children. Three of these will be discussed here: attitudes toward divorce with remarriage, toward marrying someone of another religion, and toward teenage steady dating.

Church attitudes toward these 3 practices are not equally inflexible. The first, divorce with remarriage, is never sanctioned by the Church if the marriage was valid originally; second, mixed marriage is permitted with a dispensation; third, the acceptability of steady dating is seen as contingent upon the age of the persons concerned and their prospects for marriage. The attitudes toward marriage and family will be analyzed separately, with occasional references to other index items about related subjects.

Attitudes Toward Divorce with Remarriage

ITEM 16

Even when there are serious difficulties in the family, I still believe that divorce with remarriage is always wrong.

The teaching of the Church on the indissolubility of marriage is unequivocal, so that even the elementary school respondents can be expected to be informed correctly about it. Table 72 indicates how the responses were distributed.

It is clear that the modal response was overwhelmingly a reflection of the Catholic position on divorce. Combining the 2 "agree" responses indicates that 4 out of 5 students believe divorce with remarriage to be wrong, whereas only 1 out of 7 expressed disagreement. The analysis that follows will examine only the correlates of the strongly agreeing 71%.

Boy-girl differences are not pronounced, the boys strongly agreeing 69%, the girls 72%. The elementary school and the high school are only 3% apart in "strongly agree" percentages. However, when grade level and sex are constant, only the elementary school exhibits this consensus, both boys and girls registering 71% in agreement. High school boys drop to 67% agreeing strongly, compared with 73% of high school girls.

The analytic SC-RB paradigm shows revealing relationships between background factors and the varying degrees to which different groups express agreement that divorce is wrong. The range of this agreement is from 56% to 78%.

Table 72

FREQUENCY AND PERCENTAGE DISTRIBUTION OF RESPONSES
TO THE STATEMENT THAT DIVORCE WITH REMARRIAGE IS WRONG

Response	Frequency	%
Strongly agree	10,165	70.6
Agree somewhat	1,455	10.1
Not certain	592	4.1
Disagree somewhat	1,163	8.1
Strongly disagree	1,019	7.1
Total	14,394	100.0

Social class is not a powerful discriminator among attitudes condemning divorce. All 3 social classes are at the general mean (72.1%). Religious background accounts for greater difference in response patterns, every social class manifesting a declining scale of agreement for its 6 RB groups, moving from the most to the least Catholic background. The highest percentages condemning divorce with remarriage are always found where either or both parents have had a Catholic education; the average for RB-1, 2, 3, combined is 74.9%, compared with 70.7% for RB-4, 5, 6. Ranking lowest in percentages agreeing are the RB-5 children, who are Catholic-school-educated and have one non-Catholic parent (62%).

Table 73

PERCENTAGES CONDEMNING DIVORCE WITH REMARRIAGE,
BY SOCIAL CLASS AND RELIGIOUS BACKGROUND*

	RB-1 %	RB-2 %	RB-3 %	RB-4 %	RB-5 %	RB-6 %
SC-1 (X = 72.3%)	78	73	72	70	67	68
SC-2 (X = 71.6%)	77	72	74	71	56	66
SC-3 (X = 72.5%)	76	77	74	73	64	61
RB means	77	74	74	72	62	64

* Paradigm mean = 72.1%.

A check was made to see if having a non-Catholic parent is a significant variable associated with attitude toward divorce. A cross-tabulation of father's religion against responses shows that 72% of children
of Catholic fathers condemn divorce with remarriage, whereas 61%
of children of non-Catholic fathers do—a significantly lower figure.
Comparable figures for respondents' mothers show an almost identical
ratio: 71% if she is Catholic, 61% if she is not. It is at least plausible
that the non-Catholic partner in a mixed marriage would hold more
tolerant views of divorce than the Catholic, who presumably accepts
the total value system of the Church in respect to the indissolubility
of marriage.

A comparison of the means of RB-4 and RB-6 seems to indicate that
the children's Catholic schooling makes a difference in attitude. Both
of these categories are made up of respondents who have 2 Catholic
parents, but the children in RB-4 have had a Catholic education and
those in RB-6 have not. The percentage condemning divorce with
remarriage is larger in RB-4, averaging 72%, whereas it is 64% for
RB-6. Cross-tabulations confirm the importance of schooling, for there
is a very consistent linear progression in percentages agreeing with the
statement from 64% of those who have had 1–4 years of Catholic
schooling to 74% for those with 13 years. This finding cannot be attributed merely to age and maturity, since the respondents in RB-6, as in
every other RB category, are both elementary and high school students;
yet they agree less than the others that divorce is wrong.

Next, the influence of actual religious practice in the home. As we would anticipate, children from homes that give active encouragement to religion accept Catholic teaching on divorce more than children whose families' interest in religion is very low. Children of highly religious families are 6% above the general mean, with 77% opposing divorce with remarriage; those from medium religious families fall near the mean, with 70%, the low religious group falls below the mean, with 68%. This intervening variable, family religious practice, as well as Catholicity and Catholic schooling in parents is important, although it cannot be completely dissociated from either of them.

Customary Mass attendance is reflected clearly in students' attitude toward divorce with remarriage. The irregular attenders are 15% below the general mean, with 46% opposing divorce; even the regular attenders are 4% below the mean, with 67% taking that position; but the frequent attenders are above the mean, with percentages of 74% to 76% saying divorce with remarriage is wrong. This represents a 30% gap between the most-and the least-devoted to Mass attendance as they express disapproval of divorce with remarriage.

The self-rated academic averages produced an interesting cross-tabulation with attitude toward divorce. Two things become apparent. First, the higher the scholastic average the student assigns himself, the more likely he is to oppose divorce. Thus, our percentages for A to D students run 79%, 72%, 66%, and 61%, respectively. Second, throughout the discussion of this item we have not yet observed a percentage as high as 79% opposing divorce, even when cross-tabulating that attitude against Catholicity of parents, family or personal religiosity. Whether these students have correctly assigned themselves grade averages or not, their selection of the most desirable answer, that is, the one that conforms most closely to Catholic ideals, is strongly related to the self-assigned ratings.

Respondents most of whose friends and associates chiefly attend Catholic schools are more inclined to agree that divorce with remarriage is wrong than those who only have half their friends in Catholic schools or those who associate mostly with friends not in Catholic schools. Peer group influence once more shows its strength in the comparative percentages recorded in Table 74.

Table 74

PERCENTAGES REPUDIATING DIVORCE WITH REMARRIAGE,
BY TYPE OF SCHOOL ATTENDED BY MOST FRIENDS

	Strongly agree divorce with remarriage is wrong %
Most friends in Catholic schools	73.8
Half in Catholic schools	67.3
Most friends not in Catholic schools	62.4

This apparently strong relationship between association with Catholic school students and disapproval of divorce corroborates a pilot study in which the same question was addressed to students in Catholic schools and to a control group of Catholic students in public schools. The percentages reported there not only correspond closely to those given here but also correspond linearly to the respondents' respective years of Catholic school attendance.

Table 75

PERCENTAGES REPUDIATING DIVORCE,
BY TYPE OF STUDENT RESPONDENT*

Number	Type of student	Average years of Catholic schooling	Percentages repudiating divorce
322	Catholic high	10.8	73.0
807	Catholic elementary	7.9	68.2
125	CCD high	5.8	60.8
221	CCD elementary	3.1	55.7

* Unpublished data collected for dissertation by Sister M. James Rau, O.P.

Other Measures of Family Values

Further assessment of the high value placed on family cohesion by the Catholic Church is provided by answers to 2 other questions. The first in Item 31 asks for the students' evaluation of strong family ties vis-a-vis money and possession.

ITEM 31

Money and possessions do not help a family to be successful as much as strong personal ties among family members.

Table 76 shows that more than half the students agree on the importance of personal ties over money and possessions. Boys fall below this general mean with 49% agreeing, girls exceed it with 59%. Older students give evidence of considerably greater appreciation for personal values in family life than elementary school students; 61% of them take the "strongly agree" position, compared with 49% of the younger pupils.

Table 76

DISTRIBUTION OF RESPONSES ON IMPORTANCE OF MONEY AND POSSESSIONS COMPARED WITH STRONG FAMILY TIES

Response	Frequency	%
Strongly agree	7,874	54.9
Agree somewhat	3,570	24.9
Not certain	1,377	9.6
Disagree somewhat	1,129	7.9
Strongly disagree	390	2.7
Total	14,340	100.0

However, when high school students are categorized by type of school, 2 facts about their responses emerge. First, whereas somewhat over half of the high school boys agree to the importance of family cohesion over family possessions, two-thirds of the high school girls do so. Second, there is no significant difference in the students in coeducatonal schools as compared with those in all-boy and all-girl schools.

Item 31 was directed at an intellectual commitment to the value of close family relationship. Item 40 aimed to elicit an expression of preference showing the actual commitment of students to their families. They were asked to rank their choice of activities with their families, their school friends, and their out-of-school friends. The average of those assigning first choice to family activities was 44%. Sex differences around this mean were small, but as anticipated the age differential was crucial as a discriminator. Elementary students were 23% more likely to prefer family activities over peer group activities than were high school students (55% to 32%).

ITEM 40

Which of these do you like to do best, which second best, and which third?

   a. Doing things with my family and relatives
   b. Doing things with my school friends
   c. Doing things with my out-of-school friends

High school responses vary by type of school attended. Family activities rank first only for all-girl school students. They enjoy second choice for boys and girls in coeducational institutions, and third place for boys in all-boy schools. The previous evaluation of strong personal ties among family members reported differences of only 2% in support of family cohesion; here we find differences of 3% to 12% in expressed preference for family activities (Table 77). Although girls generally

Table 77

PERCENTAGES PREFERRING FAMILY ACTIVITIES TO
ACTIVITIES WITH FRIENDS, BY TYPE OF HIGH SCHOOL

Type of school	%
All-boy	24.6
Coed boys	27.8
Coed girls	33.8
All-girl	36.6

place higher value on family activities than boys, it appears that all-girl school students do so a little more than their counterparts in coeducational institutions. It is possible that the coeducational setting has something to do with the variations in preferences.

Attitudes Toward Mixed Marriages

Item 38 was designed to discover attitudes toward entering a mixed marriage. Admittedly this is a remote consideration for many of our respondents, yet mixed marriage is of sufficient concern among Catholics that the majority of our sample would have heard it discussed and have formed some feelings about it. Again, no assumption is made about whether respondents will or will not in the future behave consistently with the attitudes they express.

ITEM 38

Which of the following best expresses your feelings about marrying someone of a different religion than yours?

a. the person I love and marry will have to be a Catholic
b. the person I love and marry will most likely be a Catholic
c. I don't intend to marry
d. the person I love and marry will not have to be a Catholic although I would like to marry a Catholic
e. the person I love and marry need not be a Catholic so far as I am concerned

In the overall responses to this question, 23% said that the person they would marry would have to be a Catholic; 25% said that the person they would marry would most likely be a Catholic; 12% said they did not intend to marry. Considering the first 2 responses as the most positive positions, students giving them are defined as "most committed." Of these there are 6850, 48% of the entire sample. On the "less committed" side, 36% said their marriage partner would not necessarily have to be a Catholic, although they would like to marry one; an additional 4% said that as far as they were concerned the person they would marry need not be a Catholic (Table 78).

Girls report 9% more than boys on the committed side (52% to 43%), and high school students exceed elementary students by 16% as committed (56% to 40%). Type of high school cross-tabulated against this item reveals a lack of consensus among secondary school students toward marrying a Catholic. All-girl school students value intrafaith marriage the most (63%), all-boy school students the least (45%). Intermediate between these extremes are the coed boys and girls, who differ

Table 78

FREQUENCY AND DISTRIBUTION OF RESPONSES SHOWING
DEGREES OF COMMITMENT TO MARRYING WITHIN THE CATHOLIC FAITH

Response	Frequency	%
The person I marry:		
Must be a Catholic	3,289	23.0
Will most likely be a Catholic	3,561	24.9
Don't intend to marry	1,676	11.7
Should preferably be a Catholic	5,140	36.0
Need not be a Catholic	620	4.4
	14,286	100.0

little in evaluating marriage to a Catholic (55% for coed boys, 56% for coed girls). Apparently this value is weakest in all-boy schools and strongest in all-girl schools.

Using only those respondents who fit into one of the 6 RB categories of the paradigm, we find 49.7% as a general average in the committed group. This average varies widely when examined according to social class and other background factors. Considering only social class variables, we find SC-1 falling below the general mean, SC-2 at the mean, and SC-3 slightly above it.

In other words, the highest degree of commitment is found in the lowest social class, as was true of the highest percentage condemning divorce, although in neither is there a great percentage difference between SC-1 and the other classes for commitment to marry a Catholic. See the findings reported so far for commitment to marrying a Catholic are consonant with those reported for correlates of opposing divorce with remarriage. Those with two Catholic parents, especially Catholic-school-educated parents, have the highest percentages in the SC-RB paradigm holding both these values.

Appreciation of marrying a Catholic as a positive value tends to increase with age and grade progression. Thus, elementary students give 41% favorable responses, high school students 56%, or 15% more. The degree of commitment also increases with the number of years the children have spent in Catholic schools.

Of the students whose self-assigned scholastic averages are A, 51% say they will marry a Catholic; also 48% of the B students, 47% of the

C students, and 41% of the D students. The range of 10% between the highest and lowest here is narrower than for almost any other attitude correlated against scholastic self-rating, considerably lower than the 18% gap between A and D students who disapproved strongly of divorce. Yet the findings are consistent in direction.

If the respondents are irregular in their attendance at Sunday Mass, they fall far below the general mean in proportions committed to marrying a Catholic (31%). If they are regular attenders they approach it (47%); and if they are frequent attenders they slightly exceed the mean (50%). These figures may not be so impressive as many would like them to be, particularly in view of the fact that from one-third to one-half of all respondents are not in this strongly committed group. Indeed, the modal response for all categories, including those who go to Mass daily, is that their marriage partner will not have to be a Catholic, although they would like to marry a Catholic. One out of 5 of the irregular Mass attenders is completely indifferent to the religion of the marriage partner (20%), but among those who attend Mass regularly this falls to 5%, and among frequent Mass attenders to 2%. The pattern of responses for this question is similar to responses condemning divorce with remarriage, but on that question a 30% difference separated the occasional Mass attenders from the frequent attenders, whereas here the percentage difference is 19%. Throughout this analysis, attitudes opposing divorce have proved to rate higher percentages than attitudes strongly supportive of marrying within the Catholic faith.

Qualities Valued in a Prospective Spouse

In Item 45, also dealing with family values, students were asked to rate in importance certain qualities they would desire in a prospective partner in marriage.

ITEM 45

Show how important to you each of the following would be if you were choosing a marriage partner:

a. a person who is a good provider or a good household manager
b. a pleasant person

    c. a morally good person

    d. a person who loves children

    e. a deeply spiritual person

The overall percentages rating each quality in degree of importance are presented in Table 79. More girls than boys rated each of the qualities very important. The largest differences were observed in evaluating "one who loves children" (girls, 85%; boys, 72%), in high school girls' evaluation of a good provider (73%) over high school boys' evaluation of a good household manager (59%), and in high school girls attributing importance to a spouse being deeply spiritual (girls, 42%; boys 27%).

Table 79

RATING OF QUALITIES IN A PROSPECTIVE SPOUSE
ON A SCALE OF IMPORTANCE*

Quality	Very important %	Fairly important %	Slightly important %	Not at all important %
A morally good person	82.3	13.7	1.2	.45
A person who loves children	79.5	15.3	1.8	.76
A pleasant person	73.5	23.1	1.5	.30
A good provider or household manager	62.5	29.1	3.8	1.7
A deeply spiritual person	36.5	42.9	9.1	3.9

* Percentages do not add up to 100 because "Not certain" responses are omitted.

It is apparent that morality in a spouse is considered highly desirable by all groups, spirituality relatively less so. The essential family values of love of children and pleasant personality are highlighted, whereas the skills of achieving a good income or being an efficient manager of a household are considered relatively less important. In this type of question one alternative receives fewer "very important" designations than the others. That fact does not necessarily imply rejection of the value of that alternative, but only rates it less in comparison with the other alternative. In this case, we would not be justified in concluding that deep spirituality is not valued by the respondents, particularly since 43% of the respondents designated deep spirituality "fairly important." On another question students were asked if they thought money and the things money can buy are likely to be harmful to one's religious and spiritual life; a measure of their evaluation of the spiritual against the material can be gleaned from the fact that two-thirds of them agreed, either strongly or somewhat, that such a danger really exists.

Questions Related To Morality

Item 36 attempted to discover how common the currently prevalent practice of steady dating is among students.

ITEM 36

Do you date the same person to the exclusion of all others?

The only response choices were "yes" and "no."

Steady dating, like all dating behavior, is strongly related to age. Therefore, we will first examine high school and elementary school responses separately. Before doing so, we might note that the proportions of our total sample who say they date one person exclusively is 22%; 78% say "no." The overall percentage of affirmative respondents obscures the great divergence between elementary and secondary students, as well as between boys and girls. Table 80 shows the order of increasing frequency of going steady by school groups. This indicates an excess of several percent on the part of boys over girls going steady regardless of school grade level.

Table 80

DISTRIBUTION OF EXCLUSIVE DATING, BY SEX AND GRADE LEVEL

| | Steady daters | |
School group	%	Mean %
Elementary school girls	9	
		11
Elementary school boys	14	
High school girls	32	
		33
High school boys	35	

When we attempt to relate background factors to going steady at the elementary school level we are speaking of only 10.5% of the total elementary school sample, or 798 children out of 7107 who answered the question (441 elementary students failed to answer, constituting a 6% "no response" group). Consequently, when we use the SC-RB paradigm of 36 cells to distribute these 798 steady daters we will expect to find some rather small cell frequencies, which will require higher significance levels to be reliable and meaningful. The paradigm shows slightly more going steady in the SC-1 group than in SC-2 or SC-3. This is not a consistent trend, however, as examination of RB categories shows. Moreover, 12 of the 35 cells in the paradigm gave frequencies under 10. Neither social class nor religious background relates strongly to going steady among elementary students. Referring once more to the relative infrequency of steady dating among students at this level, it is understandable that holding social class and religious background constant results in small percentage differences.

High school students engage in exclusive dating 3 times as much as elementary students. One out of 3 high school respondents say they date exclusively, and more high school boys go steady than high school girls (35% to 32%). Social class tends to have a definite relationship here. SC-1 students have the lowest percentage, 28.3%, going steady; SC-2 reports 33.2%; SC-3 reports 33.9%. The lowest social class is associated with the greatest amount of exclusive dating.

For purposes of comparison and brevity we again combine the age-grade levels in examining the effects of specific background factors on percentages going steady with the reminder that the overall average is 21.1%. Children of Catholic parents report going steady 2% or 3% less than children of non-Catholic parents; the former are at or slightly below the general mean, the latter 2 or 3 percentage points above it.

Percentages going steady decrease as fathers' total years of schooling increases. Thus when the fathers had only 1–7 years of schooling the children report 26% going steady; if the fathers had 17 years or more the percentage drops to 17%. When the years of Catholic education of the fathers are considered, the trend is the same, declining from 23% of those whose fathers had no Catholic schooling to 14% of those whose fathers had 17 or more years.

Similarly, mothers' total schooling correlates negatively with children's steady dating, percentages dropping from 28% to 16% as mothers' years of schooling increase. Catholic education of mothers likewise discloses a negative relationship, percentages falling from 22% to 16%. Clearly the fact of either parent's having had Catholic education tends to keep the rate of going steady moderately lower among their off-spring. Children of parents who have had some college education go steady in smaller proportions than those whose parents had no college, but the impact of college education tends to reduce steady dating slightly more if it was pursued in Catholic institutions.

Steady dating is related negatively to associating chiefly with friends in Catholic schools; 21% of these respondents go steady, but of the students who say most of their friends do not attend Catholic schools, 26% report going steady. If half their friends attend Catholic schools, 22% go steady.

Young people who go steady and who are thinking seriously of marrying soon would not be expected to plan more Catholic (or any) education, and as expected those who plan more Catholic education go steady 17% less than those who are not planning to continue their Catholic schooling (14% compared with 31%). If they are uncertain about future educational plans their rate of going steady reaches an intermediate position at 26%.

As the student rates his own scholastic average higher, he tends to go steady less. A substantial increase in proportions going steady occurs between each self-rated grade average level.

Related to the subject of dating behavior is a question on the morality of necking and petting. Although definitions of these practices vary somewhat, children in Catholic schools, especially high schools, can be expected to be informed on what is or is not permitted in this regard.

ITEM 2

I do not object to such things as necking and petting, as these are just a part of growing up.

Expected sex and grade differences appeared, with girls strongly disapproving of these practices over 2–1 more than boys (52% to 23%), and high school students disapproving 16% more than elementary students (47% to 31%). This last finding can probably be interpreted in the light of greater understanding of sex morality by older students. At both levels, boys adopt a more permissive attitude, the girls maintaining their 2–1 ratio of disapproval: high school 62% to 28%, elementary school 41% to 20%.

It was conjectured that high school students are more aware of the aspects of morality of sex behavior than are elementary students. It would be astonishing if this were not true, yet it is also conceivable that increasing maturity brings a growing awareness of variations, if not downright contradictions, between what they have been taught about sex morality and socially approved patterns of behavior. This conflict would seem to be one explanation for the fact that our high school respondents agree more than our elementary school respondents in Item 33.

Table 81

PERCENTAGES STRONGLY DISAPPROVING OF NECKING AND PETTING, BY TYPE OF HIGH SCHOOL

Type of school	% strongly disapproving	% point difference
All-girl	67	—
Coed girls	55	12
Coed boys	30	25
All-boy	4	26

ITEM 33

Sometimes I am uncertain as to what the Catholic Church teaches about what is right and wrong in behavior.

This cautiously worded statement embodying the catch-all "sometimes" elicited agreeing (strongly or somewhat) responses from 56.2% of all respondents. The most frequently selected response for all groups was "agree somewhat." One-third of the students claimed complete certainty about Catholic morals by rejecting the statement 33.3%. When sex and grade level are constant, high school students admit more uncertainty than do elementary students, 62% to 50.0%.

EDUCATIONAL ASPIRATIONS

A further dimension of student attitudes is the way they feel about future educational plans. Some research suggests that Catholics have been less oriented toward higher education than have Jews and Protestants. Recent research shows that although this may have been true in earlier immigrant days, attitude of Catholics toward higher education has changed. Here we present an analysis of the educational goals of the students as indicated by the responses to Item 29 of the SAI.

ITEM 29

The opportunity to go to college is extremely important to me.

Table 82 shows the distribution of the responses of eighth- and twelfth-grade students separately. Among the combined responses of elementary and secondary students 61% make the strongest response on the value of college opportunity. When the levels are compared, the elementary students place a higher value on college opportunity; 10% more of these younger students select the "strongly agree" category, and the 10% difference persists when the 2 "agreeing" categories are combined. It is possible that the twelfth-grade students are more realistic about college requirements, admission problems, and financial consideration.

High school boys are clearly more convinced of the importance of college for them than are the girls; 66.3% of the boys "strongly agree"

Table 82

FREQUENCY AND DISTRIBUTION OF RESPONSES
PLACING VALUE ON THE OPPORTUNITY FOR COLLEGE

Response	Elementary		High school	
	Frequency	%	Frequency	%
Strongly agree	4919	66.01	3894	56.74
Agree somewhat	1278	17.15	1176	17.14
Uncertain	510	6.84	500	7.29
Disagree somewhat	458	6.15	795	11.59
Strongly disagree	287	3.85	497	7.24

as compared with 49.6% of the girls. The boys and girls who responded to the Index were to graduate from high school in June 1963. The principals of the 2075 Catholic high schools reported that of the total graduates (155,698) of the June 1962 class, 54.2% continued their education beyond high school; this compares with the 56.7% of the respondents to the Index who placed the highest importance on attending college (Table 82). Also, the principals' reports showed that 64.1% of the boys and 46.5% of the girls who graduated in June 1962 continued their education beyond high school. These figures correspond closely with the percentages of boys and girls who identified college education as most important to them. Because of a strong proclivity to downgrade the responses of girls in attitude inquiries on the basis that they try to respond in the socially expected manner, it is most interesting that in this instance the girls' response corresponds very closely with the actual practice of the girls who preceded them only a year earlier.

Table 83 shows that boys place a higher valuation on higher education, but also that the type of high school attended affects students' evaluation. The separate schools exceed the coeducational schools; all-boy schools have the highest percentage placing the highest value on college education. This is not surprising because these separate schools are usually organized for college preparation and are highly selective in their admission policies. Social class was identified with the value that students attached to college education; the higher the social class, the greater the valuation placed on futher education. It was expected that the more successful students would have a higher

Table 83

IMPORTANCE OF GOING TO COLLEGE, BY TYPES OF HIGH SCHOOL

Response	Total Boys No.	%	Girls No.	%	Coed boys No.	%	All-boy No.	%	Coed girls No.	%	All-girls No.	%
Strongly agree	1972	66.3	1912	49.6	889	60.9	1083	71.6	727	45.6	1185	51.9
Agree somewhat	454	15.2	719	18.4	237	16.2	217	14.3	272	17.0	447	19.5
Uncertain	236	7.9	263	6.7	138	9.4	98	6.4	140	8.7	123	5.3
Disagree somewhat	216	7.2	577	14.9	136	9.3	80	5.2	280	17.5	297	13.0
Strongly disagree	93	3.1	403	10.4	59	4.0	34	2.2	173	10.8	230	10.0

regard for advanced education than they did. The extent of parents' education was significantly related to the students' valuation of college education; 77% of the students whose parents had at least a college education and 44% of those whose parents did not complete grade 8 placed their response in the highest category. Other personal and family characteristics did not prove to be strong discriminators in the attitude toward college education.

Two items in the Index probed students' attitudes toward memorization of answers and of discussion questions. Item 12 related specifically to classes in religion.

ITEM 12

In religion classes I like to discuss religious matters rather than to memorize answers.

The other item was related to the general instruction program. It seems that stronger inferences might be drawn from student responses to Item 12 in that it might be hypothesized that a more dogmatic attitude toward instruction might be encouraged. Of the total respondents (14,519), 71% strongly preferred discussion to memorization, and girls exceeded the boys in this preference 73% to 69%. The more mature high school students exhibited their preference for discussion at 78%; 65% of the elementary students made this choice. Table 84, which distributes the responses of high school students by types of schools, shows the girls in all-girl schools strongest in their desire for discussion of religious questions as opposed to memorization.

Table 84

DISCUSSION IN RELIGIOUS CLASSES RATHER THAN MEMORIZING
ANSWERS, RESPONSES BY TYPES OF HIGH SCHOOLS

Response	Total Boys No.	%	Girls No.	%	Coed boys No.	%	All-boy No.	%	Coed girls No.	%	All-girl No.	%
Strongly agree	2233	75.0	3139	80.9	1046	71.4	1187	78.4	1239	77.5	1900	83.3
Agree somewhat	481	16.1	572	14.7	250	17.0	231	15.2	291	18.2	281	12.3
Uncertain	114	3.8	62	1.6	68	4.6	46	3.0	25	1.5	37	1.6
Disagree somewhat	86	2.8	70	1.8	65	4.4	21	1.3	32	2.0	38	1.6
Strongly disagree	63	2.0	33	0.8	35	2.3	28	1.8	10	0.6	23	1.0

Once again as might be expected, the self-rated A students showed greater desire for discussion than did the D students. The group that showed the least preference for discussion was made up of those students who had a small amount of Catholic school experience and whose parents had little or no Catholic school education. These students might be exhibiting their insecurity in formal religion classes by their willingness to rely on the memorized answer rather than risk discussion in areas not familiar to them.

SUMMARY OF ICSO-2 FINDINGS

The pattern of background factors that relate most strongly to the attitudes conforming to Catholic ideals must be familiar by now. Those selecting the Catholic position most consistently are girls rather than boys, and often elementary students rather than high school students. They are likely to have had all or most of their education in Catholic schools and plan to continue their education in Catholic institutions. They perceive themselves as successful in school, rating themselves as A or B students, and their afterschool and weekend associates are selected chiefly from among other Catholic school students. They are not satisfied with attending Mass regularly on Sundays and holy days, but attend several times weekly in addition to Sundays.

As for their families, most of these students have 2 Catholic parents, one or both of whom have had considerable education, either in Catholic or in secular schools or colleges. The relationship of social class to endorsing the Catholic position differs with various questions. Upper class status is associated with less prejudice toward minority groups and more frequent Mass attendance, whereas middle and lower class status reflects stronger support of religious vocations and of Catholic family values as measured by attitudes toward divorce and mixed marriage. Finally, these supportive families take considerable interest in religion, and they make prayer and discussion of religious topics a regular part of the home life.

These personal and familial characteristics are not unexceptionably associated with the most favorable attitudes, but this happens sufficiently often to warrant the generalization, and where it does not, the text has discussed the findings completely. A clear implication of this report is that it is not warranted to refer to the attitudes of "Catholic school children" as if Catholic schooling were a unifying factor operating always and everywhere in precisely the same manner. Not only the backgrounds of the students reported here, but also the region, the diocese, and peculiar local circumstances all play a part in influencing their attitudes.

Religious-Moral Attitudes

The students combined responses ("strongly" and "somewhat") to the religious-moral values showed 82.7% antithetical to the proposition that it is unnecessary to help others in order to get to heaven. Faithful in attending Mass at least once a week were 95.9%, with more than half the respondents (52.5%) attending even more frequently. Strong support for vocations to the priesthood and the sisterhood were indicated by 85.1%, who said they would be happy to hear that one of their best friends planned to enter a seminary or a convent.

These are impressive percentages endorsing the Catholic values embodied in the items presented. Some concern might be voiced that elementary students gave stronger support to these values than did high school students. Our research does not reveal how much of this difference is due to greater idealism on the one hand or to greater sophistication on the other, but it does suggest areas of inquiry.

Almost without exception the responses showed higher percentages of girls accepting the Catholic position than boys. This was found true at both the high school and the elementary level, and it is indeed a common finding in behavioral research. The students in all-girl high schools usually ranked highest of all groups in "desirable" responses. Aside from any natural tendency of girls to be more pliable and conforming, some percentage differences were of considerable proportions. This may suggest that different approaches to religious and moral questions may be indicated for boys and for girls, especially at the high school level. Those responsible for Catholic secondary education may wish to conduct further comparative inquiries into the nonacademic outcomes of coeducational, coinstitutional, and single-sex school organizations.

The report on the "necessity of helping others" indicates that some 13% of the respondents did not think it necessary, and 4% were not sure. Those interested in Catholic education may desire to see more emphasis placed on this central Christian message of concern for one's neighbor.

Indications are clear that children who fail in their obligation to attend Mass are also significantly less Catholic in their attitudes than those who are faithful to or exceed this obligation. The high endorsement of Catholic attitudes by those who attend Mass beyond their obligation suggests that the encouragement given by home and school to frequent voluntary Mass attendance and the opportunity for the same provided by the schools is sound practice.

The affirmation that Catholic schools are logically and empirically the most fruitful source of religious vocations is further supported by a study of divinity students in which the statement is made that "Catholic religious personnel come overwhelmingly from students who have attended Catholic schools."[8] Our findings should be of interest to those responsible for the promotion of vocations and could indicate areas for further examination.

Although only 5.5% of the respondents indicated opposition to a friend's vocation, roughly twice that many expressed uncertainty about their own feelings over such an eventuality. The subject of a religious career considered as a value in itself, not simply in reference to the student's own life plans, may not have received adequate attention, leaving some of them without sufficient information or conviction to form a judgment. The pilot study mentioned earlier discovered that more Catholic students in CCD classes expressed uncertainty about their feelings over a friend's vocation to the priesthood than did students enrolled in Catholic schools.[8] A worthwhile goal might be the development of a broader and more informed view of vocations for all Catholic students, those attending CCD classes as well as those enrolled in Catholic schools.

Parents can hardly be uninterested in the obviously strong relationship between active encouragement of religion in the home and the attitudes of children as revealed in the Study. The types of encouragement specified in the questionnaire were family prayer, commemoration of religious feasts, and discussion of religion. The families where these are a part of daily life or where they occur very frequently are represented in the Study by children whose attitudes and values set them apart from those in whose homes religion is relatively weak. Parents who may have expected the Catholic school to assume full responsibility for the total religious formation of their children will perceive how essential is the collaboration of home and school.

Attitudes Toward Minorities

The second part of the attitude questionnaire showed the students rejecting bias toward minorities in varying degrees: half of them rejected the Jewish stereotype; two-thirds refused to accept the idea of native inferiority of Negroes for skilled and responsible work; and three-fourths indicated that it would not bother them to sit near some-one of another race in school. The obverse of this means that roughly 1 student in 5 or 6 expressed biased feelings or convictions; 2 in 3 were uncertain about Jews; and 1 in 2 was uncertain about Negroes. When sex and grade level were constant, the boys at both levels were shown to be more prejudiced than the girls.

Regional differences do occur, and Catholics in certain areas may disclaim any relevance of the results for their schools. However, the Christian teaching of the value of every human person in the sight of God appears to be inoperative for this minority of students in Catholic schools. Perhaps a deep diagnostic look is called for by Catholic schools and their leadership, at how or whether these principles are being presented. Indeed such an analysis would be beneficial to all schools in the United States, private or public.

Self-examination by Catholic schools may be especially necessary with respect to anti-Semitism. As reported earlier, regardless of the degree of family or personal religious devotion, the respondents in this Study were as likely to select the uncertain response about Jews being "strange and different" as they were to disagree with it. Rather than an unfavorable image of Jews, some Catholic children appear to have no image at all. Whether these findings indicate bias, ignorance, lack of contact, or inability to interpret the question, Catholic educators may desire to open a dialogue among Catholic students that will broaden their understanding of the Jewish and other minorities.

Throughout the analyses of attitudes toward minorities cross-tabulated against parents' education, it was abundantly evident that children express more totally acceptable attitudes in proportion as their parents have experienced more education. Whether the education was in Catholic institutions or not, the most highly educated parents had the least biased children. Implications are that education has more subtle values than the more obvious ones of increasing occupational and financial opportunities. The offspring of highly educated persons benefit in a broader understanding of human relations. A further implication is that favorable attitudes can be transmitted informally in the home and reinforced in the process of formal schooling. Again the focus turns on the crucial factor of collaboration between Catholic home and Catholic school if values of a specifically Catholic nature are to be encouraged successfully in all children in Catholic schools.

Family Values

Acceptance of Catholic norms with respect to remarriage after divorce characterized 80.7% of the respondents in this Study; by contrast 15.1% did not oppose divorce with remarriage. A lesser percentage (47.0%) reported that their marriage partners would have to be or would most likely be a Catholic. Thus the children's responses correspond to the relative strictness with which the Church views those 2 practices. If a third category of response—"prefer to marry a Catholic"—is added, it brings to 83.9% the respondents who value marriage within their own religious group. Only 4.4% express complete indifference to the religion of a prospective spouse. Thus 2 strongly held doctrines of the Catholic Church, Catholic marriage and the indissolubility of marriage, are upheld by these students.

The current ecumenical movement may well have an impact on the Catholic view of mixed marriages that will modify this attitude in Catholic students of the future. Indeed this may already have occurred. If the proposed changes are adopted by Vatican II, interfaith Christian marriages will become easier and will lose some of their stigma. It is noteworthy that in this Study children who have one non-Catholic parent report 22% less commitment to marrying a Catholic than do the others. If this relatively liberal view is maintained by these children, the result may well be a kind of self-perpetuating acceptance of marrying outside the faith, especially if official modification of censorious attitude toward mixed marriage is adopted by the Church.

Reactions to the numbers of elementary and high school students who report going steady will vary according to the viewpoints of those examining the proportions and the degree of their responsibility for dating practices among students. An important point here is that a highly significant 21% difference is observed in this practice between the highest (self-rated) school success and the lowest. The percentage of students going steady declines progressively as the students' perception of their own academic success improves, from 34% of the D students to 13% of those who see themselves as A students. There is a mild suggestion here that students may be substituting an easy social goal for a more difficult academic one, but the data offer no validation of this conjecture.

The relationship between steady dating and plans to continue (Catholic) education indicates that these may influence one another, since the steady daters are much less likely to plan more Catholic education than are the others. Educators who try to encourage able students to continue their studies may desire to study this relationship further. Whether exclusive dating leads to abandonment of educational aspirations, indicates plans for early marriage, or merely characterizes students intending to transfer to secular educational institutions, all would be valuable information for Catholic parents and school people, especially those responsible for counseling and guidance.

References

[1] Pope Pius XI, "Divini Illius Magistri," *Five Great Encyclicals* (New York: Paulist Press, 1939), p. 65.

[2] Commission on American Citizenship, *Better Men For Better Times* (Washington, D. C.: Catholic University Press, 1943), p. 105.

[3] Sister Mary Joan, O.P., and Sister Mary Nona, O.P., *Guiding Growth in Christian Social Living* 3 vols. (Washington, D.C.: The Catholic University Press, 1944), 1, 87.

[4] Floud, Jean, and A. H. Halsey, *"The Sociology of Education," Current Sociology*, VII, 3 (1958) (Oxford, England: Basil Blackwell).

[5] Lenski, Gerhard, *The Religious Factor* (Garden City, New York: Doubleday and Company, Inc., 1961), pp. 199–204.

[6] Davidsen, O. M., "Reliability of Self-reported High School Grades" (unpublished

research report, American College Testing Program, 1963); see also Holland, J. L., and J. M. Richards, "Academic and Nonacademic Accomplishment: Correlated or Uncorrelated?" *Journal of Educational Psychology*, 56 (August 1965), 165–174.

[7] Fichter, Joseph, S. J., *Religion as an Occupation* (Notre Dame, Indiana: University of Notre Dame Press: 1961), pp. 38–42.

[8] Smith, Robert O., "Personality and Cultural Factors Affecting the Religion of One Hundred and Forty Divinity Students," *Religious Education*, 43 (March-April, 1948), 41–42.

CHAPTER SEVEN

ICSO-3:
Student Opinionnaire

THIS THIRD INVENTORY OF CATHOLIC SCHOOL OUT-
comes was developed to assess the opinions of our 14,519 eighth- and
twelfth-grade students about selected aspects of the schools in which
they were getting their formal education. In the preparation of the
instrument and in the analysis of the data, the many influences beyond
the school that are effective in shaping the stated opinions of the students were considered carefully. The results of the analyzed data are
important because they *are* the opinions of the students, not because
they necessarily describe the schools.

The processed findings derived from 25 items to which the students
reacted are presented under 4 subheadings: (1) student opinion of the
relative importance of stated Catholic school goals; (2) student opinion of Catholic schools' level of success in meeting the stated goals;
(3) students' opinions of parental interest in Catholic schools and of
parental influence on the students' religious development; (4) student reaction to the operation of the Catholic schools which they are
attending.

STUDENT OPINION OF THE RELATIVE IMPORTANCE
OF STATED CATHOLIC SCHOOL GOALS

After 3 pilot studies to perfect the instrument and to sharpen approaches to certain research questions, 3 general hypothetical constructs
were developed:

1. that students would give primacy to the religious-moral aims of the school and would rate the schools high on achievement in this area;

2. that students would rank intellectual aims second to religious-moral aims and would rate the schools average to good in achievement;

3. that the students would rank the importance of the social, voca-tional-ocupational, and civic-patriotic aims in no particular order (other than behind the religious-moral and intellectual aims) and would rate the schools high in achieving these aims.

Many hunches and anticipations were embedded within these research questions. As the groups of items are presented and the findings analyzed, predilections resulting from the results of the pilot studies, professional experience, research literature, and "common sense" will be discussed.

The findings from 6 groups of items will be presented as answers to 2 general questions.

1. In the students' opinions, what are the important goals of Catholic schools?

2. In the students' opinions, how successful are Catholic schools in achieving their goals?

Three items requiring 15 separate responses from each student, used to assess their viewpoints, were set in the context of personal decisions for the students. We were not interested in a student's ability to parrot the "official, philosophical—pedagogical line" of the school but to discover what the student thought the Catholic schools' primary objective is. For example, one question with 5 parts was phrased:

ITEM 1

Suppose someone were to ask you: "Why are you going to a Catholic school?" Think for a moment and *then rank in the order of importance your reasons,* not those of your parents or teachers. Mark the most important reason 1, the next most important 2, and so on. *Assign all five ranks.*

a. to obtain a superior training in school subjects
b. to develop a strong moral character based on religious principles
c. to form a group of true friends
d. to prepare myself for making a good citizen
e. to become a patriotic American citizen

The other two items that probed why the students thought the schools existed were:

ITEM 9

Rank in the order of importance (1 most important, 2 next most important, and so on) *the advantages you hope to receive from your Catholic schooling. Assign all five ranks.*

- a. a group of loyal friends and companions
- b. a practical knowledge and appreciation of my duties as a Catholic
- c. a clear understanding of the various subjects I have studied
- d. a deep devotion to my country and a knowledge of my American heritage
- e. the knowledge and ability to earn a good living

ITEM 21

Different people strive for different things. Here are some things that you have probably thought about. Among the things you strive for during your school days, *just how important are each of these?* Rank from 1 to 5.

- a. living up to my religious ideals
- b. becoming a better American citizen
- c. preparing myself to make a living
- d. learning as much as possible in school
- e. being accepted and liked by other students

The Study's hypothesis was that the total response would rank the religious-moral objectives first, the intellectual objectives second, and the social, vocational, and patriotic objectives about equally but clearly behind the first- and second-ranked objectives. With a single important exception our findings confirm our hypotheses; the exception was the ranking of the vocational goal second. Figure 3 shows the combined average first-place rank given to each of the alternatives. The rankings assigned each question were sufficiently similar to permit combination for a general analysis.

Figure 3 shows that the religious-moral objective is overwhelmingly considered the most important objective. The combined first- and second-place rankings assigned this objective on the 3 items exceeded 75%. This endorsement of the religious-moral aim of Catholic educa-

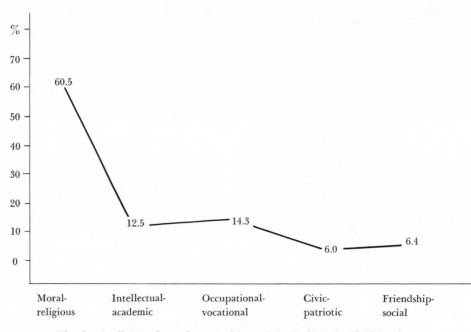

Fig. 3.   Student's first-place ranking of Catholic school objectives.

In this analysis the first-place ranks were used in discussing the findings since they were representative of the total 5-place ranking the students assigned to the question under consideration. This procedure will be used in other analyses to follow.

tion was far in excess of our pilot study results and so considerably beyond our expectations of the importance students would assign it. This great majority of responses favoring 1 alternative left little room for discrimination among the remaining 4 objectives. Even so, the slight edge of the vocational over the academic-intellectual objective was surprising. The relatively low attraction of the social and patriotic aims was anticipated. Our initial surprise that the vocational objective edged the intellectual for second rank was modified by a further look at the entire ranking of each item. When all 5 ranks are considered, the academic objective is a narrow second-place choice. The patriotic aim is a clear fourth-place choice, and the social aim a last-place choice. This overall ranking is very apparent in the average last-choice percentage for the 5 goals in the 3 items shown in Figure 4.

Figure 4 shows that there were no reversals; that is, the goals awarded many first rankings received correspondingly few last rankings, and

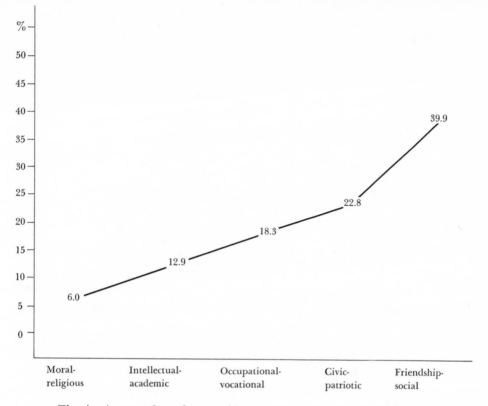

Fig. 4. Average last-place rankings of Catholic school objectives.

the reverse was also true. The differences in first-place rankings assigned the 5 educational aims by dioceses are presented in Table 85.

In sum, our sample of 14,519 students from 13 dioceses ranked the first aim (religious-moral) significantly higher than all other aims. This high percentage favoring the special educational goals of the Catholic school was in tune with our expectations. The next highest (academic-intellectual and occupational-vocational) were close in percentages and markedly above the fourth and fifth ranks (patriotic-civic and social).

These rankings usually showed variations when subgroups were isolated for comparative analyses. There were, however, no observable relationships between the personal background of most respondents and their views of Catholic schools' education objectives in patriotic, social, and occupational areas.

Table 85

DIOCESAN RANGE IN IMPORTANCE ASSIGNED TO FIVE EDUCATIONAL
OBJECTIVES AS REFLECTED IN FIRST-PLACE RANKINGS

Aim	Diocesan range of first-place rankings %	Sample average %
Religious-moral	52.9–68.9	60.5
Vocational-occupational	9.6–17.9	14.3
Academic-intellectual	7.8–18.6	12.5
Social-friendship	4.1– 9.1	6.4
Patriotic-citizenship	3.6– 8.6	6.0

Civic-patriotic and social-friendship aims are consistently ranked lowest (6%) regardless of what question is examined or what subgroup is analyzed. The only exceptions were those students who were doing poorly scholastically, according to their own evaluation. They gave more first-place choices to the social, civic, and vocational (job-preparation) aims of the schools than did the higher-achieving students.

The best and poorest students deviate significantly from the total Study average in their evaluation of the religious-moral objectives of the Catholic schools. The corresponding departures from the average percentages for the civic and social areas may be a forced concomitant of this and not a functional correlate of scholastic achievement. Apart from this single relationship there were no systematic, significant departures in the rankings of civic-patriotic and social-friendship objectives.

Table 86

ACADEMIC SELF-RATING AND FIRST-CHOICE OF
EDUCATIONAL GOALS OF STUDENTS

Self-rating	Objectives ranked first				
	Academic-intellectual	Religious-moral	Social-friendship	Occupational-vocational	Civic-patriotic
A	13.5	68.4	4.4	9.9	3.8
B	12.5	60.2	6.1	13.9	5.4
C	13.0	56.0	7.2	16.6	7.2
D	13.7	46.5	10.1	20.2	9.5
Average	12.5	60.5	6.4	14.3	6.0

Vocational-occupational aims were related to several background factors in our sample. The relationship to the students' scholastic self-assessment has been presented. Sex, type of school, and friendship patterns were also related to differential rankings of objectives. Also, there were anticipated relationships between ranking of educational objectives and personal and family religiosity. The relation of age and sex to ranking of vocational-occupational aims is not surprising. Boys were expected to be, and were, more concerned with the vocational dimension than girls, as may be seen in Table 87.

There was no measurable relationship between certain factors of students' background and the rank assigned the academic-intellectual aims. The Study had expected and found no relationship with the type of high school the students attended, the students' future plans to continue schooling under Catholic auspices, the prevalence of Catholic school attendance of the respondents' friends or the age groups.

Relationships were anticipated between the pattern of expressed opinions and the respondents' sex, the number of years spent in Catholic schools, and the educational attainment of their parents. However, few of these relationships were found. Typically, girls of high school age reflect more academically oriented responses than do their male counterparts, and our students were not exceptions. However, we reasoned that as students were exposed to the "no frills, highly academic" well-founded image of Catholic schools, they would rank the academic aims increasingly higher. Again the data did not support the assumption. And, finally, contrary to our expectations, the total

Table 87

RANKING OF VOCATIONAL-OCCUPATIONAL AIMS BY
ELEMENTARY AND HIGH SCHOOL BOYS AND GIRLS

| | Elementary | | High school | |
| | Girls (N = 4003) | Boys (N = 3476) | Girls (N = 3885) | Boys (N = 2980) |
Rank	%	%	%	%
1	9.1	11.8	5.8	12.2
2	18.2	18.7	16.9	19.6
3	26.7	27.4	30.1	29.0
4	30.1	25.9	28.1	25.0
5	15.9	16.2	19.1	14.2

years of schooling achieved by the parents was unrelated to the students' ranking of academic-intellectual aims of Catholic schools.

We had expected a positive link between the amount of Catholic schooling experienced by parents and the respondents' ranking of academic-intellectual school aims. We found, on the contrary, that those students whose fathers and mothers had not attended Catholic schools ranked academic aims significantly higher than did their classmates whose parents had attended Catholic schools.

Religious-moral educational aims also revealed many closely related student background characteristics. The age and sex groups of the sample showed different rankings of the religious-moral aims of Catholic education.

Boys ranked the religious-moral aim significantly lower than do girls. Whereas high school girls value this aim most highly, high school boys value it less when compared with the elementary school boys. We expect girls to give more conforming and desirable responses than boys, and we expect adolescent girls to be more willing to admit to religious values than boys. It appears that the difference in valuing the religious-moral goal of Catholic education may result from a number of factors. The data suggest that those students who place the highest importance on the religious-moral objectives are the self-identified high achievers, those who plan to continue their education in Catholic schools, those who have most of their friends in Catholic schools, and those who have Catholic mothers and fathers. Further, the more Catholic schooling the respondents and their parents have had, the higher they value the religious-moral objectives.

STUDENT OPINION OF CATHOLIC SCHOOLS' SUCCESS IN MEETING THE STATED GOALS

Several items inventoried students' opinions about the schools' success in achieving their formal educational objectives: religious-moral, academic-intellectual, occupational-vocational, social-friendship, patriotic-civic.

Ten items in uniform style were randomly placed in the Opinionnaire to sample students' opinions of school success. A sample item shows the format to which the student responded; this question was one of two that tapped the students' perceptions of the schools' success in achieving religious-moral objectives.

ITEM 4

In addition to "regular school subjects," Catholic schools also give special instruction in the teachings and practices of the Catholic religion. As you look back over your years in a Catholic school, *how would you describe the religious instruction you have received?* Choose one.

  a. superior
  b. very good, but could be better
  c. average
  d. below average
  e. poor

The 5 possible answers were the same for all 10 items under discussion. Pilot studies revealed no differences in response when the order was inverted or when comparable adjectives were substituted for "superior," "exceptionally well," etc. Thus the items have an identical response structure. Nine other comparable questions probed students' views regarding the schools' success in achieving their academic, vocational, social, and civic goals. Table 88 tabulates student responses on the 10 items concerned with the schools' success in achieving their goals.

Table 88

STUDENTS' OVERALL OPINIONS OF CATHOLIC SCHOOLS' SUCCESS*

| | Assessment | | | | |
| | 5 (exceptional) | 4 | 3 | 2 | 1 |
Topic	%	%	%	%	%
Academic-intellectual					
Items 3, 10, 18	26.2	39.3	25.5	6.1	2.8
Religious-moral					
Items 4, 5	36.6	33.6	21.4	5.4	2.9
Social-friendship					
Items 6, 14, 16	29.9	35.8	23.7	6.9	3.6
Vocational-occupational					
Item 13	41.8	31.7	18.1	5.5	2.7
Civic-patriotic					
Item 12	27.2	35.8	26.2	7.0	3.6
Average of 10 items	32.3	35.2	22.9	6.1	3.1

* Total number of students, 14,519

Students felt that their schools had been exceptionally successful in all tasks about 31% of the time. When we isolate the 5 areas we find considerable variation within the 31% overall rating of highest satisfaction:

Vocational-occupational	42%
Religious-moral	36%
Social-friendship	30%
Civic-patriotic	27%
Academic-intellectual	26%

These are surprising results indeed. These students had given the religious-moral objective an overwhelming first-place vote of importance (61%), followed by academic (13%) and vocational (14%) aims, and had ranked patriotic (6%) and social (6%) aims last. In general, students' ranking of the schools' success seems to indicate a considerably less favorable rank for the religious-moral and the academic-intellectual affairs of their schools. Fewer saw their schools achieving complete success in academic-intellectual affairs than they did in any of the other areas of schools' activities. We will examine each of these areas to reveal consensus and/or diversity underlying the total group's averages when the opinions of subgroups of students are considered.

Student Opinion of Schools' Success in Achieving Vocational-Occupational Objectives

Throughout the inventory boys generally viewed the schools as less successful than did the girls, with secondary school boys holding the dimmest view. The total percentages of first-place and second-place responses awarded the schools for their vocational-occupational efforts, are shown in Table 89. The differences are not striking, but the tendency is for the older students, and the boys particularly, to regard their schools as slightly less successful than do the younger students. We found earlier that the better the students the less important they felt the vocational-occupational goals; the percentage of first-place ratings for importance by average grade were A, 10%, B, 14%, C, 17%, and D, 20%. However, the more important the student felt these objectives, the less successful they felt their schools were in achiev-

Table 89

STUDENTS' VIEWS OF THE IMPORTANCE AND SUCCESS OF
VOCATIONAL-OCCUPATIONAL AIMS IN CATHOLIC SCHOOLS:
PERCENTAGE OF FIRST- AND SECOND-PLACE RANKS
BY AGE AND SEX GROUPS

| | Elementary | | Secondary | |
Opinion	Girl %	Boy %	Girl %	Boy %
Importance	27	30	23	32
Success	77	71	75	70

ing them (Table 90). The manner in which the cumulation of first-
and second-place rankings maintain the picture, is shown in Table 91.
Adding the first 2 rankings we find that low grades are related to a low
view of success, just as are the first-place rankings alone. Moreover,
if we use the last or 2 last-place ranks the same pattern obtains.

Students who ranked the importance of vocational-occupational aims
highest were those with friends who predominantly did not attend
Catholic schools. This group gave the lowest success rating in these
areas to their schools (Table 92).

It would appear that the students who associate with other students
who attend Catholic schools value higher and are less critical of the
success in vocational-occupational aims. They were also more concerned with religious and academic goals than were the students whose
friends predominantly did not attend Catholic schools.

Table 90

GRADE AVERAGES OF STUDENTS AND THEIR VIEWS OF IMPORTANCE AND
SUCCESS OF VOCATIONAL-OCCUPATIONAL GOALS
(HIGHEST-RANK PERCENTAGES)

| | Self-assigned grade average | | | |
Opinion	A %	B %	C %	D %
Importance of objectives	10	14	17	20
Success in achieving them	54	44	35	27

Table 91

RANKINGS OF SUCCESS OF CATHOLIC SCHOOLS IN ACHIEVING
VOCATIONAL-OCCUPATIONAL GOALS BY STUDENTS
IN LETTER-GRADE CATEGORIES

| | Grade average | | | |
| | A | B | C | D |
Opinion	%	%	%	%
1 exceptionally well	53.7	44.0	35.3	26.6
2 very well, but could be better	29.3	32.4	32.1	31.7
3 moderately well	12.2	16.5	22.6	21.0
4 only fairly well	3.1	5.0	6.7	11.3
5 poorly	1.7	2.2	3.4	9.4

Table 92

SUCCESS OF CATHOLIC SCHOOLS IN ACHIEVING
OCCUPATIONAL-VOCATIONAL AIMS CORRELATED WITH
STUDENT FRIENDSHIP

Success rank	Friends attend Catholic schools %	Friends half in and half out of Catholic schools %	Friends do not attend Catholic schools %
1	44.3	38.1	37.3
2	32.6	31.5	28.2
3	16.3	20.4	22.9
4	4.7	6.5	7.9
5	2.2	3.6	3.8

Student Opinion of Schools' Success in Achieving Social-Friendship Goals

In general the students were very satisfied with the schools' success in achieving social-friendship objectives. It is commonly thought that strict regimens for social activities produce dissatisfaction among Catholic school students and parents. The findings, however, give little or no support to such assumptions; 40% of all responsents assigned first-place success rank to this goal area. Although students had ranked these goals last in importance, they consider the schools' efforts in this area very successful.

Student Opinion of Schools' Success in Achieving Religious-Moral Objectives

The relationship of high academic achievement to plans for more Catholic education was discussed earlier. The students who plan more Catholic education were significantly higher on our 2 measures of religious practices.

The religious-moral objectives of Catholic schools were such an overwhelming choice (60%) as the most important aim of Catholic education that it made analyses of the other aims difficult. The students, however, did not respond in the same way to questions of how successful the schools were in achieving these same aims.

Over 34% of the sample assigned schools the highest success rating in this area, and 70% registered the combined responses "exceptionally" or "very well" to their schools' success. Although opinions about the schools' success were not significantly higher in this area than they were in all others, as was also true in ranking the importance of these objectives, they were very favorably viewed—second in perceived success to the occupational-vocational area.

We reported earlier that the highest importance for the religious-moral objectives was assigned by high school girls (73%), next highest by elementary school girls (60%), then elementary school boys (54%), and least by high school boys (48%). The age-sex dimension is modified when we look at the students' opinion of success as compared with importance in Table 93.

Table 93

STUDENTS' OPINION OF CATHOLIC SCHOOLS' SUCCESS
IN ACHIEVING THEIR RELIGIOUS-MORAL OBJECTIVES,
BY SEX AND AGE GROUPS (HIGHEST RANK PERCENTAGES)

	Age-sex group			
	Elementary		High school	
	Girl	Boy	Girl	Boy
Opinion	%	%	%	%
Importance	60.3	53.5	72.7	47.8
Success	46.2	41.3	33.4	23.3

The lesser satisfaction of the high school group was found regularly throughout the data. Probably there is an admixture of unwillingness to throw bouquets and a tendency to criticize society in general and schools in particular.

The respondents gave increasingly greater importance to religious-moral objectives of Catholic education as their number of years of Catholic education increased. Fifty-seven percent of those with 1–4 years assigned first-place importance, while 75% of those with 13 years of Catholic education assigned first-place importance. The students'

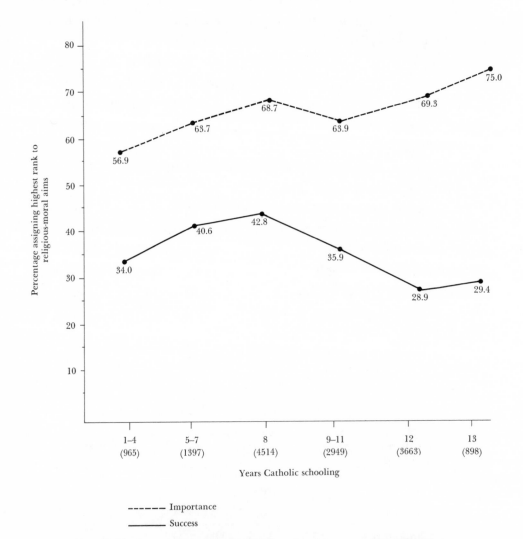

Fig. 5. Student opinion of Catholic schools' success in achieving religious-moral objectives, by years of Catholic education.

opinion of the school success reveals another quite different relationship as shown in Fig. 5. The importance assigned to religious-moral
aims of Catholic schools showed progressive increases with the amount
of Catholic school experienced by the respondent. The respondents'
view of the success of Catholic schools in achieving their aims in religious-moral education increased from 1–8 years and then showed a
steady decrease through 13 years, falling 5% below the 1–4 year group's
average. Although no formal hypothesis was tested, the findings are
somewhat surprising.

Students' scholastic averages showed a remarkable relationship to
their opinions of the importance of religious-moral aims. The higher
the grade average, the higher the student's opinion of the importance
of the aims. Similarly, students' view of the success of their schools in
achieving these aims was positively related with their academic achievement, as may be seen in Table 94. The difference between the C and
D students' views of the schools' success was not as marked as was the
difference between their opinions of the importance of these objectives.

Table 94

IMPORTANCE OF RELIGIOUS-MORAL AIMS AND STUDENTS' AVERAGE GRADES

	Percentage ranked first	
Average grade	Importance %	Success %
A	58.4	41.2
B	60.2	37.6
C	56.0	33.8
D	46.5	33.4

The type of high school in which the boys receive their schooling
seems to have no relationship to their view of the importance or success of the religious-moral objectives. But the girls, typically more concerned and more laudatory about these objectives than boys, show wide
differences in views of importance and success by high school type.
Most significant differences are in the first-place importance and success ranks awarded by students in all-girl schools.

Student Opinion of Schools' Success in Achieving Civic-Patriotic Objectives

Civic responsibility and patriotism as educational objectives for Catholic schools were only slightly more important in the opinion of the students than the last-place social and personal friendship objectives. Only 6% rated this objective as of first import (as compared with 60+% for religious-moral aims.)

Slightly over 27% indicated they were extremely satisfied with the schools' success in this area. Further, 63% assigned the combined first- and second-place ranks to their schools' success. Thus, this fourth and nearly last-place objective was given satisfactory success rating. The exploration of relation of student background to responses concerning the level of success of Catholic schools in achieving the civic-patriotic goals showed no significant patterns or trends.

Student Opinion of Schools' Success in Achieving Academic-Intellectual Objectives

The academic-intellectual goals were ranked second in importance by the respondents; however, the same respondents ranked these goals last in terms of success, with only 26% awarding "extremely success-ful" to them. When the first 2 ranks are combined, 66% of the group is included, which puts the success level of these goals in a tie for third place with social-friendship goals.

Several background factors were found related in predictable and unpredictable ways with students' opinion of success in achieving academic-intellectual goals. Contrary to expectation, grade groups did not vary in ranking the importance of academic aims (14%, 13%, 13%, and 14%). We expected and did find a strong linear relation-ship between the students' grades and their views of success in aca-demic-intellecutal matters—A, 32%, B, 27%, C, 23%, D, 22%. The proof of the pudding is in the tasting: the greater the academic success of the student the more successful he rates the school in achieving its intellectual-academic aims.

STUDENT OPINION ABOUT PARENTS' ROLE
IN THEIR EDUCATION

A measure was sought to see how students perceived their parents' part in the educative process. One item asked how they would describe the degree of their parents' interest in the schools, and a second asked them to rank, in order, 5 sources of influence on their religious development.

Table 95

STUDENTS' PERCEPTION OF THEIR PARENTS' INTEREST IN SCHOOLS

Description	Frequency	%
Extremely strong	4,459	34.09
Strong, but could be stronger	3,630	27.75
Average	3,811	29.13
Below average	668	5.11
Weak	513	3.92
Total	13,081	100.00

The distribution of responses to the first item is presented in Table 95. A third of the students described their parents' interest as "extremely strong." Only 3.9% thought of their parents' interest as "weak." Combining the 2 "strong" categories shows 61.8% using that adjective for their parents' interest, with only 9.0% designating it as "weak" or "below average."

When the SC-RB paradigm is applied to identification of parents' interest in the schools, the picture is clear: parental interest as perceived by the children is related to higher social status, Catholic education of parents, especially of mothers, and students' longer attendance in Catholic schools.

A remarkable similarity is observed in the way boys and girls answer the question, 34.04% of both rate "extremely strong," and they are within a single percentage point difference in all responses. Type of high school reflects only minor differences.

If their offspring are reporting accurately, parents are much more interested in elementary school affairs than in high school affairs. Of 9451 elementary schools, 64% reported that they had some type of parent organization connected with the school; of 2075 secondary schools, 72% reported such an organization. This would indicate a greater opportunity for display of parent interest at the high school level. At any rate, the elementary students give 42.29% of their parents credit for being very much interested, the secondary school students 25.76%. The difference of 14.53% is highly significant. The younger students likewise assign more of their parents to the "strong, but could be stronger" category (Table 96).

Table 96

STUDENTS' PERCEPTION OF PARENTS' INTEREST
IN THEIR SCHOOLS, BY GRADE LEVEL

Response	Elementary		High school	
	Freq.	%	Freq.	%
Extremely strong	2786	42.29	1672	25.76
Strong, but could be stronger	1969	29.89	1660	25.57
Average	1492	22.65	2319	35.73
Below average	192	2.91	476	7.33
Weak	149	2.26	364	5.61
Total	6588	100.00	6491	100.00

High school students appear less generous in evaluating their parents' school interest; they are more than twice as inclined to attribute weak or below average interest to parents than are elementary pupils. The pilot study in one of the 13 dioceses revealed that the parents of elementary students had substantially more education, particularly beyond high school, than parents of secondary school students. If this finding reflects the rising general educational level of presumably younger parents and if it can be generalized to the parents of the total population of the Study, we could expect higher interest to characterize the parents of elementary pupils. We find a linear progression in the relationship between the level of parents' education and degree of interest reported by the children.

Parents' interest is related to the number of years the child has attended Catholic schools, although it may well be a function of the students' present grade level, as displayed in Table 96 by the comparison of elementary and high school students' response. Those who have been in Catholic schools longest and are about to graduate think of their parents as least interested.

The students who perceive their parents as most interested and involved with their schools are also the ones who are experiencing the greatest success academically. Only a small percentage of them say their parents' interest is weak. The poorer students, that is the D students, are represented 4 times as much among those who rate their parents low on this factor and are 19.4% behind the A students in giving their parents the highest rating. It is inviting to believe that parents' interest and students' success are mutually reinforcing.

STUDENTS' PERCEPTIONS OF FIVE SOURCES OF INFLUENCE ON THEIR RELIGIOUS DEVELOPMENT

Student opinion was very clear on the relative importance of the following 5 sources of influence: religious instruction in the school, religious instruction in the Church, and the examples of parents, teachers, and peers. Table 97 combines students' rankings for all 5 sources. Students think very little of the importance of their classmates' influence (5% ranked it first), as compared with other influences on their religious development. Nearly 10 times as many students saw their parents as the most influential force on their religious development. The example of their Catholic school teachers and church sermons were third and fourth choices (12% and 13%, respectively, ranked them first in importance.)

Formal classes in religion were a distant second choice (22%), but considerably more popular than the third and fourth choices. With nearly half (48%) of our sample ranking parents first and two-thirds (66%) assigning parents a first or second rank, there can be no speculation about the unequivocal student opinion on this matter.

Both elementary and high school groups ranked parents first 48% of the time. Girls in the elementary school did so 52%, and elementary

Table 97

STUDENTS' OPINION OF THE IMPORTANCE OF INFLUENCES
ON THEIR RELIGIOUS DEVELOPMENT

			Source		
Rank	Parents' example %	School religious instruction %	Teachers' example %	Parish-church instruction %	Classmates' example %
1	48.3	22.3	12.6	11.8	5.0
2	17.2	22.5	29.4	21.3	9.7
3	15.4	24.4	26.5	20.6	13.2
4	13.0	21.4	23.0	27.4	15.2
5	6.1	9.4	8.5	19.0	57.0

school boys 44%. Similarly, high school girls ranked their parents first 52% of the time, and high school boys 44%. We can say that girls of both age groups rank their parents significantly higher in the amount of influence on their religious development than do both groups of boys.

The amount of the respondents' Catholic schooling is positively associated with ranking of parents. We find 42% of the group with least Catholic school education assigning a first rank to their parents, and 54% of the group with most Catholic school education making such an assignment. The more Catholic schooling the respondents had, the more they were of the opinion that their parents had been the primary influence on their religious development.

Better students ranked their parents' influence considerably higher than did the poorer students. Of the A students, 50.8% ranked their parents first, 48.9% of the B, 47.2% of the C. and 36.5% of the D students. The difference of 14.3% in ranking between the A and D students is significant. One might suspect that communication is probably better, rapport greater, and cooperation between parent and child more frequent in the homes of A students than in the homes of D students.

In summary we can say that two-thirds (65.5%) think of their parents as the first and second most influential factor in their religious development, and a similar proportion (61.8%) see their parents as having a strong interest in their schools.

STUDENT OPINION ABOUT SCHOOLS' OPERATION

One of the objectives of ICSO-3 was to assess the students' general level of satisfaction with the work of their schools. This section describes student responses to 3 questions regarding the schools' operation. One item was a "general satisfaction index," which permitted the students to react to the hypothetical possibility of their choosing to stay or not to stay in Catholic schools. Two other items enabled respondents to express opinions of religious and lay teachers' success in teaching regular school subjects.

The results of the general satisfaction index are reported in Table 98. Respondents were not limited to a "yes" or "no" answer, but could qualify their responses by selecting "definitely" or "probably." In conferences held with students in each of the 324 sample schools, they invariably indicated that they would choose to attend Catholic schools were the decision left to them.

Analysis of the responses shows that 77.9% answered the question affirmatively, with either "definitely" or "probably yes." Although the marginals reflect majority satisfaction, they also mirror neutrality (9.7%) and dissatisfaction (12.4%). In other words, 22.1% or more than 1 student in 5 are something less than satisfied with their Catholic school experiences. Who are these satisfied and dissatisfied students? Examination of the "definitely yes" responses reveals, that regardless of social class, half of the respondents in the SC-RB paradigm definitely would attend a Catholic school if the choice were left completely to

Table 98

DISTRIBUTION OF RESPONSE TO THE QUESTION
"IF THE CHOICE OF SCHOOL WERE LEFT ENTIRELY UP TO YOU,
WOULD YOU STILL ATTEND A CATHOLIC SCHOOL?"

Response	Frequency	%
Definitely yes	6,445	48.69
Probably yes	3,867	29.22
Uncertain	1,281	9.68
Probably no	1,012	7.65
Definitely no	631	4.76
Total	13,236	100.00

them. Higher percentages select the "definitely yes" response when the parents have been educated in Catholic schools. In RB-1, 2, and 3, 53% to 55% of the respondents express satisfaction; RB-4, in which only the child has a Catholic education, averages only a 45% affirmative response. A contrast to this cell is observed in RB-6, where the difference is that not even the child has had much Catholic education; this group average climbs to 52%. Apparently children with less Catholic schooling and whose parents have not had a Catholic education are strongly committed to Catholic school attendance. These children may be late arrivals in the system, perhaps unable to get into a Catholic school earlier, but their rate of satisfaction is higher than that of children without Catholic-school-education parents but who themselves have had considerable Catholic schooling. RB-6 children, unlike those in the other five RB categories, have been mostly educated in non-Catholic schools and are in a position to base their decisions on a comparison with other educational experiences.

A caution in interpreting these results: RB-6 where no one in the family has had much Catholic schooling is a small group compared with RB-4 (564 to 4654).

The lowest degree of satisfaction, 40%, is found among children having one non-Catholic parent. Within this category for all social classes, averages range from 1% to 20% lower than those of the other 15 cells in the paradigm.

Boys and girls show appreciable differences in their answers to the question (75.4% to 79.9% "definitely" or "probably yes"), as do elementary school compared with high school respondents (76.4% to 79.5%). The highest percentage of "yes" answers is expressed by high school girls (83%); elementary school boys and girls are almost identical with one another, with 76% "yes" and 13% "no" answers. High school boys were not far behind elementary students with 75% "yes" and 14% "no" answers. The relatively high degree of satisfaction implied in these responses can be interpreted in several ways. They may be an indication of high esteem for the Catholic school, or it may be that students in Catholic schools are the ones who want to be there. This is a sophisticated but real difference.

When the high school group is examined by school type a clear difference in responses appears. Table 99 shows the response distributions as significantly related to the type of school attended. The differences in "definitely yes" responses not only are statistically significant and unmistakably revealing of the superior satisfaction of the all-girl school students, but also demonstrate differential satisfaction of all-boy school respondents and boys in coeducational schools. Boys in coeducational schools not only answer "definitely yes" much less than do the coeducational school girls but also less than the boys attending all-boy schools, This student opinion should be of concern to Catholic school administrators, counsellors, and teachers. It would appear that all-girl schools particularly, and to a lesser degree all-boy schools, have students who are significantly more satisfied with their Catholic school education than are those in coeducational schools.

Table 99

TYPE OF HIGH SCHOOL ATTENDED AND THE RESPONDENTS'
DECISION TO STAY IN CATHOLIC SCHOOL

| | Type of school | | | |
| | Coeducational | | | |
Decision	Boys (1472) %	Girls (1604) %	All-boy (1515) %	All-girl (2288) %
Definitely yes	41.7	49.4	44.6	60.6
Probably yes	30.7	31.1	32.2	24.1
Uncertain	12.3	8.1	9.6	6.5
Probably no	9.4	6.2	8.4	6.1
Definitely no	5.9	5.2	5.2	2.6

The students' self-view as a scholastic achiever again proves to be an effective discriminator. Table 100 shows the linear relationship of scholastic index with "definitely yes" responses. The table confirms linear relationships for each level of choice across the scholastic average hierarchy. Compared with A students, D students not only select the "definitely yes" only half as often, but also are 3 times more uncertain and 3 to 4 times higher in their selection of the "no" alternatives. The story is plain: students who rate themselves academically successful like their Catholic schools; less successful students are less supportive of their Catholic schools. A similar result could probably be obtained from any group of students anywhere.

Table 100

SELF-ASSIGNED LETTER GRADES AND CHOICE OF
REMAINING OR LEAVING CATHOLIC SCHOOLS

	Average			
Decision to remain	A %	B %	C %	D %
Definitely yes	62.1	50.4	42.1	32.7
Probably yes	26.6	29.2	30.3	27.7
Uncertain	4.7	9.1	12.1	15.1
Probably no	3.9	7.0	9.8	12.0
Definitely no	2.9	4.3	5.7	12.6

Diocesan differences in students' responses to this question were also observed. The range on the "definitely yes" responses to this question were also observed. The range on the "definitely yes" response was significant (from 41.2% to 53.7%), as was the combined "definitely" and "probably yes" scores (from 71.6% to 81.8%). The "definitely no" percentages also reflected significant diocesan differences, from a low of 2.3% to 7.7%. It would appear that students' morale, school image, or level of satisfaction varies considerably from diocese to diocese. It is of no concern here whether the opinions are accurate or ill-founded; these are the opinions.

The composite of these findings is presented in Table 101 as a summation of the relationships between respondents' decisions and their personal characteristics.

A second index of student satisfaction was their view of the effectiveness of the teaching. Students' opinions of religious and lay teachers were taken from the reaction to Items 7 and 8 (14,519 respondents).

ITEM 7

You are often asked by friends or relatives, how you are doing in school. Suppose, instead, they asked you how well your teachers are doing in helping you to learn. Considering your present class as a whole, *how well do you think the religious (priests, brothers, sisters) who have taught your class have succeeded in teaching you the regular school subjects?*

Table 101

RELATIONSHIPS OF RESPONDENTS' BACKGROUND AND
CHOICE TO ATTEND OR NOT TO ATTEND CATHOLIC SCHOOL

Description of variable	Relationship to expressed choice of staying in Catholic school
All students	77.9% choose to stay
Dioceses	Moderate relationship with considerable differences at extremes
Sex	None
Elementary vs. high school per se	None
Years of Catholic schooling	None
Type of high school	All-girl school highest satisfaction; consistent relationship throughout for others
Parents' religion	Moderate difference between the 3 groups
Self-assigned scholastic index	Highly significant, positive relationship
General education of parents	None
Catholic education of parents	Moderate relationships; clearly discriminate extreme groups
Personal religiosity	Strong positive relationship
Family religiosity	Strong positive relationship

Table 102

DISTRIBUTION OF RESPONSE TO THE QUESTION OF
EFFECTIVENESS OF RELIGIOUS TEACHERS

Response	Frequency	%
No response	1,284	8.8
Exceptionally well	5,655	42.7
Very well, but could be better	4,458	33.7
Moderately well	2,216	16.7
Only fairly well	615	4.7
Poorly	291	2.2
Total	14,519	108.8
Base	13,235	

ITEM 8

In addition to religious teachers, most Catholic schools now have lay teachers as members of the faculty. Considering your present class as a whole, *how well do you think the lay teachers have succeeded in teaching the regular school subjects?*

Table 103

DISTRIBUTION OF RESPONSE TO THE QUESTION
OF EFFECTIVENESS OF LAY TEACHERS

Response	Frequency	%
No response	1,567	12.1
Exceptionally well	4,584	35.4
Very well, but could be better	4,492	34.7
Moderately well	2,704	20.9
Only fairly well	747	5.8
Poorly	425	3.3
Total	14,519	112.2
Base	12,952	

Students' opinions of their religious teachers are higher than those of their lay teachers. Religious teachers were succeeding (in regular subjects) exceptionally or very well according to 76.4% of the students, whereas 70.1% of them so ranked their lay teachers. The difference of 6.3% is statistically significant at the .05 level. Further, if the extreme (exceptionally well) is considered alone, the difference persists; indeed it increases to 7.3%, with 42.7% of the respondents so classifying the religious and 35.4% so classifying lay teachers.

The apparent satisfaction with religious and lay teachers is not distributed equally among all respondents. We find, for example, that boys are less satisfied than girls. Table 104 shows this to be true for religious and lay teachers.

High school students have considerably lower opinions of their religious and lay teachers than do elementary school students. Elementary respondents assigned "exceptionally well" to their religious teachers 52.6%, to their lay teachers 40.5%, whereas high school respondents gave 32.7% and 30.1%, respectively. This apparent drop in students' view of their teachers as professionally successful is neither perplexing nor peculiar to Catholic education. The rejection of adults' capabilities is expected of and played out by adolescents wherever they may be in contemporary American society.

Relevant here is the differential satisfaction expressed within the high school group. Coeducational boys, coeducational girls, and the all-boy high school groups are not markedly different in their appraisals, but all-girl groups showed significantly higher regard for their teachers (both religious and lay) than did the other groups. The data show a tendency for girls in all-girl schools to be more satisfied with religious and lay teachers' competency than are boys. However, the variable of sex alone does not account for the differences observed in the responses from all-girl schools. Socially desirable responses are typically elicited more regularly from girls than boys, but there is no apparent reason for girls in all-girl high schools to exhibit such a proclivity more than girls in coeducational schools. This is strong evidence that the educative processes as mediated by religious and lay teachers are more highly satisfying for girls in all-girl high schools, current educational theory notwithstanding.

Years of Catholic education reported bore no relationship to views of the success of religious or lay teachers. The religion, the general formal education, and the amount of Catholic education of each parent and both parents combined were also unrelated to respondents' views of teachers' successfulness.

Five other background dimensions were related to the students' eval-

Table 104

BOYS' AND GIRLS' RATING OF RELIGIOUS AND
LAY TEACHER COMPETENCY

Group	Evaluative rating	Religious %	Lay %
Boys	Highest	38.7	32.9
	Lower two	9.1	10.9
Girls	Highest	46.1	37.4
	Lower two	5.0	7.4

uation of the successfulness of their teachers: plans to continue Catholic education, friends' attendance at Catholic schools, scholastic average, family religiosity, and personal religiosity. The relationships were all confirmatory of the Study's predictions: highest ratings of religious teachers (and to a lesser degree of lay teachers) corresponded positively with proportions of students planning to attend Catholic schools, associating predominantly with students in Catholic schools, achieving high scholastically, coming from families with the highest incidence of religious practices, and attending Mass with frequency above minimal requirements.

In summary, the analyses of 3 opinion questions provide evidence that roughly three-fourths of the 14,519 respondents are more than moderately satisfied with the work of their schools. The most general satisfaction index shows 78% reporting that they would attend a Catholic school if the choice were theirs alone. Some 76% indicate that their religious teachers succeed exceptionally or very well in teaching regular school subjects, and 70% say the same of their lay teachers.

Girls render more favorable judgment in all 3 items than do boys, with the all-girl secondary school registering the highest degree of satisfaction on all questions. The coed girls are next, followed by the all-boy school, and not far behind are the coed boys. Elementary students show little difference based on sex, although they are slightly more favorably inclined toward their teachers than are high school students.

Children of Catholic parents are more committed to continuing in a Catholic schoool than chilren of one non-Catholic parent, but they are not significantly different in their evaluation of teachers' success in teaching regular school subjects.

Students whose friends attend Catholic schools or who see themselves as successful academically are more eager to remain in Catholic schools and to rate their teachers high in success. Also those who attend Mass frequently or whose families maintain a high level of religious interest are more favorably inclined toward Catholic school attendance and toward favorable evaluation of teachers.

It is not difficult to infer the obverse. The less-satisfied students are more likely to be boys; there is evidence that a similar sex differential would be found in a comparable age group in any school system. Dissatisfaction is higher among children whose friends do not attend Catholic schools. Which of these variables gives rise to the other is uncertain, but peer-group influence is understandably strong. Students who classify themselves as D students are much less satisfied than those who rate themselves more successful academically. Finally, students who are irregular in Mass attendance also enjoy less satisfaction in their school experiences as measured by their unwillingness to continue, and their ratings of teachers' success. Negative reactions are also true of the children in whose families religious interest and practice are low. These data suggest, but do not demonstrate, a high correlation between students' rating of teacher success and the desire to continue in Catholic schools.

SUMMARY OF ICSO-3 FINDINGS

It is clear that the students responding in this survey perceive the religious-moral goals of their schools as most important by far. The overwhelming assignment of the highest importance to the religious-moral aspect of their schools by 60% of these students narrows the range of importance of the other 4 objectives areas—to the point where occupational-vocational goals exceed intellectual-academic goals by 1.8% for the second most important ranking. To complicate this ranking further, these same students give 5.4% more last-place rankings to occupational goals than they do to intellectual goals. To repeat, these students are convinced that the religious-moral goals of Catholic schools are of prime importance, and the occupational and intellectual goals are closely related to second place.

The opinions of the students concerning the success of their schools in meeting the goals show vocational goals in first place, religious goals in second, and, most surprising, intellectual goals in last place.

In the assessment of success in occupational goals, it seems significant that the self-rated A students assigned the highest success rating to these goals twice as frequently as did the D students. This ranking coincides with the high importance these same students place on entering college and also with the large number of Catholic high school graduates who go on to post-secondary education, according to the reports of the high school principals.

The low rank assigned to the schools' success with the religious-moral goals was strongly affected by the negative outlook of the high school students. In comparing the secondary response with the elementary response, we find that only 28% of the secondary schools students gave first success rank whereas 43% of the elementary pupils assigned the highest success level to the schools in achieving religious-moral goals.

In general, opinions concerning the success level of the schools of the total group of student respondents reflect favorably on their Catholic school experiences.

CHAPTER EIGHT

What Catholic Parents Think of The Schools

IN OCTOBER 1962, THERE WERE APPROXIMATELY 6,000,-000 young people enrolled in the Catholic elementary and secondary schools of the United States. These students entered these schools and continued in them as the result of a greater or less conscious decision of their parents. The time had passed when such parental decisions were a matter of conscience or moral obligation, because Catholic schools were not available for all Catholic children. As a matter of fact, gaining admission to many Catholic schools was a difficult matter for Catholic parents. This was particularly evident in September 1962, when over 100,000 applicants for admission to Catholic elementary schools could not be accepted; this number was equal to approximately 20% of the 1962 first-grade enrollment. In view of this elementary school situation, which was duplicated at the secondary level, it was evident that Catholic parents needed a strong purpose if their children were to enter and continue in Catholic schools.

Against this background the Study staff developed an inquiry that would identify Catholic parents' expectations as they sent their children to Catholic schools. The inquiry was not aimed at identifying the purposes or goals as presented by the schools, but rather what parents hoped the schools would do for their children. Although it was clearly understood that parents' expectations would be influenced by the stated goals of the schools, the staff believed that a digest of parents' hopes would not necessarily be a reflection of the goals of the schools.

The first step in the construction of the inquiry was a series of small group meetings with parents of first-grade children who had had no other children in Catholic schools. Each parent was asked to write as many as 6 reasons why he chose to send his child to a Catholic school. To supplement the group meetings a larger group of parents of first-, eighth-, and twelfth-grade students were mailed an open-ended nondirectional questionnaire asking their reasons for choosing a Catholic school for their children. The total reponses from the meetings and the mailed questionnaires produced 250 distinguishably different goals. By content analysis of the stated goals these items were reduced to 31 categories.

A questionnaire was prepared in which 31 goal statements were presented to the respondent parent. The parent was asked to identify the level of importance he assigned to each goal and the level of success he believed the schools of his experience were achieving for each goal. The response for importance and for success was on a 5-point scale ranging from "most" to "none." A sixth response of "don't know" was offered to lessen the possibility of forced responses. Each parent was asked also to identify separately the 3 most important and 3 most successful goals. Each respondent was invited to make further comment related to the school goals; almost 1 out of every 7 parents accepted the invitation.

CHARACTERISTICS OF PARENTS

Each respondent was asked to identify himself by a set of personal characteristics including age, sex, education, religion, occupation, nationality, etc. The Parental Expectations instrument can be found in the Appendix.

The questionnaires were issued to a random sample of parents of children in first and eighth grades in 218 sample elementary schools and to parents of twelfth-grade students in 104 sample secondary schools. A total of 24,502 responses were analyzed for this report.

Although it is important to know how the total number of respondents reacted to the goal statements, equally important is an analysis of the kinds of people who were respondents. The first general characteristic of the 24,502 respondents is that they were parents who had children in Catholic schools; for this reason they represented less than 50% of Catholic parents. This group also differed from the general

Catholic population as they had children of elementary or secondary school age.

Beyond these 2 general characteristics there are specific differences that can help to describe the respondents and to analyze their responses. These characteristics, identified from the way in which the parents described themselves on the original questionnaire, are presented in Table 105.

Table 105

CHARACTERISTICS OF RESPONDENTS

(TOTAL 24,502)

1. Religion			7. Persons in family			
Catholic	22,695	92.7	2–3	2,023	8.4
Protestant	1,341	5.5	4–5	9,986	41.2
Other	229	0.9	6–7	7,750	32.0
None	178	0.8	8–9	2,913	12.0
2. Relation to child			10 +	1,537	6.4
Mother	12,869	52.5	8. Occupational status			
Father	11,498	46.9	Professional	1,751	7.4
Guardian	136	0.6	High executives	1,291	5.4
3. Age			Other			
20–29	1,080	4.5	executives	2,196	9.2
30–39	8,976	37.0	White-collar	3,130	13.2
40–49	10,636	43.7	Skilled	3,277	13.7
50–59	3,274	13.5	Small business	4,111	17.3
60 +	317	1.3	Semiskilled	5,342	22.4
4. Respondent's birth			Unskilled	1,565	6.6
Foreign-born	2,251	9.2	Disabled, etc.	1,132	4.8
Native-born	22,143	90.7	9. Years of schooling			
5. Parents' birth			8 or less	2,721	11.5
Foreign-born	10,701	44.0	9–11	4,790	20.2
Native-born	13,618	56.0	12	8,801	37.1
6. Ethnicity			13–15	3,826	16.1
Irish	6,214	27.7	16	2,114	8.9
German	4,241	18.9	17 +	1,464	6.2
Italian	2,848	12.7	10. Years of Catholic			
Polish	2,616	11.7	schooling			
English	1,628	7.3	None	9,623	39.7
French	1,186	5.3	1–8	8,086	33.4
Other N. W.			9–11	2,045	8.4
Europe	655	2.8	12	2,773	11.4
Other Europe	2,433	10.8	13–15	966	4.0
Latin America	397	1.9	16	542	2.2
All Other	192	0.9	17 or more	205	0.9

Any discrepancy between the in-item totals and the total respondents is accounted for by the "no responses." These differences are, however, very small and the percentages are related to the total response.

The parents described in Table 105 represent approximately 12,000 families (in 97% of the returned questionnaires, husband and wife each responded). As they report on their religion 7.2% are identified as non-Catholic, indicating that approximately 14% of these families are the result of mixed religious marriages. If estimates made indicating that more than 20% of married Catholics have non-Catholic spouses are well-founded, it would appear that mixed religious marriages are not proportionately represented among the families of children in Catholic schools. In addition, the fact that twice as many fathers as mothers report as non-Catholic makes it appear that there is more likelihood that the children will be sent to a Catholic school when the wife in a religiously mixed marriage is a Catholic.

The 7.2% reported non-Catholic parents substantiates the reliability of the reports of the students in these schools, who reported 7.9% of their parents as non-Catholic.

The median age of the reporting parents falls in the interval of 40–49, with the fathers averaging about 2 years older than the mothers. The parents in the youngest age interval of 20–29 had the least total education beyond grade 12 and also had the least Catholic education, with 53% reporting no experience in Catholic schools.

Parents who are foreign-born or of foreign-born parentage have appreciably smaller families and tend to have lower occupational status. The native-born have more total schooling. In addition to these factors we find that parents of Irish and German backgrounds have larger families than those of Italian or Polish descent. Only 75% of those who identify ethnically as English are Catholic, compared with 98% of the Irish and Italian. On the other hand, Irish and English show significantly higher occupational and educational attainment than either Italian or Polish. English and Italian parents are least likely to have had any Catholic schooling; of those who have had some Catholic schooling, the Italian and Polish are not inclined to go beyond the elementary grades in Catholic schools.

Mixed religious marriages show smaller families, and the small family is also related to lower job status as well as to total and Catholic education. The higher status occupations, professional and executive, show larger families, and a strong direct relationship to increased total and Catholic education. There is no attempt here to suggest causal relationships.

Clearly there is a strong relationship between total years of schooling and total years of Catholic schooling. However, the majority of the respondents have had more than half of their education in non-Catholic schools. Therefore, it would be rather difficult to assess the impact of Catholic schooling on the values, attitudes, or behavior of respondents. The proportion of the respondents who transfer to non-Catholic schools increases with total educational attainment, but an interesting feature is the high persistence rate of those who leave Catholic schools for further education.

This description of some of the characteristics of the parent respondents gives some idea of the atmosphere within which the Parental Expectations instrument was administered. As previously stated, the respondents came from parents of first-, eighth-, and twelfth-grade students in 322 schools in 13 dioceses. At the minimum these 24,502 respondents are representative of the parents in the Catholic schools of the United States.

WHAT PARENTS SAY

The 31 goals statements were not presented in related groups but were later accumulated into 6 categories for analysis and review. Even though the goals will be so grouped, each goal statement will be presented individually for additional analysis by the critical reader. The 6 groupings were developed logically, with full knowledge that other logical variations could be developed. For example, the items we identify as "academic" might be augmented by items we categorize as "school operation."

The thoughtful, even though arbitrary, analysis categories are:

1. Religious virtues
2. Personal virtues
3. Social virtues
4. Academic goals
5. School operation goals
6. Practical goals

The analyses of the parents' responses to proposed goals will be presented under 3 controls: the way in which all parents responded; the differentiated responses of mothers and fathers; and the differentiated responses of Catholic and non-Catholic parents. The analyses will follow the 6 categories outlined above and will include other parent characteristics that seem to have high significance. Further identification of the ways in which more specific groups of Catholic parents indicate their thinking, is available in the files of the Study. As examples: the responses to each inquiry item can be determined for the 7 claimed Scandinavian parents who had between 9 and 11 years of Catholic schooling and for the non-Catholic mothers in a specific diocese who had less than 12 years of total education. These examples are offered as an invitation to further exploitation of the available data by interested and qualified investigators.

As a general observation of the evaluations, parents are consistently more likely to rate the importance of goals at a higher level than they are to assign high success to schools' achievement.

Religious Expectations of Parents

In this group of 5 goal statements the total group of parents assign the highest importance to teaching children to know about God, Christ, and the Church. When the "most important" and "very important" ranks are combined, they include 96.8% of the respondents (Tables 106, 107, 108).

Table 106
RELIGIOUS EXPECTATIONS OF PARENTS
(ALL RESPONDENTS, 24,502)

Catholic schools should:			Most	Very	Some	Little	None	Don't know
Item 2 ... teach children to know about God, Christ, the Church	Importance		73.3	23.5	2.7	0.2	0.1	0.1
	Success		56.1	35.7	5.7	0.4	0.1	1.9
Item 11 ... have only religious teachers (sisters, priests)	Importance		21.7	18.6	30.1	18.4	9.2	1.9
	Success		12.8	26.8	36.3	11.8	3.9	8.9
Item 12 ... give children Catholic friends and good example	Importance		31.4	33.9	23.5	7.5	2.8	0.9
	Success		19.1	37.4	30.0	4.7	0.7	8.0
Item 19 ... train children to practice religion (Mass, etc.)	Importance		70.7	23.4	4.4	0.8	0.3	0.4
	Success		45.5	37.2	12.6	1.9	0.4	2.4
Item 30 ... foster vocations to be sisters, priests, brothers	Importance		27.4	30.5	29.2	6.3	2.6	3.9
	Success		9.4	17.3	44.3	10.9	1.1	16.9

Table 107

RELIGIOUS EXPECTATIONS OF PARENTS
(CATHOLIC, 22,695; NON-CATHOLIC, 1,748)

Catholic schools should:			Most	Very	Some	Little	None	Don't know
Item 2 ... teach children to know about God, Christ, the Church	Importance							
		Catholic	74.7	22.8	2.2	0.2	0.0	0.1
		Non-Catholic	56.1	31.9	8.8	1.5	0.6	1.1
	Success							
		Catholic	56.6	35.6	5.8	0.4	0.0	1.6
		Non-Catholic	51.6	35.9	5.3	0.6	0.0	6.6
Item 11 ... have only religious teachers (sisters, priests)	Importance							
		Catholic	21.7	18.9	30.5	18.3	8.9	1.7
		Non-Catholic	19.9	14.9	26.0	20.6	13.7	4.9
	Success							
		Catholic	12.5	26.8	37.0	12.0	3.4	8.2
		Non-Catholic	15.8	26.3	27.4	8.5	2.9	19.1
Item 12 ... give children Catholic friends and good example	Importance							
		Catholic	32.1	34.5	23.3	6.9	2.4	0.8
		Non-Catholic	21.1	24.2	27.2	14.8	9.5	3.2
	Success							
		Catholic	19.5	37.9	30.1	4.6	0.7	7.2
		Non-Catholic	15.3	30.5	28.1	6.6	1.1	18.4
Item 19 ... train children to practice religion (Mass, etc.)	Importance							
		Catholic	72.2	23.1	3.9	0.5	0.1	0.2
		Non-Catholic	49.3	27.9	12.6	4.5	2.2	3.5
	Success							
		Catholic	45.8	37.2	12.7	1.9	0.4	2.0
		Non-Catholic	41.7	36.4	11.6	1.2	0.5	8.6
Item 30 ... foster vocations to be sisters, priests, brothers	Importance							
		Catholic	28.3	31.5	29.2	5.7	2.0	3.3
		Non-Catholic	15.1	17.6	30.7	14.9	9.3	12.4
	Success							
		Catholic	9.5	17.5	45.3	11.0	1.1	15.6
		Non-Catholic	7.9	14.4	32.1	8.7	0.9	36.0

Table 108

RELIGIOUS EXPECTATIONS OF PARENTS

(MOTHER, 12,868; FATHER, 11,498)

Catholic schools should:		Most	Very	Some	Little	None	Don't know
Item 2 ... teach children to know about God, Christ, the Church	Importance						
	Mother	76.9	21.1	1.7	0.2	0.0	0.1
	Father	69.4	26.1	3.8	0.4	0.1	0.1
	Success						
	Mother	59.8	33.4	4.7	0.3	0.1	1.7
	Father	52.1	38.2	6.9	0.6	0.1	2.1
Item 11 ... have only religious teachers (sisters, priests)	Importance						
	Mother	23.2	18.9	30.1	17.6	8.2	1.9
	Father	19.9	18.3	30.1	19.3	10.4	1.9
	Success						
	Mother	12.7	26.1	36.6	12.4	3.5	8.6
	Father	12.9	27.5	36.1	11.1	3.1	9.3
Item 12 ... give children Catholic friends and good example	Importance						
	Mother	33.8	34.2	22.0	6.9	2.3	0.8
	Father	28.6	33.6	25.2	8.2	3.5	0.9
	Success						
	Mother	20.6	37.8	28.9	4.3	0.7	7.6
	Father	17.5	37.1	31.2	5.1	0.7	8.4
Item 19 ... train children to practice religion (Mass, etc.)	Importance						
	Mother	74.9	21.1	3.1	0.5	0.1	0.2
	Father	66.0	25.9	5.9	1.1	0.5	0.5
	Success						
	Mother	48.7	35.3	11.6	1.8	0.4	2.2
	Father	41.9	39.3	13.6	2.0	0.5	2.7
Item 30 ... foster vocations to be sisters, priests, brothers	Importance						
	Mother	28.6	30.9	29.2	5.3	1.9	4.0
	Father	26.2	30.2	29.3	7.3	3.3	3.6
	Success						
	Mother	9.6	17.5	43.9	9.9	1.1	17.9
	Father	9.3	17.0	44.7	12.0	1.2	15.8

Training children to practice their religion is considered almost equally important, with 94.1% of the parents assigning the highest ranks. Each of these items is also ranked high in school success, although the religion practice item is well below the religion teaching item in this regard. Tables 107 and 108, which deal with the responses of mothers and fathers and the responses of Catholics and non-Catholics, show no great differences.

The item that proposes having only religious teachers in the schools does not receive strong support; 40.3% assign high importance and 27.6% consider the item of little or no importance. The total father and non-Catholic respondents place a lower importance on this item than does the total response. The success ranking of this item shows no marked differences between the groups of respondents, and the low level of success is a rather realistic appraisal of the actual staffing in the schools, where there are few schools without some lay teachers.

Item 12, which proposes that Catholic schools give children Catholic friends and good example, received its strongest support from the mothers; 68% placed high importance on the item, whereas only 45% of the non-Catholic respondents considered this goal of high importance. The success the parents ascribe to this item coincides closely with the friendship pattern of the Inventory of Catholic School Outcomes, which indicates that their out-of-school friends were mostly Catholics.

Only 57.9% of the parents consider fostering vocations a matter of high importance, and 8.9% consider this goal of little or no importance. It is significant that almost 17% of the parents do not know whether the schools are successful in this goal.

Table 109

PERSONAL VIRTUE EXPECTATIONS OF PARENTS
(ALL RESPONDENTS, 24,502)

Catholic schools should:		Most	Very	Some	Little	None	Don't know
Item 1 . . . train children in self-discipline and hard work	Importance	47.2	43.9	7.8	0.5	0.2	0.3
	Success	23.0	38.8	30.4	2.8	0.4	4.6
Item 8 . . . train children to be honest, truthful, and moral	Importance	78.9	19.5	1.2	0.2	0.1	0.1
	Success	33.4	39.9	21.2	1.9	0.3	3.3
Item 28 . . . teach children to think for themselves	Importance	62.9	32.9	3.3	0.5	0.1	0.2
	Success	17.0	33.3	36.7	5.7	0.9	6.3

Personal Virtue Expectations of Parents

Among the personal virtues as potential goals of Catholic schools, parents award the greatest importance to the training of children in honesty, truthfulness, and morality (Tables 109, 110, 111).

Table 110

PERSONAL VIRTUE EXPECTATIONS OF PARENTS
(CATHOLIC, 22,695; NON-CATHOLIC, 1,748)

Catholic schools should:		Most	Very	Some	Little	None	Don't know
Item 1 . . . train children in self-discipline and hard work	Importance						
	Catholic	46.9	44.1	7.9	0.6	0.2	0.3
	Non-Catholic	49.7	43.4	5.6	0.2	0.2	0.9
	Success						
	Catholic	22.9	38.9	30.7	2.8	0.4	4.3
	Non-Catholic	22.9	38.6	27.4	2.6	0.3	8.2
Item 8 . . . train children to be honest, truthful, and moral	Importance						
	Catholic	79.1	19.3	1.3	0.2	0.0	0.1
	Non-Catholic	76.9	21.4	0.9	0.4	0.0	0.4
	Success						
	Catholic	33.4	40.3	21.3	1.8	0.2	2.9
	Non-Catholic	32.1	36.4	21.2	2.2	0.4	7.7
Item 28 . . . teach children to think for themselves	Importance						
	Catholic	62.8	33.1	3.3	0.4	0.2	0.2
	Non-Catholic	64.9	30.6	3.1	0.6	0.2	0.5
	Success						
	Catholic	16.9	33.4	37.2	5.7	0.8	6.0
	Non-Catholic	18.4	31.6	32.3	5.4	1.6	10.5

In fact, when the goals are examined singly this goal is rated the most important of all 31, with 98.4% giving it highest priority. The parents also award high importance to teaching children to think for themselves, placing this goal among the top 5 of all those proposed. Training in self-discipline and hard work is also given high importance by the respondents; they rank it more important than the goals of fostering vocations, having Catholic friends, and having only religious teachers.

Although the parents attached high importance to the 3 personal virtue expectations, they were considerably less willing to identify high

Table 111

PERSONAL VIRTUE EXPECTATIONS OF PARENTS
(MOTHER, 12,868; FATHER, 11,498)

Catholic schools should:		Most	Very	Some	Little	None	Don't know
Item 1 . . . train children in self-discipline and hard work	Importance						
	Mother	46.6	43.9	8.4	0.6	0.3	0.2
	Father	47.7	43.9	7.3	0.5	0.2	0.3
	Success						
	Mother	24.2	39.1	29.2	2.4	0.3	4.8
	Father	21.7	38.5	31.7	3.3	0.4	4.4
Item 8 . . . train children to be honest, truthful, and moral	Importance						
	Mother	80.6	18.0	1.1	0.2	0.1	0.0
	Father	73.1	21.1	1.4	0.3	0.0	0.1
	Success						
	Mother	34.9	38.2	21.6	1.8	0.2	3.2
	Father	31.6	41.9	20.9	1.9	0.3	3.4
Item 28 . . . teach children to think for themselves	Importance						
	Mother	63.5	31.9	3.6	0.5	0.2	0.3
	Father	62.1	34.1	2.9	0.5	0.1	0.2
	Success						
	Mother	18.3	33.1	35.4	5.5	0.8	6.9
	Father	15.5	33.6	38.4	5.9	0.9	5.6

success levels for the schools' achievement of these goals. Only 50.3% credited the schools with high success in teaching children to think for themselves, and 6.6% indicated that the schools had little or no success in this area. Considering self-discipline and hard work, 61.8% indicated high success for the schools, and 73.3% attached high success in training children to be honest, truthful, and moral. While all groups of parents agree generally in rating importance of the personal virtue goals, parents in the professional and executive group assign appreciably lower success ratings in teaching the child to think for himself.

Social Virtue Expectations of Parents

Responding to the levels of importance and success of the social goals, 95% of the parents attached the greatest importance to the goals of making children good citizens of the United States and training them to respect persons and property (Tables 112, 113, 114). They ascribe better than average success to the efforts of the schools in achieving these goals. The goal of producing leaders is rated high by 83.4% of the parents, but only 44.1% are willing to give a high rank of success to leadership development by Catholic schools.

The goal of teaching children to like other races and nationalities was ranked high by 73.1% of the parents, but only 46.3% considered the schools highly successful in achieving this objective. A second related goal that Catholic schools should teach children to get along with others such as Jews was ranked high by 82.5% of those responding, but only 48.7% considered that the goal is met on a high success level and 8.4% indicated little or no success.

The most surprising reaction to these social goals came as the parents evaluated the statement that Catholic schools should teach children to help others in foreign countries. Only 44.6% of the parents considered this goal of high importance, and 13.3% considered it of little or no importance. The parents also did not think highly of the success with which this goal was being met, as only 30.8% awarded a high success rank.

Table 112

SOCIAL VIRTUE EXPECTATIONS OF PARENTS
(ALL RESPONDENTS, 24,502)

Catholic schools should:		Most	Very	Some	Little	None	Don't know
Item 3 ... make children good citizens of the United States	Importance	55.7	38.9	4.7	0.4	0.1	0.2
	Success	30.9	44.4	18.2	1.1	0.1	5.3
Item 5 ... teach children to like other races and nationalities, as, Negroes, immigrants, Puerto Ricans	Importance	38.8	34.3	19.7	3.9	1.9	1.3
	Success	18.5	27.8	31.9	6.4	1.1	14.3
Item 15 ... produce leaders for our nation and communities	Importance	48.9	34.5	13.2	2.0	0.6	0.7
	Success	15.9	28.2	35.8	6.9	0.9	12.2
Item 17 ... teach children to get along with others such as Jews	Importance	46.9	35.6	13.2	2.5	1.0	0.8
	Success	18.1	30.6	30.6	6.8	1.6	12.3
Item 27 ... train children in respect for persons and property	Importance	60.7	34.6	4.1	0.4	0.1	0.1
	Success	23.6	38.8	29.8	3.6	0.5	3.7
Item 29 ... teach children to help others in foreign countries	Importance	19.6	25.0	40.4	10.7	2.6	1.7
	Success	10.2	20.6	38.9	9.0	1.0	20.2

Table 113

SOCIAL VIRTUE EXPECTATIONS OF PARENTS

(CATHOLIC, 22,695; NON-CATHOLIC, 1,748)

Catholic schools should:		Most	Very	Some	Little	None	Don't know
Item 3 ... make children good citizens of the United States	Importance						
	Catholic	55.6	39.1	4.7	0.4	0.1	0.1
	Non-Catholic	57.5	36.5	4.9	0.2	0.1	0.8
	Success						
	Catholic	31.2	44.5	18.1	1.1	0.1	4.9
	Non-Catholic	25.9	43.3	18.1	0.9	0.3	11.5
Item 5 ... teach children to like other races and nationalities, as, Negroes, immigrants, Puerto Ricans	Importance						
	Catholic	38.6	34.4	19.9	3.9	1.9	1.3
	Non-Catholic	41.6	33.1	15.9	4.5	3.0	1.9
	Success						
	Catholic	18.4	28.0	32.2	6.4	1.0	13.9
	Non-Catholic	18.4	24.2	30.4	5.9	1.7	19.4
Item 15 ... produce leaders for our nation and communities	Importance						
	Catholic	49.6	34.4	12.9	1.9	0.6	0.6
	Non-Catholic	41.2	35.5	16.6	3.9	1.2	1.6
	Success						
	Catholic	15.9	28.2	36.1	7.1	0.9	11.8
	Non-Catholic	16.3	27.6	31.4	5.3	0.8	18.6
Item 17 ... teach children to get along with others such as Jews	Importance						
	Catholic	46.8	35.6	13.4	2.6	0.9	0.7
	Non-Catholic	50.4	34.3	11.1	2.0	0.9	1.3
	Success						
	Catholic	18.1	30.9	30.8	6.8	1.5	11.8
	Non-Catholic	18.3	26.9	27.4	6.9	2.1	18.4
Item 27 ... train children in respect for persons and property	Importance						
	Catholic	60.7	34.6	4.1	0.4	0.1	0.1
	Non-Catholic	61.4	33.5	3.9	0.4	0.1	0.6
	Success						
	Catholic	23.5	38.9	30.1	3.6	0.5	3.4
	Non-Catholic	22.8	37.3	26.6	4.4	0.5	8.4
Item 29 ... teach children to help others in foreign countries	Importance						
	Catholic	19.4	25.1	40.7	10.7	2.5	1.6
	Non-Catholic	21.8	23.9	37.4	10.4	3.9	2.6
	Success						
	Catholic	10.1	20.8	39.3	9.1	0.9	19.7
	Non-Catholic	11.2	19.1	33.0	7.7	0.9	28.1

Table 114

SOCIAL VIRTUE EXPECTATIONS OF PARENTS
(MOTHER, 12,868; FATHER, 11,498)

Catholic schools should:		Most	Very	Some	Little	None	Don't know
Item 3 . . . make children good citizens of the United States	Importance						
	Mother	56.5	38.4	4.5	0.3	0.0	0.2
	Father	54.7	39.6	4.9	0.5	0.1	0.2
	Success						
	Mother	32.6	43.8	17.0	0.9	0.1	5.6
	Father	29.0	45.1	19.4	1.3	0.2	5.0
Item 5 . . . teach children to like other races and nationalities, as, Negroes, immigrants, Puerto Ricans	Importance						
	Mother	43.0	34.8	17.6	3.0	1.3	1.2
	Father	34.9	33.8	22.1	5.1	2.7	1.4
	Success						
	Mother	20.2	29.4	29.7	5.4	0.8	14.5
	Father	16.6	25.9	34.5	7.5	1.4	14.1
Item 15 . . . produce leaders for our nation and communities	Importance						
	Mother	50.5	33.4	12.8	1.9	0.6	0.8
	Father	47.2	35.7	13.8	2.1	0.6	0.6
	Success						
	Mother	16.7	27.9	34.3	6.2	0.8	14.1
	Father	15.0	28.4	37.5	7.8	0.9	10.3
Item 17 . . . teach children to get along with others such as Jews	Importance						
	Mother	49.9	35.0	11.5	2.0	0.8	0.7
	Father	43.5	36.0	15.3	3.1	1.3	0.8
	Success						
	Mother	19.7	30.5	28.6	6.4	1.5	13.3
	Father	16.4	30.8	32.9	7.2	1.6	11.1
Item 27 . . . train children in respect for persons and property	Importance						
	Mother	61.9	33.1	4.2	0.6	0.1	0.1
	Father	59.2	36.2	4.1	0.3	0.1	0.1
	Success						
	Mother	25.3	37.7	29.3	3.6	0.5	3.6
	Father	21.6	40.4	30.3	3.6	0.5	3.9
Item 29 . . . teach children to help others in foreign countries	Importance						
	Mother	20.7	25.8	40.0	9.5	2.0	1.9
	Father	18.2	24.0	40.9	12.0	3.2	1.6
	Success						
	Mother	11.2	21.8	37.6	7.5	0.9	21.0
	Father	9.1	19.2	40.5	10.7	1.1	19.4

Academic Expectations of Parents

As parents consider the 4 academic goals, there is surprising unanimity in their evaluation of both the importance and success levels (Tables 115, 116, 117). The goal of teaching children to read and write clearly and well is identified by 94% of the parents as highly important. Slightly more than 70% award the schools high success in meeting this goal. The 2 goals concerned with teaching arithmetic and science and teaching history and current social problems receive approximately equal treatment, with 86% indicating high importance and 48% to 53% indicating high success. The fourth goal relating to the teaching of music and art elicits a surprising common response, with only 46.1% of all parents assigning it a high priority.

It should be remembered that the proposal for evaluation was made on a one-to-one basis and not an evaluation of which item of the 31 proposed was most important. It is evident that the parents understood the request, as they frequently gave similar ratings to numbers of items. Even though parents assigned low importance to the teaching of music and art, they assigned an even lower rating of success to the goal; only 29.8% were willing to credit the schools with high success in this area, and an additional 40.6% were willing to concede that the schools achieved some success in this arts area. One of the significant deviations was that non-Catholic parents assigned higher importance and success levels to this goal.

Table 115
ACADEMIC EXPECTATIONS OF PARENTS
(ALL RESPONDENTS, 24,502)

Catholic schools should:		Most	Very	Some	Little	None	Don't know
Item 4 . . . be strong in arithmetic and science	Importance	44.3	42.4	11.8	0.9	0.1	0.5
	Success	18.3	35.5	32.5	5.3	0.4	7.9
Item 10 . . . teach children to read, write clearly and well	Importance	60.3	34.1	4.8	0.5	0.1	0.1
	Success	29.1	42.0	22.7	2.9	0.3	2.9
Item 14 . . . teach music and the arts to the children	Importance	20.2	25.9	40.6	10.9	1.8	0.6
	Success	9.1	20.7	40.3	16.4	3.2	10.2
Item 22 . . . teach children history and today's social problems	Importance	39.0	48.3	11.7	0.6	0.1	0.3
	Success	13.4	35.8	36.4	4.0	0.5	9.8

One other deviation that occurs in the evaluations of almost all goals covering both importance and success is that mothers exceed fathers in their goal evaluations.

There are many evidences that 2 groups of parents, the younger age groups and the professional-executive status parents, regularly assign lower success rankings to the proposed goals; this was particularly true of academic goals. This more critical evaluation of the schools' success level increases as the amount of Catholic schooling increases. It seems evident that the younger age groups of parents who have more total education and more Catholic education and who have higher job

Table 116

ACADEMIC EXPECTATIONS OF PARENTS
(CATHOLIC, 22695; NON-CATHOLIC, 1,748)

Catholic schools should:		Most	Very	Some	Little	None	Don't know
Item 4 . . . be strong in arithmetic and science	Importance						
	Catholic	44.2	42.5	11.9	0.9	0.1	0.4
	Non-Catholic	47.0	40.9	10.3	0.7	0.0	1.0
	Success						
	Catholic	18.2	35.6	32.9	5.3	0.4	7.6
	Non-Catholic	18.3	35.1	28.1	5.6	0.1	12.8
Item 10 . . . teach children to read, write clearly and well	Importance						
	Catholic	60.4	34.1	4.9	0.5	0.1	0.0
	Non-Catholic	60.4	34.5	3.7	0.7	0.1	0.6
	Success						
	Catholic	28.9	42.1	23.0	2.9	0.3	2.7
	Non-Catholic	29.7	41.7	18.4	2.3	0.2	7.6
Item 14 . . . teach music and the arts to the children	Importance						
	Catholic	19.8	25.9	40.9	11.0	1.8	0.6
	Non-Catholic	24.2	28.7	36.2	8.5	1.2	1.2
	Success						
	Catholic	8.9	20.7	40.7	16.7	3.2	9.8
	Non-Catholic	11.1	20.9	36.0	13.2	2.5	16.3
Item 22 . . . teach children history and today's social problems	Importance						
	Catholic	38.8	48.4	11.9	0.6	0.0	0.3
	Non-Catholic	41.5	47.2	9.9	0.7	0.2	0.5
	Success						
	Catholic	13.3	35.9	36.8	4.1	0.5	9.4
	Non-Catholic	14.4	33.9	31.7	3.5	0.7	15.7

Table 117

ACADEMIC EXPECTATIONS OF PARENTS
(MOTHER, 12,868; FATHER, 11,498)

Catholic schools should:		Most	Very	Some	Little	None	Don't know
Item 4 . . . be strong in arithmetic and science	**Importance**						
	Mother	44.6	42.5	11.5	0.7	0.1	0.6
	Father	44.1	42.3	12.1	0.9	0.1	0.5
	Success						
	Mother	19.5	35.7	31.2	4.8	0.4	8.4
	Father	17.0	35.3	33.9	5.8	0.5	7.4
Item 10 . . . teach children to read, write clearly and well	**Importance**						
	Mother	62.6	32.5	4.1	0.5	0.1	0.0
	Father	57.9	35.9	5.4	0.5	0.1	0.1
	Success						
	Mother	31.4	41.4	21.3	2.8	0.2	2.9
	Father	26.4	42.7	24.3	3.1	0.4	3.1
Item 14 . . . teach music and the arts to the children	**Importance**						
	Mother	21.9	26.5	39.6	9.9	1.6	0.5
	Father	18.1	25.5	41.8	11.9	1.9	0.8
	Success						
	Mother	9.9	21.7	39.1	16.1	3.4	9.8
	Father	8.2	19.5	41.8	16.8	3.0	10.7
Item 22 . . . teach children history and today's social problems	**Importance**						
	Mother	41.6	47.4	10.3	0.4	0.0	0.3
	Father	36.1	49.3	13.4	0.7	0.1	0.3
	Success						
	Mother	15.2	37.1	33.8	3.3	0.5	10.1
	Father	11.4	34.3	39.5	4.8	0.6	9.4

status and who chose to send their children to Catholic schools are more critical and demanding of the schools.

School Operation Expectations of Parents

The parents place a rather high priority on preparing students for college; approximately 86% assign high importance to this goal, and 61% signify that they believe the schools achieve high success in meeting this goal (Tables 118, 119, 120).

Table 118

SCHOOL OPERATION EXPECTATIONS OF PARENTS
(ALL RESPONDENTS, 24,502)

Catholic schools should:		Most	Very	Some	Little	None	Don't know
Item 7 . . . prepare children for college	Importance	48.5	37.9	12.0	1.1	0.1	0.4
	Success	22.0	39.6	26.3	2.9	0.3	8.9
Item 16 . . . have effective qualified lay teachers when needed	Importance	54.4	36.3	6.9	1.1	0.4	0.9
	Success	17.2	28.2	32.8	11.4	2.3	8.0
Item 20 . . . not have large classes (in single rooms)	Importance	46.4	31.5	15.9	3.7	0.9	1.5
	Success	8.4	14.6	31.8	27.4	11.0	6.7
Item 21 . . . have physical fitness programs for boys and girls	Importance	43.1	33.3	19.1	3.4	0.8	0.2
	Success	9.5	14.8	32.6	23.6	12.2	7.3
Item 23 . . . help gifted and slow-learning children	Importance	47.4	40.2	10.3	0.8	0.2	1.0
	Success	10.7	19.1	35.2	15.6	4.2	15.2
Item 25 . . . not give much homework to children	Importance	10.9	13.7	29.7	23.4	17.0	5.3
	Success	8.3	17.5	29.7	17.4	9.0	18.1
Item 26 . . . have effective qualified sisters, priests, and brothers as teachers	Importance	60.0	29.8	7.3	1.7	0.7	0.5
	Success	26.4	37.5	26.6	4.0	0.7	4.8

Two of the goals in this group deal with the provisions of qualified teachers, both lay and religious; the parents assign approximately the same importance to the need for qualified teachers in each group. Weighing the success of the schools in achieving this goal, 63% are willing to signify high success for the provision of effective, qualified religious teachers, whereas only 45% are willing to credit the schools with high success in providing effective, qualified lay teachers. This is another instance where the younger parents with more total and Catholic education and who have a more favorable occupational status take a dimmer view of school success; only 30% of this group indicated a high success level for the provision of adequate lay teachers.

The proposal that the schools should provide help for the gifted and for the slow-learning children was ranked by 87% of the parents as highly important, only 29% of whom thought the schools were achieving high success in meeting this objective; an additional 20% indicated that the schools were achieving little or no success in serving the gifted

Table 119

SCHOOL OPERATION EXPECTATIONS OF PARENTS
(CATHOLIC, 22,695; NON-CATHOLIC, 1,748)

Catholic schools should:		Most	Very	Some	Little	None	Don't know
Item 7 ... prepare children for college	Importance						
	Catholic	48.1	37.9	12.3	1.2	0.2	0.3
	Non-Catholic	52.3	36.8	9.2	0.9	0.2	0.6
	Success						
	Catholic	21.8	39.9	26.6	3.0	0.3	8.3
	Non-Catholic	24.5	36.3	20.6	1.9	0.2	16.5
Item 16 ... have effective qualified lay teachers when needed	Importance						
	Catholic	54.7	36.2	6.9	1.0	0.4	0.8
	Non-Catholic	48.7	37.7	8.1	1.9	0.6	2.9
	Success						
	Catholic	17.2	28.3	33.2	11.6	2.3	7.4
	Non-Catholic	16.5	27.4	27.3	8.9	2.4	17.4
Item 20 ... not have large classes (in single rooms)	Importance						
	Catholic	46.5	31.2	16.2	3.7	0.9	1.4
	Non-Catholic	46.3	34.9	12.9	3.5	0.6	1.8
	Success						
	Catholic	8.1	14.4	32.0	27.9	11.3	6.3
	Non-Catholic	12.2	17.1	30.1	20.8	7.9	11.9
Item 21 ... have physical fitness programs for boys and girls	Importance						
	Catholic	42.8	33.2	19.5	3.4	0.9	0.2
	Non-Catholic	47.0	36.7	12.9	2.3	0.6	0.5
	Success						
	Catholic	9.2	14.6	32.9	23.9	12.4	6.9
	Non-Catholic	12.3	17.3	28.9	19.2	8.6	13.6
Item 23 ... help gifted and slow-learning children	Importance						
	Catholic	47.3	40.2	10.4	0.8	0.3	0.9
	Non-Catholic	49.8	38.6	8.9	0.6	0.2	1.8
	Success						
	Catholic	10.2	19.1	35.6	15.9	4.2	14.7
	Non-Catholic	12.9	20.2	30.9	10.9	3.3	21.7
Item 25 ... not give much homework to children	Importance						
	Catholic	10.9	13.7	29.9	23.6	16.7	5.1
	Non-Catholic	10.2	13.7	25.9	21.3	20.5	8.4
	Success						
	Catholic	8.1	17.5	30.1	17.5	8.9	17.8
	Non-Catholic	10.1	16.1	24.3	15.9	9.3	24.2
Item 26 ... have effective qualified sisters, priests, and brothers as teachers	Importance						
	Catholic	60.6	29.9	7.0	1.6	0.5	0.4
	Non-Catholic	51.3	28.5	11.6	3.6	2.6	2.3
	Success						
	Catholic	26.2	37.8	26.8	4.0	0.7	4.4
	Non-Catholic	27.8	33.8	22.9	3.3	0.5	11.6

Table 120

SCHOOL OPERATION EXPECTATIONS OF PARENTS
(MOTHER, 12,868; FATHER, 11,498)

Catholic schools should:		Most	Very	Some	Little	None	Don't know
Item 7 ... prepare children for college	Importance						
	Mother	49.7	37.2	11.4	1.1	0.1	0.4
	Father	46.9	38.6	12.8	1.2	0.2	0.3
	Success						
	Mother	23.6	39.2	24.8	2.6	0.3	9.4
	Father	20.3	40.0	27.9	3.3	0.3	8.2
Item 16 ... have effective qualified lay teachers when needed	Importance						
	Mother	57.9	34.2	5.9	0.8	0.3	0.9
	Father	50.4	38.6	8.1	1.4	0.5	0.9
	Success						
	Mother	18.7	28.7	31.8	10.8	2.2	7.8
	Father	15.5	27.5	34.0	12.2	2.6	8.2
Item 20 ... not have large classes (in single rooms)	Importance						
	Mother	49.5	29.9	15.1	3.4	0.7	1.4
	Father	43.0	33.3	16.9	4.1	1.1	1.5
	Success						
	Mother	8.7	14.2	30.8	27.6	12.3	6.4
	Father	7.9	15.0	33.0	27.2	9.8	7.0
Item 21 ... have physical fitness programs for boys and girls	Importance						
	Mother	43.8	32.5	19.1	3.5	0.8	0.2
	Father	42.3	34.4	19.1	3.1	0.9	0.2
	Success						
	Mother	9.7	14.2	30.8	23.6	14.0	7.7
	Father	9.4	15.5	34.7	23.5	10.1	6.8
Item 23 ... help gifted and slow-learning children	Importance						
	Mother	49.3	38.7	9.9	0.8	0.2	1.1
	Father	45.3	41.8	10.8	0.9	0.4	0.8
	Success						
	Mother	11.1	18.9	33.4	15.9	4.5	16.2
	Father	10.2	19.4	37.4	15.3	3.8	13.9
Item 25 ... not give much homework to children	Importance						
	Mother	10.9	13.3	31.3	23.9	15.6	5.0
	Father	10.7	14.3	28.0	22.8	18.6	5.6
	Success						
	Mother	8.6	16.9	30.6	17.2	8.7	17.9
	Father	7.9	18.1	28.7	17.6	9.4	18.2
Item 26 ... have effective qualified sisters, priests, and brothers as teachers	Importance						
	Mother	63.6	28.1	6.1	1.3	0.4	0.4
	Father	55.9	31.7	8.7	2.2	0.9	0.5
	Success						
	Mother	28.5	37.1	25.3	3.8	0.7	4.6
	Father	23.9	37.9	28.1	4.3	0.7	5.1

and slow-learning students. Approximately 76% of the respondents assigned high importance to the goal of providing physical fitness programs for all children, but only 24% identified a high success level in meeting this goal.

A final goal in this group proposed that the schools should not have large classes in single rooms; 77% of the parents placed high importance on this goal, but only 23% felt that success was reached by the schools in this area, and 38% felt that the schools were achieving little or no success in controlling class size.

Practical Expectations of Parents

80% of all respondents assign high importance to Item 6, which states that Catholic schools should train children for good jobs when they grow up; 46% indicate that the schools meet this goal on a high level. However, mothers and fathers differ, with mothers attaching greater importance and success to this vocational goal than fathers (Tables 121, 122, 123).

Table 121

PRACTICAL EXPECTATIONS OF PARENTS
(ALL RESPONDENTS, 24,502)

Catholic schools should:		Most	Very	Some	Little	None	Don't know
Item 6 . . . train children for good jobs when they grow up	Importance	45.1	35.0	15.5	3.1	0.8	0.5
	Success	16.0	30.4	34.0	4.8	0.6	14.1
Item 9 . . . not be expensive for Catholic parents	Importance	40.4	26.5	24.2	5.5	1.7	1.6
	Success	13.7	21.4	33.8	18.6	5.3	7.1
Item 13 . . . get help from parents when needed	Importance	44.6	37.9	13.9	1.9	0.5	1.1
	Success	19.5	31.3	32.6	8.0	1.1	7.4
Item 18 . . . get more money from the Federal Government	Importance	44.2	21.6	15.3	6.2	6.8	5.9
	Success	5.5	3.6	9.9	26.8	32.3	21.8
Item 24 . . . have space for all Catholic children	Importance	49.7	32.9	11.7	2.8	1.0	1.9
	Success	10.7	18.7	35.3	20.5	6.9	7.9
Item 31 . . . help parents control dating of children	Importance	26.1	24.0	28.0	10.6	8.6	2.6
	Success	8.1	13.1	35.5	15.4	4.8	23.1

Table 122

PRACTICAL EXPECTATIONS OF PARENTS
(CATHOLIC, 22,695; NON-CATHOLIC, 1,748)

Catholic schools should:		Most	Very	Some	Little	None	Don't know
Item 6 ... train children for good jobs when they grow up	Importance						
	Catholic	45.1	34.9	15.7	3.1	0.8	0.4
	Non-Catholic	44.9	36.1	13.2	3.5	1.0	1.2
	Success						
	Catholic	16.0	30.6	34.5	4.8	0.6	13.5
	Non-Catholic	14.5	27.6	29.2	4.8	0.7	23.2
Item 9 ... not be expensive for Catholic parents	Importance						
	Catholic	41.0	26.6	24.2	5.4	1.5	1.3
	Non-Catholic	31.4	25.3	24.6	8.1	4.1	6.5
	Success						
	Catholic	13.6	21.3	34.2	19.1	5.4	6.4
	Non-Catholic	15.3	22.5	28.9	11.7	4.5	17.1
Item 13 ... get help from parents when needed	Importance						
	Catholic	44.6	38.1	13.8	1.9	0.6	0.9
	Non-Catholic	43.6	35.8	15.4	2.4	1.1	1.7
	Success						
	Catholic	19.3	31.4	33.1	8.2	1.1	6.9
	Non-Catholic	22.0	30.4	26.8	6.2	0.7	13.9
Item 18 ... get more money from the Federal Government	Importance						
	Catholic	44.9	21.5	15.3	6.0	6.6	5.7
	Non-Catholic	33.9	22.8	14.7	8.5	10.2	9.8
	Success						
	Catholic	5.4	3.6	9.9	27.2	32.8	21.1
	Non-Catholic	5.9	5.0	9.4	22.5	26.1	31.0
Item 24 ... have space for all Catholic children	Importance						
	Catholic	50.4	33.2	11.5	2.5	0.8	1.6
	Non-Catholic	38.7	29.9	15.3	6.6	3.7	5.7
	Success						
	Catholic	10.4	18.6	35.7	20.9	7.1	7.3
	Non-Catholic	13.9	19.5	29.6	13.8	5.4	17.8
Item 31 ... help parents control dating of children	Importance						
	Catholic	26.2	24.3	28.3	10.5	8.1	2.5
	Non-Catholic	23.0	19.6	25.2	13.2	14.4	4.5
	Success						
	Catholic	8.0	13.1	36.1	15.6	4.8	22.3
	Non-Catholic	8.4	11.5	26.3	13.3	5.7	34.7

Table 123

PRACTICAL EXPECTATIONS OF PARENTS
(MOTHER, 12,868; FATHER, 11,498)

Catholic schools should:		Most	Very	Some	Little	None	Don't know
Item 6 . . . train children for good jobs when they grow up	Importance						
	Mother	48.3	34.7	13.8	2.4	0.6	0.5
	Father	41.7	35.4	17.4	3.9	1.0	0.5
	Success						
	Mother	17.5	31.2	32.2	3.8	0.6	14.7
	Father	14.3	29.5	36.1	5.9	0.7	13.4
Item 9 . . . not be expensive for Catholic parents	Importance						
	Mother	42.2	26.5	23.2	5.0	1.4	1.7
	Father	38.4	26.6	25.3	6.1	2.0	1.6
	Success						
	Mother	13.9	20.4	33.9	19.5	5.2	7.1
	Father	13.4	22.6	33.8	17.7	5.4	7.1
Item 13 . . . get help from parents when needed	Importance						
	Mother	47.3	36.7	12.9	1.7	0.5	0.9
	Father	41.3	39.4	15.1	2.2	0.8	1.1
	Success						
	Mother	21.3	31.7	31.4	6.9	0.9	7.7
	Father	17.4	30.9	33.9	9.4	1.3	7.1
Item 18 . . . get more money from the Federal Government	Importance						
	Mother	45.4	21.3	14.9	5.4	5.7	7.2
	Father	42.9	21.7	15.8	6.9	8.2	4.5
	Success						
	Mother	5.5	3.6	9.5	25.3	31.6	24.5
	Father	5.5	3.7	10.5	28.5	33.0	18.8
Item 24 . . . have space for all Catholic children	Importance						
	Mother	51.9	32.5	10.6	2.2	0.8	1.9
	Father	47.0	33.5	12.9	3.4	1.3	1.9
	Success						
	Mother	11.2	18.0	35.0	20.2	7.3	8.2
	Father	10.1	19.3	35.6	20.8	6.6	7.6
Item 31 . . . help parents control dating of children	Importance						
	Mother	27.2	23.9	28.2	9.9	7.5	2.8
	Father	24.2	24.3	27.8	11.5	9.8	2.4
	Success						
	Mother	8.7	13.3	35.3	14.5	4.3	23.9
	Father	7.4	12.9	35.7	16.4	5.5	22.1

To the item that states that the schools should have space for all Catholic children 82% of the parents assign high importance, and realistically only 29.4% claim any high degree of success. Among non-Catholic respondents, 10% fewer assign high importance to the schools providing space for all Catholic children, and these also assign a higher level of success than the Catholic respondents. To an allied goal statement that proposes that Catholic schools should not be expensive for Catholic parents, 67% of the Catholic respondents assign high priority, and only 56% of the non-Catholics make a similar assessment. In considering the success of the schools here, only 35% of the respondents award a high success level.

In response to the proposal that Catholic schools should get Federal funds, 66% of the Catholic parents and 56% of the non-Catholic parents rank this as a high priority objective; only 9% of all parents consider there is any significant success in achieving this goal. It would

Table 124

WEIGHTED RANKINGS OF TEN MOST IMPORTANT, TEN MOST SUCCESSFUL, TEN LEAST IMPORTANT, AND TEN LEAST SUCCESSFUL GOAL ITEMS BY PARENTS' TOTAL RESPONSE

Most important	Most successful	Least important[1]	Least successful[1]
1. Honest, truthful (8)[2]	Knowledge of God (2)	Homework (25)	Federal money (18)
2. Knowledge of God (2)	Religious practice (3)	Only religious teachers (11)	No large classes (20)
3. Religious practice (3)	Honest, truthful (8)	Help others in foreign countries (29)	Dating (31)
4. Think for himself (28)	Reading, writing (10)	Music and arts (14)	Physical fitness (21)
5. Qualified religious teachers (26)	Citizenship (3)	Dating (31)	Vocations (30)
6. Respect persons and property (27)	Qualified religious teachers (26)	Vocations (30)	Gifted and slow learners (23)
7. Reading, writing (10)	Respect persons and property (27)	Catholic friends (12)	Space for all Catholic children (24)
8. Citizenship (3)	Prepare for college (7)	Like other races (5)	Music and arts (14)
9. Qualified lay teachers (16)	Catholic friends and good example (12)	Not expensive (9)	Help others in foreign countries (29)
10. Space for all (24)	Self-discipline and hard work (1)	History, social problems (22)	Homework (25)

[1] First listed is the lowest ranked in success or importance.

[2] Numbers in parentheses refer to items in original instrument.

seem that there is not an overwhelming position on the part of Catholic parents in favor of Federal funds for Catholic schools.

A goal statement proposing that parents should help the schools when needed impressed 82% of the respondents as highly important, but only 50% considered that a high level of success was being reached.

SUMMARY OF PARENT RESPONSES

To give some perspective of the way in which the total group of parent respondents reacted to individual items within the 31 goal proposals, 2 analyses are presented in Tables 124 and 125, each of which identifies those items the parents ranked as most important, most successful, least important, and least successful.

Table 125

WEIGHTED JUDGMENTS OF PARENTS ON FIRST, SECOND, AND THIRD MOST IMPORTANT AND MOST SUCCESSFUL GOALS

Most important		Most successful		Least important[1]		Least successful[1]	
1. Knowledge of God (2)[2]		Knowledge of God (2)		Help others in foreign countries	(29)	Homework	(25)
2. Honest, truthful	(8)	Religious practice	(19)	Music and arts	(14)	Music and arts	(14)
3. Qualified religious teachers	(26)	Honest, truthful	(8)	Catholic friends	(12)	Federal money	(18)
4. Think for himself	(28)	Qualified religious teachers	(26)	Homework	(25)	Physical fitness	(21)
5. Self-discipline, hard work	(1)	Citizenship	(3)	Help from parents	(13)	Large classes	(20)
6. Citizenship	(3)	Self-discipline, hard work	(1)	Get along with others	(17)	Get along with others	(17)
7. Space for all Catholic children	(24)	Respect for persons and property	(27)	Only religious teachers	(11)	Only religious teachers	(11)
8. Religious practice	(37)	Reading, writing	(10)	Physical fitness	(21)	Help others in foreign countries	(29)
9. Gifted and slow learners	(23)	Prepare for college	(7)	Dating	(31)	Dating	(31)
10. Federal money	(18)	Think for himself	(30)	Vocations	(10)	Schools not expensive	(9)

[1] First listed is the lowest ranked in success or importance.

[2] Numbers in parentheses refer to items in original instrument.

In Table 124 the listings are developed from the total responses, each of which is weighted to produce a graded list starting with the item to which the combined respondents assigned the highest importance and the item to which they assigned the highest success, and likewise for the least importance and least success.

By inspecting Table 124 we find 7 stated goals common to the importance and success columns. The 3 first places in each of these columns are occupied by the same goals but in an inverse order. It is of interest that only 1 academic goal appears in these columns, the reading and writing well goal, which is seventh in the importance column and fourth in the success column. Even though the goal of encouraging students to think for themselves is given a fourth place in the importance column, it does not appear in the success column. In a reverse procedure, the goal of providing Catholic friends and good example appears in seventh place in the least important column and in ninth place in the most successful column. The goal of having only religious teachers in Catholic schools is placed in thirtieth place in importance. We find the goal of helping others in foreign countries in the least important column and in the least successful column, and the goal of fostering vocations received the same rank of low importance and low success.

In Table 125 the analyses are developed from the opportunity each parent had to identify the first, second, and third most important and most successful goal statements of the 31 presented, a completely different opportunity from his evaluation of each item separately.

There is a surprising consistency as we compare the corresponding columns in the 2 tables; for example, 7 of the most important goals which appear in the first table are also found in the second table. Among the repetitions are the emphases on the religious and personal virtues and the lack of academic emphasis; only 1 academic goal appears in the second table, where it is identified in the most successful column. There is strong agreement between the 2 analyses of the goal of teaching children to help people in foreign lands; in each approach the parents assign a low success value and an even lower importance value. In each analysis the goal of preparing students for college is in the most successful column, although it does not appear in the most important column of either table. It seems of consequence to point up 2 goal proposals related to the staffing of the schools, that they should be staffed entirely by religious teachers and that the staff should consist of well-qualified religious teachers and lay teachers. The possible goal of staffing only with religious teachers is identified in both analyses as unimportant. The provision of qualified religious and lay teachers, presented in 2 separate items, is identified as of high importance, but only the provision of qualified religious teachers is included in the most successful column.

In this day of encouraged broad dialogue, it would seem that inviting opportunities for fruitful discussions concerned with the future of Catholic schools and with the future of the youth they serve are available for those who wish to grasp them. All the members of the staff who worked in this Study have been continuously impressed with the high interest of the parents and the general Catholic laity and the great desire of those who service Catholic schools to extend every effort in finding the paths to increased quality education for Catholic youth.

Appendix

STUDY OF CATHOLIC EDUCATION

SCHEDULE I
FACULTY DATA
Please read Instructions on reverse side before completing this form.

Name _____

School _____

School Address _____

(Street)   (City) (Zone) (State)

1. Check Appropriate Lines:

   a)[1] Teacher _____   Administrator _____
                    1   2

   b) Elementary _____   Secondary _____
                    1   2

   c) Priest _____   Brother _____   Sister _____
               1   2   3

   Layman _____   Laywoman _____
            4   5

2. Catholic _____   Non-Catholic _____
              1   2

3. Full-Time[2] _____   Part-Time[2] _____
                  1.0   O.X.

4. Age (last birthday): _____ yrs.

5. Specify Grade and/or Subject (s) Which You Teach:

   _____

6. a) Hours per Week Spent in Classroom Instruction.[3] _____

   b) (For Elementary Teachers only)[4] Is your grade on double shift?   Yes _____   No _____
                                                                              1   2

   c) If your answer to (b) is yes, do you teach morning _____, afternoon _____ or both shifts _____?
                                                              1   2   3

7. Preparation (check highest level attained):

   One year or more beyond master's degree _____   Two or more years of college, but no degree _____
                                               8   4

   Master's degree _____   One year of college _____
                      7   3

   Bachelor's degree plus _____   Less than one year of college _____
                             6   2

   Bachelor's degree _____   High School only _____
                        5   1

8. Was your undergraduate degree received from a Catholic institution?

   Yes _____   No _____   Do not have degree _____
        1   2   3

9. a) Number of Semester Hours of Professional Education Courses:[5] _____

   b) (For Principals only) Number of Semester Hours of Professional Preparation in Administration and Supervision _____

10. Teaching Experience (indicate number of years):

    Catholic Schools   Public Schools   Independent Schools   Total

    _____   _____   _____   _____
                                                                                      M

285

11.   Number of Years in Present School: _____
12.   For Full-Time Lay Teachers Only:
       What is your gross salary (i.e., before deductions) for the school year, 1962-63? $_____

———————
[1] SEE INSTRUCTIONS 1
[2] SEE INSTRUCTIONS 2
[3] SEE INSTRUCTIONS 3
[4] SEE INSTRUCTIONS 4
[5] SEE INSTRUCTIONS 5

INSTRUCTIONS

NOTE: The small letters or number subscripts which appear in this form are for data analysis purposes only, and should be ignored by the person completing this questionnaire.

1.   Each principal should also fill out this Schedule I. If the principal also functions part time as a teacher, a **second** form should be filled out as a teacher; in each case the general instructions governing "Part Time Equivalent" should be followed. If a principal spends half-time in teaching, this item is reported as .5 principal, .5 as teacher.

2.   All part time instructional personnel are reported in decimal terms of 1. If a part-time teacher spends the equivalent of one day a week in the instruction of children, this teacher is reported as .2 (one day a week is the equivalent of two-tenths of a week). A priest who spends the equivalent of one-half day a week in the class room is reported as .1. Report to the nearest upper tenth, e.g., .25 is reported as .3. Each full-time person reports as 1.

3.   These hours are those which are assigned to teachers for face-to-face relations with pupils.

4.   **Double shift** signifies separate morning and afternoon sessions for different groups of children in the same grade.

5.   **Semester Hours of Professional Education Courses** refers to the credit hours which have been acquired by faculty members in the technical field of education as opposed to the content fields. A course titled "Teaching Reading in the Primary Grades" would be a professional education course, whereas "Elizabethan Literature" would be a content course.

Please return this form to the Principal of your school no later than SEPTEMBER 30, 1962.

APPENDIX B
STUDY OF CATHOLIC EDUCATION

SCHEDULE II
PRINCIPAL'S SUMMARY (ELEMENTARY)
INSTRUCTIONS

It is requested that each school principal devote some faculty meeting time to a discussion of Schedule I, which is the individual Faculty Data form. All Faculty Data sheets (Schedule I) are to be returned with Principal's Summary (Schedule II) to the Diocesan Superintendent's office by October 15, 1962.

In filling out this summary the small letter or number subscripts, which appear throughout the form, should be ignored. These subscripts are for later data analysis purposes.

These blanks have been glued together and four sheets of carbon paper are supplied for your convenience. Please re-assemble and staple securely the original when you have it ready for return in order to avoid stray pages or a mix-up in questionnaires.

TYPES OF SCHOOLS refer to the source of administrative control.

"**Parochial**": When the administration is the responsibility of a single parish.

"**Interparochial**": When the administration is shared by two or more parishes.

"**Private**": When the administration is the responsibility of a religious community or of a private corporation under approval of the Ordinary.

"**Diocesan**": When the administration is under the direct control of the Ordinary or of the Diocesan Office of Education. Included here will be "Central" and "Regional" schools as distinguished from "Interparochial" schools.

"**Institutional**": When the administration is established to fulfill a child-care function, e.g., orphanages, care of delinquents, full-time care of the deaf, etc.

Instructions (Footnote references throughout are to these numbered instructions.)

1. Part-Time and Full-Time Equivalent:

   All full-time personnel are each reported as 1. All part-time personnel are reported in decimal terms of 1. If a principal spends half time teaching and half time as a principal, this time distribution is reported as .5 principal, and .5 teacher. If a part time teacher spends the equivalent of one day a week in the instruction of children, this teacher is reported as .2; and a priest who spends the equivalent of one-half day a week in the classroom is reported as .1, or one-tenth of a week. Full Time Equivalent is the sum of the full time total plus the accumulation of the decimal terms of the part-time personnel, e.g., 10 full time teachers (10) plus three part-time teachers at .2 each (.6) plus one part-time teacher at .5 (.5) totals 11.1 Full Time Equivalent. Use the upper tenth in reporting, e.g., .25 should be reported as .3.

2. Do not accumulate number of additional classrooms, e.g., if ten additional classrooms are anticipated for 1963 and none for 1964 or 1965, this is reported as 1963 <u>**10**</u>;   1964 <u>**0**</u>;   1965 <u>**0.**</u>

3. Age of School Buildings—Report the age of each building segment, e.g., if the original building was completed in 1942, its age would be reported as 20 years, and if an addition was completed in 1952, its age would be reported at 10 years under Addition (1).

4. In choosing the facilities' group which most closely describes your school, go below in the grouping rather than above. With good judgment, evaluation of facilities to approximate the proposed groupings may be made.

5. In many instances the school principal will need the assistance of others in order to make a close approximation of the percentages of sources of Financial Support. It is urged that special care be given to this whole item.

6. From this item an analysis of class size in the elementary school will be developed. If in your school you have three first grades and the enrollment figures are 34 pupils in one class, 38 pupils in the second class, and 42 pupils in the third class, record them as follows: Grade 1 <u>**34**</u> <u>**38**</u> <u>**42**</u> __ __

   Please return the **white original** and the **yellow copy** to your Diocesan Superintendent's office on or before **OCTOBER 15, 1962.** The **blue copy** is for your files.

STUDY OF CATHOLIC EDUCATION

SCHEDULE II
PRINCIPAL'S SUMMARY (ELEMENTARY)

School _____

Address _____

(Street)   (City)   (Zone)   (State)

Principal's Name _____

1. TYPE (check appropriate line):

    Parochial   _____   Private   _____   Diocesan   _____
                          1   2   3

    Interparochial   _____   Institutional _____
                          4   5

2. ADMINISTRATION:

    a) **Principal**

        Full time (non-teaching)   _____
                                            1.0
        Part time [1]   _____
                                            O.X

    b) **Assistant Principal**

        Number full time (non-teaching) _____
                                             M
        Number part time [1]   _____
                                             M
        Total full time equivalent [1]   _____
                                             XX

    c) **Clerical Workers**

        Number full time   _____
        Number part time   _____

3. FACILITIES:

    a) **Number of classrooms** in use as of September, 1962 (do not include gym, multipurpose room, cafeteria, music room, audio-visual room, etc.)

        _____

    b) **Number of classrooms** vacant as of September, 1962   _____

    c) **Number of additional classrooms** which definitely will be constructed

        September, 1963 [2] _____   September, 1964 [2] _____   September, 1965 [2] _____

    d) **Age of School Buildings** (in years) [3]

        Original plant

        _____ yrs.

        Additions

        (1) _____ yrs.
        (2) _____ yrs.
        (3) _____ yrs.
        (4) _____ yrs.

    e) **Special Facilities** (check that group below which most closely represents the special facilities available in your school) [4]

        _____ (1) Gym
             1   Auditorium   Music
                         Cafeteria   Art
                         Library   Home Economics
                         Audio-visual   Industrial Arts

_____ (2) **Gym**
2   Auditorium
     Cafeteria
     Library
     Music
     Art

_____ (3) Multipurpose
3   Cafeteria
     Library
     Music
     Art

_____ (4) **Multipurpose**
4   Cafeteria
     Library

_____ (5) Multipurpose
5

f) **Televised Instruction**

(1) Number of television sets available for use in the school _____

(2) Are closed circuit television facilities available within the school, including studio transmission?

Yes _____   No _____
    1   2

(3) Have provisions been made for the future use of televised instruction?

Yes _____   No _____
    1   2

4. TESTING PROGRAM:

a) **Listed below** are the mental ability and achievement tests which are among the tests most commonly **in use**. Each test is identified by a code number. (See next page.) Using **only** the code numbers and **not** the title of the tests, indicate on the grade chart the tests which are used regularly in your school.

	A. Achievement	M. Mental Ability
Grade One	_____	_____
Grade Two	_____	_____
Grade Three	_____	_____
Grade Four	_____	_____
Grade Five	_____	_____
Grade Six	_____	_____
Grade Seven	_____	_____
Grade Eight	_____	_____

Achievement Tests:

Code	Title
1	California Basic Skills Tests
2	Iowa Tests of Basic Skills
3	Gray-Cotaw Achievement
4	S.R.A. Achievement Tests
5	Scholastic Achievement Series
6	STEP
7	Stanford Achievement Tests
8	Metropolitan Achievement Tests
9	Other

Mental Ability Tests:

Code	Title
1	California Test of Mental Maturity
2	Metropolitan Readiness
3	SCAT
4	Henmon-Nelson Tests of Mental Ability
5	Kuhlman-Anderson Intelligence Tests

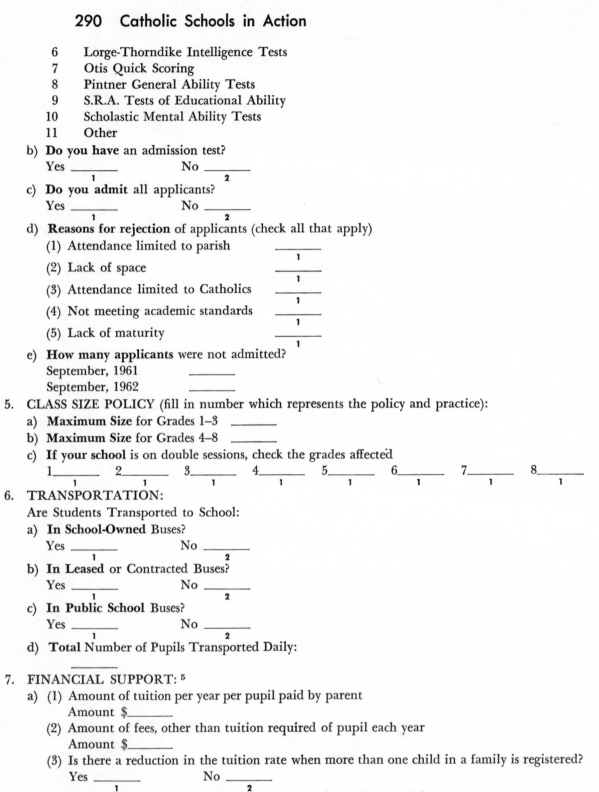

    6   Lorge-Thorndike Intelligence Tests
    7   Otis Quick Scoring
    8   Pintner General Ability Tests
    9   S.R.A. Tests of Educational Ability
    10   Scholastic Mental Ability Tests
    11   Other
  b) **Do you have** an admission test?
     Yes _____   No _____
           1   2
  c) **Do you admit** all applicants?
     Yes _____   No _____
           1   2
  d) **Reasons for rejection** of applicants (check all that apply)
     (1) Attendance limited to parish   _____
                                                  1
     (2) Lack of space   _____
                                                  1
     (3) Attendance limited to Catholics   _____
                                                  1
     (4) Not meeting academic standards   _____
                                                  1
     (5) Lack of maturity   _____
                                                  1
  e) **How many applicants** were not admitted?
     September, 1961   _____
     September, 1962   _____

5. CLASS SIZE POLICY (fill in number which represents the policy and practice):
  a) **Maximum Size** for Grades 1–3   _____
  b) **Maximum Size** for Grades 4–8   _____
  c) **If your school** is on double sessions, check the grades affected
     1_____   2_____   3_____   4_____   5_____   6_____   7_____   8_____
           1   1   1   1   1   1   1   1

6. TRANSPORTATION:
   Are Students Transported to School:
  a) **In School-Owned** Buses?
     Yes _____   No _____
           1   2
  b) **In Leased** or Contracted Buses?
     Yes _____   No _____
           1   2
  c) **In Public School** Buses?
     Yes _____   No _____
           1   2
  d) **Total** Number of Pupils Transported Daily:

     _____

7. FINANCIAL SUPPORT: [5]
  a) (1) Amount of tuition per year per pupil paid by parent
         Amount $_____
     (2) Amount of fees, other than tuition required of pupil each year
         Amount $_____
     (3) Is there a reduction in the tuition rate when more than one child in a family is registered?
         Yes _____   No _____
               1   2
     (4) Approximate % of financial support provided by tuition and fees

None _____ 1   Less than 25% _____ 2   25%– 50% _____ 3

51%–75% _____ 4   76%–100% _____ 5

b) **Approximate % of Financial Support Provided by Parish Subsidy**

None _____ 1   Less than 25% _____ 2   25%– 50% _____ 3

51%–75% _____ 4   76%–100% _____ 5

c) **Approximate % of Financial Support Provided by Diocesan Subsidy**

None _____ 1   Less than 25% _____ 2   25%– 50% _____ 3

51%–75% _____ 4   76%–100% _____ 5

d) **Approximate % of Financial Support Provided by Religious Community, Excluding Contributed Services**

None _____ 1   Less than 25% _____ 2   25%– 50% _____ 3

51%–75% _____ 4   76%–100% _____ 5

e) **Approximate % of Financial Support Provided by Endowments, Gifts or Miscellaneous Sources**

None _____ 1   Less than 25% _____ 2   25%– 50% _____ 3

51%–75% _____ 4   76%–100% _____ 5

8. IS THERE A PARENT-TEACHER ORGANIZATION OR A HOME AND SCHOOL ASSOCIATION IN THE SCHOOL?

Yes _____ 1   No _____ 2

9. HEALTH SERVICES:

a) **Are Health Services Provided by the School?**

Yes _____ 1   No _____ 2

b) **Are Health Services Provided by a Municipal or County Department?**

Yes _____ 1   No _____ 2

c) **Are Health Services Provided by a Public School Department?**

Yes _____ 1   No _____ 2

d) **If the Answer Is "Yes" in either "b" or "c," Are the Services Equivalent to Those Provided in the Public Schools?**

Yes _____ 1   No _____ 2

10. STAFF SALARY:

a) **What Is the Annual School Yearly Salary Paid for Full-Time Religious Teachers?** (Do not include contributed services.) $_____

b) **Indicate the Number of Full-Time Lay Teachers Who Are Paid Salaries at the Various Intervals Presented Below.** (Salaries are for the full school year, 1962–63.)

Salary Category	Number
Under $2500	_____
2500–2999	_____
3000–3499	_____
3500–3999	_____
4000–4499	_____
4500–4999	_____
5000–5499	_____
5500–5999	_____
6000 and over	_____

c) **Are Salaries Determined** by a Salary Schedule Which Is Related to Training and Experience?

Yes _____   No _____
         1   2

11. STAFF UTILIZATION AND TECHNOLOGICAL AIDS:

a) **Staff** (check if employed in instruction)

Teacher aides   _____
                              1
Team teaching   _____
                              1
Other (specify)

_____   _____
                                 M
_____   _____
                                 M

b) **Technological Aids** (check if used consistently in instruction)

Radio	_____	Overhead projection	_____
Televised instruction	_____	Programed learning	_____
Tapes	_____	Other (specify)	_____
Films	_____	_____	_____
Transparencies	_____		M

12. GRADUATES:

	Boys	Girls	Total
Number for June, 1962	_____	_____	_____ M
Number who went to Catholic High Schools	_____	_____	_____ M

13. ENROLLMENT BY GRADE (September, 1962):

	Boys	Girls	Total
Kindergarten	_____	_____	_____ M
First Grade	_____	_____	_____ M
Second Grade	_____	_____	_____ M
Third Grade	_____	_____	_____ M
Fourth Grade	_____	_____	_____ M
Fifth Grade	_____	_____	_____ M
Sixth Grade	_____	_____	_____ M
Seventh Grade (not part of Jr. H.S.)	_____	_____	_____ M
Eighth Grade (not part of Jr. H.S.)	_____	_____	_____ M
Ninth Grade (not part of Jr. or Sr. H.S.)	_____	_____	_____ M
Total	_____	_____	_____ M

14. CLASS SIZE BY GRADES (give the number of students enrolled in each class at each grade level; use the space opposite "&" for combination classes) [6]

Grade 1   _____ _____ _____ _____ _____
    &   _____ _____ _____ _____ _____
Grade 2   _____ _____ _____ _____ _____

&	——	——	——	——	——
Grade 3	——	——	——	——	——
&	——	——	——	——	——
Grade 4	——	——	——	——	——
&	——	——	——	——	——
Grade 5	——	——	——	——	——
&	——	——	——	——	——
Grade 6	——	——	——	——	——
&	——	——	——	——	——
Grade 7	——	——	——	——	——
&	——	——	——	——	——
Grade 8	——	——	——	——	——
&	——	——	——	——	——
Grade 9	——	——	——	——	——

15. **CLASSIFICATION OF INSTRUCTIONAL PERSONNEL**

Note: Please give the total number of persons on instructional staff, both full and part time.

Religious			Lay		GRAND TOTAL
Priests	Brothers	Sisters	Men	Women	

[1] SEE INSTRUCTIONS 1
[2] SEE INSTRUCTIONS 2
[3] SEE INSTRUCTIONS 3
[4] SEE INSTRUCTIONS 4
[5] SEE INSTRUCTIONS 5
[6] SEE INSTRUCTIONS 6

APPENDIX C
STUDY OF CATHOLIC EDUCATION
SCHEDULE III
PRINCIPAL'S SUMMARY (SECONDARY)
INSTRUCTIONS

It is requested that each school principal devote some faculty meeting time to a discussion of Schedule I, which is the individual Faculty Data form. All Faculty Data sheets (Schedule I) are to be mailed to N.C.W.C. Department of Education, 1312 Massachusetts Ave., N.W., Washington 5, D.C., along with Principal's Summary (Schedule III) by October 20, 1962.

In filling out this summary the small letters or number subscripts, which appear throughout the form, should be ignored. These subscripts are for later data analysis purposes.

These blanks have been glued together and four sheets of carbon paper are supplied for your convenience. Please re-assemble and staple securely the original when you have it ready for return in order to avoid stray pages or a mix-up in questionnaires.

TYPES OF SCHOOLS refer to the source of administrative control.

"Parochial": When the administration is the responsibility of a single parish.

"Interparochial": When the administration is shared by two or more parishes.

"Private": When the administration is the responsibility of a religious community or of a private corporation under the approval of the Ordinary.

"Diocesan": When the administration is under the direct control of the Ordinary or of the Diocesan Office of Education. Included here will be "Central" and "Regional" schools as distinguished from "Interparochial" schools.

"Institutional": When the administration is established to fulfill a child-care function, e.g., orphanages, care of delinquents, full-time care of the deaf, etc.

Instructions (Footnote references throughout are to these numbered instructions).

1. Part-time and Full-time Equivalent:

   All full-time personnel are each reported as 1. All part-time personnel are reported in decimal terms of 1. If a principal spends half time teaching and half time as a principal, this time distribution is reported as .5 principal, and .5 teacher. If a part-time teacher spends the equivalent of one day a week in the instruction of children, this teacher is reported as .2; and a priest who spends the equivalent of one-half day a week in the classroom is reported as .1, or one-tenth of a week. Full-Time Equivalent is the sum of the full-time total plus the accumulation of the decimal terms of the part-time personnel, e.g., 10 full-time teachers (10) plus three part-time teachers at .2 each (.6) plus one part-time teacher at .5 (.5) totals 11.1 Full-Time Equivalent. Use the upper tenth in reporting, e.g., .25 should be reported as .3.

2. For purposes of this report, "Superintendents" of Co-institutional Schools are to be reported as Principals; and principals of the boys' and of the girls' departments are to be reported as Assistant Principals.

3. Age of School Buildings—Report the age of each building segment, e.g., if the original building was completed in 1942, its age would be reported as 20 years, and if an addition was completed in 1952, its age would be reported at 10 years under Addition (1).

4. Do not accumulate increased capacity, e.g., if a two hundred increased capacity is anticipated for 1963 and none for 1964 or 1965, this is reported as 1963—200; 1964—0; 1965—0.

5. In choosing the facilities grouping which most closely describes your school, go below in the grouping rather than above. With good judgment, evaluation of facilities to approximate the proposed groupings may be made.

6. In many instances the school principal will need the assistance of others in order to make a close approximation of the percentages of sources of Financial Support. It is urged that special care be given to this whole item. Please return the **white original** to the Department of Education, N.C.W.C., 1312 Massachusetts Avenue, N.W., Washington 5, D.C., by **October 20, 1962.** The **yellow copy** should be mailed to your Diocesan Superintendent of Education for his files. The **blue copy** is for your files.

SCHEDULE III
PRINCIPAL'S SUMMARY (SECONDARY)

School _____

Address _____

(Street)   (City)   (Zone)   (State)

Principal's Name_____

1. TYPE of school (check appropriate lines):

    a) Parochial _____   Private _____
                1   2

        Interparochial _____   Diocesan _____
                   3   4

        Institutional _____
               5

    b) Boarders accepted: Yes _____   No _____
                           1   2

    c) Boys Only _____   Coeducational _____
               1   2

        Girls Only _____   Co-institutional _____
               3   4

    d) **Grade Organization**

        7– 8 _____   8–12 _____
              1   4

        7– 9 _____   9–12 _____
              2   5

        7–12 _____   10–12 _____
              3   6

        Other _____
            7

    e) **Program Offering** (check the items which describe your school)

        College Preparatory _____
                             1

        General _____
               2

        Vocational-Technical _____
                         3

2. ADMINISTRATION:

    a) **Principal**

        Full-time (non-teaching) _____
                              1.0

        Part-time [1] _____
                  O.X.

    b) **Assistant Principal** [2]

        Number full-time (non-teaching) _____
                                  M

        Number part-time [1] _____
                      M

        Total full-time equivalent [1] _____
                        XX

    c) **Clerical Workers**

        Number full-time _____

        Number part-time _____

3. INSTRUCTIONAL PERSONNEL (do not include aides or substitutes):

    a) **Guidance Personnel**

        Number full-time _____
                       M

        Number part-time [2] _____
                      M

        Total full-time equivalent _____
                       XX

b) **Teacher's Normal** Daily Assignment
   (1) Number of classroom teaching periods   ————
   (2) Number of other assigned periods   ————
   (3) Total of daily assigned periods   ————
   (4) Length of school day (hours)   ————
   (5) Number of periods per day   ————

c) **Maximum Class Size** (policy)
   (1) For academic subjects   ————
   (2) For physical education   ————
   (3) For industrial arts   ————
   (4) For home economics   ————

d) **If your school** is on double sessions, check the grades affected

7 ————   8 ————   9 ————   10 ————   11 ————   12 ————
   1   1   1   1   1   1

4. FACILITIES:

a) **Number of Classrooms** in Actual Use as of September, 1962 (do not include gym, multipurpose room, music room, cafeteria, etc.)   ————

b) **Number of Vacant Classrooms** as of September, 1962   ————

c) **Age of School Buildings** (in years) [3]
Original plant
———— yrs.
Additions
(1) ———— yrs.   (3) ———— yrs.
(2) ———— yrs.   (4) ———— yrs.

d) **Additional Pupil Capacity** Which Will Be Available (express in number of additional pupils who will be accommodated)
September, 1963   ————
September, 1964 [4]   ————
September, 1965 [4]   ————

e) **Science Laboratories in Use** (indicate number)

Chemistry	————	Combination Laboratory	————
Physics	————	Other (specify)	
Biology	————	————————————	
General Science	————	————————————	[M]

                                              [M]

f) **Academic Services** (check that group below which most closely represents the special facilities available in your school) [5]

———— (1) Library	———— (2) Library
[1] Language Laboratory	[2] Language Laboratory
Reading Laboratory	Reading Laboratory
Home Economics	Home Economics
Industrial Arts	Industrial Arts
Drafting (Mechanical Drawing)	Drafting (Mechanical Drawing)
Typing	Typing
Office Practice	Office Practice
Choral Room	
Band and Orchestra Room	
Audio-visual Center	

_____ (3) Library
  3

      Language Laboratory
      Reading Laboratory
      Drafting (Mechanical Drawing)
      Typing
      Office Practice

_____ (5) Library
  5

      Typing

_____ (4) Library
  4

      Language Laboratory
      Reading Laboratory
      Typing

g) **Other Facilities** (check that group below which most closely represents the special facilities available in your school) [5]

_____ (1) Gymnasium
  1

      Auditorium
      Cafeteria
      Pool
      Chapel

_____ (3) Gym-Auditorium
  3

      Cafeteria
      Chapel

_____ (5) Multipurpose
  5

_____ (2) Gymnasium
  2

      Auditorium
      Cafeteria
      Chapel

_____ (4) Multipurpose
  4

      Cafeteria or Auditorium
      Chapel

h) **Televised Instruction**

(1) Number of T.V. sets available for use in the school _____

(2) Are closed circuit T.V. facilities available within the school, including studio transmission?

    Yes _____   No _____
        1   2

(3) Have provisions been made for the future use of televised instruction?

    Yes _____   No _____
        1   2

5. **TESTING PROGRAM**

a) Listed below are the mental ability and achievement tests which are among the tests most commonly in use. Each test is identified by a code number. Using the code numbers and not the title of the tests, indicate on the grade chart the tests which are used regularly in your school.

	A. Achievement	M. Mental Ability
Grade Seven	_____	_____
Grade Eight	_____	_____
Grade Nine	_____	_____
Grade Ten	_____	_____
Grade Eleven	_____	_____
Grade Twelve	_____	_____

Achievement Tests

Code	Title
1	California Achievement Tests
2	Cooperative General Achievement Tests
3	Cooperative English Tests
4	High School Placement Tests (Scholastic)
5	Iowa Tests of Educational Development
6	National Merit Qualifying Test

Code   Title
7   SRA High School Placement Test
8   STEP
9   SRA General Educational Development
10   Essential High School Content Battery
11   Other

Mental Ability Tests

Code   Title
1   ACE Psychological Examination
2   California Mental Ability
3   CEEB Scholastic Aptitude Test
4   SCAT
5   Henmon-Nelson Tests of Mental Ability
6   Kuhlman-Anderson Intelligence Tests
7   Lorge-Thorndike Intelligence Tests
8   Pintner General Ability Tests
9   SRA Tests of Educational Ability
10   Otis Mental Ability Tests
11   Terman-Merrill Intelligence Tests
12   Other

b) **Do You Have** an Admission Test?

Yes _____ 1   No _____ 2

c) **Do You Admit** All Applicants?

Yes _____ 1   No _____ 2

d) **Check Reasons** for Rejection of Applicants (check all that apply)

(1) Attendance limited to parish or region _____ 1

(2) Lack of space _____ 1

(3) Attendance limited to Catholics _____ 1

(4) Not meeting academic standards _____ 1

(5) Lack of maturity or stability _____ 1

e) **How Many** Applicants Were Not Admitted?

September, 1961 _____   September, 1962 _____

6. FINANCIAL SUPPORT: [6]

a) (1) Amount of tuition per year per pupil paid by parent

Amount $_____

(2) Amount of fees, other than tuition required of pupil each year

Amount $_____

(3) Is there a reduction in the tuition rate when more than one child in a family is registered?

Yes _____ 1   No _____ 2

(4) Approximate % of financial support provided by tuition and fees

None _____ 1   Less than 25% _____ 2   25%– 50% _____ 3

51%–75% _____ 4   76%–100% _____ 5

b) **Approximate % of** Financial Support Provided by Parish Subsidy

None _____ 1   Less than 25% _____ 2   25%– 50% _____ 3

51%–75% _____ 4   76%–100% _____ 5

c) **Approximate % of** Financial Support Provided by Diocesan Subsidy

None _____ 1   Less than 25% _____ 2   25%– 50% _____ 3

51%–75% _____ 4   76%–100% _____ 5

d) **Approximate % of** Financial Support Provided by Religious Community, Excluding Contributed Services

None _____ 1   Less than 25% _____ 2   25%– 50% _____ 3

51%–75% _____ 4   76%–100% _____ 5

e) **Approximate % of** Financial Support Provided by Endowments, Gifts or Miscellaneous Sources

None _____ 1   Less than 25% _____ 2   25%– 50% _____ 3

51%–75% _____ 4   76%–100% _____ 5

7. IS THERE A PARENT-TEACHER ORGANIZATION OR A HOME AND SCHOOL ASSOCIATION IN THE SCHOOL?

Yes _____ 1   No _____ 2

8. HEALTH SERVICES:

a) **Are Health Services** Provided by the School?

Yes _____ 1   No _____ 2

b) **Are Health Services** Provided by a Municipal or County Department?

Yes _____ 1   No _____ 2

c) **Are Health Services** Provided by a Public School Department?

Yes _____ 1   No _____ 2

d) **If the Answer Is "Yes"** in either "b" or "c," Are the Services Equivalent to Those Provided in the Public School?

Yes _____ 1   No _____ 2

9. STAFF SALARY:

a) **What Is the Annual** School Year Salary Paid to Full-Time Religious Teachers? (Do not include contributed services.)

$_____

b) **Indicate the Number** of Full-Time Lay Teachers Who Are Paid Salaries at the Various Intervals Presented Below. (Salaries are for the full school year, 1962–63.)

Salary Category	Number	Salary Category	Number
Under $2500	_____	4500–4999	_____
2500–2999	_____	5000–5499	_____
3000–3499	_____	5500–5999	_____
3500–3999	_____	6000 and over	_____
4000–4499	_____		

c) **Are Salaries Determined** by a Salary Schedule Which Is Related to Training and Experience?

Yes _____ 1   No _____ 2

10. STAFF UTILIZATION AND TECHNOLOGICAL AIDS:
   a) **Staff** (check if employed in instruction)   Other (specify)
      Teacher aides _____   _____
                          1   M
      Team teaching _____   _____
                          1   M
   b) **Technological Aides** (check if used consistently in instruction)
      Radio _____   Overhead Projection _____
                    1   1
      Televised instruction _____   Programed learning _____
                                1   1
      Tapes _____   Other (specify)
                    1   _____
      Films _____   M
                    1
      Transparencies _____
                          1
11. GRADUATES:
   a) **From Grade 12**   Boys   Girls   Total
      Number for June, 1962   _____   _____   _____
                                                                          M
      Number who entered Catholic colleges   _____   _____   _____
                                                                          M
      Number who entered private non-Catholic
      colleges   _____   _____   _____
                                                                          M
      Number who entered public colleges   _____   _____   _____
                                                                          M
      Number who entered religious life   _____   _____   _____
                                                                          M
      Number who entered diocesan seminaries _____   _____   _____
                                                                          M
   b) **From Grade 9** (for Jr. H.S.)   Boys   Girls   Total
      Number for June, 1962   _____   _____   _____
                                                                          M
      Number who went to Catholic High Schools _____   _____   _____
                                                                          M
12. ENROLLMENT BY GRADE: (September 30, 1962)
   Seventh grade (only if part of Jr. H.S.)   _____   _____   _____
                                                                          M
   Eighth grade (only if part of Jr. H.S.)   _____   _____   _____
                                                                          M
   Ninth grade   _____   _____   _____
                                                                          M
   Tenth grade   _____   _____   _____
                                                                          M
   Eleventh grade   _____   _____   _____
                                                                          M
   Twelfth grade   _____   _____   _____
                                                                          M
   Total   _____   _____   _____
                                                                          M
13. IS YOUR SCHOOL ACCREDITED BY A REGIONAL AGENCY OR COMMISSION?
   Yes _____   No _____
            1   2
14. CLASSIFICATION OF INSTRUCTIONAL PERSONNEL
   Note: List the total number of persons who are on your instructional staff, both full and part time.

Religious			Lay		GRAND TOTAL
Priests	Brothers	Sisters	Men	Women	

APPENDIX D

STUDY OF CATHOLIC EDUCATION
INVENTORY OF RELIGIOUS OUTCOMES
DIRECTIONS FOR ADMINISTRATORS

I. General Directions for Administering—Total Administration Time = 90 minutes.

A. Proposed Schedule for Administering

	Time in Minutes
1. First Sitting	
Distribute materials, fill out Information Sheet	10
Part I Understandings	35
Total	45 minutes
2. Second Sitting	
Part II Attitudes	25
Part III Opinions	20
Total	45 minutes

B. Detailed Directions for Administering have been set up according to this time schedule. Before beginning the test the administrator should make certain he has the following materials in his possession.

1. Inventory booklets for each student and one for himself.
2. Answer booklets for each student and one for himself.
3. Additional pencils. Electrographic pencils are **not** required.
4. A "Testing—Do Not Disturb" sign for the door.
5. A copy of these Directions.
6. A watch.

C. Just before starting to administer the Inventory do the following:

1. See that all students' desks are cleared.
2. See that each student has a sharpened pencil.
3. Place the "Testing—Do Not Disturb" sign on the door.
4. Maintain a natural classroom situation.

D. During the administration of the Inventory proceed as follows:

1. Read the Directions exactly as they are written. Make sure that all students understand the directions and the sample item before telling the class to start work.
2. After each part has started, move about the room to make sure that the instructions are being followed. Give additional instructions to individual students if there is apparent misunderstanding, e.g., correct way to mark answer sheet. Check to make sure students are working on the correct page and are marking the answer sheets as instructed. Do **not** give help on specific questions in the Inventory.
3. Follow exactly the time limits for the three parts of the Inventory. Keep a record of starting time, working time and finishing time for each part.

II. Detailed Directions for Administering

Note: These directions are printed in regular margins or in indented margins. The material in the regular margins is for the information of the administrator. All directions to be read aloud to the students are in indented margins. These directions should be read word for word exactly as printed.

Upon entering the room where the students are gathered say:

"I am _____, a field worker for the national Study of Catholic Education.

This morning (afternoon) you are asked to respond to an Inventory of Religious Outcomes.

First I will pass out the Answer Booklets."

Count out the booklets and have them passed back by rows.

"**Next** I will pass out the Inventory Booklets. Please do not open the booklets until you are told to do so."
Count out the Inventory Booklets and have them passed back by rows.

"**Each** student should have a sharpened pencil with an eraser. If you should break the point of your pencil during the Inventory, put up your hand and I will provide you with another."

"**Now** look at the cover page of the second booklet I gave you. Read silently to yourselves as I read aloud the Instructions **To the Student:**"
Read slowly and distinctly the cover page: **To the Student.**

STUDENT INFORMATION SHEET

"**Now** take the Answer Booklet and fill out the cover page, The Student Information Sheet. Pay no attention to the small numbers on this page as they are for coding purposes. Please print or write very carefully.

"**After** the name of your school, print the name of this diocese which is _____. The date today is
_____. Continue to answer all of the questions. Raise your hand if you have difficulty with the questions.
As students raise their hands, go to their places and answer their questions. If it appears that the entire class is having difficulty with an item, explain that item in detail to the entire class.

The following explanations are intended to help the administrator answer questions on the Student Information Sheet.

Item 5   Some students may have difficulty with this question, especially if they have attended several different schools.

Item 6   This question includes grown-up brothers and sisters living away from home.

Item 8   May cause difficulty for some. A detailed response is preferable to a general answer. Have the student put the answer in his own words. He should not give the name of the employer unless this is significant.

Item 9   The rule for "Unknown" applies to all the questions on the parents' ethnic origin and education.

Item 19   May cause difficulty for students who are not used to class standings. A simple graph on the chalk board may help them to locate themselves in their class.

PART I

When all students have completed the Student Information Sheet say:

"**Now** fold over the Student Information Sheet so that the Answer Sheet to Part I is showing.

Next open your Inventory Booklets to the second page entitled "Directions for Part I." Read silently to yourselves as I read aloud the Directions for Part I."
Read slowly and distinctly the Directions for Part I.

Now follow as I read the Instructions at the top of the Answer Sheet for Part I.
Read the Instructions.

"Are there any questions?" (Answer any pertinent questions).

"**Open** your Inventory Booklet and begin to work on Part I. Continue until you have answered all fifty questions. You will have 35 minutes for Part I. If you finish early go back over your answers. Do not begin Part II until told to do so."
Note the beginning time. Call time after 35 minutes. This will conclude the first sitting. If the inventory is to continue after a recess, have the students close their booklets and leave them at their places. If, under unusual circumstances, the Inventory is to continue at another time, have the students print their three initials at the top right hand corner of the Answer Booklet and pass them to the front of the room. Then collect the Inventory Booklets.

PART II

When the students have reassembled either after recess or at another time, check the preparations as explained in the General Directions above. When the students are settled and ready to begin say:

"Now open your Answer Booklet to Part II. Next open your Inventory Booklet to the Directions for Part II.
Read silently to yourselves as I read aloud the Directions for Part II."
Read slowly and distinctly the Directions for Part II.

"**Now** follow as I read the Instructions at the top of the Answer Sheet for Part II."
Read the Instructions.

"Are there any questions?" (Answer any pertinent questions).

"Turn to Part II of your Inventory Booklet and begin work. Continue until you have answered all the questions. You will have 25 minutes for Part II. If you finish early go back over your answers. Do not begin **Part III** until told to do so."

Note the beginning time. Call time after 25 minutes. Go on immediately with Part III.

PART III

"We will continue with Part III of the Inventory. First turn your Answer Booklet to the Answer Sheet for Part III. Then open your Inventory Booklet to the Directions for Part III. Read silently to yourselves as I read aloud the Directions for Part III.

Read slowly and distinctly the Directions for Part III.

"**Now** follow as I read the Instructions at the top of the Answer Sheet for Part III."
Read the Instructions.

"**Are** there any questions?" (Answer any pertinent questions).

"**Turn** to Part III of your Inventory Booklet and begin work. Continue Part III. If you finish early go back **over** your answers."

Note the beginning time. Call time after 20 minutes.

END OF INVENTORY

"**Close** your Inventory Booklets and your Answer Booklets. First pass the Answer Booklets to the front of **the** room. Next, pass up the Inventory Booklets.

Thank you very much for your fine cooperation."

APPENDIX E
AN INVENTORY OF CATHOLIC SCHOOL OUTCOMES
A THREE PART QUESTIONNAIRE FOR STUDENTS ATTENDING CATHOLIC ELEMENTARY AND SECONDARY SCHOOLS IN THE UNITED STATES OF AMERICA

PART I   RELIGIOUS UNDERSTANDINGS
PART II   STUDENT ATTITUDES
PART III   STUDENT OPINION CONCERNING CATHOLIC SCHOOLS

COPYRIGHT, 1965
THE UNIVERSITY OF NOTRE DAME DU LAC
NOTRE DAME, INDIANA

INVENTORY OF CATHOLIC SCHOOL OUTCOMES
To the Student

In the following pages you will find an Inventory in three parts concerned with the outcomes of Catholic schools.

It is most important that you answer the questions according to how **you** think or feel. Some of the questions have to do with your knowledge of the teachings of the Catholic religion. Other questions ask how you feel about certain things. Still other questions ask you for your frank opinion. In all cases your answer should be the one which agrees with how you really think or feel.

Before answering the questions in the booklet, please fill out the information requested on the first page of the Answer Booklet entitled, "Student Information Sheet." Please answer all the questions. If you have difficulty in filling out the "Student Information Sheet," raise your hand and the administrator will help you.

Editors:
> Terry P. Denny
> Rev. Xavier Harris, O.F.M.
> Reginald A. Neuwien

INVENTORY OF CATHOLIC SCHOOL OUTCOMES
PART I
RELIGIOUS UNDERSTANDINGS
DIRECTIONS

Part One of the Inventory is concerned with religious understandings. Some of the chief teachings of the Catholic Church are here presented. Several statements are made about each these teachings. **More than one of these statements is correct.** In this respect the Inventory differs from most tests you have taken.

You are to select the answer which **you** think is best. After reading the statements pick the one which comes closest to your understanding of the question. Be sure to read all of the statements before selecting the best answer. Do not spend too much time on any one item.

Now study the following example. All of the other items in Part I of the Inventory are similar to this:
"The seven sacraments are best understood as:
a.   Direct encounters with Christ at critical moments in our lives;
b.   Material symbols which remind us of God's spiritual grace;
c.   Automatic dispensers of the graces of Redemption;
d.   Sensible signs producing grace in the souls of the worthy;
e.   Means of sanctification instituted by Christ."

To answer this question you must know what a sacrament is. You will recall the answer of the catechism: "A sacrament is an outward sign instituted by Christ to give grace." Notice that none of the choices uses these exact words. You are to select the answer which, in your judgment, gives the best explanation of what a sacrament really is.

After reading all of the choices, check the one which you think is best. If you are not sure you know the answer, check the answer that seems best to you. **Always check only one answer.**

Suppose in the above example you decide that d. is the best explanation of a sacrament, you would mark the answer sheet as follows:

( ) a.   ( ) b.   ( ) c.   (√) d.   ( ) e.

Now find the Answer Sheet for Part I in your Answer Booklet and make sure you know how to answer the questions.

PART I

1. The best way to strengthen our faith is:
( ) a. To avoid the company of non-Catholics;
( ) b. To read and study and thus learn more about our faith;
( ) c. To live by faith so that all our actions are directed by faith;
( ) d. To use every opportunity to profess and practice our faith;
( ) e. To look to the Church for guidance in every event of life.

2. The Holy Eucharist is the greatest of the sacraments because:
( ) a. It nourishes our soul with Christ's own life;
( ) b. It rewards us for leading a virtuous life;
( ) c. It unites us most intimately with Christ;
( ) d. It consoles us with the comfort of Christ's presence;
( ) e. It contains Christ's body and blood, soul and divinity.

3. The chief point of the Old Testament prophecies concerning the coming Redeemer is that the Messias would:
( ) a. Reopen the gates of heaven;
( ) b. Belong to the Jewish race;
( ) c. Proclaim the glad tidings of the Kingdom;
( ) d. Repair the damage done by sin;
( ) e. Conquer the enemies of Israel.

4. When we say that the only-begotten Son of God "became man for our sakes" we mean that the Second Person became man:
( ) a. To set us a good example;
( ) b. To rescue us from the devil;
( ) c. To teach us the ways of Salvation;
( ) d. To make us the children of God;
( ) e. To redeem us from sin.

5. The chief reason we love and honor Mary is because:
( ) a. She helps us to stay pure;
( ) b. She is one of the most perfect of God's creatures;
( ) c. She is the most admired woman who ever lived;
( ) d. She has been appointed by God to be our spiritual mother;
( ) e. She is the Mother of God and therefore deserves highest honor.

6. For a Catholic the principal teacher of the faith is:
( ) a. The pope and bishops of the Church;
( ) b. The pastor and the religious teachers;

( ) c. Christ teaching through the Church;
( ) d. The clear voice of conscience;
( ) e. The holy, Roman Catholic Church.

7. The sacrament of Confirmation is intended most of all:
( ) a. To strengthen the Christian as a soldier of Christ;
( ) b. To make the Christian ready to fight for his religion;
( ) c. To prepare the Christian to take part in the work of the Church;
( ) d. To complete the consecration of the Christian begun in Baptism;
( ) e. To conclude the formal instructions in the Catholic religion.

8. When we pray our chief concern should be:
( ) a. To grow in the love of God;
( ) b. To lead a better moral life;
( ) c. To keep our mind on what we are saying;
( ) d. To obtain favors, if it be God's will;
( ) e. To drive away the devil.

9. The most important reason why religious take vows of poverty, chastity and obedience is:
( ) a. To follow more completely the way outlined by Christ;
( ) b. To free themselves from worldly cares and concerns;
( ) c. To insure the efficient operation of religious organizations;
( ) d. To devote themselves more perfectly to the practice of charity;
( ) e. To inspire them with a dislike for worldly things.

10. The best way to preserve the virtue of chastity (purity) is:
( ) a. To protect one's good reputation at all costs;
( ) b. To avoid anything that might cause regrets later on;
( ) c. To be unselfish, self-controlled and considerate in all one's actions;
( ) d. To avoid all occasions of sin and to resist temptations;
( ) e. To treat one's own body and the bodies of others with reverence.

11. We can best understand the importance of Baptism by recalling that:
( ) a. It introduces the Christian into the Body of Christ;
( ) b. It removes our inborn tendency to sin;
( ) c. It admits the baptized to the other sacraments;
( ) d. It takes away Original Sin by conferring grace;
( ) e. It sets us apart from those who are not members of the True Church.

12. We can best show due respect for our bodies by:
( ) a. Regarding the body as the co-principle of our life in Christ;
( ) b. Keeping the body fit to avoid suffering and ill health;
( ) c. Making our body serve the best interests of the soul;
( ) d. Building up our body as an efficient "machine";
( ) e. Taking proper care of our life and health.

13. The liturgy (Mass, Sacraments, etc.) may best be described as:
( ) a. The Body of Christ worshipping the Trinity;
( ) b. The prayer life of the people of God;
( ) c. The vestments and sacred music used in Church;
( ) d. The greatest religious drama ever enacted;
( ) e. The official public worship of the Church.

14. Heaven may best be understood as:
( ) a. An eternal chorus of praise and adoration;

( ) b. A loving, personal union with the Blessed Trinity;
( ) c. A state of eternal blessedness;
( ) d. A never-ending feast without boredom;
( ) e. Unending possession of the Beatific Vision.

15. We make the best use of private property when we:
( ) a. Are thrifty and conscientious in our use of property;
( ) b. Are openhanded toward our neighbor who is in need;
( ) c. Regard ourselves as stewards to whom God has lent property;
( ) d. Avoid theft and other wilful violations against justice;
( ) e. Are content with our state in life and do not try to change it.

16. To remain in the "state of grace" requires us to:
( ) a. Seek to "walk with God" in an attitude of friendship;
( ) b. Live the life of grace through acts of charity;
( ) c. Hear no evil, see no evil, do no evil;
( ) d. Avoid sin, so that our soul is always pleasing to God;
( ) e. Keep our baptismal robe pure and spotless.

17. The seven sacraments are best understood as:
( ) a. Direct encounters with Christ at critical moments in our lives;
( ) b. Material symbols which remind us of God's spiritual grace;
( ) c. Automatic dispensers of the graces of Redemption;
( ) d. Sensible signs producing grace in the souls of the worthy;
( ) e. Means of santification instituted by Christ.

18. We prove our love for God especially by:
( ) a. Repaying His love for us with gratitude;
( ) b. Never missing our daily prayers;
( ) c. Avoiding sin and keeping His commandments;
( ) d. Seeking to love Him on account of His goodness;
( ) e. Forgetting ourselves and going against our natural desires.

19. The chief reason why work is necessary for man is because:
( ) a. Work in a special way gives glory to God;
( ) b. Work makes man self-reliant and independent;
( ) c. Work is the natural condition of man in this life;
( ) d. Work serves as a penance for our sins;
( ) e. Work brings satisfaction for a job well done.

20. The chief value of truthfulness is:
( ) a. It gives us the reputation for honesty;
( ) b. It directs our life toward truth;
( ) c. It makes our character noble;
( ) d. It leads others to trust us;
( ) e. It keeps us from worrying over lies.

21. The Mass is a true sacrifice because:
( ) a. The Mass can be offered only by an ordained priest;
( ) b. Christ as priest offers Himself as a victim to the Father;
( ) c. The Mass reminds us to offer our own sacrifices to God;
( ) d. The Mass is the unbloody renewal of the sacrifice of the Cross;
( ) e. The two-fold consecration mystically separates Christ's Body and Blood.

22. The best way to treat venial sin is:
( ) a. To hate the suggestion of insulting God by any sin;

( ) b. To be careful lest venial sins add up to a mortal sin;
( ) c. To fear to offend God even in the slightest matters;
( ) d. To realize that venial sin is unworthy of a Christian;
( ) e. To reject the brief pleasure held out by sin.

23. The chief value of the life, sufferings and death of our Lord is that He hereby:
( ) a. Earned for us God's grace and everlasting life;
( ) b. Showed his unlimited love for us;
( ) c. Taught us how to live, suffer and die;
( ) d. Set us free from sin and sin's penalty;
( ) e. Proved to doubters that He was a real man.

24. The best time to call a priest when someone is sick is:
( ) a. When there is some doubt about the right to Church burial;
( ) b. When the person is near death;
( ) c. When the family is in need of consolation;
( ) d. When the person is seriously ill;
( ) e. When the doctor decides there is no hope.

25. We should practice the Corporal and Spiritual Works of Mercy:
( ) a. Constantly, at least in intention;
( ) b. Whenever called upon to do so by those in authority;
( ) c. As often as we receive recognition for our generosity;
( ) d. As often as our circumstances and means allow;
( ) e. Whenever we tend to be selfish and self-centered.

26. We can best prove our love for our neighbor by:
( ) a. Performing the Corporal and Spiritual works of mercy;
( ) b. Giving ourselves unselfishly to our fellowman for the love of God;
( ) c. Recommending our neighbor to God in our prayers;
( ) d. Loving our neighbor as Christ in disguise;
( ) e. Loving our neighbor so that he will return our love.

27. Children can best fulfill their duties toward their parents by:
( ) a. Doing their best to please them;
( ) b. Praying to God for them;
( ) c. Helping them in all their needs;
( ) d. Imitating their good example;
( ) e. Confiding in them at all times.

28. The best way to join in the liturgy (Mass, Sacraments, etc.) is:
( ) a. To attend Church services regularly;
( ) b. To read about the vestments, music and ceremonies;
( ) c. To follow the rites and rituals in approved books;
( ) d. To learn how to serve Mass or help in the sacristy;
( ) e. To take an active part in performing the liturgical acts.

29. We can best cooperate with a priest in performing his sacred ministry by:
( ) a. Honoring him as God's representative, "Another Christ";
( ) b. Helping him in his ministry in whatever way we can;
( ) c. Taking part in his priestly acts at Mass and through the sacraments;
( ) d. Defending the priest against all objections;
( ) e. Assisting the priest in parish activities.

30. Sanctifying grace or the grace-life may best be explained as:
( ) a. A special gift of God making the soul pleasing to Him;
( ) b. The personal possession of God Himself;
( ) c. An attitude of friendship between the soul and God;
( ) d. A safe and sure ticket to heaven;
( ) e. A spiritual garment clothing the soul with beauty.

31. The strongest reason we have for going to confession often is:
( ) a. To gain self-knowledge by a careful examination of conscience;
( ) b. To make up to God for past and present sins;
( ) c. To remain on terms of friendship with God;
( ) d. To grow in grace whose principle is God's forgiving love;
( ) e. To stir up feelings of remorse and guilt for past sins.

32. The principal effect of the sacrament of Extreme Unction (Anointing of the Sick) is:
( ) a. To prepare the soul to face death;
( ) b. To assure the dying person of Church burial;
( ) c. To remove the last traces of sin;
( ) d. To heal both the body and the soul;
( ) e. To console the family of the dying person.

33. The finest way to show gratitude for the grace of Baptism is to:
( ) a. Pray that others might be as fortunate as we are;
( ) b. Use our baptismal right to receive the other sacraments;
( ) c. Refuse to associate with non-baptized persons;
( ) d. Live fully the Christ-life which Baptism confers;
( ) e. Do our best to remain in the state of grace.

34. A couple about to be married should regard the sacrament of Matrimony as:
( ) a. An abiding union of bodies and souls continually blessed by God;
( ) b. A sacred partnership to make their love holy;
( ) c. A pledge of loyalty to the directions of the Church;
( ) d. A source of grace and blessing to each partner;
( ) e. A bond uniting them as a couple to God in a special way.

35. We best prove our love and devotion to Mary, the Mother of God by:
( ) a. Trusting in her as our loving mother;
( ) b. Conforming our lives to the teachings of her divine son;
( ) c. Honoring her as the world's greatest woman;
( ) d. Being pure in thought, word and deed;
( ) e. Admiring her excellence and singing her praises.

36. We can best enter into the Mystery of the Resurrection and Ascension by:
( ) a. Believing firmly in the "Empty Tomb";
( ) b. Seeing these events as the high points in the work of redemption;
( ) c. Condemning Easter eggs and the Easter bunny;
( ) d. Living so as to bring about Christ's Second Coming;
( ) e. Understanding how these mysteries prove Christ's divine power.

37. We can best cooperate with the graces of Confirmation by:
( ) a. Fighting fearlessly for the rights of the Church;
( ) b. Studying hard to pass the test before Confirmation;
( ) c. Entering fully into the sacramental life of the Church;
( ) d. Defending our faith when called upon to do so;
( ) e. Devoting ourselves where possible to the works of the Church.

38. We should receive Holy Communion often because:
( ) a. We are rewarded for leading a virtuous life;
( ) b. We are nourished and strengthened by this food of our souls;
( ) c. We become more like Christ through sacramental contact with Him;
( ) d. We are inspired to be very holy;
( ) e. We thus honor Christ, the author of this sacrament.

39. When we accept the teaching of the Church, we profess our faith in:
( ) a. The oldest and largest Church in the world;
( ) b. The authority of the pope and bishops;
( ) c. Divine revelation as guaranteed by the Church;
( ) d. The word of God enlivened by the Holy Spirit;
( ) e. The pastor and Sisters in the parochial school.

40. The chief value of prayer is:
( ) a. It unites us with God;
( ) b. It wins for us rich graces;
( ) c. It gives us peace of soul;
( ) d. It inspires us with good thoughts;
( ) e. It strengthens us against evil.

41. Christ founded the one, true Church because He wanted thereby:
( ) a. To satisfy man's desire for religious fellowship;
( ) b. To unite all men with Himself to glorify the Father;
( ) c. To save all men through a visible society;
( ) d. To distribute the graces of redemption;
( ) e. To prove that all other religions are man-made.

42. We should look forward to heaven with joy because:
( ) a. We shall have eternal pleasure without interruption;
( ) b. We shall see God face to face;
( ) c. We shall know and love God as He knows and loves Himself;
( ) d. We shall no longer have to suffer;
( ) e. We shall be completely happy there.

43. The strongest reason for observing the Ten Commandments is because:
( ) a. They will give us peace of soul and a good conscience;
( ) b. They will give instructions in the practice of charity;
( ) c. They will tell us what to do and what to avoid;
( ) d. They will give us a detailed blueprint to follow;
( ) e. They will help us over rough spots on the way to heaven.

44. The Fourth Commandment is primarily concerned with:
( ) a. Relations between God our Father and His loving children;
( ) b. Community relationships of all kinds;
( ) c. Relations of obedience between parents and minor children;
( ) d. All relations between parents and children;
( ) e. All relations between superiors and subjects.

45. The most important act of a person going to confession is:
( ) a. A sincere sorrow for sin inspired by the love of God;
( ) b. An exact examination of conscience before confession;
( ) c. The humble acknowledgement of his sins to Christ's representative;
( ) d. Doing a penance in atonement for his sins;
( ) e. Feeling sad and depressed because of his sins.

46. The chief reason we must respect our body is because:
( ) a. Our body "gets even" if we fail to take care of it;
( ) b. Our body is a holy temple of God destined for immortality;
( ) c. Our body is the instrument of our soul;
( ) d. Our body was created by God;
( ) e. Our body works better when properly cared for.

47. The Bible teaching that God created man "in His own image and likeness" means:
( ) a. Man's spiritual powers of intellect and will are Godlike;
( ) b. All men are equal in God's eyes;
( ) c. Man's soul somehow looks like God;
( ) d. Man's spirit has a capacity for the divine;
( ) e. Man reflects the qualities of God.

48. The best explanation of why God created the world and all it contains is because God wanted:
( ) a. To overcome His loneliness;
( ) b. To make creatures subject to Him;
( ) c. To reveal His unlimited goodness;
( ) d. To manifest His great glory outwardly;
( ) e. To share His goodness with others.

49. Young men and women during their pre-marriage days should be:
( ) a. Considerate by regarding each other as possible marriage partners;
( ) b. Wide-ranging in their choice of friends and acquaintances;
( ) c. Interested in learning all about marriage from experts;
( ) d. Cautious lest they be led into sin;
( ) e. Common-sense in dealing with each other before marriage.

50. Being born with Original Sin means:
( ) a. Our natures are diseased by sin;
( ) b. It is only natural for us to sin;
( ) c. We have a strong inclination to sin;
( ) d. We share in Adam's guilt;
( ) e. We lack the life of grace.

STOP AND WAIT FOR FURTHER INSTRUCTIONS
IF YOU FINISH EARLY GO BACK OVER YOUR ANSWERS

APPENDIX F

INVENTORY OF CATHOLIC SCHOOL OUTCOMES
ANSWER BOOKLET
STUDENT INFORMATION

Name of School_____ Diocese_____ Date_____

1. Are you a boy or girl? Please circle   Boy   Girl
                                     1   2

2. What is your present age? Count birth month but not present month.   _____
            Years   **Months**   1   2   3

3. Do you plan to continue your education in a Catholic school? Circle the correct response   Yes   No   Uncertain
                                                               1   2   3

4. How many years have you attended a Catholic school? Count this year.
Count part years as whole years.   _____
                                        Total   1   2   3   4

5. How many different Catholic schools have you attended?   _____
                                        Total   1   2   3   4

6. How many brothers and sisters do you have?
Count half brothers and sisters and step brothers and sisters.   _____
                                        Total   1   2   3

7. Is (was) your **father** a Catholic? Circle response.   Yes   No   Uncertain
                                                 1   2   3

8. What is (was) your **father's** occupation?_____
                                          1   2   3   4
Describe the kind of work he does: Owner of farm, high school teacher, welder, etc. If you do not know, write "Unknown" in blank. This applies to questions below.

9. What nationality was your **father's** family predominantly? _____
                                        1   2   3   4   5   6   7

10. What was the highest grade your **father** completed in school? Circle number below.
   1   2   3   4   5   6   7   8   9   10   11   12   13   14   15   16   17 +   Unknown
      1   2   3   4   5   6   7   8

11. How many years did your **father** attend Catholic schools?
Circle response or fill in blank.   Didn't attend _____   Uncertain _____   Years _____
                                   1   2   3   4   5   6

12. Is (was) your **mother** a Catholic? Circle response.   Yes   No   Uncertain
                                               1   2   3

13. What is (was) your **mother's** occupation? _____
                                        1   2   3   4   5
Describe the kind of work she does **if** she works outside the home.

14. What nationality was your **mother's** family predominantly? _____
                                      1   2   3   4   5   6   7

15. What was the highest grade your **mother** completed in school? Circle number below.
   1   2   3   4   5   6   7   8   9   10   11   12   13   14   15   16   17 +   Unknown
      1   2   3   4   5   6   7   8

16. How many years did your **mother** attend Catholic schools?
Circle response or fill in blank.   Didn't attend _____   Uncertain _____   Years _____
                                   1   2   3   4   5   6

17. What was your average grade **last** year?   A   B   C   D
Circle the appropriate letter.   Best grade   Next best   Average   Below average
                                       1   2   3   4

18. What is your average grade **this** year?   A   B   C   D
Circle the appropriate letter.   1   2   3   4

19. Over-all what kind of student are you?   A   B   C   D
Circle the appropriate letter.   Top ¼   Top ½   Lower ½   Lower ¼
                                       1   2   3   4

20. Do most of the friends you associate with after school and on weekends go to a Catholic school?
Circle response.   Yes   No   ½ & ½
                   1   2   3

THE UNIVERSITY OF NOTRE DAME DU LAC
Notre Dame, Indiana

Editors:
TERRY P. DENNY
REV. XAVIER HARRIS, O.F.M.
REGINALD A. NEUWIEN

APPENDIX G

INVENTORY OF CATHOLIC SCHOOL OUTCOMES
ANSWER SHEET FOR PART I

Instructions: There are fifty questions in Part I. Each question requires one and only one answer. Place a check mark (√) inside the parentheses to the left of the letter of the statement of your choice. Make sure that the number of the question and the number of your answer agree.

1.	( ) a.	( ) b.	( ) c.	( ) d.	( ) e.	26.	( ) a.	( ) b.	( ) c.	( ) d.	( ) e.
2.	( ) a.	( ) b.	( ) c.	( ) d.	( ) e.	27.	( ) a.	( ) b.	( ) c.	( ) d.	( ) e.
3.	( ) a.	( ) b.	( ) c.	( ) d.	( ) e.	28.	( ) a.	( ) b.	( ) c.	( ) d.	( ) e.
4.	( ) a.	( ) b.	( ) c.	( ) d.	( ) e.	29.	( ) a.	( ) b.	( ) c.	( ) d.	( ) e.
5.	( ) a.	( ) b.	( ) c.	( ) d.	( ) e.	30.	( ) a.	( ) b.	( ) c.	( ) d.	( ) e.
6.	( ) a.	( ) b.	( ) c.	( ) d.	( ) e.	31.	( ) a.	( ) b.	( ) c.	( ) d.	( ) e.
7.	( ) a.	( ) b.	( ) c.	( ) d.	( ) e.	32.	( ) a.	( ) b.	( ) c.	( ) d.	( ) e.
8.	( ) a.	( ) b.	( ) c.	( ) d.	( ) e.	33.	( ) a.	( ) b.	( ) c.	( ) d.	( ) e.
9.	( ) a.	( ) b.	( ) c.	( ) d.	( ) e.	34.	( ) a.	( ) b.	( ) c.	( ) d.	( ) e.
10.	( ) a.	( ) b.	( ) c.	( ) d.	( ) e.	35.	( ) a.	( ) b.	( ) c.	( ) d.	( ) e.
11.	( ) a.	( ) b.	( ) c.	( ) d.	( ) e.	36.	( ) a.	( ) b.	( ) c.	( ) d.	( ) e.
12.	( ) a.	( ) b.	( ) c.	( ) d.	( ) e.	37.	( ) a.	( ) b.	( ) c.	( ) d.	( ) e.
13.	( ) a.	( ) b.	( ) c.	( ) d.	( ) e.	38.	( ) a.	( ) b.	( ) c.	( ) d.	( ) e.
14.	( ) a.	( ) b.	( ) c.	( ) d.	( ) e.	39.	( ) a.	( ) b.	( ) c.	( ) d.	( ) e.
15.	( ) a.	( ) b.	( ) c.	( ) d.	( ) e.	40.	( ) a.	( ) b.	( ) c.	( ) d.	( ) e.
16.	( ) a.	( ) b.	( ) c.	( ) d.	( ) e.	41.	( ) a.	( ) b.	( ) c.	( ) d.	( ) e.
17.	( ) a.	( ) b.	( ) c.	( ) d.	( ) e.	42.	( ) a.	( ) b.	( ) c.	( ) d.	( ) e.
18.	( ) a.	( ) b.	( ) c.	( ) d.	( ) e.	43.	( ) a.	( ) b.	( ) c.	( ) d.	( ) e.
19.	( ) a.	( ) b.	( ) c.	( ) d.	( ) e.	44.	( ) a.	( ) b.	( ) c.	( ) d.	( ) e.
20.	( ) a.	( ) b.	( ) c.	( ) d.	( ) e.	45.	( ) a.	( ) b.	( ) c.	( ) d.	( ) e.
21.	( ) a.	( ) b.	( ) c.	( ) d.	( ) e.	46.	( ) a.	( ) b.	( ) c.	( ) d.	( ) e.
22.	( ) a.	( ) b.	( ) c.	( ) d.	( ) e.	47.	( ) a.	( ) b.	( ) c.	( ) d.	( ) e.
23.	( ) a.	( ) b.	( ) c.	( ) d.	( ) e.	48.	( ) a.	( ) b.	( ) c.	( ) d.	( ) e.
24.	( ) a.	( ) b.	( ) c.	( ) d.	( ) e.	49.	( ) a.	( ) b.	( ) c.	( ) d.	( ) e.
25.	( ) a.	( ) b.	( ) c.	( ) d.	( ) e.	50.	( ) a.	( ) b.	( ) c.	( ) d.	( ) e.

APPENDIX H
INVENTORY OF CATHOLIC SCHOOL OUTCOMES
PART II
STUDENT ATTITUDES
DIRECTIONS

Part II of the Inventory asks you how you think and feel about a number of things that are related to your present life as a student. Some of the items have to do with your future life after you leave school. There is **no** right or wrong answer; the best answer is the one which you decide, after giving it some thought, best agrees with your feelings. None of the answers can be associated with you personally, now or later, since no names or numbers are being used in the Inventory. You may feel free to be perfectly frank in answering the questions.

The first thirty-five items are statements with which you are asked to agree or disagree. To help you **express** how you feel about these statements, the Answer Sheet offers you these five choices:

Strongly Agree	Somewhat Agree	Don't know or Uncertain	Disagree Somewhat	Strongly Disagree
1	2	3	4	5

Notice that there is a number beneath each of these headings. To record your response on the Answer Sheet all you have to do is to circle the number under the heading which best expresses your attitude.

Study the following example. The first thirty-five items are all answered in the same way:

"When I make new acquaintances, I want them to know that I am a Catholic."

If you strongly agree with this statement, circle number 1 on the Answer Sheet. If you agree, but not strongly, circle number 2. If you are not certain, circle number 3. If you disagree, but not strongly, circle number 4. Finally, if you disagree strongly, circle number 5.

The last ten items also ask you to circle numbers, but the meaning of the numbers is explained in the Inventory Booklet. To answer these items you simply decide on the number of the statement of your choice and circle the number. Here is an example of that type of item:

"Which of the following best expresses your attitude toward modern art"? 1) I don't like it at all; 2) I like some things about it; 3) I don't know enough about it to say; 4) I like it very much; 5) I like it best of all kinds of art.

1   2   3   4   5

The example gives the answer of someone who likes some things about modern art.

Now find the Answer Sheet for Part II in your Answer Booklet and make sure you know how to answer the questions.

PART II

1. The whole family should pray together frequently.
2. I do not object to such things as necking and petting, since these are just a part of growing up.
3. While I do not like to admit this even to myself, I sometimes have the ambition to become a great man like Einstein, Beethoven or Shakespeare.
4. The kind of life work I will choose to do as an adult will not have any effect on my being a good Catholic.
5. Generally, I do not believe in all these community drives, like the Community Chest or the United Fund. People on relief and in need should be taken care of by their own relatives.
6. A boy who has a good job in a grocery store under a very fair employer finds that when the boss is away he can get by with doing less work than is expected of him. I believe that it is morally wrong for the boy to do this.
7. Manual labor and unskilled jobs seem to fit the Negro mental and physical ability better than more skilled or responsible work.
8. My parents do not know very much about what is going on in my school.
9. If one of my best friends said she wanted to become a Sister, I would pray that she would succeed in that vocation.

10. In the present struggle against Communism every young man should be willing to serve in the armed forces even at the risk of losing his life or his future occupation.

11. A good education stresses doing things for others even though you do not get anything out of it yourself.

12. In religion classes I like to discuss religious matters rather than to memorize answers.

13. In the long run the best way to live is to pick friends and associates whose tastes and beliefs are the same as your own.

14. It makes no difference to me whether I receive Holy Communion from a white or a colored priest.

15. To reach heaven it is enough to live our own lives well without looking for ways of helping others.

16. Even when there are serious difficulties in the family, I still believe that divorce with remarriage is always wrong.

17. There is something different and strange about Jews; it is hard to tell what they are thinking and planning, and what makes them tick.

18. It makes me happy to hear that one of my best friends is going to the seminary to become a priest.

19. We have a responsibility in Christian charity to give money and make sacrifices to help oppressed people in other parts of the world.

20. Generally speaking, the world we live in is a pretty lonely place.

21. If I were going to college, and money presented no problem, I would prefer to go away to school rather than attend a college where I could live at home.

22. I do not admire boys and girls who do more work than the teacher assigns.

23. I feel that a strong interest in money and the things money can buy is likely to hurt a person's religious and spiritual life.

24. Wherever I work, I hope that I will be able to help the people I work with to be good Christians.

25. Getting a good job depends more on the pull or luck a man has than on his real ability or hard work.

26. Since the President has asked for volunteers to serve in the Peace Corps in other countries, I should be willing to spend two years helping some other country.

27. I don't bother reading about political questions; I think that is why we have paid government officials—to look after these things for us.

28. No matter how stupid or vulgar a person may be, we should still try to be kindly toward him because he is a son of God.

29. The opportunity to go to college is of extreme importance to me.

30. America would be more of a Christian nation if it used more of its tax money to help other nations of the world.

31. Money and possessions do not help a family to be successful as much as strong personal ties among family members.

32. I prefer teachers who teach rather than those who make me find out things for myself.

33. Sometimes I am uncertain as to what the Catholic Church teaches about what is right and wrong in behavior.

34. It would bother me to sit next or near a person of another race (e.g., a Negro, a white person) in school.

35. No difficulty can hold us back if we have enough will power.

36. Do you date the same person to the exclusion of all others? If **yes,** circle number **1** on the answer sheet; if **no** circle number **2.**

37. If the answer to the preceding question was **no,** skip this question. If **yes,** then indicate below how long you have been dating this person exclusively by circling the appropriate number on the answer sheet.
    1) less than a month
    2) one to three months
    3) four to six months
    4) six months to a year
    5) a year or more

38. Which of the following best expresses your feelings about marrying someone of a different religion than yours?
    1) The person I love and marry will have to be a Catholic
    2) The person I love and marry will most likely be a Catholic
    3) I don't intend to marry
    4) The person I love and marry will not have to be a Catholic, although I would like to marry a Catholic
    5) The person I love and marry need not be a Catholic so far as I am concerned.

39. Which of the following best represents your usual practice with respect to attendance at Mass:
    1) occasionally on Sundays and/or holy days
    2) regularly on Sundays and holy days
    3) besides Sundays and holy days, 1 to 3 times a month when not obliged to go
    4) besides Sundays and holy days, 2 or 3 times a week when not obliged to go
    5) besides Sundays and holy days, 4 or more times a week when not obliged to go

40. Which of these do you like to do best, which second best, and which third?
    a) Doing things with my family and relatives
    b) Doing things with my school friends
    c) Doing things with my out-of-school friends

41. How frequently do your mother and/or father encourage interest in religion and its practice—for example, by family prayer, celebration of religious feasts, discussion of religion, etc.?
    1) every day
    2) very frequently
    3) fairly frequently
    4) once in a while
    5) very seldom

42. Here are three different jobs. If you had your choice, which one would you pick?
    1) a job which pays a moderate income but which you are sure of keeping
    2) a job which pays a good income but which you have a 50-50 chance of losing
    3) a job which pays an extremely good income if you make the grade, but in which you lose almost everything if you don't make it

43. Please indicate whether or not you date, and how frequently:
    1) I do not date, or date only occasionally
    2) I date about once a month
    3) I date about every two or three weeks
    4) I date once or twice a week
    5) I date three or more times a week

44. Indicate how important each of the following is to you as you look forward to choosing a life work:
    a) a chance to gain recognition for outstanding work
    b) a chance to exercise personal judgment and responsibility
    c) a chance to raise the moral standards of the place in which I live
    d) a chance to exercise leadership in the community
    e) a chance to make people more conscious of God and religion

45. In the same way as in the preceding question, show how important to you each of the following would be if you were choosing a marriage partner:
    a) a person who is a good provider or a good household manager
    b) a pleasant person
    c) a morally good person
    d) a person who loves children
    e) a deeply spiritual person

APPENDIX I

INVENTORY OF CATHOLIC SCHOOL OUTCOMES
ANSWER SHEET FOR PART II

Instructions: The first 35 items are marked by circling the number under the heading which best describes how you feel.

	Strongly Agree	Agree Somewhat	Uncertain Don't Know	Disagree Somewhat	Disagree Strongly
1)	1	2	3	4	5
2)	1	2	3	4	5
3)	1	2	3	4	5
4)	1	2	3	4	5
5)	1	2	3	4	5
6)	1	2	3	4	5
7)	1	2	3	4	5
8)	1	2	3	4	5
9)	1	2	3	4	5
10)	1	2	3	4	5
11)	1	2	3	4	5
12)	1	2	3	4	5
13)	1	2	3	4	5
14)	1	2	3	4	5
15)	1	2	3	4	5
16)	1	2	3	4	5
17)	1	2	3	4	5
18)	1	2	3	4	5
19)	1	2	3	4	5
20)	1	2	3	4	5
21)	1	2	3	4	5
22)	1	2	3	4	5
23)	1	2	3	4	5
24)	1	2	3	4	5
25)	1	2	3	4	5
26)	1	2	3	4	5
27)	1	2	3	4	5
28)	1	2	3	4	5
29)	1	2	3	4	5
30)	1	2	3	4	5
31)	1	2	3	4	5
32)	1	2	3	4	5
33)	1	2	3	4	5
34)	1	2	3	4	5
35)	1	2	3	4	5

The next 8 items are answered by circling the numbers which correspond to your choice of items as explained in the Inventory. Be sure to mark each of the items as directed.

36)   1   2

37)   1   2   3   4   5

38)   1   2   3   4   5

39)   1   2   3   4   5

40)   1st_____   2nd_____   3rd_____
    Fill in letter of choice in rank order.

41)   1   2   3   4   5

42)   1   2   3   Choose one.

43)   1   2   3   4   5

The last two items have special headings to indicate the degree of importance.

44)   How **important** is each to you?

	Very	Fairly	Don't know	Slightly	Not at all
a)	1	2	3	4	5
b)	1	2	3	4	5
c)	1	2	3	4	5
d)	1	2	3	4	5
e)	1	2	3	4	5

45)   How **important** is each to you?

	Very	Fairly	Don't know	Slightly	Not at all
a)	1	2	3	4	5
b)	1	2	3	4	5
c)	1	2	3	4	5
d)	1	2	3	4	5
e)	1	2	3	4	5

APPENDIX J
INVENTORY OF CATHOLIC SCHOOL OUTCOMES
PART III
STUDENT OPINION CONCERNING CATHOLIC SCHOOLS
DIRECTIONS

This part of the Inventory is an Opinionnaire (a questionnaire which asks for opinions). There are twenty-five questions which seek your frank opinion about the Catholic school or schools you have attended.

In an Opinionnaire there are no right or wrong answers. **Your** opinion is the right one for you. In answering the questions be sure to give your opinion, not the opinion of your parents or teachers or schoolmates, unless they happen to agree with yours.

Please read each question carefully and then select the response which best agrees with your opinion. Most of the items are like the following:

"One of the goals of Catholic schools is to produce loyal and patriotic American citizens. Insofar as you can observe your fellow schoolmates, how well would you say your school is succeeding in citizenship training"?
Choose one.
a.   exceptionally well;
b.   Very well, but could be better;
c.   Moderately well;
d.   Only fairly well;
e.   Poorly

Again, it is important to stress that it is your opinion which counts. Select the answer which comes closest to your opinion.

Some of the items ask you to rank certain things by voting for first place, second place, third place and so on. An example of this type of question is the following:

"Some day you will hold a job or follow a profession. Looking forward to this time of your life, rank the five items below in terms of their importance to you. (Rank from 1 to 5)
a.   The security of steady work;
b.   The opportunity for rapid rise;
c.   The enjoyment of the work itself;
d.   Friendly people to work with;
e.   A high income.

Many people answer such a question by selecting the most important item and then the runner-up. This gives them the first and second choice. Next they pick the least important item. This gives them the fifth choice. Finally they decide between the two remaining answers which become their third and fourth choices.

Now study the examples at the top of the answer sheet for Part III and make sure you know how to answer the two types of questions.

PART III

*1.   Suppose someone were to ask you: "Why are you going to a Catholic school?" Think for a moment and **then rank in the order of importance your reasons for attending a Catholic school.** Be sure to give your reasons, not those of your parents or teachers. Mark the most important reason 1, the next most important 2, and so on. **Assign all five ranks.**
Rank:
a. To obtain a superior training in school subjects;
b. To develop a strong moral character based on religious principles;
c. To form a group of true friends;
d. To prepare myself for making a good living;
e. To become a partriotic American citizen.

2. If the choice of school were left entirely up to you, **would you still attend a Catholic school? Choose one.**
    a. Definitely yes;
    b. Probably yes;
    c. Uncertain;
    d. Probably no;
    e. Definitely no.

3. Catholic schools like other schools train their students in what might be called the "regular school subjects" such as English, mathematics, social studies and science. As you look back over your years in a Catholic school, **how would you describe the academic training you have received? Choose one.**
    a. Superior;
    b. Very good, but could be better;
    c. Average;
    d. Below average;
    e. Poor.

4. In addition to "regular school subjects," Catholic schools also give special instruction in the teachings and practices of the Catholic religion. As you look back over your years in a Catholic school, **how would you describe the religious instruction you have received? Choose one.**
    a. Superior;
    b. Very good, but could be better;
    c. Average;
    d. Below average;
    e. Poor.

5. As you know, one of the objectives of a Catholic school is to help the student develop a strong moral character. From your own experience and from observing your friends, **how well do you think the Catholic school you attend is succeeding in character training? Choose one.**
    a. Exceptionally well;
    b. Very well, but could be better;
    c. Moderately well;
    d. Only fairly well;
    e. Poorly.

6. You are probably aware that Catholic schools strive to develop the character traits of respect and obedience. From your own experience and from observing your friends, **how well do you think the Catholic schools you have attended are succeeding in developing these traits? Choose one.**
    a. Exceptionally well;
    b. Very good, but could be better;
    c. Moderately well;
    d. Only fairly well;
    e. Poorly.

7. You are often asked by friends or relatives, how you are doing in school. Suppose, instead, they were to ask you how well your teachers are doing in helping you to learn. Considering your present class as a whole, **how well do you think the religious (priests, brothers, sisters), who have taught your class, have succeeded in teaching you the regular school subjects? Choose one.**
    a. Exceptionally well;
    b. Very well, but could be better;
    c. Moderately well;
    d. Only fairly well;
    e. Poorly.

8. In addition to religious teachers, most Catholic schools now have lay teachers as members of the faculty. Considering your present class as a whole, **how well do you think the lay teachers have succeeded in teaching the regular school subjects? Choose one.**
   a. Exceptionally well;
   b. Very well, but could be better;
   c. Moderately well;
   d. Only fairly well;
   e. Poorly.
*9. **Rank in the order of importance** (1 = most important, 2 = next most important, and so on) **the advantages you hope to receive from your Catholic schooling. Assign all five ranks.**
   Rank:
   a. A group of loyal friends and companions;
   b. A practical knowledge and appreciation of my duties as a Catholic;
   c. A clear understanding of the various subjects I have studied;
   d. A deep devotion to my country and a knowledge of my American heritage;
   e. The knowledge and ability to earn a good living.
10. Some of the traits which all schools seek to develop in their students are studiousness, interest in learning new things and a strong liking for reading. Considering your present class as a whole, **how well do you think your school has succeeded in developing these scholastic traits? Choose one.**
    a. Exceptionally well;
    b. Very well, but could be better;
    c. Moderately well;
    d. Only fairly well;
    e. Poorly.
*11. Sometimes you think about the job or profession you will one day hold. **Which of the following careers appeals most to you?** Put your preference in rank order from 1 (most appealing) to 5 (least appealing). **Assign all five ranks.**
    a. A career in which I can take part in community affairs;
    b. A career in which I can be creative and original;
    c. A career in which I can work with people rather than things;
    d. A career in which I can be helpful to those in need;
    e. A career in which I can earn a good deal of money.
12. One of the goals of Catholic schools is to produce loyal and patriotic American citizens. Insofar as you can observe your fellow schoolmates and classmates, **how well would you say your school is succeeding in citizenship training? Choose one.**
    a. Exceptionally well;
    b. Very well, but could be better;
    c. Moderately well;
    d. Only fairly well;
    e. Poorly.
13. It is generally recognized that education has a "dollar and cents" value—that your schooling will help you later on to obtain a good job and earn a suitable living. **How well do you think the Catholic school is preparing you for your life work? Choose one.**
    a. Exceptionally well;
    b. Very well, but could be better;
    c. Moderately well;
    d. Only fairly well;
    e. Poorly.

14. The maintenance of good order and respect for authority reflected in good behavior in and out of school, is often referred to as "discipline." From your own experience and observation, **how would you describe the discipline of your school? Choose one.**

    a. Exceptionally good;

    b. Very good, but could be better;

    c. Average;

    d. Weak;

    e. Extremely weak.

*15. **Rank in the order of importance** (1 = most important, 2 = next most important, and so on), **the following influences in your religious development.** This includes your knowledge of Catholic beliefs, your appreciation of Catholic values and your performance of Catholic duties. **Assign all five ranks.**

    a. The instruction and example of my parents;

    b. The example and personal guidance of my teachers;

    c. Religious instruction provided in the parish, Church;

    d. Religious instruction provided by the school;

    e. The example of my schoolmates and classmates.

16. Catholic schools expect that their graduates will be "socially responsible," aware of the problems of their fellowmen and anxious to help them solve these problems. **How well do you think your Catholic school has made you and your classmates "socially responsible?" Choose one.**

    a. Exceptionally well;

    b. Very well, but could be better;

    c. Moderately well;

    d. Only fairly well;

    e. Poorly.

17. In addition to religious and moral training Catholic schools are often known for the courtesy, good manners and politeness of their students. From your own experience and observation, **how well do you think your school has succeeded with your class in developing good manners? Choose one.**

    a. Exceptionally well;

    b. Very well, but could be better;

    c. Moderately well;

    d. Only fairly well;

    e. Poorly.

18. All schools strive to develop the intellectual traits of their students. Some of these qualities are a keen desire for knowledge, willingness to work at intellectual tasks, and studying beyond class assignments. From your experience and observation, **how well has your school developed these scholarly traits in your class? Choose one.**

    a. Exceptionally well;

    b. Very well, but could be better;

    c. Moderately well;

    d. Only fairly well;

    e. Poorly.

*19. **Rank in the order of importance** (1 = most important, 2 = next most important, and so on) **the outcomes which you expect from your years in a Catholic school.** Later on, as you look back on your school days, what outcome will you value most? **Assign all five ranks.**

    a. A well-developed loyalty to my country as well as my school, which will last throughout life;

    b. A well-developed Christian character formed in the image and after the example of Jesus Christ;

c. A well-equipped personality enabling me to compete successfully in the business of making a living;

d. A well-balanced intellectual development, including both religious and non-religious knowledge;

e. A well-adjusted social awareness whereby I might be of greater benefit to my fellowman.

20. Since Catholic schools must be financed for the most part by Catholic parents, these parents are often very interested in the school and are willing to cooperate with the plans and programs of the school. From your own experience, **how would you describe your own parents' interest in your school? Choose one.**

   a. Extremely strong;

   b. Strong, but could be stronger;

   c. Average;

   d. Below average;

   e. Weak.

*21. Different people strive for different things. Here are some things that you have probably thought about. Among the things you strive for during your school days, **just how important are each of these?** (Rank from 1 to 5)

   Rank:

   a. Living up to my religious ideals;

   b. Becoming a better American citizen;

   c. Preparing myself to make a living;

   d. Learning as much as possible in school;

   e. Being accepted and liked by other students.

22. If you could be any of these things you wanted, **which would you most want to be? Choose one.**

Boy	**Girl**
a. Jet pilot;	a. Airline stewardess;
b. Doctor;	b. Nurse;
c. Missionary;	c. Sister;
d. Atomic scientist;	d. School teacher;
e. Famous athlete.	e. Actress or artist.

*23. Some day you will hold a job or follow a profession. Looking forward to this time of your life, rank the five items below in terms of their importance to you. (Rank from 1 to 5)

   Rank:

   a. The security of steady work;

   b. The opportunity for rapid rise;

   c. The enjoyment of the work itself;

   d. Friendly people to work with;

   e. A high income.

*24. Looking forward to your years in **college,** how important do you think each of the following will be to you? (Rank from 1 to 5)

   Rank:

   a. Campus activities and social life;

   b. Preparation for making a living;

   c. The stimulation of new ideas;

   d. Opportunity to strengthen my faith;

   e. Becoming a more productive American citizen.

25. If you could be remembered here at school for one of the five things listed below, which would you want it to be? **Choose one.**

   a. Most highly respected;

   b. A brilliant student;

c. Most popular;
d. Athletic star or cheerleader;
e. Leader in student government.

STOP AND WAIT FOR FURTHER INSTRUCTIONS
IF YOU FINISH EARLY GO BACK OVER YOUR ANSWERS

APPENDIX K

INVENTORY OF CATHOLIC SCHOOL OUTCOMES
ANSWER SHEET FOR PART III

Instructions: There are twenty-five questions in Part III. Each question has five choices. Mark only one choice except for the starred (*) items which ask you to rank the statements. On the starred items, five answers are required. Be sure to assign all five ranks.

Example of a single choice item: **Choose one.**

x.   ( )a._____   ( )b._____   ( )c._____   ( )d._____   ( )e._____

Example of a ranked (five choice) item: **Assign all five ranks.**

*y.   ( )a._____   ( )b._____   ( )c._____   ( )d._____   ( )e._____

*1.   ( )a._____   ( )b._____   ( )c._____   ( )d._____   ( )e._____

2.   ( )a._____   ( )b._____   ( )c._____   ( )d._____   ( )e._____

3.   ( )a._____   ( )b._____   ( )c._____   ( )d._____   ( )e._____

4.   ( )a._____   ( )b._____   ( )c._____   ( )d._____   ( )e._____

5.   ( )a._____   ( )b._____   ( )c._____   ( )d._____   ( )e._____

6.   ( )a._____   ( )b._____   ( )c._____   ( )d._____   ( )e._____

7.   ( )a._____   ( )b._____   ( )c._____   ( )d._____   ( )e._____

8.   ( )a._____   ( )b._____   ( )c._____   ( )d._____   ( )e._____

*9.   ( )a._____   ( )b._____   ( )c._____   ( )d._____   ( )e._____

10.   ( )a._____   ( )b._____   ( )c._____   ( )d._____   ( )e._____

*11.   ( )a._____   ( )b._____   ( )c._____   ( )d._____   ( )e._____

12.   ( )a._____   ( )b._____   ( )c._____   ( )d._____   ( )e._____

13.   ( )a._____   ( )b._____   ( )c._____   ( )d._____   ( )e._____

14.   ( )a._____   ( )b._____   ( )c._____   ( )d._____   ( )e._____

*15.   ( )a._____   ( )b._____   ( )c._____   ( )d._____   ( )e._____

16.   ( )a._____   ( )b._____   ( )c._____   ( )d._____   ( )e._____

17.   ( )a._____   ( )b._____   ( )c._____   ( )d._____   ( )e._____

18.   ( )a._____   ( )b._____   ( )c._____   ( )d._____   ( )e._____

*19.   ( )a._____   ( )b._____   ( )c._____   ( )d._____   ( )e._____

20.   ( )a._____   ( )b._____   ( )c._____   ( )d._____   ( )e._____

*21.   ( )a._____   ( )b._____   ( )c._____   ( )d._____   ( )e._____

22.   ( )a._____   ( )b._____   ( )c._____   ( )d._____   ( )e._____

*23.   ( )a._____   ( )b._____   ( )c._____   ( )d._____   ( )e._____

*24.   ( )a._____   ( )b._____   ( )c._____   ( )d._____   ( )e._____

25.   ( )a._____   ( )b._____   ( )c._____   ( )d._____   ( )e._____

APPENDIX L
STUDY OF CATHOLIC EDUCATION
PARENTS' QUESTIONNAIRE

Parents:
  Please fill out these questionnaires, one for father and one for mother.
  Return them by your child tomorrow. Thank you.
Dear Parent or Guardian:

Through the generous help of the Superintendent of Catholic Schools of your diocese we are asking you to express your honest ideas on how important certain goals of Catholic schools seem to you. In this part of our national study of Catholic schools there are no **right or wrong answers,** so we are asking you to consider each possible goal carefully and then check an alternative which best represents your viewpoint. Very little writing is needed and it takes only about twenty minutes of your time. **Your name is not requested,** but your opinion is highly valued.

Special stress must be placed on the response from the parents of children in Catholic schools and also **parents of children not in Catholic schools.**

The procedure is very simple. After mother and father have filled out separate answers, fold the sheets and **seal them in the enclosed envelope.** Then, have your child take the sealed envelope back to the school. Parents of children not in Catholic schools should have the envelope put in the **mail box of the Sisters' convent** of your parish, or given to the teacher of the religious instruction class.

Finally, we ask you to fill out the answers immediately so that the **envelopes can be returned tomorrow.** The sealed envelopes will then be returned to the Superintendent of Schools, who will send them directly to us at the University of Notre Dame. Many thanks for your kind help and interest. May we ask you not to leave any spaces blank, because your opinion is very important to us.

1. (Check one) Are you mother_____, or father_____, or guardian_____ of the child?
2. (Check one) Are you Catholic_____, Protestant_____, other religion_____, no religion_____.
3. How old are you?_____.   4.   How many years of schooling did you have?_____.
5. How many years did you have in **Catholic elementary** school?_____.
6. How many years did you have in **Catholic high** school?_____.
7. How many years did you have in **Catholic college** or **university?**_____.
8. Indicate the **kind of work you do,** such as salesman, machine operator, secretary-typing, truck driver, officer clerk, office manager, middle executive in large business, senior executive in smaller corporation. Do NOT give name of company you work for.
   If now **unemployed** or **retired** give your usual work._____
9. Were you born in another country? Yes_____, No_____. If Yes, where?_____
10. Were either of your parents born in another country? Yes_____, No_____. If Yes, where?_____
_____
11. What **nationality** is your family predominantly, for example, Polish, Irish?_____.
12. **How many people** are in this, your immediate family?_____.
13. For each of your children (0 to 17 years of age) in your present family, please answer the questions at the top of each column on the next page (an example is given on the first line to indicate how it can be done—please fill all spaces for each child).
14. Is your spouse living at home? Yes_____, No_____.

Age	Boy or Girl (Check One)	Present School Grade	Kind of School Catholic Public		Is Child Receiving Religious Instruction (from school, parish) Yes No		How Many Years of Catholic School Do You Plan for Each Child	Tell Briefly Why You Do Not Plan More Catholic School for Each Child
13	X	8	X		X		None	No bus transportation

The statements below describe some **possible** things about Catholic schools. After thinking over each statement, please remember that there are **no right or wrong answers** and that you are asked to express your frank opinion. Then, we ask you to do two things in regard to each statement: 1) check how important this is (to you) for the Catholic schools you know of; 2) **check** how successful in doing this are the Catholic schools you know of? Be sure to make two checks after each statement, one on its importance, and one on its success. Catholic schools refer only to elementary and high schools.

Statements	How Important (to you) is This for the Catholic Schools You Know of? Most Imp.	Very Imp.	Some Imp.	Little Imp.	Of No Imp.	Don't Know	How Successful in Doing This Are the Catholic Schools You Know of? Most Succ.	Very Succ.	Some Succ.	Little Succ.	No Succ.	Don't Know
1. Catholic schools should train children in self-discipline and hard work.												
2. Catholic schools should teach children to know about God, Christ, the Church.												
3. Catholic schools should make children good citizens of the United States.												
4. Catholic schools should be strong in arithmetic and science.												
5. Catholic schools should teach children to like other races and nationalities, as Negroes, immigrants, Puerto Ricans.												
6. Catholic schools should train children for good jobs when they grow up.												
7. Catholic schools should prepare children for college.												
8. Catholic schools should train children to be honest, truthful, moral.												
9. Catholic schools should not be expensive for Catholic parents.												

Statements	How Important (to you) is This for the Catholic Schools You Know of?						How Successful in Doing This Are the Catholic Schools You Know of?					
	Most Imp.	Very Imp.	Some Imp.	Little Imp.	Of No Imp.	Don't Know	Most Succ.	Very Succ.	Some Succ.	Little Succ.	No Succ.	Don't Know
10. Catholic schools should teach children to read, write clearly and well.												
11. Catholic schools should have only religious teachers (Sisters, priests).												
12. Catholic schools should give children Catholic friends and good example.												
13. Catholic schools should get help from parents when help is needed.												
14. Catholic schools should teach music and the arts to the children.												
15. Catholic schools should produce leaders for our nation and communities.												
16. Catholic schools should have effective qualified lay teachers, when needed.												
17. Catholic schools should teach children to get along with others, such as Jews.												
18. Catholic schools should get more money from federal government.												
19. Catholic schools should train children to practice religion (Mass, Communion).												
20. Catholic schools should not have large classes (in single rooms).												
21. Catholic schools should have physical fitness programs for boys and girls.												
22. Catholic schools should teach children history and today's social problems.												
23. Catholic schools should help gifted and slow-learning children.												
24. Catholic schools should have space for all Catholic children.												
25. Catholic schools should not give much homework to children.												
26. Catholic schools should have effective qualified Sisters, priests as teachers.												
27. Catholic schools should train children in respect for persons and property.												
28. Catholic schools should teach children to think for themselves.												

Statements	How Important (to you) is This for the Catholic Schools You Know of?						How Successful in Doing This Are the Catholic Schools You Know of?					
	Most Imp.	Very Imp.	Some Imp.	Little Imp.	Of No Imp.	Don't Know	Most Succ.	Very Succ.	Some Succ.	Little Succ.	No Succ.	Don't Know
29. Catholic schools should teach children to help others in foreign countries.												
30. Catholic schools should foster vocations, to be Sisters, priests, brothers, etc.												
31. Catholic schools should help parents control dating of children.												

Finally, will you pick out the **most important statement** from the list above and **put its number in the space below.** Similarly we ask you to pick out the second most important, third most important; and also the most successful thing done by the Catholic schools you know of, the second and third most successful.

Most Important_____   Most Successful_____

Second Most Important_____   Second Most Successful_____

Third Most Important_____   Third Most Successful_____

Many, many, thanks for your help and interest. If you wish, you may write any added comments which occur to you. Then, please **seal your reply in the enclosed envelope** and have your child return it to the teacher or to the mail box of the Sisters' convent. **May we ask you to do this quickly, today if possible.**